In this three-part study of the serious plays which Corneille wrote between 1630 and 1643, David Clarke first explores the Norman experience and identity of the dramatist himself. A second section reviews the principles and distinctiveness of his poetics in a period when literary activity, and particularly historical drama, became increasingly subject to central government pressures. The third and final section discusses the political and tragic significance of Corneille's plays, and seeks to re-establish a link between their reflection of contemporary ideological tensions and the 'collective mind' of their intended audience with reference to popular, but now little-read, contemporary moralists and political theorists.

PIERRE CORNEILLE

PIERRE CORNEILLE

Poetics and political drama under Louis XIII

DAVID CLARKE

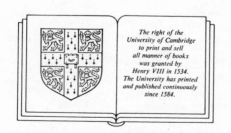

The right of the
University of Cambridge
to print and sell
all manner of books
was granted by
Henry VIII in 1534.
The University has printed
and published continuously
since 1584.

CAMBRIDGE UNIVERSITY PRESS

Cambridge   New York   Port Chester
Melbourne   Sydney

Published by the Press Syndicate of the University of Cambridge
The Pitt Building, Trumpington Street, Cambridge CB2 1RP
40 West 20th Street, New York, NY 1011-4211, USA
10 Stamford Road, Oakleigh, Melbourne 3166, Australia

© Cambridge University Press 1992

First published 1992

Printed in Great Britain at the University Press, Cambridge

*A cataloguing in publication record for this book is available
from the British Library*

Library of Congress cataloguing in publication data
Clarke, David R.
Pierre Corneille: poetics and political drama under Louis XIII /
David R. Clarke.
p.   cm.
Includes bibliographical references.
ISBN 0 521 40434 7 (hardback)
1. Corneille, Pierre, 1606–1684 – Political and social views.
2. Political plays, French – History and criticism. 3. France –
Politics and government – 1610–1643. 4. Mythology, Greek, in
literature. 5. Tragedy. I. Title.
PQ1785.P6C57   1992
842′.4 – dc20   91-14037   CIP

ISBN 0 521 40434 7 hardback

For Lesley Gilbert

Contents

Acknowledgements

First acknowledgement of indebtedness must go to Professor Odette de Mourgues. Of all others, she most revealed to me the pleasures of the seventeenth-century French stage and I much regret that she did not live to see this small tribute to the spell of her teaching. I would also like to express my gratitude to Professor W. D. Howarth, Professor W. Barber, and Dr E. Jacobs, and to my colleagues at King's College, London, especially Professor Richard Griffiths, Mr Martin Hall, Dr Anne Green, and Dr Valerie Worth. Without their wise counsel and support, nothing would have been possible. I am also grateful for the good offices of Sarah Stanton and the Cambridge University Press.

Note on the text

All abbreviations are self-explanatory short forms of titles set out in full on their first appearance in the main text. Fuller bibliographical details are entered in the Bibliography. I follow standard practice for the abbreviation of titles of journals in the case of *Forum for Modern Language Studies* (FMLS), *French Studies* (FS), the *Modern Language Review* (MLR), the *Revue d'Histoire Littéraire de la France* (RHLF), the *Romanic Review* (RR), and the *Revue des Sciences Humaines* (RSH).

With the exception of quotations from the reference editions of Corneille's works, the spelling of all period quotations has been modernized, as have capitalization and punctuation.

Introduction

It is a measure of Richelieu's success in transforming the country he governed that many still believe that the grass of Parnassus grows only in Paris. One consequence of such intellectual centrism has been that Corneille's historical and political drama has almost invariably been discussed in terms of Parisian taste or 'national' political preoccupations, or even assumed to be unambiguously expressive of his patron's policies. Few critics have related the plays to their author's provincial context, and then it was to see allusions to contemporary events, despite the aesthetic impropriety of reducing the universals of Classical drama to the particulars of history. Thus, before discussing the political interest of Corneille's serious drama written in the reign of Louis XIII, this study proposes both to re-examine the historical facts of this Norman dramatist's experience of politically momentous times (Part I) and, as a preliminary control to critical assessment of the plays, to explore the principles upon which Corneille believed that the drama, by transmuting history into tragedy, offered a means to the better understanding of his times (Part II).

Corneille was no different from many of his contemporaries in having a special interest in history and political theory as essential instruments in the understanding of present political events. But his disagreements with theoreticians in Paris on the proper dramatic imitation of history remind us of an intellectual independence which was already apparent in his private life. In an age when so many 'robins de province' left for Paris in pursuit of patronage, he was decidedly unusual in holding to a career as *officier* in the Palais de Justice in Rouen at the same time as successfully pursuing in Paris another literary career which was to bring him the patronage of Richelieu. Since that illustrious patron was also the man most responsible for a series of economic miseries and institutional

I

humiliations in Corneille's native Normandy, it is unlikely that the Rouennais political dramatist read the course of events with the Minister's eyes. Indeed, the tensions between Corneille's twin careers go far to explain his independence in discussion of the principles underpinning the dramatic recreation of history and the problematic nature of his dramatic illustration of political issues.

Apart from his plays and a small amount of occasional poetry, Corneille left little to tell us of his response to fundamental political debates which characterized the ministry of Richelieu, or to decisions made in Paris which severely affected his native Normandy. How Corneille's experience of his times contributed to the larger significance of his drama will only become clear if, by turning first to the external historical evidence of what it was to live in Normandy, we recognize that, educated in the rich humanistic culture of his Jesuit teachers and a proud participant in the cultural inheritance of the *officier* caste to which he belonged, he was also heir to a specifically Norman patrimony.[1] Part I can do little more than set out the major perspectives and bare facts of Corneille's provincial context, but it should suffice to show how a sense of 'Normanness' is likely to have affected the way in which he envisaged the dramatist's art and inflected the ways in which his plays recreated ancient history in the light of moral and political issues of immediate concern to the audiences of his day.

The very variety of the studies of Corneille which have appeared in the last forty years suggests that it would also be useful to look at his own description of his art before turning to direct discussion of his plays. Although Corneille wrote what is arguably the most original and distinguished body of seventeenth-century French dramatic theory, it is surprising how few critics have consistently tried to apply its lesson to the ways in which they approach the texts themselves.[2] As Corneille himself observed of the various interpretations which had been laid upon the *Poetics*, 'Je crois qu'il est à propos de parler de ce qu'il [Aristotle] a dit, avant que de faire effort pour deviner ce qu'il a voulu dire.'[3] And yet, despite the fact that Corneille's developing understanding of the practice of his art indicates his sensitivity to institutional changes and political pressures in a period when matters of poetics were never very far from matters of political ideology, critical discussion has traditionally been more concerned with exploring the literary influences and traditions which bear upon his work.[4] Thus, in offering a preliminary exploration of the attendant moral and aesthetic assumptions which informed the creation of his plays and their presentation to their audience, Part II of this study also aims to show how Corneille's work assumed and exploited habits of mind and intellectual structures specific to a period when there was no other generally current theory of art than the didactic theory of poetic imitation which ultimately derived from Aristotle. This view of poetry as a means to knowledge was not unaffected by the changing political circumstances of Corneille's long lifetime: indeed it came to be much modified by influential theorists whose establishment and political allegiances were of a very different kind to Corneille's, and whose conclusions on the obligations of the poet and on the nature and ends of poetry were correspondingly different, for all that each claimed to respect the spirit of the *Poetics*. In consequence, an awareness of the tensions which existed between provincial *officier* traditions and the interventionism of centralizing ministerial rule can give valuable relief to Corneille's theoretical originality, since prescriptive theorists close to the centres of power undoubtedly influenced him by their differences about what priorities governed literary judgements.

By noting such differences of theory and practice, I hope to show how Corneille's serious drama, so closely bound up with the intellectual inheritance and political evolution of his age, was particularly liable to misunderstanding once times changed and its supporting poetics fell into discredit or neglect. Since this happened even before Corneille's death, it is not surprising that twentieth-century readers are even less familiar with fundamental aspects of the theory within which he worked. Even at the most commonly received level, Corneille's poetics and their accompanying philosophy and moral psychology are at some remove from the literary sensibility and critical expectations of modern audiences and readers. The result has sometimes been perplexity and impatience or, worse, incautious invocations of 'realism' or 'anti-didacticism' which lead us yet further away from Corneille's explicit assertions on his art. In seeking, however tentatively, to re-establish the particular view which Corneille entertained of the artist's imitative relationship to 'reality' and – through his plays – to his audiences, we surely stand a better chance of appreciating the specific character and interest of his work. The twentieth-century mind, more attentive to the literal than to the figurative, and working within the pervasive assumptions of modern psychological terminology, all too easily falls into a language which, because foreign to seventeenth-century habits of thought, may not offer the most sympathetic means by which to describe Corneille's achievement, or define the relationship he envisaged between dramatic performance and spectator.

Since my principal concern is to isolate those elements of Corneille's poetics which are most distinctive in telling us about his understanding of his art, little time is spent on aspects of his theory where he is largely in accord with contemporary practice and which have been amply treated elsewhere. On the other hand, my discussion of Corneille's position under Louis XIII must necessarily include some consideration of the much later *Discours* of 1660. This is because, despite the special problems posed by their polemic context and by the fact that they are an author's retrospective reading of his own work, the *Discours* maintain an astonishing continuity with earlier major expressions of principle and offer insights into Corneille's earliest practice which are too valuable to leave aside. Furthermore, Corneille's later explanation and defence of his work defines what he understands by tragedy, an issue which he did not directly address in the period 1629 to 1643 but which is central to critical assessment of his plays.

Since it is intended that this preliminary study of Corneille's poetics should serve in some degree to control subsequent critical discussion of the plays themselves, I shall be more concerned with those elements of his theory which bear most heavily upon the moral and political significance of historical drama. For instance, it is of exemplary importance that Corneille so emphasizes the importance of the dramatic action as a whole and is so attentive to the fortunes of individual roles in an extended political conflict. Of similar interest is his enduring preoccupation with immediacy of meaning in the drama, since this throws into special relief the retrospective political significance of his *dénouements* which 'place' previous elements of the unfolding action and serve to order and weigh those elements, whether they be actions or earlier expressions of sentiment or principle. Only with the completion of the hero's destiny can audience or critic come to final judgement on the quality of individual motivation and choice as they had earlier been illustrated by various *dramatis personae* in the course of the action. Thus, when Corneille suggests that his plays pleased their audiences because they made immediate moral sense, he offers a salutary reminder to the critic that the leisurely interpretative pleasures of the expert scholar in his study are at some remove from the ways in which his plays' performance stimulated an audience to political reflexion.

If we are to recapture something of this effect with which Corneille's political plays first unfolded in performance, we need not only to respect the aesthetic assumptions which governed their creation and reception but also to situate their illustration of conflicts of values within the ideological controversies and institutional changes of the times when they were written. This is not to confine Corneille's drama to a dusty corner of literary history by evoking the preoccupations and prejudices of times none too close to us, for the plays, like Corneille's own theoretical works, make amply clear that it was the enduring necessities of our political condition which he sought to elucidate. Thus a primary aim of my discussion of Corneille's political drama in Part III is to explore the enduring appeal of those plays by setting them in relationship to the common assumptions of the seventeenth-century audience for which they were written. Others have amply established Corneille's affinity with the learned humanistic culture of the late sixteenth and early seventeenth centuries, but that culture extended, albeit in dilute form, to the far wider social spectrum of his first audiences. If we hold to the fact that Corneille's plays were enjoyed by many more than a cultured few, and remember that analogy was central to the intellectual habits of seventeenth-century France, then an interesting critical field emerges. As long as the obvious risk of confusing analogy with identity is borne in mind, a re-examination of Corneille's plays in the light of the minor moral and political writers of the period can serve to re-establish the link between the text and the moral and political convictions which governed the judgement of the reflective, if less expertly learned, spectators who formed the bulk of Corneille's seventeenth-century theatre public.

While Plato, Aristotle, St Thomas Aquinas, or Machiavelli were certainly familiar names to many of those spectators, their actual teaching was more likely to be known to them through the many popular, but minor, writers of the period who peddled moral commonplaces nicely adjusted to the understanding of a larger public. In fact Corneille's first audiences were likely to be far more familiar with the truisms contained in works by these largely forgotten contemporary moralists and political theorists than through direct acquaintance with the thought of the intellectual fathers of humanistic culture, or indeed with the major originals of contemporary French literature. For this reason such authors figure little in this attempt to pick up the calculated resonances of Corneille's 'peinture parlante' as it addressed itself to the collective 'mind' of its seventeenth-century audience. Indeed it is the very lack of originality of minor seventeenth-century moralists and political theorists, who rehearsed common belief rather than broke new ground, which links us to Corneille's first spectators and tells us something of the ways in which his plays challenged or appealed to the emotions and understanding of that intended audience. In discussing the significance of his plays, then, it is not my intention to extend yet further the literary biography of the dramatist himself, much less to treat the plays as a pre-text to the demonstration of a single preoccupation governing their overall development. This attempt to recapture something of the moral and political resonances of the serious drama which Corneille wrote under Louis XIII may reveal certain ideological sympathies and recurrent preoccupations, but these should emerge as no more and no less than the characteristic intellectual coherence to be expected of an uncommonly thoughtful and gifted dramatist's attempt to penetrate the significance of his times and set it before his public.

PART I

'Une muse de province'

'Une muse de province'

La première fois que je le vis, je le pris pour un marchand de Rouen : Son extérieur n'avait rien qui parlât pour son esprit... Il n'a jamais parlé bien correctement la langue française : peut-être se ne mettait-il pas en peine de cette exactitude ; mais peut-être aussi n'avait-il pas assez de force pour s'y soumettre.

Corneille était assez grand, et assez plein, l'air fort simple et fort commun, toujours négligé et peu curieux de son extérieur... Il parlait peu, même sur la matière qu'il entendait parfaitement. Il n'ornait pas ce qu'il disait : et pour trouver le grand Corneille il le fallait lire... Il avait l'humeur brusque, et quelquefois rude en apparence : au fond il était très aisé à vivre, bon mari, bon parent tendre et plein d'amitié... Il n'aimait point la Cour, il y apportait un visage presque inconnu, un grand nom qui ne s'attirait que des louanges et un mérite qui n'était point de ce pays-là.[1]

These descriptions of Corneille in old age, with his undistinguished appearance and Norman accent, show a man quite content with his provincial origins and who had no interest in acquiring 'le bel air de la cour'. All who met Corneille in later life remark on his lack of the social graces which had come to be expected in the brilliant world of Paris and the Court during the last forty years of the century. All suggest that the famous dramatist remained in many respects a provincial for all his life, and all show a striking lack of interest in his Normanness as they separate his incorrigibly provincial accent and unpolished appearance from the distinction of his plays. This metropolitan distaste for Corneille's obstinate provincialism is already apparent in Chapelain's letters to Balzac in the early days of the young Rouennais lawyer-poet's rising fortunes. Having complained of Corneille's 'bourru' manners in the 1630s, in 1640 Chapelain referred to his vulgar interest in the profits his pen could earn him. *Horace* would only be published after a profitable run on the stage and Balzac would have to wait for the pleasure of reading it: 'telles sont les conventions des poètes mercenaires et tel le destin des pièces vénales'. Six months on, when Balzac had still not got his copy, Chapelain returned to Corneille's provincial concern for his money:

Pour les *Horaces* de Corneille, on ne vous en saurait servir parce que le poète est à Rouen, et que le poème est de ces marchandises qui sont à vendre et non à donner.[2]

For his part, Corneille was well aware of his differences with the experts on the merit of his play, and deliberately marked out his chosen distance from the capital when he dedicated *Horace* to the Cardinal as the work of 'une muse de province'.[3]

The tenacity with which Corneille held to his roots provoked open scorn and mistrust in his literary adversaries. To D'Aubignac, who had been much more closely linked to Cardinal Richelieu's côterie than Corneille and whose view of the proper pursuit of literature made the drama symbiotic with the cultivation of central power and patronage, Corneille's enjoyment of the literary life of a provincial capital was almost incomprehensible.[4] But Corneille knew his real worth, and when he finally removed to the capital in 1662, he was too old and too confident of that worth to be convinced of the necessity of acquiring new social graces. His pen spoke better for him than ever could his tongue with an accent which he would not reform simply to please the ears of Paris society. This defensive pride seems to have been a major feature of Corneille's character, constantly showing itself in an obstinate independence which strained relations even with the best-intentioned of his contemporaries. Chapelain perhaps hit on the truth in 1662 when, reporting on the literary talents of the day, he observed that Corneille had prodigious poetic talents as well as 'de la doctrine et du sens', but added that he entirely lacked other qualities essential to success in the world of 'les grandes affaires': 'Hors du théâtre on ne sait s'il réussirait en prose ou en vers, agissant de son chef, car il a peu d'expérience du monde et ne voit guère rien hors de son métier.'[5] Corneille's failure to adapt to Paris manners, his flagging conversation and apparently narrow interests seem to reflect a social unease which stemmed from being appreciated only for that part of himself which complemented a world with which, in other respects, he had less in common. As Fontenelle implies, Corneille's qualities were too deeply rooted in another provincial world to be much appreciated in 'ce pays-là'.

Present-day readers, less convinced that the centres of power alone express the proper order of things, may well suspect that the repeated contrast of poet and man tells us more about the exclusive viewpoint of the capital than about the author of *Le Cid* and *Horace*. What is missing in contemporary references to the poet's worries about his profits or to his carelessness about his accent or appearance is an awareness of how important Corneille's Norman roots were to him. These pundits simply did not consider that an interest in money was characteristic of life in a province where times were a good deal harder than in Paris, or that Corneille's concern for the profitability of his plays might stem from a healthy respect for the pleasures of an audience rather broader then an élite group of literary experts. For our part, we should be careful not to adopt the same intellectual centrism which so discounts aspects of Corneille's character and preoccupations which may seem to have little to do with a 'great French dramatist'. Notoriously miserly and unkempt himself, Chapelain was nonetheless General Secretary of the Académie Française and Corneille's provincial habits were easy to misinterpret from the relative comfort of the capital.[6] And yet, had Chapelain given a little thought to the way Corneille was marked by his Norman background, even he might have been struck by the irony that the man whose decisions most cruelly affected Corneille's province was also his patron in Paris. If we are to understand the paradox of that position, and its implications to the drama which transformed plain Pierre Corneille into 'le grand Corneille', we need to recall the Norman context and eventful times in which the poet began his long career.

Of Corneille's thirty-two complete plays, no less than twenty-six were written during the first fifty-six years of a life firmly rooted in Normandy. Corneille had tried his hand as a poet in his student days, but his true career began with the attachment to the local Palais de Justice and the purchase of a double *office* in the Rouen Parlement in 1628. Twenty-one of his plays were composed while he fulfilled his obligations as 'Avocat du Roi à l'Amirauté de France, et des Eaux et Forêts à la Table de Marbre'. As such, Corneille represented the third generation of his family to belong to the

humbler levels of the Rouennais *officier* caste. Since the day when his
forebears had moved to the provincial capital and begun to buy their
way into the dignities which made them a part of the growing
'Fourth Estate' of the *robe*, his family had followed the pattern of
social ascent characteristic of the provincial bourgeoisie in service of
an increasingly powerful monarchy. In January 1637 Corneille's
father, Pierre, was ennobled in reward for this solid tradition of
provincial service to the Crown. Corneille's own growing success as
a dramatist undoubtedly played its part in this ennoblement,[7] and
that literary career would so broaden the narrowly provincial
horizons of his family's interests and ambitions that Corneille and his
younger brother Thomas would move house to Paris in 1662.
Meanwhile, in 1635, Corneille's literary success would earn him the
patronage of the man whose policies were irrevocably to alter the
future of France – and at considerable cost to the poet's native
Normandy.

On the Day of Dupes (11 November 1630), Richelieu mastered
any effective opposition in the King's Council, and thereafter
pursued an aggressive foreign policy of national grandeur which was
to bring about an extraordinary revolution in France's institutions
and European destiny.[8] French involvement in the Thirty Years'
War before 1635 had meant costly subsidies to the Holy Roman
Emperor's Protestant enemies, but entry into open war with Spain
made the Cardinal's 'politique de gloire' still more expensive and
the possibility of much needed internal reforms still more remote. As
Richelieu observed: 'Si le Roi se résolvait à la guerre – and he made
sure that the King did so – 'il fallait quitter toute pensée de repos,
d'épargne et de règlement du dedans du royaume'.[9] Well aware of
the country's need for reorganization and reconciliation, he knew
that a greater danger lay beyond her frontiers in the ambitions of the
House of Habsburg. Internal reforms would have to wait upon the
reduction of the threat of Habsburg encirclement, and a stern policy
of discipline and repression would have to serve at home if he was to
find the money necessary to a successful prosecution of the war.

A rapid rise in taxation, forced by the iron logic of financing open
hostilities, was the most generally felt consequence of Richelieu's
reversal of the traditional policy of alliance with Spain. Furthermore,
the ways in which the money was raised were perceived by many to
be profoundly at variance with tradition, as the government of
France moved from a judicial exercise of sovereign power towards

more expeditious and pragmatic methods. This change, in which a fundamentally religious view of the body politic ruled by a king revered as God's viceroy on earth was forced to yield before a more secular view of government in which the King embodied the modern State's sovereign executive authority, has been interpreted as but one illustration of the larger ideological revolution which took place in the early modern Europe of Corneille's long lifetime.[10] Certainly Richelieu's shift from a religious view of government towards more harshly pragmatic political methods prompted a vigorous revival of political theory and debate, which was in turn reflected in the historical drama written in the latter years of Louis XIII's reign and during the minority of Louis XIV.

A sense of traditional order in peril was common in the first half of the century, as belief in the ordered and purposive security of an Aristotelian interpretation of the world was increasingly shaken by the confusion of contemporary events. Behind the expression of personal bereavement, Donne's *Anatomie of the World* of 1611 already tells of the failure of traditional certainties as it laments the decay of Nature:

> And new Philosophy calls all in doubt,
> The Element of fire is quite put out...
> And freely men confess that this world's spent,
> When in the Planets, and the Firmament
> They seek so many new; then see that this
> Is crumbled out again to his Atomies.
> 'Tis all in pieces, all coherence gone;
> All just supply, and all Relation.[11]

This theme of disorientation was repeatedly to be evoked as the emerging nation-states of Europe experienced the convulsions of the Thirty Years' War and the revolutions and revolts of the 1630s and 1640s. During the ominous preliminaries to the execution of Charles I in the most spectacular institutional revolution of the period, Sir Robert Fanshawe remarked that war seemed now to govern the crooked order of the times:

> Now war is all the world about
> And everywhere *Erynnis* reigns,
> Or else the Torch so late put out,
> The stench remains.[12]

To many men of culture this was very evidence of a drift away from ancient sanctities, as the rulers of the seventeenth century, trusting to will and artifice alone, stumbled into the confusions of an age of iron.

In comparison with her neighbours, France was relatively fortunate and largely escaped the upheavals which shook so many nations at the time. Yet there could be little doubt that a revolution of a sort was afoot in the country and the theme of order lost recurs most commonly amongst those who, like Corneille with his special interest in history and politics, had been nurtured in the humanistic ideals of late Renaissance culture. All were impressed by the way the time-hallowed traditions of a 'tempered' absolutism were yielding before 'la nécessité évidente' and more autocratic methods of governance.[13] Even amongst more pragmatic thinkers, men convinced that this move to a more strongly centralized power was the only guarantee of stability, it was far from easy to agree what were – or ought to be – the principles upon which that order should be grounded. Those principles were fiercely debated in every country in Europe, but France was distinctive in the way in which contentious institutional change was fuelled by the government itself. As Richelieu pursued his 'politique de gloire' in the face of a series of rebellions and conspiracies which under Mazarin were to culminate in the Frondes (1648–52), the tensions generated by France's involvement in the Thirty Years' War provoked so widespread a sense of anxiety and nostalgia for more innocent and ordered times that many felt driven to express their concern. In vividly practical terms the *Lettre d'un gentilhomme français bon catholique* (probably written in 1632) bemoans the changed social and political climate:

Paris n'est plus Paris; et notre siècle est pire cent fois que celui des premières années de Tibère; deux personnes n'osant converser familière-ment comme amis, ni se parler à l'oreille, sinon portes serrées, et après avoir secoué les tapisseries, et examiné s'il y a quelques trous au plancher, ou aux serrures des portes, de là où leurs gestes puissent être aperçus…Bien que jamais je n'aie rien écrit qui puisse offenser le Roi ou l'Etat, je n'ai pour autant osé confier jusqu'à présent aucune de mes lettres à mes domestiques, ayant pris le soin et la peine de les aller consigner en personne chez le messager.[14]

Repeatedly a kinder past is contrasted with the present war and harsh repression at home. In an uneasy mixture of exhilaration before national triumphs abroad and weariness and uncertainty about the morality of hostilities against fellow-Catholics, many anxiously reflected on the way present policies seemed to signal the end of the traditional sanctities of French monarchical rule.

Of Corneille's acquaintances, Chapelain himself had to admit that times had changed for the worse and that he envied Balzac's bucolic pleasures in his Charentais retreat:

Je vous envie votre siècle d'or et je me contenterais bien d'en passer ici un d'argent, mais la guerre qui ne finit pas encore nous en fait vivre un d'aussi mauvais fer qu'il en ait encore été employé dans le monde.[15]

With his personal investment in the new order, Chapelain did not blame the Cardinal for the war or for the drift towards an increasingly autocratic exercise of power. Balzac, however, did not hesitate to do so – at least in private. While he was never Corneille's friend, Balzac admired his work and in August 1637 had written publicly in defence of *Le Cid*. Privately he had also expressed his astonishment at Corneille's ability to delight his audiences by renewing 'par le théâtre la terreur et la pitié que Richelieu fait régner sur la scène de la réalité'. In 1640 he again confided his disgust for political triumphs bought at such a cost to the people, and in January 1643 wrote to Corneille fervently to applaud in *Cinna* an Augustan vision of a monarchical legitimacy capable of bringing an end to civil disorder and political dissent.[16] In 1644, his *Relation à Ménandre* eloquently expresses his disenchantment and his hopes that the world might yet be brought to rights:

La corruption est grande mais le genre humain, quoique fort gâté a encore des parties entières, et il y a encore quelques restes de justice sur la terre... L'erreur ne gagne pas tant de pays ni se déborde si généralement qu'elle ne laisse place à la vérité: et la vérité n'est pas si seule ni si mal assistée qu'elle ne subsistera dans le temps contraire en attendant qu'elle puisse vaincre quand le temps favorable sera venu.[17]

By Balzac's death in 1654, the ineluctable evidence of the new political order had turned all such hopes to ashes, and Corneille himself recognized the inapplicability of the providentialism of his drama to present times. The reassuring conclusion of *Pertharite* was remote indeed from recent events in a Cromwellian England ruled by a regicide commoner. Sadly he drew his conclusions:

Il est temps que je sonne la retraite... je commence à m'apercevoir que je deviens trop vieux pour être à la mode. (*Pertharite*, 'Au Lecteur', GC, II, 715)

When later he began to write again for the stage, his work would above all provoke a sense of scandal before the irrelevance of older ideals of heroic and civic virtue in a world now irredeemably given over to the cynical pursuit of political advantage and brutal calculations of force.

The experience of the Frondes stands between Balzac's attenuated hopes in his *Relation à Ménandre* and Corneille's withdrawal on the failure of *Pertharite*. As the Frondes came to an end, it had become apparent how insufficient was any appeal to tradition in protest against the advance of political pragmatism and royal authoritarianism. In this respect the Frondes were but the last of a series of ideologically conservative and reactionary revolts unavailingly mounted against Richelieu, whose transformation of the government of France Mazarin made it his business to complete. Mazarin's return to Paris early in 1653 marked the end of any effective role in political decision for the *noblesse d'épée* and for a *noblesse de robe* which, by religious conviction and constitutional tradition, claimed to play an essential tempering role in the royal dispensation of justice. In the years which followed, traditionalists who had sought to put reason and knowledge to the service of a State grounded in religion would be increasingly on the retreat as the pursuit of truth and political ambition came to rest in the hands of more disillusioned and pragmatic men.[18] By 1662, Louis XIV's reduction of the *noblesse d'épée* to little more than a military or decorative role, like his denial to the Sovereign Courts of any participation in the conduct of government through their rights of remonstrance and review, spectacularly illustrated the triumph of an essentially executive concept of government. Completing the logic of a process which Corneille's old patron had hastened thirty years earlier when the necessities of war drove him to expand a directly appointed executive bureaucracy, the King made it clear that he would govern without regard to institutions or orders who grounded their claim to importance in a fundamentally religious view of the nature and delegation of his royal authority.[19] Henceforth all eyes would look only to the Conseil du Roi, and to a monarch who seemed to assume in himself a divinity of which earlier he had been simply the earthly representative. Whether as Apollo in the splendid iconography of the Sun King's court or when, in his daily devotions in the chapel at Versailles, he eclipsed the altar as sole object of his courtiers' attention, Louis XIV magnificently embodied an idea of the monarchy as final repository of truth and authority, sole centre of power and patronage in the nation-state. It was both apt and inevitable that the playwright, who despite earlier patronage had held to his provincial roots in Rouen, finally packed his bags and moved to the capital in the same year of 1662 when Louis XIV peremptorily completed the political humiliation of the *officier* caste in which Corneille had served so long in his home province.[20]

THE NORMAN CONTEXT

If we look to Normandy and to Corneille's place within the institutional changes of the period, it is clear that his family's social ambitions were built on close association with the judicial admini-stration of the provincial economy.[21] As the eldest son of quietly respectable *bourgeois* in Rouen, Corneille's entry into his twin *offices* continued a tradition which had become the most important guarantee of his family's standing within the local community.[22] The means which enabled his father to ensure that continued par-ticipation in the dignities and ideological patrimony of the Rouennais *officier* caste were founded on the prudent acquisition and letting of local property. Since 1584, when Corneille's grandfather first became a citizen of Rouen, the family had farmed or rented small parcels of land, mostly in the neighbourhood of the city. Comfortably off if not rich, they owned two houses in Rouen – one of which they let – and as *bourgeois* of a *ville franche* they enjoyed exemption from the *taille*. This put them at a financial advantage over other modestly prosperous *laboureurs* outside the city walls in acquiring agricultural holdings on the outskirts of Rouen in a classic instance of the movement of wealth to the towns in the period. None of these properties outside the city walls was particularly large and, until Pierre Senior's ennoblement in 1637, they would have enjoyed no fiscal exemptions on income gained from them.

Inheritance as well as careful investment helped these townsfolk gradually increase their modest family patrimony, and Corneille and his younger brother Thomas jointly inherited a manor house and some 125 hectares of land in Les Andelys. Apart from investing in *charges* bought for the rising generation and their activity as petty landlords, the Corneille family also loaned money to others of the *officier* caste in Rouen, loans repaid by *rentes* on properties which were themselves security for the principal sum borrowed. They do not seem to have invested in the more risky area of loans to the Crown.[23] In sum it seems that Corneille's family, despite its brand new title of nobility, valued its roots in the local countryside quite as much as its modest standing in the Rouennais *officier* society. Corneille's sons, rather than the poet himself, made the real break with family tradition when they bought commissions in the King's armies and began the next stage of seventeenth-century social ascent. As for the dramatist himself, his attachment to the Rouennais simply continued family tradition, for all that his literary talents had become an important source of income. When he removed to Paris it was principally to further his younger brother's literary career and his sons' ambitions, since he himself had been content to pass fifty-six years in Normandy as petty land-owner and provincial lawyer. His enduring attachment to his *terroir* is touchingly evident in the fact that he finally sold the house in the rue de la Pie and his little property of Petit Couronne only a year before his death – some twenty years after he moved to Paris – and then he made his will.

Corneille's pride in his Rouennais *offices* and his affection for his properties reminds us that more is at issue here than money. By recognizing the importance which many of his generation attached to local loyalties, we may better understand the tensions which existed between Corneille's literary patronage and his provincial identity. In the sixteenth and early seventeenth centuries the term *patrie*, as referring to a national entity, remained the possession of learned, and particularly neo-Stoic, scholars such as Guillaume du Vair. As a term to rally national loyalties it first came to prominence in the ministerial apologetics of the 1630s and early 1640s, and it is far from certain that Corneille himself offers an instance of this later usage in his plays.[24] Not until the latter part of the seventeenth century was the term *patriote* commonly used in association with the nation-state and in the modern sense of 'a man conscious of his loyal participation in, and obligation to serve, the larger national entity of the state'. It is a telling reminder of the strains which earlier existed between particularist provincial tradition and the hardening profile of state authority in the time of Richelieu that those at the centre of power then used the term in a derogatory sense to describe anyone who supported the interests of his province rather than those of King and Court.[25] And indeed, to a Rouennais in the 1630s, a sense of *patria* first meant the moral entity of the family *domus*, with its extended relationships by descent and marital alliance. After that it embraced a vocational community such as the magistrature to which Corneille belonged in Rouen. In turn these loyalties contributed to a broader sense of identity as a subject of the King in his province of Normandy. Thus the major components of a sense of *patria* would be 'a sense of kinship and unity with others sharing the same allegiance' and 'a sense of community as a legal and historical entity with distinctive characteristics, specific obligations, rights and privileges'. Ultimately, and only very hazily, might it have stretched to include the community of the realm.[26]

For Corneille, to be born a Frenchman of Normandy would have implied a sense of belonging which linked him to his provincial countrymen through shared allegiance to the King of France in a community recognizable by local custom and by the way its history and laws guaranteed proudly distinctive Norman rights and obligations under the Crown. To be a citizen of Rouen in the 1630s and to be an *officier* of the King in his provincial Parlement was to be at the heart of a *patrie* whose distinguishing rights and liberties were recalled all the more vividly because they were now threatened by ministerial policy. In the 1620s and 1630s the promise of literary patronage and fame drew many Norman writers to Paris, and Corneille was exceptional in choosing, despite his success in the capital, to remain in Rouen. In fact his early work offers an occasional hint of his special sense of 'Normanness', for the 1632 sonnet in praise of Richelieu is likely to have conveyed a double-edged meaning particularly to be appreciated by Norman readers.[27] He was also proud to remind his Paris audience of how many successful writers were Normans when, in *La Galerie du Palais*, a discussion of the fashion for theatre-going leads Lysandre to observe that 'Beaucoup font des vers, mais peu la comédie.' Dorimant his friend then remarks that 'Ton goût, je m'en assure, est pour la Normandie' (*La Galerie du Palais*, I, vii, 145–6). As La Pinelière noted in 1635, 'maintenant pour se faire croire excellent poète, il faut être né dans la Normandie', and in the same year he wrote that Corneille was at present engaged on a play about a Duke of Normandy.[28] The sensation of *Le Cid* proved the information wrong, but the rumour shows how Corneille's name was associated with a specifically Norman character and preoccupations in the years when first he made his reputation as a playwright.

Rouen's proximity to Paris both confirmed and threatened this Norman sense of identity, rendering the local Parlement especially

sensitive to events in the national capital. In the 1630s some of its
officiers were quick to follow the lead set by their Parisian colleagues
in obstructing the Cardinal's will and behind both popular protest
and local Parlement obstructionism there was a fervent reaffirmation
of the province's distinctively Norman privileges under the King's
justice.[29] Most important of the ancient and distinguishing rights on
which the King's Norman subjects grounded their protests were the
liberties guaranteed to them by the Chartre Normande. This had
originally been granted in perpetuity by Louis X in 1315 and, in the
Duchy at least, it was believed to give Normandy a uniquely
favourable position under the governance of the Crown. Notably it
gave every Norman subject the right of direct appeal to his liege-lord
the King, who, in response to this *clameur de haro*, undertook
immediately to suspend all exercise by delegation of the royal justice
and investigate, either in person or through a specially appointed
representative, the claim that his Norman subjects had been wronged
by the malfeasance or incompetence of his officers. More importantly, in a period during which the King's greatest servant
forced crushing increases of taxation on Normandy, certain articles
of the Charter were deemed still to guarantee the King's Norman
subjects freedom from all 'extraordinary' taxation, obliging them to
pay only the normal feudal dues and the *taille*. The single limitation
set upon this special fiscal status lay in the Charter's recognition that,
in cases of extreme necessity, the King might request extra moneys
from his Norman subjects. The amount of such a contribution would
never be imposed, but would instead by freely agreed to by the
provincial Estates and paid in the form of a *don gracieux*.[30] These
privileges remained alive in the popular Norman awareness of a
distinctive identity, and the *clameur de haro* survived at least notionally
as part of the customary law of the province. But the reality was that
the Charter had ceased to be recognized by the Crown since the
early years of the seventeenth century. Henri IV had been the first
king to exclude it from the long list of 'Lois Fondamentales' and
traditional rights which every King of France swore to observe at his
sacre and, in his turn, the infant Louis XIII had not sworn to uphold
the Charter. These royal tactics, curtailing local particularisms by
default and omission rather than by active opposition, were not
however believed by the common people of Normandy to have
invalidated their hallowed and distinctive liberties. Indeed the more
Richelieu imposed extraordinary taxes and forced levies in the 1630s

and 1640s, the more the men of Normandy recalled those ancient privileges. This was particularly evident in the Nu-Pieds uprising of 1639, when Rouen became involved in one of the most spectacular manifestations of provincial resistance to Richelieu's policies.[31]

A Norman born and bred but trained in the law, Corneille would have been well aware of the technically obsolete character of the Charter: he would also have been quick to see how the traditional liberties of his native province were being set aside. That process was all the more apparent because it exacerbated hard times which left few in the province unaffected. But here it should be said that Corneille's own feelings are likely to have been mixed, since he stood to gain from the misfortunes of fellow-Normans whose livelihood was solely based on cultivation of the land. Many of the townsfolk of Rouen – and particularly those of the *officier* class – considerably increased their holdings of local land during times of sudden and harsh rises in taxation when debtors, unable to maintain repayment on their loans, were forced to surrender to creditor townsfolk the deeds of agricultural property which had secured their borrowing. It is unlikely that Corneille's family refrained from such profitable transactions at the time, and there is evidence that he later acquired land by foreclosing on secured loans to debtors who had got into difficulties of repayment.

The less agreeable side of the matter was that, as a petty land-owner and minor *officier* in the provincial Parlement, Corneille himself could not entirely have escaped the harsh consequences of his Cardinal-patron's policies in Normandy. To understand how this happened we have to begin with natural calamities which were seriously aggravated by Richelieu's costly pursuit of his 'politique de gloire'. From 1620, the climatic hiccup which has been called the little ice age of the seventeenth century resulted in a series of such poor harvests that food shortages became both cause and conse-quence of a dramatic fall in the population working the land.[32] This precipitated an agricultural crisis and serious economic difficulties even in so rich a province as Normandy. Cruelly, the full weight of the government's impositions was imposed just when a prolonged economic recession really began to bite. By the 1630s hard cash had become scarce and prices rose sharply, while income levels remained generally stagnant until general recovery in the 1660s. To make matters worse, the plague – a natural companion of hunger in the countryside – became endemic in Normandy and lingered on until

1640 in parts of the province and especially in the Rouennais.[33] A series of *mortalités*, the worst of which occurred in 1630, further depressed the province's prosperity, with Rouen suffering particularly badly in the years between 1636 and 1640.

By the closing years of Richelieu's ministry, Normandy was in the unenviable position of enjoying the reputation, but no longer the reality, of possessing a wealth which Government was determined to tap in order to keep the King's armies in the field. The province's own Estates and Parlement should have afforded it some protection, but their repeated protests between 1635 and 1638 did nothing to stem ministerial demands. This disregard of Normandy's Sovereign Courts was a severe blow to local pride and foreshadowed the province's extreme institutional disgrace after the Nu-Pieds revolt in 1639, when its Parlement was suspended and a commission of sixteen men was sent in to administer the province. In terms of taxation, Normandy in the 1630s seemed speedily to be becoming subject to the relatively unfavourable conditions of other provinces which had no representative courts and whose contribution was decided in Paris. By 1639, in the larger context of a nation already taxed at five times the level which had obtained under Henri IV, the three *généralités* of the province's fiscal structure contributed no less than a quarter of the total revenue raised in France, half of which was spent on the war. Institutionally and economically enfeebled, Normandy's difficulties in that year were so extreme that eighty-two out of a list of 183 villages were unable to settle their taxes.[34]

There is no doubt that Richelieu was well aware of the discontent caused by his demands for money, and his letters urged those involved in collecting taxes to avoid excessive severity so as not to destroy the people's loyalty. But the practical realities of finding the money brought painful measures which were as unavoidable as they were offensive to the local *officiers* who traditionally administered taxation. The Cardinal himself had no choice but to establish, in the name of 'la nécessité évidente', a directly appointed system of commissaries and *intendants de finances*. Sent in from Paris and attached to the Hôtel de Ville, such appointments had been made on a temporary and *ad hoc* basis since the sixteenth century. But as the war dragged on their duties were extended from merely inspecting the provincial fiscal administration to directly settling the amount to be contributed in forced loans and to seeing that the cash was indeed collected. Only thus could government expedite the collection of funds by bypassing the regional fiscal courts whose *élus* and *trésoriers* claimed to be the only true delegates of the King's authority and argued that such direct impositions of royal taxation offended liberties guaranteed by the Fundamental Laws of the Realm. Their lofty appeals to tradition cut little ice with the Cardinal. Too often they were a cover for personal interests and regional or institutional particularism; as a result they often made matters worse, since they forced Richelieu to rely even more on his henchmen.[35]

But the local Parlement in Rouen also contained traditionalist *officiers* whose reverence for the sanctity of their relation to the Crown inspired genuinely high-minded protests backed by a profound humanistic and juridical culture. In their view a position in the Parlement, whether of Paris or of Normandy, imposed on them a solemn obligation to the King as members of tempering Sovereign Courts which enjoyed inalienable rights of advice and review. Jérôme Bignon, Avocat Général in the Paris Parlement, was a distinguished example of these *officiers* whose culture and religious sense of the institutional dignity of the magistrature led them to oppose the Cardinal's conduct of affairs. Bignon courageously argued in the Paris Parlement for the particular dignity of that Sovereign Court as the successor to the ancient *Curia Regis* to whose wisdom the King was bound to pay heed. In his *Remonstrance d'Ouverture* of 1627 he eloquently set out the claims of his caste as a veritable living temple of wisdom and justice in the realm, portraying the Parlement as a kind of public conscience essential to the legitimacy of royal governance.[36] In 1636 this formidably cultured lawyer returned to his theme before Louis XIII himself in his *lit de justice*, but it was in vain that he protested that, if Richelieu's exceptional measures advanced the power of the King, they did so in contravention of the sacred and conciliating traditions of royal justice.

Draping themselves in the stately toga of dignities appropriate to their inheritance of a long-hallowed judiciary function, provincial *officiers* echoed their Paris colleagues and asserted that they too had an essential role to play in local administration as a kind of conscience to the royal will. To such men obstructive remonstrance was a principled means to preserve the King's justice in their province. In no sense did they consider that their opposition to the Cardinal's expedients implied disloyalty to the King. On the contrary, they believed that they were defending the just exercise of kingly rule against the taint of bad counsel and ministerial tyranny. This line of argument was held to be particularly strong in the matter of taxation, since universally respected authorities like Bodin considered the right freely to review and advise on the Crown's demands for money to be an essential distinguishing feature between the sanctity and excellence of the 'most Christian' French monarchy and the *monarchie seigneuriale* of pagan antiquity, totally unrestrained in the possession and use of its subjects' lives and wealth.[37] The view that the Sovereign Courts constituted a 'puissance seconde' in the realm had been forcefully expressed earlier in the uncertain years of Louis XIII's minority, but under Richelieu's ministry it persisted in the safer and more general form of political theory which repeatedly characterized government by 'coup d'état' as contrary to the French monarchy's respect for natural justice in ordering the body politic.[38] Intense public interest in this debate is reflected on the stage during the period, and not least in *Le Cid*, *Horace*, and *Cinna*. As might be expected of plays written by an *officier* with a particular interest in politics and history, all three plays variously illustrate the conflicting claims bearing on royal decision and explore the ideological and economic price of national glory.

Money, as well as local solidarity and an offended sense of institutional dignity, prompted opposition in the provinces, even amongst men whose rank and office often guaranteed them personal immunity from the bulk of taxation which fell on peasants, merchants, and artisans. The more privileged still stood to lose by the impoverishment of their tenants and found themselves increasingly out of pocket as a result of rising taxation on goods and their movement. A number of Corneille's colleagues in the provincial Parlement gave covert support to popular protest in Normandy because the Cardinal's taxes affected their own income as landlords. Too many tenants, unable to meet both the exactions of the state commissaries and pay their rent, satisfied the tax-collector backed by a troupe of *fusiliers* and then pleaded penury to their landlords when the time came for settling dues. This explains why many more than the wretched *taillables* so resented the special commissaries sent into the province, especially after enforcement of the *levée de subsistence* (November 1637) which paid for the maintenance of unwelcome troops and fell principally upon the towns, whether or not they were *villes franches* like Rouen.

Another reason for discontent among petty land-owners and

officiers was that some of the peasantry, particularly hard hit by poor harvests, abandoned the land and joined a swelling vagabond population which drifted towards the greater affluence of the towns. Not only was the town-dweller's investment in workable agricultural land at risk, he also had to lay out good money in order to cope with this increase of beggars in the city. Unenviable choices arose between running further into municipal debt in an attempt directly to help the destitute, curtailing movement between city and surrounding countryside, and raising the municipal income by setting higher tolls. The last two measures were most often adopted because they were less painful in the short term, but they disrupted trade, further impoverished the local tenantry, and so diminished their landlords' returns.[39] While no direct evidence exists to show that Corneille or his family suffered from this spiral of misfortune, he could hardly have remained indifferent to it, since his own accounts as treasurer of the Parish of St Sauveur show that in 1650 the Hôtel de Ville had still not fully recovered from its financial difficulties and was able only partially to repay the interest on loans raised from the parish.

Government simply turned a deaf ear to the city fathers' vehement protests that Rouen was in no state to meet further demands of money. Yet even the Cardinal knew that Normandy was in such serious difficulties that it actually needed extra funds if its collapsing economy were to recover. Unfortunately the province was not alone in this and the hard-pressed Minister for Finance knew that, when it came to funds, right across France the Crown had come near to scraping the bottom of the barrel. Even the greatly increased number of *offices* for sale was giving diminishing returns. This matter of government attempts in the 1630s and 1640s to supplement revenue by selling *offices* draws attention to yet another cause for discontent among the incumbent *officiers* of the Rouen Parlement. Between 1635 and 1637 the latter fiercely resisted the creation of any new *offices* by delaying registration of the relevant edicts, since many of these new posts duplicated existing ones. This devalued the worth of the original *office* as an investment, diminished its holder's particular dignity, and halved the fees which he might expect from it. In 1638 Corneille himself petitioned to prevent a similar devaluation of his own *office* but in July 1640 his pleas were dismissed, to the government's profit and his financial loss. Other governmental manipulations of the cost of selling and inheriting *offices* did not affect him, but it is hard to imagine that he remained indifferent to government initiatives which so offended many of his kind in Rouen.[40]

Of course Corneille, with his very minor *offices*, is not to be identified with the powerful families who led the Parlement's resistance to the Cardinal. We should not underestimate, however, the elaborately hierarchical character of the Ancien Régime, nor how important was a corporate sense of identity and institutional dignity to the *officier* caste in which Corneille's participation gave him his principal sense of social status. His dignities participated in those of more influential fellow magistrates, and he would have been well aware of the collective affront represented by Richelieu's expedients. Furthermore, his duties as 'Avocat du Roi en l'Amirauté de France et à la Table de Marbre' were to defend the King's interests in matters principally relating to ship-building and the use and exploitation of the rivers and forests of the province. Since this called for a thorough knowledge of the King's rights and of those of his Norman subjects in two areas of major significance to the provincial economy, he certainly could not have ignored the damage caused by the impoverishment of his province.[41] For this to be clear we need only note the importance of timber to local industry and the peasant economy, and recall that it had been a question of forestry rights and the sale of firewood which provided the initial pretext for the revolt of the salt-workers of lower Normandy. As for the 'waters' which were Corneille's concern as the King's representative in any irregularities or disputes, they too represented a major source in the rural economy. They were an important source of energy in the milling of grain and played a major role in the increasingly heavily taxed transport of goods in the province. Like the woods and forests they were also a source of food, and the protection of the King's rights against poaching must have assumed growing importance as famine became more common and the agricultural economy flagged.[42] It would be rash indeed to assume that, as one of the *gens du roi* in the Rouen Parlement, Corneille's attitude to ministerial policy was predefined by the fact that he represented the King's interests in court. It is rather more likely that his duties brought sharply home to him the plight of his province and the deteriorating relationship between Crown and *patrie*, as the latter paid the price of a war for which many held Richelieu to be responsible.

That war had begun none too well since, by 1636, the Spanish armies had advanced from the north as far as Corbie and their outriders had even been seen near Pontoise. This invasion of Picardy brought further misfortune to northern Normandy, which began to suffer all the miseries of a frontier province without any of the fiscal privileges which such regions traditionally enjoyed. Villages and towns were driven yet further into debt, since they were forced to pay to equip the able-bodied men who were marched off to join the King's armies. It is well known that, despite Richelieu's efforts to ensure that officers had the money to pay their troops and maintain sound discipline, dread of the French soldiery was little different from fear of occupation by the enemy. In 1637 Sublet des Noyers noted that all France was complaining of irregularly paid and ill-controlled French soldiery, and the geography of hostilities meant that Normandy bore the brunt of the costly and disruptive consequences of quartering and maintaining them.[43] Furthermore the very morality of the Cardinal's war was widely questioned, since many considered the disastrous early campaign in the Low Countries to be conclusive evidence of divine displeasure at a policy which had abandoned the traditional Catholic alliance and divided the brotherhood of true Christendom. The outburst of rejoicing in Paris at news of the relief of Corbie is to be assessed against this previous record of dismal military failure which many believed to be providential confirmation of their worst doubts. Over-ruling widespread misgivings both at Court and in the provinces, Richelieu had to wait until the last year of his life to see the first glimmerings of the solid success which alone could justify him. Until then, in a land which looked anxiously for a conclusion to the war, ruthless severity would serve to deter anyone whose thoughts strayed to conspiracy or revolt.

So when the salt-makers of lower Normandy rebelled in 1639 at the rumour that their region would no longer be exempt from the *gabelle*, not a few of the minor local gentry and Rouennais *officiers* tacitly encouraged or supported them. When the weavers and dyers, the tanners and leather-workers of Rouen, incensed by new controls and taxes on their products, destroyed the tax offices of the Crown there were many in the Rouen Parlement who, despite their mistrust and fear of the mob, felt some sympathy for the people's sense of injustice. Years of governmental exactions had so badly affected local prosperity that large numbers of men were now driven to protest and, almost inevitably, that meant that things would get out of hand. The local Parlement knew that when the rioters killed a

collector and looted and burnt the house of a *traitant* who had made
a fortune out of provincial misfortune, these excesses were inspired
not by disloyalty to the King but by exasperation with the servants
of a minister whose exactions had estranged the King from his loyal
subjects. They understood how, by the late 1630s, the King's
presence in Normandy was most obviously represented by commissaries and *fusiliers* who looked more like the agents of an alien
tyranny, as they enforced the hated levies from which popular
tradition held the province to be exempt. Such servants of the
Minister were very proof that the identity of the province was
threatened in its traditional relationship to the Crown, and that the
King's true representatives in the provincial institutions had been
reduced to impotence. Thus they also knew that the Nu-Pieds'
adoption of the old slogan of 'Vive le Roi sans la gabelle' expressed
the fervently loyal convictions of men who still believed in the vigour
of a Charter which guaranteed that the King himself would deliver
his Norman subjects from the oppression of a minister and his
servants who were doing the province a grave series of wrongs.[44] As
Richelieu's critics bitterly pointed out, his apologists might strive to
identify the ministerial will with that of the King so that they could
condemn any adverse comment as 'lèse-majesté', but the Nu-Pieds
had no doubts about their loyalty. For all that there was wild talk
in Paris that Normandy might secede and that the war would bring
about a civil war in France, the Nu-Pieds marched because they
believed that, once he knew the facts, the King would honour the
ancient privileges of Normandy in the sacred exercise of his supreme
function as fount of justice. Trusting in the traditional equity of the
monarchy, they even hoped to see re-established that golden age of
provincial prosperity under Louis XII, a monarch who was
particularly cherished in Normandy because he had first established
its Sovereign Courts and whose reign was popularly believed to have
been exempt from taxation.

It has been suggested that the severity of Séguier's repression of
the troubles in Normandy has been exaggerated, since only a few
ringleaders were hanged. But this underestimates both the harshness
of the circumstances which provoked the revolt and the impact of the
institutional humiliation visited on provincial *officiers* whom the
government accused of 'mauvaise volonté' because they had been
too slow to restore public order.[45] As an *officier* and citizen of Rouen,
Corneille is likely to have had little sympathy for the mob itself and

even less for the half-dozen man hanged a step away from his front door. But he knew that neither peasantry nor Parlement was disloyal to the Crown and he must have been appalled by the punitive suspension of the Sovereign Court in which he served and which was so central to his sense of dignity. As for his own financial position, he must have considered himself fortunate indeed in having received, in 1637, the provincial Parlement's ratification of his ennoblement. Since then the city had only been able to avert governmental threats of confiscation by paying yet further sums of money, and this when much of the Hôtel de Ville's income was already being diverted straight into the Crown coffers in order to pay for the maintenance of troops in Normandy. And despite his new nobility, between 1637 and 1639 Corneille himself would have had to contribute to 'exceptional' levies of 100,000 *livres* 'en subsistence' in order to avert the yet worse fate of having troops quartered in the town itself. In the course of those three years the city had paid the exchequer close on 1,240,000 *livres* in a series of exactions which many of his *officier* colleagues believed to be quite sufficient to explain, if not excuse, the slowness with which they had acted to curb the violence of the simple people.[46]

Thus the fervent loyalty to the King expressed even by men who opposed the methods and policies of the Cardinal was no mere form of words. Instead it shows how reverence for the monarchy was not necessarily extended to his servants, and even inspired a desire to see the dismissal of a minister widely perceived to be governing in the name of the King but against the traditional character of the monarchy. The crucial issues of the theoretical debate of the period – in which the Society of Jesus played a not inconsiderable part both as panegyrists of the monarchy and as the most eloquent opponents of the moral thrust of the Cardinal's policies – were never posed in terms directed against the King. What was really at issue in the fierce polemics over 'la raison d'état' and increasing appeals to expediency was a more sophisticated variant of the protests of the Nu-Pieds. All called for a return to the harmonizing justice which was believed traditionally to inform the King's exercise of his undisputed authority, whether that justice was expressed directly by the King himself or by delegation through his ministers and servant *officiers*. Against such a background it is far from certain that Corneille, as an ex-pupil of the Jesuits who served as one of the *gens du roi* attached to the Table de Marbre in Rouen and a poet who went out of his way to celebrate the monarchy in his poetry, was *ipso facto* an unconditional supporter of Richelieu's policies. Such a view falls into the trap set by ministerial apologists who identified the Cardinal's will with that of the King. Like all his Norman compatriots Corneille was undoubtedly the King's man, both as magistrate and as poet, but his loyalty was entirely compatible with an independent assessment of the quality of the Cardinal's governance and of its relation to past and present definitions of the distinctive character of the French monarchy. As we shall see, unmistakable echoes of the broader debate on the nature of royal governance are to be found in the plays which Corneille wrote in this period, conveying as they do both exhilaration at the prospect of conquest and uncertainty about the human cost and problematic morality of political decision in time of war.

If, finally, we turn to Corneille's patrons and acquaintances during the reign of Louis XIII in search of evidence of Corneille's own political sympathies, we are likely to be disappointed. A comparison of Corneille's circumstantial poetry with the considerable amount of praise heaped on the Cardinal by other writers who were either Richelieu's literary *protégés* or actively sought his patronage does show, however, that Corneille wrote very little in praise of his patron. With the one exception of the dedication of *Horace*, Corneille's few occasional pieces directly concerned with the Cardinal date from either before the period of his patronage or were written after Richelieu's death.[47] The most we can deduce from so limited a contribution to the contemporary flood of verse in the Cardinal's honour is that Corneille was not one of the sycophantic admirers in the Cardinal's literary côterie. Furthermore the period 1635 to 1642, when Corneille received an annual purse from Richelieu, also suggests that there was room for some independence of mind in the relationship. Not only did Corneille not forfeit the Cardinal's generosity when he withdrew from the company of the Five Authors, but the history of the Querelle du *Cid* – once we bear in mind the unrepentantly independent poetics which Corneille expressed on publishing *Médée* (1639) and in his dedication of *Horace* to Richelieu (1641) – makes it clear that Corneille did not believe that Richelieu's patronage imposed on him the poetic orthodoxy and propagandist subservience so evident in the work of other dramatists in the service of the Cardinal. If we are to believe Claude Sarrau when he urged Corneille to write something in honour of the

recently dead Cardinal's memory, it would appear that Richelieu
even respected an obstinately independent talent who was better tied
to himself than wooed by others.[48] Corneille refused to respond to
Sarrau's request, but this is not surprising since the latter had been
one of the sixteen appointed to replace the suspended Rouen
Parlement after the Nu-Pieds disturbances. Instead, when he did
write a sonnet on Richelieu's death, he marked out the distance
between himself and those who had once praised the Cardinal:

> Non, je n'étale point d'illustres déplaisirs,
> D'ambitieux regrets, ni de pompeux soupirs,
> Comme de ton vivant je m'abstins à me taire.[49]

It seems that the poet did not love his old patron – and from a
Norman's point of view it is not hard to see why – but the sonnet
makes it clear that he respected him and acknowledged a personal
debt to him for his patronage, despite an enduring bitterness over the
matter of *Le Cid*.

As for other possible patrons and dedicatees of Corneille's drama
in the period, a possible link with the Vendôme family, which was
prominent in its opposition to Richelieu, has been suggested. If that
link existed, it would again confirm what looks to have been
Corneille's skill in combining artistic and intellectual independence
with financial opportunism.[50] Corneille was too prudent to strike
public attitudes, and it is notable that he never sought to dedicate his
work either to anyone closely attached to the malcontent circle of
Gaston d'Orléans or to families in Rouen like that of Le Tellier or
Faucon de Ris, whose closeness to government made them very rich
but extremely unpopular in Normandy.[51]

Of more local admirers of Corneille, the most interesting are the
Campion brothers, Rouennais aristocrats who claimed the dramatist's friendship and left a contemporary assessment of the Cardinal's
rule.[52] No hard conclusions can be drawn about this association,
since it is not Corneille but Alexandre and Henri de Campion who
claim the friendship, yet there can be little doubt that the
acquaintance was warm enough some twenty years later when
Corneille contributed a liminary sonnet to Alexandre de Campion's
Hommes illustres.[53] The Campion *Entretiens* refer to Corneille as a poet
who found it impossible to submit to the tyranny of the Cardinal's
taste (*Entretiens*, pp. 443–4), but their account of the dramatist's
withdrawal from the Cardinal's team of authors has so obvious a

political slant within a wider attack on Richelieu that it cannot be
taken at face value. Furthermore, even if these aristocratic
conspirators and Corneille really were on friendly terms in the
closing years of Richelieu's ministry, that in itself would offer no
certain indication that they either agreed or disagreed on the merits
and demerits of the Cardinal's politics. Yet this acquaintance with
the three Campion brothers, two of whom were involved in the
abortive rebellion led by Soissons (1641) and caught up in the
Vendôme family's subsequent disgrace, does make another tenuous
link with Richelieu's enemies and, at the least, suggests that
Corneille was familiar with the arguments advanced by those
prominent noblemen who contested the changes that the Cardinal
had wrought in the government of France.

On a number of occasions the *Entretiens* vividly remind us of the
oppressive political climate of the last years of Richelieu's ministry,
as the brothers and their friends risk some highly critical views in the
privacy of their own home: 'A peine on ose parler de sa propre
misère dans sa propre maison et avec sa famille: j'ai peine à
reconnaître la France dans un état si réformé' (pp. 346–7). Another
of the friends, describing the impossibility of finding any kind of
reconciliation between the great families of France and the methods
of Richelieu's government, bewails the way in which many
honourable noblemen have been put to death by the Minister.
Indeed, no man is safe these days from the calumnies of the
Cardinal's spies: 'Il n'y a point de religieux dans les couvents les plus
réformés que les commissaires que l'on donne aujourd'hui aux
accusés ne trouvassent moyen de convaincre de quelque crime digne
de mort sur les instructions qu'on leur fournit' (pp. 337–8). Another
friend agrees, since he knows that his only security lies in his
usefulness to the Cardinal in a Court where justice counts for little:
'Je ne fonde ma sûreté ni sur mon innocence, ni sur la justice du
Ministre dont vous parlez, mais sur sa prudente politique et sur la
qualité de mon emploi' (p. 339). The Ninth, Tenth and Eleventh
Entretiens all turn on the rights and wrongs of Richelieu's 'prudente
politique' in terms of obvious relevance to major political themes in
the plays which Corneille was writing during the closing years of
Richelieu's ministry. The majority hold that the Cardinal's prudence
derives from Machiavellian principles, since he governs by force and
fear rather than in reliance on love as the primary force for social
harmony. In particular Richelieu has failed to govern in accordance

with the Christian principle that no distinction be made between public and private morality. With some reluctance the friends accept that there might be a case for present severities, but they prefer instead to stress the oppressiveness of policies which make short shrift of ancient liberties. One of the company, however, is asked to defend Richelieu's methods and scandalizes the rest with the argument that the Cardinal is to be approved for having constrained 'une nation si folle à devenir sage'. This view, so forcefully advanced in Richelieu's own *Testament Politique*, is countered by the observation that it is a bitter thing to have deprived 'un si grand peuple d'une liberté dont il a joui plus de douze cent ans' (p. 347). In response to the objection that the French had invariably abused that liberty, the speaker holds to his conviction that the people have the right even to misuse their liberty. Not unreasonably this is dismissed in turn as the naive idealism typical of a theorist ignorant of the practical necessities of statecraft: 'Je vois que vous êtes du nombre du ceux qui font consister la félicité des peuples dans la liberté qu'ils ont de se perdre, et que c'est pour cette raison que vous trouvez beaucoup de tyrannie à les contraindre de vivre en repos' (p. 349). But this 'realist' line of attack is itself effectively parried by another who dryly observes that of all things peace has hardly been the hallmark of the Cardinal's rule. It is then the turn of Richelieu's defender to find himself condemned as one of that sorry band of modern political thinkers 'qui mettent le bonheur et la gloire du Prince à voir trembler et gémir les peuples sous le joug de sa puissance' (pp. 349–50).

The Campion *Entretiens* hardly offer a balanced judgement of Richelieu's ministry, but they do give a lively account of protestatory arguments voiced in private at the time. In this they vividly reflect the ideological polarization of a period in which practical necessity and hard political realism were repeatedly set against an idealist defence of the traditional and conciliating sanctities of a Christian monarchy respectful of Divine and Natural Law and the Fundamental Laws of the Realm. Corneille might also have been impressed by an assessment of the moral ambiguity of the Cardinal (pp. 469–72), which offers interesting points of comparison with his own characterization of the eponymous hero of *Horace*. Although the political significance of that play is decidedly more balanced than are the Campion brothers' discussions, *Horace* is also much concerned with the problems of discipline and sacrifice in the interests of national glory, and airs similar doubts about the cost of war and the morality of those who set State necessity over individual rights. These themes were also treated, but with less subtlety, in the work of a number of other dramatists who openly supported the Cardinal, and it is likely that something of Bignon and Balzac's admiration of Corneille's plays derived from their perception that his drama was uniquely effective in its more shaded presentation of political issues. While avoiding the 'set pieces' of slanted debate so favoured in other plays written at the time with an eye to the Cardinal's approval, *Le Cid*, *Horace*, and *Cinna* all explore matters of considerable concern to the traditional humanist culture of the French magistrature, 'déchiré entre sa pente libérale et républicaine et son désir d'une monarchie puissante et respectée'.[54] In the last analysis then, and in default of any unequivocal personal expression of political allegiance by this most prudent of dramatists, it is likely to be the plays themselves which will tell us most about their author's response to the issues of his day.

CONCLUSION

Corneille's experience in Normandy during the reign of Louis XIII repeatedly suggests a situation which would only confirm the dramatist in that pride and independence of mind which contemporary accounts so emphasize. His steady refusal to be anything other than his own man may disappoint those who prefer to annexe the author of *Horace* into the history of France as a noble propagandist of exemplary national loyalties, but the historical facts point to a more complex and ambiguous reality. If Corneille's own attitude to the Minister was equivocal this was because, as a provincial *officier* and political dramatist who enjoyed the Cardinal's patronage, his position made it so. It is not difficult to lift out of *Le Cid* or *Horace* a number of passages which argue eloquently in favour of one set of moral or political values, but such passages take their place in a larger dramatic exposition in which equally eloquent counter-argument forces us to reflect on the sufficiency of each view expressed. It has been observed that the relationship of patronage in the seventeenth century did not invariably impose a propagandist function on the beneficiary poet, and the even-handedness with which Corneille's plays set out the political argument makes it clear that the dedication of his work did not bring with it a servile adhesion to the interests and preoccupations of a particular patron.[55] *Horace* may well have pleased Richelieu by its brilliant illustration of the heroic virtues of devoted service to the destinies of a nation at war, but it also orchestrated a series of tragic conflicts which powerfully challenged its spectators to reflect more generally on the morality and cost of Rome's pursuit of universal dominion.

As we shall see, the same indications of intellectual independence are to be found in Corneille's defiance of the prescriptions of Richelieu's Académie, even when – as one of those who 'belonged' to the Minister – he dedicated *Horace* to the Cardinal himself. His independence is again apparent in the brilliant political morality of *Cinna* and in his evocation of contentious theological subject-matter in *Polyeucte*, neither of which was entirely of a kind to please the Cardinal.[56] Both the distinctiveness of Corneille's poetics and the problematic nature of his dramatizations of political conflict confirm that this Rouennais poet's ability to see both sides of an argument was central to the creative processes which lay behind his work. His plays may certainly be seen to take up a position on the ideological and political conflicts of the times, but they do so with a thoughtfulness which can only be betrayed once we pursue univocal equations with any contemporary party or local faction. This greater moral richness will become immediately apparent once we look to the texts themselves and measure the distance between Corneille's practice and that of dramatists who, like Scudéry or Guérin de Bouscal, sought to ingratiate themselves with the Cardinal by turning history to the advantage of the Minister's 'politique de raison'. It is frankly impossible to confuse such programmatic exercises with Corneille's eloquent exposition of the full spectrum of contemporary political debate within the fierce pressures of an extreme situation. Historical drama of the kind represented by *Horace* urgently challenges the spectator to exercise his own moral judgement before the spectacle of men entangled in the necessities of choice and political responsibility, and there is an enormous distance between the intellectual ambition apparent in Corneille's works and the narrower intentions of those who made it their task to educate the public in the Cardinal's policies and celebrate his triumphs.

However, if Corneille was not unreservedly the Cardinal's man, this should not lead us to the contrary oversimplification of associating him equally unequivocally with other voices raised in condemnation of his patron. Unavoidably the poet's eyes turned towards the centres of power and patronage and contemplated horizons wider than those of his native Normandy. Ample evidence of that broader vision is to be found in his drama and it would be surprising indeed if this were not the case. In looking to political philosophy and history for the means to understand his times, Corneille was but one of many loyal servants of the King who found reason for exhilaration as well as disquiet in the new perspectives which Richelieu's policies set before the country. The comprehensiveness and humanity of the great historical tragedies which made Corneille's fortune as a dramatist derive not only from his learning or the arguments of colleagues who served in the Palais de Justice of his native Normandy, but from an understanding of the reasons of those who governed the country. The result is a realism and profundity of political reflection which saves Corneille's plays from being either simple vehicles for propaganda or allegorical illustrations of abstract political ideals. Instead they transmute contemporary political debate into dramatic themes of great personal urgency, as Corneille's own reflections on his times re-emerge transformed into the tragic ambiguities and often insoluble conflicts of his heroes.

Corneille's convictions about the nature of the art which could achieve such a transformation are there to be studied in the many theoretical statements which he made about his practice. His unremitting efforts to define what he understood to be the true character of his work resulted in a consistent and in many respects very individual statement of position, the culmination of which were the three *Discours* of 1660. We shall see, however, that the theoretical statements he made during the reign of Louis XIII already show that, in opposition to a more politically servile doctrinaire tradition, he placed his dramatic poetry squarely within the scholarly tradition to which he belonged by education and by participation in the *officier* culture of his day. It may have taken the literary furore which followed the success of *Le Cid* to open Corneille's eyes to the ways in which that literary tradition was threatened, as a gulf widened between the spirit and intentions of the servants of Richelieu and the example and influence of prudent and reflective dissentients, like Balzac or Bignon, who applied and adapted to the times the rich inheritance of their humanistic culture. But Corneille's earliest statements on *Le Cid* bear witness to an enduring conviction that the seductions of the drama were consubstantial with the most elevated of poetry's traditional claim to communicate higher truths, rather than the orthodoxies of the moment.[57] Before looking to Corneille's plays written in the reign of Louis XIII, we need to see how his view of the poet's obligation to serve those higher truths sets into critical perspective this initial review of an *officier*-dramatist's personal experience of the Palais de Justice in Rouen and the Cardinal's palace in Paris. Many of his contemporaries may have liked to look for simple equations between life and literature, and did so long before Molière's *Précieuses ridicules* made such fools of themselves over the relationship of fiction to experience. But Corneille's own discussion of his art precludes any consideration of the historical events and figures of Louis XIII's France as so many elements simply to be transposed into 'des pièces à clef'. His double career as a cultured Norman *officier* and dramatist, like his special interest in history and politics, is above all significant because it gave him a privileged vantage-point from which, at the most general level, he could assess the meaning of his times and transform it into the broadly human truths of tragedy. Thus the second part of this study will serve as a necessary preparation for critical discussion of his plays, in so far as it examines the ways in which Corneille believed that, through a stage recreation of history, he could transform the local truths of contemporary ideological conflict into a poetic expression of their more enduring significance.

PART II

Corneille's conception of poetic drama

Theoretical controversy: 1629–43

THE EARLY YEARS AND THE QUERELLE DU *CID* (1629–37)

Critics have long recognized the distinctiveness of Corneille's poetic theory, and the key to his independence is generally held to be his insistence that pleasure is the prime end of his art. By so forcefully asserting the importance of delight, whether in the 'Epître dédicatoire' of *La Suivante* (published September 1637) or in the more sober opening of the three *Discours* of 1660, Corneille stands almost alone against the moralistic emphasis of doctrinaire opponents whose semi-official status and regulatory concerns indicate how intimately seventeenth-century literary theory was connected with the changes wrought by Richelieu's Ministry. The Cardinal's institution of the Académie Française in 1635, and his patronage of a number of men whose brief it was to develop a body of prescriptive theory, show how important a role public policy was to play in a remarkable revival of interest in the nature of poetry and the poet's place within the polity. Thus Corneille's fidelity to a dissentient view of the obligations and ends of the artist is as ideologically significant as is his political drama, since both show a cultured lawyer-poet's distinctive response to political developments which called into question the traditional values and culture of his caste. But only with the controversy over *Le Cid* (1637) does Corneille seem to become fully aware of the broader political implications of contemporary literary debate. Before then the success of his plays was sufficient reason for the independent-mindedness of his earliest theoretical statements. In fact the applause of his audiences would always remain a constant reassurance to him, and not least because, of all his contemporaries, he alone grounded his theory in the practice of the art he sought to define. The result is that Corneille's many theoretical statements show a unique interplay

between his own understanding of his place as poet within the
political evolution of his times, his reading and reflection on the art
of poetry, and the varying success of his plays with the public. Over
some thirty years of increasingly sophisticated theoretical writings,
the combination of these three factors was to lead Corneille into
conflict with influential men whose regulatory theory, because they
stood much closer to the centres of power, was far less attentive to the
practical realities of the contemporary stage.

By 1637, and Corneille's first and most bitter conflict with
doctrinaire theory over *Le Cid*, he already had nine plays to his
credit, none of which had failed and several of which had been very
successful. On the other hand Chapelain, Secretary of the Académie
required to pass judgement on *Le Cid*, had little practical experience
of writing plays and had already had his disagreements with
Corneille in co-ordinating the Five Authors' work on the *Comédie des
Tuileries* (first performed on 4 March 1635). As for La Mesnardière,
who published his anti-Cornelian *La Poétique* in 1639, he had even
less experience of writing for the stage. This is woefully apparent in
his remarkable unconcern for the realities of contemporary performance and his scorn for all but an élite of spectators whose taste
coincides with his own. The rest of La Mesnardière's hypothetical
audience seems to be composed of undiscriminating spectators whose
role is envisaged principally to be the beneficiaries of a form of
drama designed to advance their moral and social education. The
Abbé d'Aubignac may later have established himself as a considerable authority in matters of theory and cherished the ambition
to become a kind of minister in control of the public stage, but this
most acrimonious and persistent of Corneille's critics met with little
success when he practised what he preached. Not surprising then
that Corneille began and ended his *Discours* with reminders of the
gap which yawned between the doctrinaires' dismal lack of stage
success and their claims to prescriptive expertise:

Il faut...savoir quelles sont ces règles, mais notre malheur est...que ceux
qui leur...ont voulu servir ici ne les ont souvent expliqués qu'en
grammairiens, ou en philosophes. Comme ils avaient plus d'étude et de
spéculation, que d'expérience du théâtre, leur lecture nous peut rendre plus
doctes, mais non pas nous donner beaucoup de lumières pour y réussir.
(First *Discours*, LF, 38; GC, III, 119)

Voilà mes opinions, ou si vous voulez, mes hérésies touchant les principaux
points de l'Art...Je ne doute point qu'il ne soit aisé d'en trouver de

meilleurs moyens, et je serai tout prêt de les suivre, lorsqu'on les aura mis en pratique, aussi heureusement, qu'on y a vu les miens. (Third *Discours*, LF, 148; GC, III, 190)

Independence of spirit and a sharp awareness of the realities of performance were always major characteristics of the manner in which Corneille approached any theoretical exposition of the 'rules', and they constantly illuminate his exploration of his successes and failures. By directly appealing to Aristotle's *Poetics* in the light of his own experience as a dramatist, he avoided a debate which often distracted attention from stage to study and fogged perception of substantive practical issues by fruitless displays of erudition in secondary commentary.

Since Corneille's first comedy *Mélite* (1629) had been well received at a time when the public was none too concerned about the play's irregularity, his earliest statements on the rules display a liberal flexibility, drawing on both ancient example and modern prescription whenever they can help him to write successfully for his audience. But the Querelle du *Cid* (1637) put an end to the rather light-hearted tone of these earlier statements. As argument about his play became increasingly heated, Corneille was drawn willy-nilly into a complex debate about poetry and the civic obligations of the artist which had arisen under Richelieu's ministry during the 1630s. Since the one major certainty to which Corneille clung was that his play was a sensational success with the public, the controversy over *Le Cid* confirmed his pragmatism rather than weakened it. Any criticism was suspect, no matter what the position and reputation of the theoreticians from whence it came, if it argued that popular applause was evidence of popular ignorance.

But it would be wrong so to stress Corneille's pragmatism that we under-rated his interest in learned theory, even at this early stage in his career. That he began in total ignorance of the rules is hardly surprising, given the likely date of *Mélite's* first performance in 1629. Only recently, and amongst a fashionably Italianizing few in Paris, had there been the first indications of a specifically French interest in matters of dramatic regularity. By 1630, when Chapelain wrote to Godeau on the twenty-four-hours rule, he did so as something of a pioneer in French taste, but his erudition relied upon direct acquaintance with fewer authorities than his judicious manner suggested.[1] Much later, when Corneille wrote to Huyghens on the 6 March 1649, he looked back on those days prior to *Le Cid* and described his first works as 'les péchés de ma jeunesse et les coups d'essai d'une muse de province qui se laissait conduire aux lumières purement naturelles, et n'avait pas encore fait réflexion qu'il y avait un art de la tragédie, et qu'Aristote en avait laissé des préceptes'.[2] But ignorance is a relative thing, and this modest disclaimer offers something less than the truth. Corneille may have begun his career as an innocent, but as early as the 'Préface' to *Clitandre*, there are signs that he has set himself to acquire at least a fashionable competence in matters of regularity, for all that he maintains a freely pragmatic view of how to apply the rules. Whatever his ignorance in writing *Mélite*, Corneille had become well aware of the unities when he wrote *Clitandre* (first performed in 1632), and it was characteristic of his determination to impress the cognoscenti that he should try to perform the unprecedented feat of making this rattling tragicomedy conform to the twenty-four-hours rule. It was equally characteristic of his independence that he made this temporal regularity even more of a virtuoso exercise by breaking another rule, when he rejected narrated action in favour of setting everything helter-skelter upon stage. Such a novel combination of regularity and irregularity, which Corneille claims to have devised for the greater pleasures of his audience, shows us a self-assured young poet who claims the right to experiment with traditional forms in order to advance the practice of the art he has inherited from antiquity:

Je me donne ici quelque sorte de liberté de choquer les Anciens, d'autant qu'ils ne sont plus en état de me repondre, et que je ne veux engager personne en la recherche de mes défauts. Puisque les Sciences et les Arts ne sont jamais à leur période, il m'est permis de croire...que de leurs instructions on peut tirer des lumières qu'ils n'ont pas eues. (GC, 1, 95)

Already we can see an amusing but dangerously self-congratulatory note and a tendency to trail his coat which will lead Corneille into quite unnecessary extra trouble during the storm over *Le Cid*. He already has some knowledge of the *Poetics* and cites Horace's *Art of Poetry*, but on the substantial matter of conformity or not to the rules it is clear that he prefers a median position of flexible independence.

By 1634 and *La Veuve*, Corneille's interest in theory is still more to the fore. Another reference to the *Art of Poetry* suggests that Horace had assumed a more prominent part in his thinking since he holds his own play to illustrate the view that comedy is the poetic imitation of a certain sphere of society, expressed in appropriate language and with entertaining complexities of plot: 'La Comédie n'est qu'un portrait de nos actions, et de nos discours, et la perfection des portraits consiste en la ressemblance. Sur cette maxime je tache de ne mettre en la bouche de mes acteurs, que ce que diraient vraisemblablement en leur place ceux qu'ils représentent, et de les faire discourir en honnêtes gens, et non pas en Auteurs' (GC, I, 202). This first appearance in Corneille's work of the key commonplace of the poetry/painting comparison shows that he assumes his reader to be familiar with the traditional concept of significant imitation, central to the humanistic theory of poetry.[3] Rather prematurely, he also makes the first of several promises to give a full theoretical exposition of his views. By 1634 the mode was for theory and Corneille intends to shine amongst a select band of theoretical experts as well as in his plays:

Ce n'est pas que je méprise l'antiquité, mais comme on épouse malaisément des beautés si vieilles, j'ai cru lui rendre assez de respect de lui partager mes ouvrages, et de six pièces de Théâtre qui me sont échappées, en ayant réduit trois dans la contrainte qu'elle nous a prescrite, je n'ai point fait de conscience d'allonger un peu les vingt et quatre heures aux trois autres. Pour l'unité de lieu et d'action, ce sont deux règles que j'observe inviolablement, mais j'interprète la dernière à ma mode, et la première tantôt je la reserre à la seule grandeur du théâtre, et tantôt je l'étends jusqu'à toute une ville ... Quelque jour je m'expliquerai davantage sur ces matières, mais il faut attendre l'occasion d'un plus grand volume. (GC, I, 203).

All the signs are that Corneille's grasp of poetic theory was growing, together with an interest in finding ways of applying it to best advantage in his work. Theory was not to be despised, and indeed might usefully support his conviction that he had a superior natural talent as a dramatist. Never throwing in his hand either with the 'réguliers' or the 'irréguliers', Corneille accepted here, rejected there, and most often adapted and experimented. In no way does he seem to have felt overawed or constrained by the semi-official authority of Chapelain or other theorists of the mid-thirties.

But with the extraordinary success of *Le Cid* in the first weeks of 1637 and the fatal misjudgement of publishing the *Excuse à Ariste* (written in 1633 and previously circulated in manuscript), Corneille became the target of rivals whose work he had overshadowed. Isolated by his arrogance and success, Corneille was forced to abandon his carefree liberalism in the matter of the rules. The worst of publishing the *Excuse* at this time was that, while certain lines seemed to the beleaguered Corneille appropriately defiant, others looked outrageously self-congratulatory and ungrateful to the Cardinal:

> Les vers à present
> Aux meilleurs du métier n'apportant que du vent,
> Chacun s'en donne à l'aise, et souvent se dispense
> A prendre par ses mains toute sa récompense.
> Nous nous aimons un peu, c'est notre foible à tous,
> Le prix que nous valons, qui le sait mieux que nous?...
> Je sais ce que je vaux, et crois ce qu'on m'en dit:
> Pour me faire admirer je ne fais point de ligue,
> J'ai peu de voix pour moi, mais je les ai sans brigue,
> Et mon ambition pour faire plus de bruit
> Ne les va point quêter de Réduit en Réduit,
> Mon travail sans appui monte sur le Théâtre...
> Je ne dois qu'à moi seul toute ma Renommée,
> Et pense toutefois n'avoir point de rival
> A qui je fasse tort en le traitant d'égal.
> (GC, I, 780)

Much of this was satisfactorily offensive to Scudéry and Mairet but, by so discounting the benefits of distinguished patronage, made Corneille an easy target for other authors attached to the Cardinal's entourage. Confronted by Scudéry's condemnation of *Le Cid* in the self-consciously expert *Observations* and by the *Sentiments sur 'Le Cid'* in which the Académie publicly endorsed prescriptive regularity (early December 1637), Corneille realized that he would have to defend himself with the very weapons with which his play was currently being attacked. With a new polemic urgency he was to hold to the unarguable success of his play with the wider public, venturing into the theoretical arena with still more emphatic assertions of the primacy of delight.

The circumstances and character of what Corneille interpreted as his condemnation during the episode of the Querelle left a lasting impression on him. One important lesson he learned from the experience was how theoretical argument, once abstracted from the realities of performance, could gather such momentum that any consideration of audience response to the play itself receded into unimportance. A yet more important lesson was that, under the Cardinal, questions of literature were never very far from questions of politics. Early in 1637 Corneille had regarded the affair as nothing more than a squabble got up by jealous literary inferiors who were exploiting the debate on regularity in order to disparage the success of his play. With this personal rivalry in mind he had been slow to grasp the larger political implications of the controversy, even when the Cardinal's Académie was called to show its paces for the first time in a judgement which would give a more official dimension to the dispute. That others had seen how things were moving is shown by Mersenne's letter to Descartes of the same year. In a general complaint against the way freedom of expression was increasingly under threat, the well-informed Mersenne saw that the Cardinal's Académie had a specific role to play within his broader system of governmental control: 'Jamais on ne fut plus exact qu'à présent pour l'examen des livres, car Monsieur le Chancelier a des agents affidés pour juger de ce qui est pour la théologie, d'autres pour la politique, l'Académie de Paris pour les pièces d'éloquence tant en vers qu'en prose, et des mathématiciens pour le reste.'[4] It has been observed that the *officier* class and the literary world were Richelieu's first targets in imposing a 'politique de raison' which would assert the absolute authority of the King and his Minister.[5] Certainly, in keeping with the obstructionism discussed in the first part of this study, the Paris Parlement dragged its feet in completing the verification of the Académie's letters-patent. These 'hommes de loi' in Paris had been quicker than the provincial lawyer and dramatist to recognize the threat to their own cultural and political traditions. Corneille seems only to have become fully aware of the awkwardness of his position when the Cardinal himself insisted, through Boisrobert, that *Le Cid* be submitted to the Académie's judgement and refused him the right of a reply. This sharply revealed the consequences and obligations arising from generous, but not always disinterested, patronage and made clear how Richelieu's manipulation of literary activity raised crucial questions about the moral authority of the poet and his relation to the political order of the moment.

Balzac was later to deplore the pursuit of *pensions* as the seductive path to intellectual servility; when Corneille later presented *Le Cid* in the edition of 1648 he too hinted that his patron had taken a hand in events through his creatures in the Académie.[6] Balzac knew of what he spoke, and had already paid the price for mixing literary eloquence and politics in the suddenly shifting perspectives of France under the Cardinal's rule.[7] His literary pre-eminence might ensure his membership in the Académie, but he had opted for the country life and did not attend the institution, many of whose members he regarded as mortgaged to their pensions and patronage. With his letter to Scudéry on *Le Cid* (27 August 1637) he intervened in support of the play, expressing the view that any technical irregularities were amply justified by its success.[8] But by then Corneille was publicly at odds with appointed arbitrators who were already unfavourably disposed to *Le Cid* and closely associated with the Cardinal's interests. 'Messieurs de l'Académie' were keenly aware that they had the express brief of elaborating and imposing a literary order which would carry with it a number of constraints upon a more traditional, and less political, view of the poet's art. We have only to look at Chapelain's allusions to the 'puissantes considérations' which bore upon the Académie's deliberations to realize that these were as much political as aesthetic. In a letter to Boisrobert Chapelain even expressed his willingness to abdicate his own judgement in favour of the Cardinal's wishes when it came to a final verdict on *Le Cid*. The same sense of political accountability lay behind Chapelain's relief at the news that Richelieu broadly approved the *Sentiments*, just as it inspired his final description of the published version as yet another superhuman achievement of the Cardinal's will.[9]

It is easy to imagine the comfort Corneille found in Balzac's letter to Scudéry, and the 'Epître' prefacing *La Suivante* (published at the height of the Querelle in September 1637) may well have been addressed to this exiled man of letters who had already paid for venturing into that shadowy area where literary activity and interests of government merged. By daring, in *Le Prince*, directly to express himself on political issues, Balzac had more obviously run the risk of offending the Cardinal. But that a literary quarrel over a tragicomedy could now be regarded as a matter for public concern made it crystal clear how inclusive had become the perspectives of Richelieu's preoccupation with public order, as he enlisted the literary world to serve his ends. Corneille's change of tone in the 'Epître' prefacing *La Suivante* is striking. All the flippant self-assurance of 1634 has disappeared and the liberal attitudes of a *moderne* are now reiterated with defiant energy and bitter passing ironies. Scudéry and Mairet are dismissed with haughty disdain in an echo of the rondeau, *Qu'il fasse mieux*.[10] 'Si je ne fais bien, qu'un autre fasse mieux, je ferai des vers à sa louange, au lieu de le censurer. Chacun a sa méthode, je ne blâme point celle des autres, et me tiens à la mienne: jusques à présent je m'en suis trouvé fort bien, j'en chercherai une meilleure quand je commencerai à m'en trouver mal.' Insistence on the pleasures of the drama is now linked to open scepticism about the pretensions of doctrinaire prescription. Citing the irregularity of antiquity, Corneille tries to confound the 'réguliers' by invoking Scaliger himself (the doctrinaires' most revered modern authority) and ironizing about his own comedy's regularity: 'les règles des Anciens sont assez religieusement observées en celle-ci'. The whole 'Epître' breathes a combative independence which will never be absent from Corneille's subsequent defence and definitions of his art. Characteristically proposing a flexible application of the rules, he draws a sharp distinction between practising poets and critics in their study:

J'aime à suivre les règles, mais loin de me rendre leur esclave, je les élargis et reserre selon le besoin qu'en a mon sujet...Savoir les règles, et entendre le secret de les apprivoiser adroitement avec notre Théâtre, ce sont deux sciences bien différentes, et peut-être que pour faire maintenant réussir une pièce, ce n'est pas assez d'avoir étudié dans les livres d'Aristote et d'Horace. J'espère un jour traiter ces matières plus à fond...Cependant mon avis est celui de Térence. Puisque nous faisons des Poèmes pour être représentés, notre premier but doit être de plaire à la Cour et au Peuple, et d'attirer un grand monde à leurs représentations. Il faut, s'il se peut, y ajouter les règles, afin de ne déplaire aux Savants, et recevoir un applaudissement universel, mais surtout gagnons la voix publique: autrement notre pièce aura beau être régulière, si elle est sifflée au Théâtre. (GC, 1, 385 and 386–7)

Corneille's appeal to the 'lecteur désintéressé...à prendre la médaille par le beau revers' underlines his doubts about the integrity of his critics and barely disguises his conviction that the *Sentiments* of the Académie will be far from impartial.

According to Pellisson, Corneille had reluctantly agreed in June 1637 that *Le Cid* should be submitted to the Académie's arbitration. Since that was the pleasure of His Eminence, this agreement was obviously something of a formality. In November his political naiveté still allowed him to believe that he would get a chance to defend himself and to hope that the Cardinal, as a connoisseur of the drama, would accept the dedication of his reply to the Académie. Corneille was quickly undeceived, and the formal courtesies of his letter (23 December) barely conceal his sense of injury at being refused a public reply to this official publication of unacceptable criticism.[11] We know how bitterly he took this rebuff from the remarkable fact that for the rest of his life he repeatedly asserted its injustice, but this enduring resentment was not simply a matter of personal pride. Corneille repeatedly returned to the matter because the artistic issues evoked by the Querelle remained live ones long after Corneille himself had died, and because he knew they raised crucial questions about the poet's role within the larger framework of the State. René Bray has pertinently remarked how the Académie's elaboration and expression of a 'Classical' doctrine represented a direct continuation of policies which had powerfully contributed to the advance of centralized absolutism and bureaucratic autocracy. After the Cardinal's death Corneille was to declare with even greater clarity his fidelity to the poetics of the humanistic tradition to which he was heir, even if this meant continued disagreement with a doctrinaire tradition behind which stood 'l'Etat autoritaire, dont la continuité de dessein devait assurer le succés'.[12] The pressures to which he yielded in late 1637 were still there in later years, as Richelieu's oversight of the world of literature was perpetuated in an official system of literary authority which was an important part of his political legacy to France.

Later, in the 1648 collected edition, Corneille made it clear that his enforced silence did not imply acceptance of the criticisms expressed in the *Sentiments*. In fact we shall see that this was already evident in theoretical statements prefacing *Médée* and *Horace* (1639), *La Suite de Menteur* (1645) and *Héraclius* (1647). In all of these he grasped the opportunity implicitly to defend *Le Cid*, as he dealt with the moral content of serious drama and the relationship between truth and verisimilitude on stage. Much later in 1660, the *Discours* show that Corneille was still concerned to justify his stand on *Le Cid*, notably on the 'vrai' and the 'vraisemblable', and the 'Examen' of the play shows him still anxious to deal with a point raised long ago in Scudéry's *Observations*. That the continued pressure to which Corneille felt himself subject was far from imagined can be seen from the writings of his opponents. D'Aubignac's *Pratique du théâtre*, originally commissioned by the Cardinal in 1640 for the better regulation of the public stage, was finally published in 1657, and Corneille's three *Discours* were conceived partly as a reply to D'Aubignac's treatment of the issue of the 'vrai' and the 'vraisemblable' which had been so central to argument over *Le Cid*. Later still, in 1663, when D'Aubignac's *Dissertations* again renewed the argument, the 'Préface' to *Sophonisbe* returned once more to these long-standing differences.

The full significance of the running argument with doctrinaire theory from 1637 into the 1660s can only be understood once this long debate is placed within its political context. A number of distinguished studies of the ideology and literary movements of the time have observed how the years 1637 to 1645 were a period of crisis for the traditional humanistic culture of seventeenth-century France, and particularly that of the magistrate tradition in the Parlements under pressure from an ascendant and increasingly autocratic monarchical absolutism.[13] When both Balzac and a major figure in the Paris Parlement, Jérôme Bignon, publicly expressed their admiration for *Le Cid*, their interventions were significant responses to a controversy which revealed how the brief of the Cardinal's Académie could run counter to the graver pleasures of a literary eloquence more closely associated with the humanist *officier* tradition. As for Richelieu, if he threw his weight behind a rehabilitation of the public stage in the 1630s, he did so not only from a genuine love of the theatre but also because he saw how powerful an instrument it could be in presenting the rationale of his policies. This instrumental view of the role of the liberal arts within the larger order of State posed, in inescapable form, a conflict between tradition and the new order. Balzac, less agile or less supple than Corneille, had held to his convictions and retreated to the comfortable eccentricities of his 'hermitage' in the Charente. Corneille, like the Norman he was, opted for both sides, swallowing his pride and restoring his standing with his patron by dedicating his next play to him. But even as he did so he kept faith with his cultural inheritance by yielding nothing on his poetic principles, as the dedication of *Horace* itself makes clear. He then spent the next thirty years defending the means to realize the historical 'beau sujet' with the profundity already apparent in the play he had dedicated to the Cardinal. That many of the Académie's strictures on *Le Cid* related to manner rather than to content, and that their preoccupation with the impropriety and 'invraisemblance' of its subject led them to disregard popular enthusiasm for *Le Cid*, was entirely characteristic of an institution whose first function was to establish a fitting style for the communication of truths imposed 'from above'.[14] Corneille's response was to defend an artistic autonomy, first defined in Aristotle's *Poetics*, which never ceased to be threatened by the prescriptive narrowness of an 'official' theory of prudential admonition within which the poet's first obligation was to celebrate the favourite truths of an established order. In the years following the Querelle du *Cid*, Corneille was to develop his understanding of the dramatic illustration of moral and political truths with steadily increasing theoretical expertise. By the *Discours* of 1660, for all that he wears his learning lightly, it is clear that the erstwhile innocent of *Mélite* has become not only a master of his craft but also formidably expert in the history of its theory. Citing Robortello, Vettori, Minturno, Castelvetro, Heinsius, and Vossius, Corneille makes his 'quelques courses' in matters of doctrine with total mastery of his material. Most striking of all, however, is the perfect consistency with which those *Discours* define poetic convictions which had been central to Corneille's position during the Querelle du *Cid* and which he had since developed as occasion arose.

DOCTRINAIRE POETICS AND THE 'EPÎTRE' OF *MÉDÉE* (1639)

The first and most important of these occasional theoretical pieces was the prefatory 'Epître' of *Médée* (March 1639). Published some eighteen months after his enforced silence on *Le Cid*, it was Corneille's first chance publicly to reply to the *Sentiments*, and it both offered a definition of the principles governing his own practice of the drama and prepared the ground for *Horace*.[15] In November he wrote to Boisrobert (15 November 1637), expressing his impatience to know the Académie's views, and may already have been at work on *Horace*. By the time he wrote again to Boisrobert (3 December 1637), the Académie's criticisms were published and he could draw his own conclusions about the nature of that verdict, as he yielded to the 'autorité si souveraine' of the ministerial interdict:

Je me résous, puisque vous le voulez, à me laisser condamner par votre illustre Académie...Mais je vous supplie de considérer qu'elle procède contre moi avec tant de violence, et qu'elle emploie une autorité si souveraine pour me fermer la bouche, que ceux qui sauront son procédé auront sujet d'estimer que je ne serais point coupable si l'on m'avait permis de me montrer innocent...*Le Cid* sera toujours beau, et gardera sa réputation d'être la plus belle pièce qui ait paru sur le Théâtre, jusques à ce qu'il en vienne une autre qui ne lasse point les spectateurs à la trentième fois...Maintenant que vous me conseillez de n'y répondre point [à l'Académie], vu les personnes qui s'en sont mêlées, il ne me faut point d'interprète pour entendre cela...et j'aime mieux les bonnes grâces de mon Maître que toutes les réputations de la terre: je me tairai donc, non point par mépris, mais par respect. (GC, I, 805–7)

Evidently there was consolation in the hopes he placed on the success of the new play, already conceived in the unrepentant mood of defiance so apparent in the 'Epître' prefacing *La Suivante* in September 1637.[16]

Earlier, in April 1637, soon after the first performance of *Le Cid*, Corneille had somewhat naively asked Chapelain to persuade Balzac to intervene in the affair on his behalf. Chapelain's letter to Balzac (1 April 1637) recounts this request for help and how he did not respond to it. It shows that he considered *Le Cid* to be barbarously irregular and also reveals a combination of malice and metropolitan self-importance which amply explains Corneille's later mistrust of him. Despite these officious obstructions, Balzac received a copy of the play and liked it – which made Chapelain rather more cautious when he wrote again in June. In deference to Balzac, he is rather kinder in the *Sentiments* (to be published in December) but is still anxious to write down the uncultured taste of those who applauded *Le Cid*. Echoing Scudéry's attack on the play's 'borrowed' beauties, he limits Corneille's contribution to the invention of 'les ornements' and makes it clear that he believes that refined literary taste must decide in favour of Scudéry:

Il est bien vrai, entre nous, que le *Cid* se peut dire heureux d'avoir été traité par un français et en France, où la finesse de la poésie du théâtre n'est point encore connue. En Italie, il eût passé pour barbare…ce qui a donné beau jeu à Monsieur de Scudéry, corival de Corneille, de lui objecter les fautes que vous verrez remarquées dans le volume qui je vous envoie. (13 June 1637)[17]

There is a pleasant irony in seeing Chapelain, who had been unwilling to send a copy of the play itself, now hasten to offer Scudéry's *Observations* as a guide to the most distinguished critic of his generation. Nonetheless, having read both *Le Cid* and the *Observations*, Balzac wrote two months later to Scudéry in support of the play. By late 1637 Corneille had concluded that Chapelain was unlikely to act as a disinterested intermediary, and when the latter next mentioned him in a letter to Balzac (15 January 1639) he had no idea that Corneille was again at work. Indeed the 'bourru' Corneille had simply let Chapelain know that he resented and rejected his views on *Le Cid*. If, as is likely, *Horace* was on the way to completion by this time, Corneille must have found some satisfaction in hiding the fact as he listened to Chapelain's back-handed encouragements to produce 'quelque nouveau *Cid* qui attire encore les suffrages de tout le monde, et qui montre que l'art n'est pas ce qui fait la beauté' (15 January 1639).[18] By March of that year, publication of *Médée* gave Corneille his first public opportunity to set out his own views on the vexed question of what kind of moral significance was specific to poetic drama. Preparing the way for a new play which would indeed be in the same vein as *Le Cid* and defy the general tenor of the Académie's preferences, the 'Epître' still more firmly asserts the primacy of delight[19] even as it claims to spare the dedicatee a display of doctrinaire precepts which

doivent être fort mal entendus et fort mal pratiqués quand ils ne nous font pas arriver au but que l'art se propose. Celui de la Poésie dramatique est de plaire, et les règles qu'elle nous prescrit ne sont que des adresses pour en faciliter les moyens au Poëte, et non pas des raisons qui puissent persuader aux spectateurs qu'une chose soit agréable quand elle leur déplaît. (GC, i, 535)

As early as 1633, in a preface to Marini's *Adone*, Chapelain sought to give authority to his understanding of the rules by invoking another kind of 'raison universelle', which was less to be perceived in the world of common experience than directly preconceived by the poet, whose function it was to communicate such prior truths through carefully chosen 'probable' fictions. Indeed Truth was to be banished from Parnassus, for Justice and Reason alone prevailed there, and it was only re-admissible disguised as 'la vraisemblance, laquelle...et non la vérité, sert d'instrument au poète pour acheminer l'homme à la vertu'.[20] Scudéry's *Observations sur 'Le Cid'* conform to this moralizing view of poetic probability when they argue that, since the subject matter of *Le Cid* involved reprehensible conduct, it followed that such material was unacceptable within the bounds of poetic regularity: 'Il n'est pas vraisemblable qu'une fille d'honneur épouse le meurtrier de son père. Cet évènement était bon pour l'historien, mais il ne valait rien pour le poète.' In recording Chimène's love for Rodrigue, history made it regrettably clear that she was no 'fille d'honneur'. Worse, her marriage to him rewarded 'cette fille, mais plutôt ce monstre' for her shameful love. Corneille had set before the Paris public a reprehensible imitation of unedifying historical material in which 'l'on...voit une fille dénaturée ne parler que de ses folies, lorsqu'elle ne doit parler que de son malheur'. In *Le Cid* both 'les bonnes moeurs comme les règles de la poésie dramatique' were offended:

Et pour connaître cette vérité il faut savoir que le poème de théâtre fut inventé pour instruire en divertissant, et que c'est sous cet agréable habit que se déguise la philosophie, de peur de paraître trop austère aux yeux du monde; et par lui, s'il faut ainsi dire, qu'elle semble dorer les pillules, afin qu'on les prenne sans répugnance, et qu'on se guérit presque sans avoir connu le remède. Aussi ne manque-t-elle jamais de nous montrer sur la scène la vertu récompensée, et le vice toujours puni...et c'est ainsi qu'insensiblement on nous imprime en l'âme l'amour de la vertu.[21]

Curiously enough Chapelain's own second draft of the *Sentiments* opened with an outline of a more 'hedonist' position. In a review of opinions about the ends of poetry he first observes that 'les uns soutiennent qu'elle (la poésie) n'a pour but que le plaisir des peuples, les autres que sa dernière intention est leur profit'. Subsequent expansion of this opposition is already prejudiced by the assertion that the drama appeals either to 'les sens' or to 'la raison', typically distorting the Horatian tag into 'docere aut delectare'. While there is little room for doubt about which of these opinions is to be preferred, he briefly describes a third, and median, view of a 'moderne', 'lequel, sans s'attacher à [l'opinion] qui fait de la poésie une morale déguisée, estime que le plaisir en est la seule fin, mais fait distinction de plaisir et ne lui attribue que celui qui est raisonnable'. Thus a play might be considered well realized if the pleasure offered is 'fondé en raison [et produit] par les voies qui le rendent régulier, lesquelles à peu près sont les mêmes qui sont requises pour le rendre profitable'. One wonders whether this interesting attempt at a compromise had not originated in Balzac's Charentais retreat. Unfortunately its implications are not more fully explored, for Chapelain introduces it only to reject it as incompatible with his regulatory brief, 'parce que nous ne croyons pas que sans de puissants motifs ceux qui tiennent pour le profit l'aient assigné à la poésie'.[22] Fairly obviously these motives relate to more 'eminent' authorities than either Scaliger or Heinsius. Any published version of the Académie's deliberations would have to reflect its appointed place in the Cardinal's national programme of political education. Obedience was to be associated with virtue within the Académie's official commission to 'proposer des exemples de vertu en faisant l'éloge des grands serviteurs du pays, et en particulier le Roi'.[23]

The finally approved and published version of the *Sentiments* makes this political accountability amply clear. The third option is now completely suppressed in favour of the argument that, if pleasure is an end of art, this is only so because poetic drama is 'l'instrument de la vertu, qui purge l'homme, sans dégoût et insensiblement, de ses habitudes vicieuses, qui est utile parce qu'il est honnête...Si ce plaisir n'est l'utilité même, au moins est-il la source d'où elle coule nécessairement.' Pleasure is reduced to the purely instrumental function of rendering agreeable the morally improving effect of the drama. This leads directly to a fully-developed utilitarian argument in which a theory of public education by stealth is much more elaborately set out than ever were the three possibilities of Chapelain's earlier draft:

Les mauvais exemples sont contagieux, même sur les théâtres; les feintes réprésentations ne causent que trop de véritables crimes, et il y a grand péril à divertir le peuple par des plaisirs qui peuvent produire un jour des douleurs publiques. Il nous faut bien garder d'accoutumer ni ses yeux ni ses oreilles à des actions qu'il doit ignorer...si nous ne lui en apprenons en même temps la punition, et si au retour de ces spectacles il ne remporte du moins un peu de crainte parmi beaucoup de contentement.'[24]

With rather less bluster than Scudéry, the Académie agrees that the subject of *Le Cid* is 'de très mauvais exemple' and so is inappropriate for the public stage. With a characteristic political inflexion of the concept of verisimilitude towards conventionally received ideals of moral respectability, the *Sentiments* set strict limits to the poet's choice and treatment of his source material:

Toutes les vérités ne sont pas bonnes pour le théâtre, et...il en est de quelques-unes comme de ces crimes énormes dont les juges font brûler les procès avec les criminels. Il y a des vérités monstrueuses...qu'il faut supprimer pour le bien de la société...C'est principalement en ces rencontres que le poëte a droit de préférer la vraisemblance à la vérité, et de travailler plutôt sur un sujet feint et raisonnable que sur un véritable qui ne fût pas conforme à la raison. Que s'il est obligé de traiter une matière historique de cette nature, c'est alors qu'il la doit réduire aux termes de la bienséance, sans avoir égard à la vérité, et qu'il la doit plutôt changer toute entière que de lui laisser rien qui soit incompatible avec les règles de son art, lequel se proposant l'idée universelle des choses, les épure des défauts...que l'histoire...est constrainte d'y souffrir.

Chimène's behaviour is treated no more kindly than is the historical truth of human behaviour:

Ses mœurs sont du moins scandaleuses, si en effet elles ne sont dépravées. Ces pernicieux exemples rendent l'ouvrage notablement défectueux, et s'écartent du but de la poésie, qui veut être utile. Ce n'est pas que cette utilité ne se puisse produire par des mœurs qui soient mauvaises; mais pour la produire par de mauvaises mœurs, il faut qu'à la fin elles soient punies, et non récompensées comme elles le sont et cet ouvrage.[25]

For all its attempted accommodation of pleasure with profit, the Académie's regulatory concern that poetry function as an instrument of prudential admonition is clearly to the fore, as Aristotle's discussion of poetic probability is abusively invoked in support of a concept of verisimilitude which constantly drifts towards assertions of ideal moral propriety. After unavailing attempts to find 'improving' modifications to the play's original historical material, the Académie's conclusion is overwhelmingly favourable to Scudéry when it asserts that 'le plus expédient eût éte de n'en point faire de poème'. The implication of this is that, since the original facts could not be manipulated in such a way as to conform to conventional preconceptions of proper behaviour, a vaguely Platonizing invocation of 'l'idée universelle des choses' as a pre-existent benchmark of acceptable conduct should direct the dramatist either towards silence or exemplary illustrations of a 'better' world than the one in which we live.

When Aristotle said that men take pleasure in learning from artistic imitation, he certainly had not meant that the poet should in some way offer a lesson in virtuous living. But, like the *Sentiments*, La Mesnardière's *La Poétique* (1639) takes the view that dramatic poetry should indeed serve civic virtue by persuasion and example.[26] Characteristically careless with his Aristotelian sources, La Mesnardière confuses the *Poetics* with the *Rhetoric* and his argument quickly drifts towards the presentation of poetic drama as illustrating an ideal 'golden' world, rather than expressing universal truths through the proper imitation of historical particulars. Balzac had already noted this doctrinaire peculiarity when he wrote to Scudéry on *Le Cid* in 1637. Scudéry held that poetic imitation should present a better world of ideas for the edified contemplation of the spectator, and that the rules were in accordance with – and existed to serve – this ideal order.[27] Balzac's reply gracefully alluded to Plato's *Republic* in a warning which went straight to the heart of the argument:

S'il faut que Platon le banisse [*Le Cid*] de sa République il faut qu'il le couronne de fleurs en le bannissant et ne le traite pas plus mal qu'il n'a traité Homère. Ne vous attachez point avec tant de scrupule à la souveraine raison; qui voudrait la contenter et satisfaire à sa régularité serait obligé de lui bâtir un plus beau monde que celui-ci: il faudrait lui faire une nouvelle nature des choses, et lui aller chercher des idées au-dessus du Ciel.[28]

Like Scudéry, La Mesnardière's sharply reduced interest in resemblance to the original flows from the pre-eminence he too gives to the cautionary function of a play in which the hero may display but should finally master 'quelque fragilité qui mérite d'être excusée' and in which villains display vices which are finally punished (*Poétique*, p. 141). True to his Scaligerian loyalties, La Mesnardière derides Castelvetro's preoccupation with the satisfactions of the common audience and his argument never loses sight of this basic conviction that the public spectacle of tragedy should serve pleasantly to inculcate moral and civic virtues.

Despite the crudity of his position, the way in which La Mesnardière submits the poet to the needs of the city has at least the merit of brutal clarity: 'Je n'introduis rien au théâtre que je n'approuve au barreau' (*Poétique*, p. 72). Such a statement reposes on concepts of moral and civil orthodoxy which are quite extrinsic to any arguably Aristotelian view of poetic truth, and its disastrously limiting consequences become clear as soon as it is applied to historical tragedy. With all the severity of Plato banishing 'the sweet lyric or epic muse' from his Republic, the author of *La Poétique* holds that a major part of experience has to be either suppressed or at least severely condemned at the socially responsible poet's tribunal: 'Or encore que dans le monde des bons soient souvent affligés, et que les méchants prospèrent...le poème tragique donnant beaucoup à l'exemple et plus encore à la raison...[est] toujours obligé de récompenser les vertus, et de châtier les vices' (*Poétique*, p. 107). Despite the assertion that tragedy can only properly be appreciated by a sophisticated élite and should only be written with such an audience in mind, La Mesnardière has little faith in the moral discrimination even of this ideal audience. The poet must strictly censor himself in his choice of subject-matter and must guide and protect the spectator by inserted moral comment, spelling out an exemplary morality for the benefit of unreasonable weaker brethren in the audience who presumably would not otherwise realize when they should be gratified or horrified. It is characteristic of La Mesnardière's insensitivity to the realities of the spectator's moral and aesthetic response to stage performance that he assumes that, once the poet has reminded the spectator that he should be scandalized, he will indeed be appropriately shocked. Such is the poet's obligation to 'penser à la morale et donner beaucoup à l'exemple' (*Poétique*, p. 21), that it is simply not enough to trust in the spectator's natural good sense in response to the vivid depiction of vice. Coarsening almost beyond recognition the rich moral possibilities of the Aristotelian theory of imitation, La Mesnardière presents the art of tragedy as 'une prédication active et un sermon délicieux' (*Poétique*, p. 217). In so recasting a poetics of stage portraiture into a programme of pulpitry and propaganda, he follows the Jesuit Cellot's praise of tragedy as the most powerful force for social and political regulation: 'O art précieux, supérieur à toute autre, puisqu'il pourvoit au bien suprème de l'Etat, en retenant dans leur devoir, et en conduisant par les voies les plus douces à la vertu non seulement les cités, mais même les provinces et les royaumes.'[29]

This is not a simple matter of retouching or even of applying fig-leaves to individual roles. The very world in which La Mesnardière's heroes move is so profoundly modified a version of real experience that the recommended dénouement becomes what Bray wittily called 'une sorte de distribution de prix ou plutôt un Jugement Dernier'.[30] But even La Mesnardière has to admit that the poet cannot wholly fabulate, for all that it is in that direction that his prejudices are leading him. Vice triumphant is, alas, almost unavoidable at some time in the course of the play. The solution is found in a tragic 'raisonneur' who praises virtue unjustly persecuted, execrates triumphant vice, and reminds the audience that final judgement and punishment, if slow to come, is sure to come (*Poétique*, pp. 223–4).[31] Following Chapelain and Scudéry, La Mesnardière also suggests that, if historical events fail to offer the requisite spectacle of virtue finally triumphant, the poet should suppress the awkward truth in favour of such probable fictions as will spare or confirm his audience's moral prejudices. This view, together with its accompanying assertion of the poet's social obligations, vigorously persists into the second half of the century, notably in D'Aubignac's criticism of Corneille's *Sophonisbe* and its unedifying spectacle of a Queen's adultery: 'Il n'est point nécessaire que le poète s'opiniâtre à faire historien, et quand la vérité répugne à la générosité, à l'honnêté, ou à la grace de la scène, il faut qu'il l'abandonne et qu'il prenne le vraisemblable pour faire un beau poème, au lieu d'une méchante histoire.'[32] Thus do doctrinaire theories of the 'vraisemblable' and the 'bienséant' – ostensibly dawn from Aristotle's original statements on poetic truth and probability – exploit poetic imitation to the ends of social order and moral improvement. D'Aubignac again succinctly expresses this intention with a revealing turn of phrase: 'Nous ne voulons point croire que les Rois puissent être méchants, ni souffrir que leurs sujets...se rebellent contre leur puissance, non pas même en peinture.'[33]

All this may well prompt the reader into wondering whether the doctrinaires' ideal of tragedy is not in danger of losing any right to be called a poetic imitation of the real world. So narrow and embellished an account of human conduct seems to propose to the poet a field of vision almost as limited as that of the nervous ostrich. La Mesnardière concedes that 'les belles descriptions...font passer dans notre âme avec un plaisir sensible la propre essence des choses dont elles tracent les images' (*Poétique*, p. 314). But this imitative vividness, which Corneille holds central to his art in perfect accord with a more traditional understanding of the didactic theory of poetry, La Mesnardière considers insufficient of itself to ensure the special moral efficacy he believes to be essential to the drama. Any such delightfully vivid imitation is quickly hedged with censorious limitations: 'Ces merveilleuses peintures...ne doivent figurer que des choses qui soient plaisantes, ou pour le moins supportables. Il faut qu'un si beau coloris soit employé en des sujets qui ne soient point odieux, et que l'on ne travaille pas comme ces peintres bizarres qui mettent toute leur science à pourtraire une couleuvre, ou quelque autre vilain reptile' (*Poétique*, p. 314). All 'vilaines choses qui travaillent ou scandalizent toutes les âmes bien nées par leurs représentations odieuses ou affligeantes' are proscribed matter for imitation, for the greater edification and pleasure of an ideal audience of 'gens d'esprit connaissants et raisonnables' (*Poétique*, pp. 314–15 and 325).[34] The latter would surely have found very little stimulus to reflection in so unreal and, in the worse sense, conventional a representation of human behaviour.

The doctrinaires neither trust the audience's judgement nor value the poet's ability to show the intrinsic truth of whatever subject he imitates. Instead they transform the drama into an agreeable depiction of an alternative poetic universe of ideas, far superior to the wretched world of experience. In their works, the humanistic concept of artistic imitation has undergone a quite remarkable shift of sense, since the obligation to imitate now lies not so much with the artist as with the spectator, who is expected to shape his life in accordance with what the artist has directly created and bodied forth through the 'golden world' of his stage spectacle. Despite all their expressions of reverence for Aristotle, the doctrinaires' political and utilitarian bias constantly leads them away from the *Poetics* and towards the *Republic's* emphasis on the civic obligations of the poet, as they create rule-books for the fabrication of an ideal world of pre-conceived virtues within the formal framework of classical regularity.

In this context, Sidney's description of Canidia's portrait offers a useful reminder of the fundamental inefficacy of so misguided an enlistment of poetry to the ends of moral improvement: 'As to a lady that desired to fashion her countenance to the best grace: a Painter should more benefit her to portray a most sweet face, writing Canidia upon it, than to paint Canidia as she was, who Horace sweareth was full ill favoured.'[35] The doctrinaires' proposed poetic spectacle is conceived rather in the same spirit, as it too becomes the means whereby the poet expresses 'divine consideration of what...should be'. It is not hard to see that such a portrayal of human behaviour is likely to have had as little practical effect on the seventeenth-century spectator's conduct as had Canidia's portrait on her frightful looks. The comparison may do scant justice to the nobility of Sidney's argument elsewhere, but at least it shows why the doctrinaires' utilitarian preoccupations lead them to forget the realities of audience response in the theatre. Fortunately for the development of seventeenth-century French literature, common sense prevailed in poetic practice if not in poetic theory. As every student knows, the 'vilain reptile' – so abjured by La Mesnardière and so spectacularly and successfully portrayed in human form in Corneille's *Médée* – retained an honoured place in poetry as the 'serpent' and 'monstre hideux...par l'art imité' of Boileau's later review of the century's literary achievement.[36]

However, Chapelain's third and suppressed option of a poetics of 'reasonable pleasure' reappears transformed in the 'Epître' with which Corneille replied to his critics, when he published *Médée* in March 1639. Clearly much depends upon what is meant by 'reasonable', and it is notable that Corneille describes the pleasure offered by his depiction of Medea in terms of a 'reason' which conforms neither to the narrowly political sense of exemplary social behaviour nor to the cautionary effect of an action in which wickedness is finally punished. Instead reason is understood in the more commonly accepted sense of the faculty which permits the spectator to perceive those universal truths which proper poetic imitation expresses. While the *Discours* of 1660 will repeat this argument with greater care and precision, it will not be one which much interests D'Aubignac in *La Pratique du théâtre* (1657), even when he asserts that 'le poète ne travaille que pour leur plaire [aux spectateurs]'. This passage refers to the satisfaction of 'les doctes' in the audience, and the rest of the argument seeks to allay traditional Church prejudice against the theatre by repeatedly stressing the moral and social profit to be found in the drama.[37] It is no surprise then that D'Aubignac, piqued by the *Discours*, published in 1663 an unambiguously utilitarian *Troisième Dissertation* on Corneille's *Œdipe*. Reviving the Académie's condemnation of *Le Cid*, D'Aubignac now rigorously circumscribes the poet's choice of subject and insists on his obligation to foster social and political order: 'Il faut enseigner des choses qui maintiennent la société publique, qui servent à retenir les peuples dans leur devoir, et qui montrent toujours les Souverains comme des objets de vénération environnés des vertus comme de la gloire'.[38] This as strikingly illustrates the continuing political constraints implicit in the doctrinaire argument of profit as, twenty-six years earlier, the 'Epître' prefacing *Médée* exemplifies the claim to poetic autonomy implicit in what has been called Corneille's 'hedonist' opposition to the Académie's views.

It is important to note, however, that a simple opposition of hedonism to didacticism, attractive as it may seem, is insufficient to describe Corneille's argument with the doctrinaires, since the second part of the 'Epître' discusses *Médée* in relation to the more subtle – and traditional – contention that pleasure itself may be a means to knowledge of the most ambitious kind. Corneille prefaces his illustration of heroic atrocity in *Médée* by arguing that just such an insight into human nature is central to the pleasure which his play offers. As a result he can present a view of the higher moral significance of poetic drama which totally escapes the limitations imposed by a concept of verisimilitude governed by essentially local notions of political and social propriety. Instead the poet's freedom to present his *personnages* in a way which makes their intrinsic qualities and defects immediately apparent to the spectator is held to be a central aspect of the pleasure to be derived from the play's performance:

Ici vous trouverez le crime en son char de triomphe, et peu de personnages sur la scène sont les mœurs ne soient plus mauvaises que bonnes; mais la peinture et la Poésie ont cela de commun entre beaucoup d'autres choses, que l'une fait souvent de beaux portraits d'une femme laide, et l'autre de belles imitations d'une action qu'il ne faut pas imiter. Dans la portraiture

il n'est pas question si un visage est beau, mais s'il ressemble, et dans la
Poésie il ne faut pas considérer si les mœurs sont vertueuses, mais si elles sont
pareilles à celles de la personne qu'elle introduit. Aussi nous décrit-elle
indifféremment les bonnes et les mauvaises actions, sans nous proposer les
dernières pour exemple, et si elle nous en veut faire quelque horreur, ce
n'est pas par leur punition qu'elle n'affecte pas de nous faire voir, mais par
leur laideur qu'elle s'efforce de nous représenter au naturel. Il n'est pas
besoin d'avertir ici le public que celles de cette Tragédie ne sont pas à
imiter, elles paraissent assez à découvert pour n'en faire envie à personne.
Je n'examine point si elles sont vraisemblables ou non... il me suffit qu'elles
sont autorisées ou par la vérité de l'histoire, ou par l'opinion commune des
Anciens. (GC, I, 535–6)

By illustrating the realities of human behaviour *and* misbehaviour,
Corneille's play is both interesting and enjoyable because it raises
serious moral issues. 'Proper' imitation of the realities of human
conduct – whether or not they are punished or rewarded – may
challenge conventional expectations, but it also preserves a fully
moral dimension to the pleasures of understanding them. Since
Horace, Emilie, Cinna and Polyeucte all pursue courses of conduct
which (if judged in terms of the Académie's notions of civic and
social propriety) can only be termed scandalous, Corneille's
argument here is as relevant to his dramatic practice after *Médée* as
to the play itself.

Corneille's use of the poetry/painting comparison, like his faith in
the moral efficacy of vivid likeness in significant imitation, places the
'Epître' squarely within the broadly didactic tradition of humanistic
poetic theory. His argument has a long pedigree and draws heavily
on Plutarch's celebrated discussion of 'How a Young Man should
study Poetry'. There it had been argued that poetry was a source of
wisdom particularly suited to the preparation of an unformed mind
before it graduated to the more arduous discipline of philosophy.
Poetry was profitable precisely because it offered a pleasurable
comparison of both the wicked and the good. Even shameful actions,
once imitated by art, were a source of both pleasure and profit in so
far as they were matter for the exercise of moral judgement:
'Children rightly nurtured amid poetry will in some way or other
learn to draw some wholesome and profitable doctrine even from
passages that are suspect of what is base and improper.' Quoting the
'oft-repeated saying' that 'poetry is articulate painting and painting
inarticulate poetry', Plutarch exhorted his reader to impress upon
the young man,

that when we see a lizard or an ape or the face of Thersites in a picture we are pleased with it and admire it not as a beautiful thing but as a likeness. For by its essential nature the ugly cannot become beautiful; but the imitation, be it concerned with what is base or what is good, if only it attain to the likeness is commended.

If Plutarch admitted to some doubt about the propriety of painting 'unnatural acts, as Timomachus painted a figure of Medea slaying her children', he nevertheless concluded in favour of such disturbing representations – and in terms which Corneille echoes in the 'Epître':

In these matters...what we recommend is not the action which is the subject of the imitation, but the art, in case the subject in hand has been properly imitated. Since then poetry also gives an imitative recital of base deeds or of wicked experiences and characters, the young man must not accept as true what is admired and successful therein, or approve it as beautiful, but should simply commend it as fitting and proper to the character in hand.[39]

By so presenting the poet's task as the fit representation of the character and actions of Medea through a dramatic portrait 'au naturel', Corneille is not proposing a theatre of 'realism' in today's sense of the word. The true worth of the dramatic poem resided in the lucidity with which it revealed the essential nature, good or evil, of whatever action was imitated. This required the seventeenth-century poet to render the essential truth of his subject 'assez à découvert' to penetrate the audience's understanding in both its affective and intellective aspects, thereby stimulating the spectator to form his own judgement on what he had witnessed.[40] In Corneille's scheme of things, *Médée* realized the truth of its heroine, not in the sense of the Platonizing 'Idée' with which the utilitarians made such play, but in the more traditional Aristotelian sense of a pleasurable understanding of her essential nature. This perception possessed a more enduring moral validity than any arbitrary equation of verisimilitude with essentially local ideas of propriety. Corneille's play 'painted' both Médée's claim to justice as a wronged wife and her terrible vengeance on her betrayers in an even-handed representation of her situation and her deeds, their motivation and their consequences. If this challenged the audience to reflect on right and wrong in a way which stretched their understanding beyond narrow and received social orthodoxies tricked out as 'l'Idée universelle des choses', that surely was not a matter for public disquiet. It was sufficient that the audience found pleasure in the heightened moral understanding which resulted from the decorum and luminosity with which both playwright and actors had skilfully imitated the particular events of the Medea legend and ensured an immediate perception of their broader human significance.

It is an unkind irony that Corneille, who was so concerned in the 'Epître' to preserve the moral profundity of his art by rejecting any restriction on the dramatist's portrayal of human action, has been understood on the evidence of the same text to have been the exponent of a heroic drama not to be appreciated 'sur le plan d'une morale de valeurs'.[41] In fact nothing could be further from the truth. Certainly the 'Epître' rejects the narrow prescriptions of the doctrinaires, but only to present, under the banner of delight, a much profounder theory of moral significance. Like Castelvetro before him in his attacks on Scaliger, Corneille was closer to Aristotle in this than were his self-styled Aristotelian opponents, because he was convinced of poetry's capacity to express a reality seen in the essential nature of the thing or action imitated.[42] In replying to the *Sentiments*, the 'Epître' prefacing *Médée* is strikingly close to those learned seventeenth-century commentators on Aristotle who were happily uninvolved in literary and political wrangles about the relationship of the poet to the governing order. Like Corneille, these theologians and philosophers preserve the careful distinctions which Aristotle had first established between the *Poetics*, the *Politics*, and the *Rhetoric*, stating without equivocation that art is morally 'indifferent' because its office is to imitate nature as it is, rather than moralize by imitating only a reassuring part of it. They thus make a clear distinction between the office of imitation and the nature of the subject: 'les actions sont honnêtes ou déshonnêtes, mais les ouvrages qui se font par art ne sont honnêtes ni déshonnêtes à parler proprement … C'est le propre de l'art de pouvoir peindre toute sorte de représentation.'[43]

It is not difficult to understand how Corneille's view of the poet as portraitist 'au naturel' has been misconstrued in terms of more recent concepts of 'realism' and 'naturalism', imprecise though these terms are.[44] The twentieth-century audience is familiar enough with the idea of the accurate presentation of particulars, but less so with the seventeenth-century poetic commonplaces of 'nature' and 'the natural' as descriptive of the essential significance of the thing imitated.[45] Again, the twentieth-century reader finds himself at some distance from seventeenth-century poetic assumptions in so far as present-day habits of mind tend more sharply to distinguish between profit and delight. As has been tartly observed elsewhere, our understanding of what seventeenth-century poets meant by utility 'has become what Bacon would call a poor shrunken thing'.[46] The same may be said of our understanding of delight, but we are not entirely to be blamed for this since, even by the time of *Médée*, there were already authoritative and powerful voices in France who themselves impoverished both concepts by opposing profit and delight. However, to persist in such a misunderstanding, in discussion of a poet whose theory so consistently resisted the doctrinaires' denial that pleasure was consubstantial with the perception of truth, seems less permissible. Thus modern critical discussion of Corneille's poetic 'hedonism' or of the 'amorality' of his drama once again polarizes terms which, to Corneille, were essentially complementary, and thereby draws us back into the very same false dichotomy which bedevilled the views of Chapelain or La Mesnardière.

The arguments of the 'Epître' diverge most significantly from those of the Académie in that area where doctrinaire theory modified the properly didactic character of humanist poetic theory, the better to serve contemporary political ends quite foreign to the original implications of a theory of poetry which treated of imitation as a means to knowledge. For Corneille, poetry would always remain a powerful means to the expression of universals perceived in his subject. For his opponents, poetry served agreeably and persuasively to propagate 'given' and conventional moral truths extrinsic to the subject itself. The difference is crucially important and, in its extreme form, distinguishes the poet from the literary propagandist. Since both relied heavily on the same rhetorical methods, their differences of literary practice are not always immediately apparent, except in the depth and scope of their vision and the subtlety and power with which they exploit this shared repertory of skills.[47] It has been observed that the doctrinaires' narrow pedantry 'aboutissait à entraver l'effort créateur de l'artiste, à le soumettre au faux bon sens des esprits médiocres...L'idée de vraisemblance que rejette Corneille, c'est celle d'un classicisme abâtardi.'[48] The shallowness of the 'Classical' tradition of doctrinaire theory which formed a constant counterpoint to Corneille's own statements calls attention to one of the more extraordinary paradoxes of the century. Nowhere more than in seventeenth-century France is the gap more apparent between the poverty of officially sanctioned definitions of the poet's function and the quality of the literary achievement over which 'Messieurs de l'Académie' so theoretically presided. It was Corneille's misfortune that, for reasons specific to the political evolution of France, there were not 'a few persons' but an influential number, neither good poets nor perceptive critics, who sought to clip the wings of artists convinced that poetry commended itself to its public because it was concerned with Truth, and not with the 'Favourite Truths' of the age.

ACCOMMODATION AND CONTINUITY: THE DEDICATIONS OF *HORACE* (1640–1) AND *POLYEUCTE* (1643)

Since the subject and political significance of *Horace* were quite unrealizable within the Académie's terms of reference, Corneille had a compelling reason to insist that even the most disquieting aspects of human behaviour might be fit matter for poetic imitation and offer both pleasure and enlightenment to the spectator. Corneille's new play was to eclipse his rivals and critics as a resounding demonstration of the true profundity with which the historical subject might be treated, and the imposing superiority of the masterpieces which followed *Horace* were to confirm the importance of his impenitently independent stand in the late 1630s. From now on we can observe, in Corneille's practice and occasional theoretical statements, a careful elaboration of the fundamental convictions about his art which had first crystallized during the Querelle du *Cid*.

Of course, if Chapelain and La Mesnardière were closely attached to the Cardinal's interests, Corneille himself for the last four years had also enjoyed his pension of 1,500 *livres* from Richelieu. The difficulties of his position are apparent in a correspondence with Boisrobert which makes it clear that, despite differences of literary judgement, Corneille was obviously anxious not to offend his powerful patron. Richelieu's acceptance of the new play suggests that Corneille had made his accommodations by the second half of 1640, but the very flatteries of the dedication reveal that this had been achieved without yielding on any of the fundamental principles involved in the Querelle. His earlier plays and prefatory statements had already shown that he was no enemy of the rules, rather did he value them in so far as they served the proper ends of poetry. Where

Corneille differed was on a definition of the ends which 'regularity'
served, unimpressed as he was by any claim that the rules themselves
enshrined and expressed an ideal order more obviously to be
associated with political considerations than with those 'more
philosophical' truths of which Aristotle had written. The formal
regularity of *Horace* certainly belongs in the general triumph of 'the
rules' as the means to economy and force which is characteristic of
French drama after 1637, but we would be wrong to interpret this
play's greater regularity as if a youthful flirtation with the rules had
ended in the scandal of *Le Cid*, a shotgun marriage with doctrinaire
poetics, and *Horace* as the first-born of so improbable a union.
Greater formal regularity in *Horace* brought Corneille within the
limits of respectability, but the play's subject and circumstances of
composition show that it was the offspring of a bride of Corneille's
own choosing – an older love certainly, but not an 'ancient beauty'
forced upon him by authority. The contiguity of the 'Epître'
prefacing *Médée* reminds us that *Horace* continues principles essential
to *Le Cid*, notably with regard to the poet's choice of material and
treatment of 'historical' fact in relation to the 'vraisemblable' and
the 'bienséant'.

When Corneille read his new tragedy in late 1639 to an assembly
of *cognoscenti*, most of whom had been hostile to *Le Cid*, he almost
certainly knew that Camille's murder and the judgement of Act v
would be badly received. That expected criticism was sufficient to
make him hesitate, but finally he refused to make any substantial
changes to his play.[49] Despite its favourable public reception, *Horace*
soon looked likely to provoke another expert controversy, and
Chapelain write to Balzac on the 19 February 1640 in terms which
suggest that he recognized the new work's affinity with its
predecessor:

Corneille a fait une nouvelle pièce...où il y a une quantité de belles choses
et du même esprit du *Cid*. Néanmoins je voudrais pour sa perfection qu'il
eût inventé et disposé autrement qu'il n'a fait, et s'il l'imprime bientôt, je
vous enverrai mes sentiments dessus et la manière que je voudrais qu'il eût
tenue pour en faire une chose accomplie. (19 February 1640)[50]

Well aware of the importance of the poetic issues at stake, the
Secretary of the Académie was tempted to start the war of words
again.

Since Corneille's play still disregards the central lesson of the

Sentiments on 'le vraisemblable' and on the choice of a historical subject, it is likely that defiance, quite as much as a desire to conform, played a part in the greater dramaturgical regularity of *Horace*. To brilliant and individual effect Corneille adopts the Roman subject popularized by rival dramatists, clearly intending to excel on his opponents' ground just as he had done before when *Clitandre* regularized the unregularizable in reply to criticism of the imperfections of *Mélite*. Indeed Corneille's crushing popular success in the 1640s is only fully comprehensible once we recognize how unfavourably similar Roman history plays by his contemporaries compare with the scope and political profundity of the sequence of plays with which he followed *Le Cid*. Only a superior talent and the ambitious view Corneille took of the possibilities of historical drama explain a series of masterpieces which makes even the best of his competitors' work in the late 1630s and 1640s look third-rate. We shall return to some of these rival works in discussion of Corneille's plays, but the difference between Corneille's poetic ambitions and those of other dramatists of his day is equally apparent in the way his rivals discuss their art. Grenaille, presenting his *Innocent malheureux* in 1639, only offers a trite confusion between the qualities necessary to tragedy and those necessary to its author. Others variously embroider on the familiar theme of the primacy of edification: for instance even Du Ryer follows the line set in Sarasin's praise of Scudéry's *Amour tyrannique* (played 1638, published 1639) and prefaces his *Saul* of 1642 with the assertion that tragedy is 'la plus agréable école où l'on puisse apprendre la vertu'. This chimes remarkably well with the views of the Jesuit dramatist Bartollomei, who wrote that dramatized history 'enseigne comme Reine à toutes les autres vertus la conservation des Républiques et des Royaumes et le bonheur des Peuples'.[51] Later, Gillet de la Tessonerie even goes so far as to compose *L'Art de régner, ou le Sage Gouverneur* (1645) as a kind of dramatic lesson from history for the young Louis XIV. It is of little significance that he seems to agree with Corneille on the matter of presenting facts both pleasant and unpleasant, for the point serves the emphatically moralizing conviction that both have to be shown to ensure the cautionary effect of a lesson in which profit comes before pleasure.[52]

In all likelihood the prospect of a second Querelle over *Horace* was ended by the Cardinal's acceptance of the dedication of the published edition (January 1641). The circumstances and terms of

this dedication have been interpreted in a sense which makes the
play and its successor into two of the greatest political lessons in
dramatic form of the period, and the dedication itself has been held
to present *Horace* as a dramatic illustration of the 'grandes idées' of
the Cardinal. According to this reading, the dedication is an act of
political allegiance and the play a brilliant practical realization of
Richelieu's desire that the public stage serve the political education
of the Paris public.[53] We shall leave interpretation of the play until
later, but this dedication is itself a text of greater subtlety than a
forthright expression of the unconditional adhesion to the Cardinal's
views. Instead it shows the extent and limits of the accommodation
which Corneille achieved with a powerful master who, whatever the
true facts of his involvement and role in the Querelle du *Cid*, was
certainly understood by Corneille to have favoured Scudéry's views
and to have been the principal instigator of the Académie's
condemnation of his play.

It was perhaps fortunate for Corneille that, at the time of
Richelieu's acceptance of the dedication, the King had commanded
that Boisrobert and his unseemly impertinences be banished from
the Cardinal's household. By a nice irony, this link-man between the
Cardinal and the Paris literary world had been 'exiled' to Rouen.
But he had also been one of the few who admired *Horace* on its first
reading in his house in late 1639 and, even if he wrote to the
Cardinal inviting him to make fools of his unfriendly Norman
neighbours, he may have helped Corneille patch up what, on the
poet's side at least, was an undoubtedly strained relationship.[54]
Whether Boisrobert helped or not, Corneille's refusal to modify his
play after that earlier reading of *Horace* suggests that his reconciliation with the Cardinal was essentially a formal one. There is
little evidence, either in the play or in the dedication, that Corneille
had made an unlikely *volte face* of poetics and been suddenly converted
to Academic orthodoxy or the propagandist dissemination of the
Cardinal's political ideas. Indeed Corneille as much as admits that
Horace was not conceived in such a spirit since, after conventional
deprecations of his work, he promises another work better suited to
his patron. Furthermore, he goes to some lengths to point out, in
appropriately flattering terms, that he is not one of the literary
côterie close to the Cardinal – and small wonder, since La
Mesnardière, Scudéry, and Sarasin had all been trying to belittle *Le
Cid* as late as 1639.[55] Instead *Horace* is described as the product of a

provincial poet living in Rouen who, unlike that favoured few, lacks the benefit of close association with the Cardinal and his ideas. As Corneille carefully picks his way back into the Cardinal's graces, he still manages to assert his own convictions by presenting *Horace* as of a piece with what he had written since joining the Five Authors in 1635 (GC, I, 833–4). But the facts of those five years of patronage belie this flattering description of docile provincial simplicity. Whether he had been excluded or had withdrawn of his own choice, Corneille had ceased to work with Boisrobert, Rotrou, Colletet, and L'Estoile by June 1638. If we are to believe the Campion brothers, this was because he could not 'assujettir la force et la sublimité de ses pensées toutes libres, à des conceptions si délicates et si spiritualisées, qu'elles n'avaient pas assez de corps pour se soutenir elles-mêmes'.[56] A more likely reason, however, was that the growing seriousness of his own dramatic preoccupations sat ill with the other four authors' interest in the *ballet de cour* and the romanesque and allegorical tragicomedies which Richelieu most enjoyed. Corneille already had very different ambitions as a dramatist of political subject-matter, and was uninterested in the confection of programmatic history-plays or spectacular political allegories. But he did not forfeit his pension in 1638 and still received it in 1641, which suggests that Corneille had not given too much offence to the Cardinal, even if his refusal to collaborate may have contributed to the latter's willingness to see a gifted but awkward *protégé* called to order by the Académie. In the last analysis, the precise significance of Corneille's profession of indebtedness to the Cardinal's 'grandes Idées' must remain a moot point, not least because the rhetorical question in which it is couched artfully leaves it to the Cardinal to give the answer. But somewhat remarkably, if we compare it with other dedications to Richelieu in the period, the dedication barely touches on the Cardinal's greatness as a political figure. Instead it flatters Richelieu as a connoisseur of dramatic poetry, shrewdly aiming to please his patron by presenting him as Muse rather than Minister.

What follows is much less equivocal and offers sure evidence of Corneille's own position in recent literary polemics. This is established with all the wit which Richelieu had come to expect of a poet who until recently had been largely a comic dramatist:

Il faut, Monseigneur, que tous ceux qui donnent leurs veilles au Théâtre publient hautement avec moi que nous vous avons deux obligations très signalées; l'une d'avoir ennobli le but de l'Art, l'autre de nous en avoir

facilité les connaissances. Vous avez ennobli le but de l'Art, puisqu'au lieu
de celui de plaire au peuple, que nous prescrivent nos Maîtres... vous nous
avez donné celui de vous plaire et celui de vous divertir; et qu'ainsi nous
ne rendons pas un petit service à l'Etat, puisque contribuant à vos
divertissements, nous contribuons à l'entretien d'une santé qui lui est si
précieuse et si nécessaire.

With this Corneille sticks to his literary principles and makes his
accommodations unmistakeably on his own terms. To those, like
Richelieu, who were well aware of the poetic issues raised by the
debate on *Le Cid*, there is considerable humour in the way Corneille's
flatteries manage to reconcile two hitherto irreconcilable views on
the ends of art. Still clinging to essentials, he re-asserts the primacy
of pleasure but ingeniously equates the Cardinal's pleasures with
public profit.[57] Of the same order is the extravagantly flattering
description of the Cardinal's face during a performance of a play as
worth more than ten years spent reading learned theory – a
compliment which disarmingly sustains Corneille's pragmatic
conviction that the applause of one 'eminent' spectator is worth
more than all the bookish theory of his Académie:

Vous nous en avez facilité les connaissances puisque nous n'avons plus
besoin d'autre étude pour les acquérir, que d'attacher nos yeux sur Votre
Eminence quand elle honore de sa présence et de son attention le récit de
nos Poèmes. C'est là que lisant sur son visage ce qui lui plaît, et ce qui ne
lui plaît pas, nous nous instruisons avec certitude de ce qui est bon, et de
ce qui est mauvais, et tirons des règles infaillibles de ce qu'il faut suivre et
de ce qu'il faut éviter. C'est là que j'ai souvent appris en deux heures ce que
mes livres n'eussent pu m'apprendre en dix ans; c'est là que j'ai puisé ce qui
m'a valu l'applaudissement du Public. (GC, I, 834)

This made elegant amends indeed for the *Excuse à Ariste*, while
simultaneously wittily co-opting the Cardinal's auspices in a public
statement of his own position on *Le Cid*. Richelieu's failing health
meant that Corneille's promise of work more worthy of his patron
was never fulfilled, and it is difficult to imagine what it might have
been, since Corneille refused to contribute any kind of panegyric
when his patron died.[58]

    The ingenuity with which Corneille both spoke his mind and kept
silent in response to the Cardinal's death is already apparent in the
witty flatteries of the dedication of *Horace*. We would be wrong to be
over-impressed by Corneille's fulsomeness or suspect a note of irony,
except in so far as his choice of phrase offers a brilliant reminder of

the skill with which the seventeenth-century writer could exploit the conventions within which he was working, even the normally hollow conventions of a formal dedication. Richelieu, unlike the sober-sided Louis XIII, enjoyed a joke so long as it was not at his own expense, and he would certainly not have missed – and does not seem to have been offended by – this ingeniously unrepentant dedication which so nicely mocked the Académie.[59] In dedicating *Horace* to Richelieu Corneille not only restored his position as the *protégé* of a formidable master, but also contrived to do so with a public display of devotion which made it very clear that he had not yielded an inch on matters of poetic principle.

The aesthetic significance of the dedication and preliminary notice of *Polyeucte* is another matter, however. Corneille had nothing of interest to say in presenting *Cinna*, but publication of his saint's tragedy at the end of 1643 produced the only occasion in all his work when Corneille submits his poetic endeavours to the prior certitudes of a greater order. Even here, though, where the poet's pride yields to the piety of the Christian sinner and Corneille sets his skills in service of the imperatives of Christian Revelation, *Polyeucte* is presented as a source of delight to the pious Anne of Austria. But in Corneille's prefatory account of his historical sources those pleasures serve the solemn meaning of a martyr's sacrifice, as his art is set to the task of revealing the Christian verities exemplified by Polyeucte's triumphant death. For once in his career, and for evident reasons of sound doctrine, Corneille presents delight as the servant of the prior 'Idea' and, in much the same sense as both Jesuits and doctrinaires argued, describes poetic imitation in instrumental terms, as a 'vehicle' for the communication of a preconceived and directly apprehended higher truth.[60] Of the historical facts behind this Counter-Reformation 'portrait des vertus chrétiennes' he observes:

Comme il a été à propos d'en rendre la représentation agréable, afin que le plaisir pût insinuer plus doucement l'utilité, et lui servir comme de véhicule pour la porter dans l'âme du peuple: il est juste aussi de lui donner cette lumière pour démêler la vérité d'avec ses ornements, et lui faire connaître ce qui lui doit imprimer du respect comme Saint, et ce qui le doit seulement divertir comme industrieux. (GC, I, 976)

The exceptional nature of this statement within the body of Corneille's theory is entirely attributable to the character of the play and to Corneille's religious convictions. Only as a devout son of the

Counter-Reformation does he humble his art before the sinner's faith in the Christian message. Never again will he adopt such a turn of phrase. He has no cause to do so, since *Théodore* (1646) is his only other saint's play, and there he contents himself with wry reflections on his audiences' changing moral sensibility (GC, II, 269).

By 1644 Corneille had already become undisputed master of the Paris stage, and the 'Au Lecteur' prefacing the first volume of his collected works reveals his confidence in a manner successfully applied over the preceding years. For the first time Corneille was sufficiently sure of himself to set his plays prior to *Le Cid* into the category of work blemished by early inexperience and even in need of correction by eliminating 'ce qu'il y a de plus insupportable'. These modifications were to be made in the collective edition of 1648, but Corneille's closing remarks of 1644 show that, if five successful years made it easier for him to admit to the imperfections of his early work, he was still wary of giving his critics a chance to discuss any emendations:

Je ne m'étendrai point à vous spécifier quelles règles j'y ai observées, ceux qui s'y connaissent s'en appercevront aisément, et de pareils discours ne font qu'importuner les savants, embarasser les faibles, et étourdir les ignorants. (GC, II, 188).

By now Corneille had acquired a very adequate theoretical competence and this passage needs to be set against the erudition he parades five years later in a letter to the scholar Huyghens (6 March 1649). Presenting a first volume of the 1648 amended edition of his works up to *Le Cid*, Corneille describes *Médée* as something rather better than his other early works and displays an expertise only comparable with that of the dedication of *Don Sanche* to Huyghens in May 1650.[61] There he outlines the novel concept of a 'comédie héroique' in an important theoretical piece which, together with the earlier 'Epître' prefacing *La Suite du Menteur* (1645) and the prefaces of *Rodogune* and *Héraclius* (both of 1647), shows his growing ability to exploit considerable learning in defence and elaboration of principles which earlier had been attacked in the Querelle du *Cid*.[62]

Furthermore, in the five collective editions published between 1648 and 1657, Corneille's 'Avertissement' preceding *Le Cid* at last publicly mentions Balzac's letter to Scudéry as the favourable verdict of a truly independent and distinguished critic. Again he protests at having been denied the right of the reply to the verdict of his opponents. With the benefit of hindsight he records how the literary debate had been obscured by the intrusion of higher powers which had both influenced the Académie's deliberations and forced him to accept their judgement as final:

A moins que d'être tout à fait stupide, on ne pouvait pas ignorer que comme les questions de cette nature ne concernent ni la religion ni l'Etat, on en peut décider par les règles de la prudence humaine, aussi bien que par celles du théâtre, et tourner sans scruple le sens du bon Aristote du côté de la politique. Ce n'est pas que je sache si ceux qui ont jugé du *Cid* en ont jugé selon leur sentiment ou non... mais seulement que ce n'a jamais été de mon consentiment qu'ils en ont jugé, et que peut-être je l'aurais justifié sans beaucoup de peine, si la même raison qui les a fait parler ne m'avait obligé à me taire. (GC, 1, 695)

Corneille then goes on to outline the kind of truth which, in his view at least, he had always sought to express in his works. Invoking Robertello's 'Aristotelian' conditions for the 'perfect tragedy' he argues (rather unconvincingly) that *Le Cid* meets these conditions, but makes the more important point that the *Poetics* enshrine artistic principles which transcend local and favourite truths. These principles, he says,

sont de tous les temps et de tous les peuples; et bien loin de s'amuser au détail des bienséances et des agréments, qui peuvent être divers, selon que ces deux circonstances sont diverses, il [Aristotle] a été droit aux mouvements de l'âme dont la nature ne change point. Il a montré quelles passions la tragédie doit exciter dans celles de ses auditeurs... il en a laissé des moyens qui auraient produit leur effet partout dès la création du monde, et qui seront capables de le produire encore partout, tant qu'il y aura des théâtres et des acteurs. (GC, 1, 695–6)

Once again Corneille's belief in the dignity of the drama and the fruitfulness of the poetics he has inherited prompts him to refer his practice back to the most respected of all literary authorities, pending the long-promised formulations of the *Discours*. That strength of purpose and continuity of inspiration was to guarantee Corneille's remarkable capacity to combine coherence of thought and constant self-renewal during another twenty-five years of writing for the stage.

2

Tradition and originality

Corneille's statements on his art during the reign of Louis XIII take it as axiomatic that poetry's moral effect operates through the pleasurable perception of truths which Aristotle had called 'something more philosophical than history'. This places his work within a long and venerable 'Classical' tradition – didactic certainly, but only in so far as it conceived of moral profundity as consubstantial with a certain kind of delight in learning and understanding. But ever since rhetoric had come to be considered central to the art of poetry, later authorities came to be nearly as much revered as Aristotle. If, in defending the moral authority of the poet, Corneille so emphasized immediacy of significance in the dramatic poet's imitation of an action, this was because Plutarch had stressed the importance of vivid concretion, while Cicero and Quintilian had offered influential accounts of the means whereby such telling vividness of representation could be achieved by 'painting' in words. Subsequent Renaissance and seventeenth-century theorists had persistently misread Horace's 'ut pictura poesis' as suggesting that poetry in some way imitated 'to the life' – a general proposition which was certainly implicit in the *Art of Poetry*, as Corneille had seen in the 'Au Lecteur' of *La Veuve* when he described good comedy as an apt and lively portrait of social manners. No one, however, understood this characteristically Roman inflexion of the idea of imitation towards a greater 'truth to life' as encouraging the poet to apply himself to the artless transcription of particulars. The still inexperienced Chapelain had come perilously close to such a naiveté in 1630 when, writing to Godeau on the twenty-four-hours rule, he equated the original action imitated in a play with an exactly congruent stage representation, but he had quickly abandoned the

idea as incompatible with his belief that poetry had fundamentally
moralizing ends.[1] All were agreed that the poet's imitative skills in
selection and ordering, when combined with the power of words
vividly to bring subject-matter to mind, surpassed simple one-to-one
imitation by showing a more generally applicable meaning latent in
local particulars. Without the presence and lucidity which was the
hallmark of proper imitation, this more philosophical truth could
only lie dormant and unperceived in its local habitation.[2]

Plutarch first fatally confused the sister arts (which Aristotle had
simply compared) in the famous statement that painting was dumb
poetry and poetry speaking painting, and his portraits in the parallel
Lives offered a notable illustration of how powerfully the arts of
selection and contrast could reveal enduring moral truths through
the particulars of history. The Roman rhetoricians, however, offered
a more systematic outline and example of how to realize the
desirable quality of *evidentia*, and their heirs in the sixteenth and
seventeenth centuries all considered rhetorical manuals indispensable to proper poetic imitation. Frequent seventeenth-century use of
the poetry/painting equation reminds us that the rhetorician's skills
were believed to offer a repertory of devices which ensured that the
forms of representation were indivisible from expression of a larger
truth. In such a scheme of things 'le sujet' implied something rather
more ambitious than a simple résumé of the events which formed the
narrative basis of an epic or a play. The term embraced the higher
truth communicated by the poet's depiction of the world of
particulars, and the 'sujet' of historical drama was not so much
history simple as history shaped in a way which made clear to the
spectator its more universally applicable moral significance.[3] Thus
plot was 'l'argument de la pièce' in the fullest sense, because the
dramatic force and persuasiveness of action and dialogue ensured
the communication of much more than a simple narrative of human
deeds. By the poet's able disposition and presentation of action and
speech, he 'painted' justice, injustice, the qualities of vengeance,
clemency, or Christian martyrdom, rendering their essential nature
immediately intelligible through spectacle and dialogue. In this
sense Corneille could argue that his portrait of Medea was both
terrible and delightful, because it offered a truth to nature which
only a skilled poet could make apparent in the original history,
revealing an otherwise hidden structure of meaning which powerfully challenged the spectator to reflection. Corneille's artifices did

not make his dramatic imitation of Medea less true, rather did they make nature more 'natural', in the sense that his 'peinture parlante' pleasurably conveyed the essential truth of the things it depicted. As such he could be justly proud of his play as an 'imitation au naturel' which was vividly and decorously delightful in so far as it revealed the lasting significance of moral uglinesses and beauties inherent in the actions it presented on stage.

Such a depiction of human conflict was inextricably bound up with moral issues and moral effects, and this was particularly the case of the drama, where dialogue gave to each voice all the force and persuasiveness of the rhetorician's art. Each participant in the action in turn moved the spectator to believe more strongly or challenged his previously held beliefs, leading him to a dénouement which called him to final judgement on the significance of all that he had witnessed. But while such effects made dramatic poetry a potent means to modify the moral sensibility of the spectator, it might also be that an inferior exercise would leave the spectator aware that the dramatist-rhetorician's skills in praise or dispraise had been harnessed not to the expression of the essential truth of events, but turned instead to serve a shallower purpose. As Tuve explains, a less honest poet might well 'push' a preconceived message, exploiting particulars as allegorical vehicles for a given propagandist point, or appeal to the emotions of spectators or readers in a manner which, on later reflection, would be seen to lack true coherence with the essential nature of the subject. Such tricks were to give rhetoric its bad name, but a more honest dramatist could quite properly use the arts of eloquence and disposition the better to address the faculties and affections of his spectator, subtly calculating how the vividness and relief of the drama's imitation of an action would move him to strong feelings, 'to will, to act, to understand, to believe, to change his mind'.[4] Corneille's discussion of 'effet' in relation to the poet's painting 'au naturel' shows that he relies heavily on an assumed understanding of how the collective mind of his audience worked when, in the course of performance and in final judgement, it recognized and evaluated the ugly and the beautiful, the bad and the good. In this process Right Reason was the common moral currency which linked dramatist and individual spectator and underpinned both the poet's authority and the audience's enjoyment of a stage depiction of men in conflict. Thus Corneille's unvarying attention to the success or failure of his work in the theatre relates to something much more important than financial profit: it is entirely characteristic of an age in which every great artist appealed to a shared patrimony of Right Reason, as he assessed the efficacy of his art in relation to the public 'mind' for which it was intended.

Such a reliance on the powers of vivid concretion could only operate securely within a framework of common assumptions about the nature of the soul and man's condition and context. For instance, the importance Corneille gives to credibility in his own discussion of 'le vraisemblable' makes important assumptions about how the human intellect and will function when the spectator relates his own convictions and experience to the poet's imitation of the world. By relying on Right Reason, Corneille trusts that every spectator is as naturally capable of discriminating between qualities of behaviour as he is capable of perceiving the difference between light and dark in the physical world. If Corneille understood verisimilitude principally as dramatic credibility, this was because it was essential to that powerful conviction of the truthfulness of events which would stimulate and illuminate the spectator's innate capacity to discern the enduring significance of human conduct. In this, like the devout humanists of his times, Corneille made no clear separation of reason from emotion in assessing the spectator's response to his stage illustration of the good and the beautiful, the bad and the ugly. The twentieth century may limit the operations of reason to intellect alone, but for Corneille and his spectators it was self-evident that passions like love and hatred had a proper part to play in the recognition and rational pursuit of virtue.[5] Thus the dramatist's capacity to produce natural and immediate movements of the will through the affections of his audience formed a necessary part of any theoretical discussion of a play's ability to enlist belief and thereby please and profit by expressing a higher moral truth. This combination of passion and reason, of will and understanding, is so fundamental to Corneille's conception of dramatic effect that it cannot be ignored in critical discussion of plays which were written in expectation of a series of moral and political convictions shared by the audience whose judgement and emotions the dramatic action was intended to challenge or seduce.

If Corneille does not question, any more than did Castelvetro himself, the generally didactic character of the humanistic theory of poetry, we may well wonder why he renewed the Italian's 'hedonist' opposition to Scaliger and his heirs and so distanced himself from the regulatory concerns of doctrinaires who argued that the poet's civic obligation was agreeably to teach directly preconceived truths.

Why, of all dramatists, should this Rouennais *officier* and poet, himself a pupil of the Jesuits and in culture the son of the Counter-Reformation, have argued so doggedly against a moralizing theoretical tradition which was very much a Counter-Reformation phenomenon? A brief survey of how the didactic theory of imitation developed during the sixteenth and early seventeenth centuries can help us here. While it is certain that the moralistic emphasis became increasingly apparent in the latter half of the sixteenth century, something of it was already apparent in earlier humanist commentary of the *Poetics*. The intrinsic didacticism of the theory was of course decided from the outset and was not at issue, since all agreed that good poetic imitation communicated higher truths. However, as the original theory of imitation came to be modified by the rhetorical cast of mind of sixteenth-century commentators particularly sensitive to the persuasive power of the word, differences emerged on what Aristotle had meant by such truths. In Robortello's *De Arte Poetica* (1548) it is clear that the argument of moral profit has come to the fore, for all that Robortello never felt the need to declare himself on one side or other of the profit and delight issue. This first and much respected commentary established a pattern which lent itself particularly well to subsequent development of a fully utilitarian reworking of Aristotle's text. Intent upon the recuperation of the art of antiquity and the study of its methods, sixteenth-century humanists were embarrassed that Plato had considered artistic imitation to be no better than third best to the truth, and was only prepared to discuss the poet in relation to his moral and political context. For Robortello and for later commentators on the recently rediscovered *Poetics*, Aristotle's assertion that the poet dealt in universal truths offered a welcome answer to Plato's general condemnation of poetic imitation as the lowest of all forms of imitation, 'the poor child of poor parents'.

In amplification of this supposed apologetic intention behind the *Poetics*, humanist commentators returned with more confidence to Plato's discussion of the moral and social context of art and took heart from his concession that the poet might have a certain political utility in the Republic. The result was that Aristotle's arguments were much transformed, for all that he had originally been so careful to differentiate the aesthetics of the *Poetics* from the ethical preoccupations of the *Politics* and the *Rhetoric*. Keen to justify their studies of the great works of antiquity, commentators on the *Poetics* gave a moral gloss to Aristotle's discussion of poetic probability which went well beyond his original meaning. Developing the twin concepts of *hamartia* and *catharsis* in a distinctively regulatory sense, they transformed the tragic hero of middling virtue into a cautionary example and *catharsis* into a socially improving experience in itself. This essentially Platonizing recourse to a 'political' justification for art undoubtedly lies behind the development of poetic theory under the influence of the Council of Trent (1545–63). The potency of a view of art which held poetry to be the vehicle for some kind of morally profitable pre-existent 'idea', once it was allied with a thoroughly rhetorical cast of mind convinced of the persuasive power of the word, is already apparent in the typically moralistic flavour of J-C. Scaliger's influential *Poetices* (1561), which downgrades the imitation of things in favour of the communication of a directly conceived idea through the allegorical significance of the *exemplum*. Not surprisingly, in these later years of the sixteenth century the prestige of Aristotle's text waned as fast as 'allegorical' readings of the theory of imitation gained in popularity and Counter-Reformation theoreticians urged the poet towards exemplary expressions of a preconceived philosophical, moral, or theological message.[6] Discussion of the *Poetics* was only to revive with any conviction, if not always with greater understanding, in French literary debates between 1630 and 1660.

Castelvetro's contribution to this French revival of interest in the *Poetics* has long been recognized with regard to the three unities and definitions of verisimilitude. Yet he also deserves attention for the way in which he offered a prestigious model for Corneille's disagreements with Scaliger's heirs amongst the French doctrinaires. When Castelvetro's *La Poetica* (1570–2) heretically referred the art of poetry to the art of history, its author, motivated by his distaste for the Counter-Reformation utilitarians of his own time, wished to deny the latters' claim that the poet not only could, but also should, directly create higher universals. In this he foreshadowed Corneille's own motives in France when he in turn disagrees with the prescriptive utilitarian theory of established literary authority and offers his own 'hérésies' on historical truth and verisimilitude in the *Discours*. Corneille's opponents might follow Castelvetro on the unities and the importance of verisimilitude, but they were profoundly mistrustful of his concern for pleasure and his belief in the soundness of the spectator's judgement. Yet it is precisely Castelvetro's respect for the larger public of the groundlings, his practical recognition of the realities of the theatrical experience, and his

consciously provocative and speculative methods of argument,
which Corneille revives as a minority of one in his own debate with
the doctrinaires in the years following the Querelle. Corneille shares
a manner with Castelvetro which, on more than one occasion, leads
to what has been called, rather unsympathetically, a replacement of
Aristotle's ideas by the theorist's own pet theories.[7] Certainly
Corneille and Castelvetro were conscious of their own originality
and claimed an interpretative freedom which permits them to
speculate beyond the limits of the *Poetics*, but in both cases Aristotle
remained their most respected authority, and one whom they
exploited in a more generous and fruitful sense than was possible
within the un-Aristotelian spirit of their opponents. This is not the
place to explore the extent of Corneille's debt to Castelvetro, but
that there exists a large number of telling similarities is beyond
question.[8] Suffice to note, with the benefit of hindsight, that a greater
flexibility of method and a shared distaste for the moralizing cast of
mind permitted both Castelvetro and Corneille to argue with
greater sensitivity to the original spirit of the *Poetics* than did
pedantic opponents who so reverentially claimed to give Aristotle's
text a weight and authority normally reserved for Holy Writ. Like
Castelvetro before him, whenever Corneille is faced with an obscurity
in the *Poetics*, he does not turn to learned gloss and the resources of
sixteenth-century grammarians and philosophers. Instead, like the
Italian, he feels free to doubt the completeness of the master-text and
tries to make sense of it in the light of his own experience.

Why Corneille should have done this becomes clear if we recall his
position under Richelieu's ministry. As we might expect of a pupil of
the Jesuits, he conformed loyally to the Counter-Reformation
aesthetic in the instance of *Polyeucte: tragédie chrétienne*. There Corneille
stated with characteristic terminological precision that he
had indeed set his poetic skill and the pleasures of the theatre to serve
the prior truths of Christian Doctrine. But political drama of a
secular nature was another matter, and, once faced by opponents
whose commission and patronage linked them closely to the machine
of state, Corneille again waved the banner of delight because – by
his provincial position and illustrious patronage – he was particularly sensitive to the way in which political concerns had become
entangled with issues of literary activity. The Querelle du *Cid*
directly involved him in a controversy over the ends of art which, for
reasons peculiar to France in the 1630s, revived an earlier Counter-
Reformation enlistment of the didactic theory of poetry to the

propagation of truths quite other than the 'truths more philosophical than history' to which Aristotle had referred. As is apparent in Chapelain and D'Aubignac's pretensions to allegorical significance in their epic poetry, their Scaligerian sympathies led them to a view of poetry profoundly analogous in spirit to the Counter-Reformation exploitation of the arts in service of previously defined concepts of orthodoxy. But where the Counter-Reformation recruitment of the poet to express prior truths served the ends of faith, in the hands of the Cardinal's servants in France it served the secular ends of a new and much debated political order and celebrated values which, in many respects, had profoundly affected the fortunes of Corneille's province and were profoundly at variance with the humanistic culture of the *officier* caste to which he belonged.[9] For the enemies of this champion of the spectator's pleasures in the theatre it was easy to insinuate that Corneille was coarsely preoccupied with maximum returns from the box-office. It is just as easy, and even further from the truth, for the modern critic to conclude that Corneille's 'hedonism' is evidence of a supposed fascination with little more than the 'émotions fortes' which can be induced by virtuoso manipulations of stagecraft. Master-dramatist he certainly was, but Corneille's 'effets' relate to higher intellectual ambitions than may be explained by a simple fascination with dramatic excitement, above all because he entertained nobler convictions about the moral comprehensiveness of political drama and the dignity of his art than could be contained within the narrow limits set by his theoretical opponents.

What has been called the intellectual sensuousness of the times lies at the heart of Corneille's appeal to Right Reason in his use of the poetry/painting comparison, just as his confidence in the audience's powers of passionate judgement, in a natural conjunction of sense and intellect, is characteristic of a devout humanist moral theology particularly associated with his Jesuit teachers. This pervasive sensibility also lies behind the extraordinary popularity of allegory and emblematics.[10] But reference to such popular, and particularly Jesuit, artistic forms reminds us how important it is to judge the spirit in which such a sensibility and its attendant poetic could be exploited. The religious poetry, Court ballet, collegiate and some public drama of the period all show how it could be harnessed to narrowly propagandist ends, as emblem and allegory were variously used to contemplative and polemic effect in both religious and secular spheres. The temptation to exterior moralizing or to trimming a subject the better to serve some preconceived and favourite truth was always latent in a theory which owed so much to the rhetorician's traditional purposes to move and to persuade. It was not, however, in that spirit that Corneille exploited his art, and his theoretical statements after the Querelle show that he was aware that the humanistic theory of poetry itself set firm limits to moralizing excess and propagandist bias.[11] If we are not to confuse Corneille with others who also worked and theorized within the broad traditions of the didactic theory of imitation, we need to bear in mind that the 'Epître' prefacing *Médée* cautions us against hasty reference to that flourishing contemporary tradition of allegory as a direct poetic model. From start to end of the 'Epître', Corneille's defence of the profitable pleasures of the 'portrait au naturel' reads true to Plutarch's own scorn for allegory and otiose moralizing explanations, 'as though the poet himself did not afford the right solutions'.[12]

College dramatic theory and Counter-Reformation dramatic practice undoubtedly influenced the subject-matter and formal development of seventeenth-century French tragedy after the late 1630s. But the late sixteenth-century Italian and Jesuit tradition so emphatically sets tragedy at the service of a prior truth that it is less obviously to be associated with Corneille's theory and practice than with the convictions of his doctrinaire opponents during and after the Querelle du *Cid*. Comparisons between Corneille's drama and the stage tradition of the Jesuits are likely to be critically fruitful only so long as Corneille's carefully phrased statements on the nature and ends of his drama are recognized as setting certain limits to the exercise.[13] As has been pointed out elsewhere, the Jesuit drama represents 'une activité purement didactique et doctrinale' and is better considered as a distinctive dramatic sub-genre.[14] The illustration of a providential view of history or an aversion to political machiavellianism was not a monopoly of the Society of Jesus, and, if Corneille's plays may be called historical tragedies, 'à valeur religieuse' or 'à valeur morale', that offers no certain indication that they were written in the same deeply utilitarian spirit which inspired the Jesuit dramatists, much less in the spirit of doctrinaire theorists with whom Corneille was in public disagreement.

Recent studies of the cultural background of the theatre in the age of Louis XIII do, however, make it easier to see the continuity which exists between, on the one hand, a Counter-Reformation enlistment of the didactic theory of poetry in the interests of civil morality and propagation of the faith and, on the other, the socially regulatory and propagandist concerns of the seventeenth-century doctrinaires in the Académie.[15] It is notable how the revival of interest in historical subject-matter and the use of Jesuit sources claimed so many adherents in the late 1630s amongst the Cardinal's côterie of writers. There is, furthermore, an interesting parallel to be drawn between the Jesuits' hesitant acceptance of the commercial theatre (provided it fell within the orthodoxies of the moral teaching of the church) and the carefully prescriptive deliberations of the Cardinal's Académie as it exercised its brief to regulate stage production and public eloquence within the secular perspectives of the Cardinal's 'politique de raison'. Almost certainly the Jesuit model of historical drama was not to the romanesque tastes of the Cardinal himself, but the political drama of his protégés shows that, even if his actual policies were at variance with those of the Society of Jesus, Richelieu shared the Jesuits' conviction that the stage could be made a force for public edification more potent than the pulpit.

In the case of Corneille's dramatic practice we shall see that matters are very different. However important the Jesuit example may have been to the greater formal regularity of the plays Corneille wrote after Le Cid, it was his doctrinaire opponents, with their programmatic and regulatory aesthetic, who were the true heirs of the Counter-Reformation stage tradition. Perhaps there still exists somewhere a copy of an earlier Jesuit version of Horace, but the importance of finding it diminishes considerably once we remember that Corneille reworked the subject at a time when he was emphatically at odds with a utilitarian view of the drama which owed so much to Jesuit theory and practice. It is also worth noting that even in Polyeucte, where his theoretical position is of perfect religious orthodoxy, Corneille still departs from the practice of his erstwhile masters by presenting a hero whose scandalous conduct fails to conform with the more passive models of sanctity favoured by Jesuit tradition.

The Jesuit Caussin's encyclopaedic works certainly offer a possible source for a number of the historical figures which appear in Corneille's plays. However, the way in which Corneille treated those common subjects cannot easily be identified with Caussin's appeal to rhetoric and allegory in the service of utilitarian ends. To assert that the spirit of Caussin's writings is essentially 'conforme à l'optique Cornélienne' in its preoccupation with the 'formation d'une morale pratique' begs too many questions about Corneille's own statements of position.[16] It is more to the point to note how Caussin's peculiar concern for public edification finds a sympathetic echo in the works of Chapelain and La Mesnardière – men with whom Corneille was in public disagreement. The important problem is to define the spirit in which Corneille exploited his own poetic training and rhetorical skills in his dramatic imitations of an action. Very early in his career Corneille had grasped the difference between the orator-philosopher's concern to carry his point and the dramatist's use of rhetoric in the more problematic presentation of contrasted characters and motives. On a number of occasions he indicates an awareness of the distance which lies between the playwright's creation of *dramatis personae* and those repertories of character models commended by Caussin in the orator's depiction of the passions. As early as *La Veuve* ('Au Lecteur', GC, I, 202) and *La Galerie du Palais* (I, vii, 165–76; GC, I, 313) he had mocked the intrusiveness of literary effects into the drama, and in the first *Discours* the distinction between displays of eloquence and dramatic dialogue remains as fundamental as it had been for Aristotle: '[L'orateur] peut étaler son art, et le rendre remarquable avec pleine liberté... [le poète] doit le cacher avec soin, parce que ce n'est jamais lui qui parle, et ceux qu'il fait parler ne sont pas des orateurs... Ceux que le poëte fait parler ne sont pas des poëtes' (LF, 62–3; GC, III, 134). Unlike the orator, the poet must efface himself if he is to achieve the more freely reflective effect of a dramatic presentation of contrasted character and conflicting action. Furthermore, as Corneille observed in his 'Préface' to *La Place Royale*, 'un Poète n'est jamais garant des fantaisies qu'il donne à ses Acteurs' (GC, I, 740). If criticism of Corneille's plays is not to commit the same naiveté as Castelvetro mocked in Scaliger, when the latter mistook the subject of his beloved Virgil and interpreted Aeneas as an allegorical *exemplum* of *pietas*, some caution is needed before we draw analogies between the rhetor's arts and intentions and the dramatist's task in creating his play.[17] The 'Epître' prefacing *Médée* already expressed an aesthetic standpoint specific to dramatic imitation which cannot directly be identified with the arts of the orator as Cicero, Quintilian, or even Father Caussin define them. Before publishing the *Discours*, Corneille himself wrote that matters of rhetoric – together with problems of moral and political doctrine – were no more than a minor 'broderie' to be treated in a fourth *Discours* which he never got round to writing (GC, III, 7). Furthermore, in the third *Discours*, he makes it clear that he is writing of an art only wholly realizable in the theatre, advising the inclusion of stage directions in the published text for the benefit of the reader in his study, so that 'la tragédie soit aussi belle à la lecture qu'à la représentation, en rendant facile à l'imagination du lecteur tout ce que le théâtre présente à la vue des spectateurs' (LF, 137; GC, III, 183). This perception that the theatre is not to be confused with the study stands as a clear warning to the twentieth-century critic not to attach too much importance to the learned seventeenth-century rhetoric of 'allégorisme' as he tries to hunt down meanings which would only have been accessible to the *eruditi spectatores*.

HISTORICAL AND DRAMATIC TRUTH: POETIC TRUTHS AND POETIC NECESSITIES

Despite the fact that the *Discours* were published in 1660, over fifteen years after the death of Louis XIII and long after the tribulations of *Le Cid*, they represent an indispensable completion and systematization of Corneille's occasional and fragmentary earlier theoretical statements. They also remain so true to the spirit of Corneille's earlier theoretical statements that they are likely to be a surer guide to our reading of his plays than later commentary by other parties. Drawing on some thirty years of stage experience, this privileged reader's account of the fundamentals of his practice stands in such perfect continuity with previous statements of principle that it can hardly be passed over, and is particularly important to the critic when it deals with issues which had not previously been raised or fully explored.[18] Of these issues I shall only be concerned with what Corneille considers necessary to the dramatic imitation of an historical subject, with tragic characterization, and with the subject, structure, and effect of tragedy – all matters bearing heavily on a critical appreciation of the political drama he wrote in the period.

We have seen how Corneille's long argument with 'Messieurs de l'Académie' had always revolved around definitions of poetry's ends and of its relation to the truth. In his letter to De Pure Corneille makes it clear that, in discussing 'de quelle utilité elle [la poésie dramatique] est capable', his conclusions in the *Discours* derive from a practical understanding of the theatre and that he has no wish to discuss the profit that 'should be' present in poetry. When this

defender of a poetics of delight opens his three-part discussion with
a *Discours* entitled 'de l'Utilité...du Poëme Dramatique', he makes
it clear that his project is both a personal statement of principles and
a limiting and defining exercise in response to the prescriptive theory
of the doctrinaires. The resounding opening quotation of Aristotle,
to the effect that the end of poetry is pleasure of a specific kind, at
once associates that pleasure with the proper interpretation of the
rules relating to verisimilitude and the necessities of the dramatist's
art. By immediately raising these two closely interdependent issues,
Corneille leaves no doubts about the distance between his own
position and that of those who associated verisimilitude with
conventional concepts of moral orthodoxy. Asserting the falsity of
the belief that 'il faut que le sujet d'une tragédie soit vraisemblable',
he marks out the central ground upon which, as a practising poet of
historical tragedy, he intends to argue his differences (LF, 36; GC,
III, 117). This is also to defend *Le Cid* once again in terms already
used in the 'Au Lecteur' of *Héraclius* (1647), where he had defended
as acceptable the extraordinary and morally shocking historical
instance of a mother's deliberate sacrifice of her child: 'L'action
étant vraie...il ne faut plus s'informer si elle est vraisemblable, étant
certain que toutes les vérités...sont recevables dans la poésie,
quoiqu'elle ne soit pas obligée à les suivre. La liberté qu'elle a de
s'en écarter n'est pas une nécessité, et la vraisemblance n'est qu'une
condition nécessaire à la disposition, et non pas au choix du
sujet' (GC, II, 357). This holds true to the 'Epître' prefacing
Médée in so far as it presents poetry in service of the truth, whether
it be disturbing or not, and makes the important point that, while
historical subject-matter itself does not fall under considerations of
verisimilitude, the poetic fictions with which the poet elaborates the
basic material are indeed governed by such considerations. Where
his opponents' concern for 'probability' refers us directly back to
received standards of behaviour, Corneille is principally interested in
questions of morality in so far as they affect the credibility of his
poetic imitation. The result is that 'probability' becomes a matter of
practical aesthetics, bearing on the spectator's readiness to believe in
the dramatic action: 'Tout ce qui entre dans le poëme doit être
croyable, et il l'est, selon Aristote par l'un de ces trois moyens, la
vérité, la vraisemblance ou l'opinion commune' (GC, II, 357).
Underlining Corneille's distaste for any moralistic limitations to
poetic imitation, the 'Au Lecteur' claims Aristotle's authority in
stating that 'le sujet d'une belle tragédie doit n'être pas

vraisemblable', since the *Poetics* had observed that tragedy is particularly concerned with unnatural crimes between people of close parentage.

Faithful to *Médée* and *Le Cid*, the first *Discours* goes yet further, stating that 'unnatural' actions, 'qui remuent fortement les passions, et en opposent l'impétuosité aux lois du devoir ou aux tendresses du sang', are even to be enthusiastically welcomed by the poet as subjects upon which he may most brilliantly exercise his art and deeply move his audience. Such subjects need no other sanction than their historical or legendary authenticity, for without that they might indeed be unbelievable: '[Ils] ne trouveraient aucune croyance parmi les auditeurs s'ils n'étaient soutenus, ou par l'autorité de l'histoire qui persuade avec empire, ou par la préoccupation de l'opinion commune qui nous donne ces mêmes auditeurs déjà tout persuadés' (LF, 36; GC, III, 118). The second *Discours* again contends that these extraordinary historical truths offer subjects capable of the most brilliant and morally challenging development and are not subject to judgements of verisimilitude and consequential modification. Their credibility is assured simply by virtue of the fact that they happened, and Corneille quotes Aristotle as his ostensible authority here. But the audience will only readily accept a dramatization of such events if they are also shown the reasons which lie behind them. Thus a concern for verisimilitude only enters Corneille's scheme of things at the point where it governs the ways in which the poet fleshes out the bare bones of history with his own explanatory inventions. Corneille calls these elucidating fictions the 'circonstances' or 'moyens de parvenir à l'action' – 'action' being understood as the significant imitation in dramatic form of historically recorded human deeds (LF, 101; GC, III, 159). It is in the use of these fictions that the poet most brilliantly shows his skill in weaving a seamless combination of truth and verisimilitude which never exceeds our capacity to believe:

Lorsqu'elles [les histoires] sont vraies, il ne faut point se mettre en peine de la vraisemblance, elles n'ont pas besoin de son secours... Ce que nous ajoutons à l'histoire, comme il n'est pas appuyé de son autorité, n'a pas cette prérogative... C'est pourquoi ce que nous inventons a besoin de la vraisemblance la plus exacte qu'il est possible pour le rendre croyable. (LF, 112; GC, III, 166)

In limiting considerations of verisimilitude to the poet's explanatory fictions Corneille holds to the properly aesthetic principle that the stage action be recognized as fundamentally true to human

experience. This goes to the heart of Corneille's differences with
Scaligerians for whom 'toutes les vérités ne sont pas bonnes pour le
théâtre', and who condemned Chimène's behaviour in the name of
public morality.[19] By welcoming the extraordinary and even
disturbing historical subject, Corneille prepares the ground for
stating his own convictions about the moral profundity of 'le beau
sujet'. As a poet of political 'tragédie d'histoire' capable of setting
out the full moral implications of human behaviour, he obviously
needs to be unhampered by moralizing preconditions if he is to
explore and express all aspects of that truth. This was bound to lead
him away from La Mesnardière's golden world. Credibility has
become the very precondition of that kind of passionate involvement
which alone can permit the spectator to experience moral effects and
moral insights more compelling than those offered by a careful
interpretation of the play as allegorical *exemplum*.

When the first *Discours* returns to its opening assertion that delight
is the end of art, it makes it clear that an insistence on pleasure
implies no trivialization of the effect of poetic drama. In Corneille's
view the debate over profit and delight is an arid one because it
opposes the two elements:

Cette dispute même serait très inutile, puisqu'il est impossible de plaire selon
les règles, qu'il ne s'y rencontre beaucoup d'utilité... Ainsi, quoi que l'utile
n'y entre que sous la forme du délectable, il ne laisse pas d'y être nécessaire,
et il vaut mieux examiner de quelle façon il y peut trouver sa place, que
d'agiter... une question inutile touchant l'utilité de cette sorte de poëmes.
(LF, 38–9; GC, III, 119)

Corneille is using his words with extreme care here, for he is dealing
with a particularly sensitive area of debate and presenting a view
wholly alien to those who preferred the looser relationship of
'admitting' pleasure as sugar on the bitter pill of profit. In practice
the perception of the play's moral significance is consubstantial with
the pleasure of watching it, and delight is the form without which
profit could not exist. What he means by 'nécessaire' will become
fully apparent later, but his use of the term 'forme' would have been
immediately recognizable to the seventeenth-century reader as a
properly Aristotelian and scholastic reference to the distinguishing
and particular mode in which a thing exists and without which it is
not manifest: *forma dat esse rei*. Corneille's wry dismissal of any
separation of the two elements permits a re-formulation of the
problem which has the supreme virtue, for him at least, of precluding
any discussion about what kind of message 'should be' propagated

and ensures that any further discussion of the moral effect of poetic imitation both takes into account what actually happens in performance and also respects the poet's freedom to imitate 'toutes les vérités'.

On this basis Corneille lists four different ways in which the moral significance of dramatic poetry may constitute a source of pleasure – (i) 'les sentences', (ii) 'la naïve peinture des vices et des vertus', (iii) the dénouement as a cautionary lesson, and (iv) the theory of tragic purgation. The first and third of these will be mainly of interest for the way they show Corneille's pragmatic independence of the utilitarian tradition, but the second and fourth need fuller examination, since Corneille discusses them in relation to 'nécessités' which relate directly to what he believes the poet must do if he is to achieve specifically tragic effects. On the first 'utilité' – the proper and strictly limited use of 'sentences' – Corneille's practical advice permits no distortion of dramatic imitation towards the kind of moralizing intervention which is better suited to the pulpit (LF, 40–2; GC, III, 121). His preference that the poet should remain hidden behind the dramatic action is of course shared, in theory at least, by his contemporaries. But his care to integrate moral generalizations into the contingencies of action and individual characterization is of rather greater importance, since it reflects his distaste for any mode of imitation which aims directly to express preconceived truths, rather than make an intrinsic truth pleasurably apparent through dramatic contrasts and conflicts of behaviour. In Corneille's view the drama has a very limited place indeed for overt philosophizing and should never lose that unbroken credibility which is a prime characteristic of good dramatic poetry.

Implicit in Corneille's short discussion of the 'sentence' is his unshakable confidence that the public is competent to understand his play without the assistance of authorial pointers to a 'correct' interpretation.[20] The same conviction lies behind 'la naïve peinture des vices et des vertus, qui ne manque jamais à faire son effet, quand elle est bien achevée, et que les traits en sont si reconnaissables qu'on ne les peut confondre l'un dans l'autre, ni prendre le vice pour la vertu. Celle-si se fait alors toujours aimer, quoique malheureuse; et celui-là se fait toujours haïr bien que triomphant' (LF, 42; GC, III, 121). This outlines what Corneille believes to be by far the most important source of dramatic significance.[21] In so far as 'naïveté' involves clarification rather than simplification and entails that special relief which can only result from poetic ordering and vivid expression, its implications will only be fully developed in his later discussion of 'les mœurs bonnes' and the poetic *nécessités* which apply to the dramatic imitation of history. At this point, however, Corneille simply refers to it in order to dismiss the view that criminal behaviour should invariably be punished, and discussion moves on to the third kind of 'utilité' listed – the 'dénouement en leçon morale'.

The reminder that *Médée* was a success, despite the fact that it concluded with the triumph of wickedness, makes it clear that Corneille's position has not changed since 1634 and that he still has little enthusiasm for providential moralizing. While he does observe that the success of *Médée* was a rarity and that few dramatists may care to risk such a challenge to the audience's moral prejudices, this does not weaken his confidence in his seventeenth-century audience's capacity to judge. As a result he does not believe that the reassuring triumph of approved moral principles should be a binding obligation on the poet:

[Ce] n'est pas un précepte de l'art, mais un usage que nous avons embrassé, dont chacun peut se départir à ses périls... En effet, il est certain que nous ne saurions voir un honnête homme sur notre théâtre sans lui souhaiter de la prosperité, et nous fâcher de ses infortunes. Cela fait que quand il en demeure accablé, nous sortons avec chagrin, et remportons une espèce d'indignation contre l'auteur et les acteurs; mais quand l'évenement remplit nous souhaits, et que la vertu y est couronnée, nous sortons avec pleine joie, et remportons une entière satisfaction et de l'ouvrage, et de ceux qui l'ont représenté. Le succès heureux de la vertu, en dépit des traverses et des périls, nous excite à l'embrasser; et le succès funeste du crime ou de l'injustice est capable de nous en augmenter l'horreur naturelle, par l'appréhension d'un pareil malheur. (LF, 43–4; GC, III, 122)

This nicely shows how Corneille manoeuvres to give the poet maximum freedom in pleasurably moving the affections of his audience by moral insights which are not to be identified with moral reassurance. Whether he is right or wrong in claiming Aristotle's authority here, he presents profit as consubstantial with delight in so far as the poet may flatter the spectator's moral preferences by satisfying his hopes of a triumph of right and justice. His refusal to go any further by raising the moral 'distribution des prix' to the dignity of a 'précepte' shows that, while he acknowledges the pressures of public taste, he still wants to reserve for himself a perilous freedom to paint the unpleasant spectacle of vice and injustice triumphant. Given his belief that the pleasures of serious drama stem from the perception of moral truths, he leaves the poet free to make his individual artistic choice. Everything will depend on the skill with which he presents his subject to the spectators since, in principle at least, a morally challenging ending may quite properly be preferred and still please the more sophisticated and discriminating modern audience. The most scandalous instances, like that of the Medea legend, certainly represent a risk which Corneille himself will not often take in his plays, but *Le Cid* and *Horace*, as well as a number of his later works, succeed in exploiting moral disquiet to profound effect. By preserving at least the principle of the dramatist's freedom of imitation and invention Corneille once again refuses to confine the choice and disposition of his subject-matter to the horizons of La Mesnardière's golden world, and thereby remains closer to the sense in which Aristotle first discussed the poet's use of the 'probable' in his imitation of events.

To grasp the full implications of 'la naïve peinture des vices et des vertus' we have to move forward to the second *Discours*, where Corneille discusses verisimilitude in relation to what he considers to be 'necessary' aspects of the poetic imitation of history. Having extended the area and character of permissible poetic imitation well beyond the confines of a verisimilitude governed by ideals of socially acceptable behaviour, Corneille lists the artistic 'nécessités' which will have to be observed. This leads him into a series of careful definitions in which he lists no less than four kinds of verisimilitude – (i) 'le general', (ii) 'l'ordinaire', (iii) 'le particulier', and (iv) 'l'extraordinaire'. Happily matters are not quite so bad as they seem, since the first two relate to any invented action in conformity with general notions about what is commonly likely to happen or, in the case of characterization, how men of a certain kind commonly behave (or would probably behave) in given circumstances (LF, 100; GC, III, 158). As for the third kind – 'le particulier' – this concerns the way in which action or character need to be matched to specific knowledge of definite historical events or of particular individuals such as Alexander the Great (LF, 112–15; GC, III, 166–8). Not surprisingly, the last kind of verisimilitude – 'le vraisemblable extraordinaire' – is of most interest to our understanding of Corneille's ambitions as a dramatist since, by referring to a willingness to believe in extraordinary events because they have occasional and extraordinary historical precedents, he is able to include the brilliant and rare possibility amongst the poet's legitimate inventions:

L'extraordinaire est une action qui arrive, à la vérité, moins souvent que sa contraire [*namely that kind of action 'qui arrive plus souvent ou du moins aussi souvent que sa contraire'*] mais qui ne laisse pas d'avoir la possibilité assez aisée pour n'aller point jusqu'au miracle, ni jusqu'à ces événements singuliers qui servent de matière aux tragédies sanglantes par l'appui qu'ils ont de l'histoire ou de l'opinion commune…Ainsi la victoire du Cid contre le Comte se trouverait dans la vraisemblance extraordinaire, quand elle ne serait pas vraie. (LF, 116; GC, III, 168–9)

Since precedents like the victory of David over Goliath happen against all probability, Corneille prefers to call this 'vraisemblance extraordinaire' credible or possible, rather than probable, and restricts their invention to occasions when they are 'necessary' to the poet's satisfactory imitation of his subject. This invocation of a specifically aesthetic necessity is particularly interesting, since nowhere do we come closer to Corneille's intentions than when he describes what must be done if he is successfully to dramatize history. By admitting the extraordinary invention as a poetic necessity on purely aesthetic grounds, Corneille gives yet another indication of how remote his purpose is from moralizing prescription and how attracted he is to the more reflective pressures offered by a drama which challenges audience expectations.

Corneille invokes Aristotle in the most practical dramatic sense when he considers it necessary that events be prepared and be seen to be the consequence of previous causes, either of circumstance or character: 'le nécessaire en ce qui regarde la poésie n'est autre chose que le besoin du poëte pour arriver à son but ou pour y faire arriver ses acteurs'. Revealingly he stretches this a little further, stating that the Greeks included in the term not only that which is 'absolument nécessaire, mais aussi quelquefois ce qui est seulement utile à parvenir à quelque chose'. In the first place this poetic necessity bears on characterization and defines, for instance, what a lover should do if he wants to win his lady: 'Le but des acteurs est divers, selon les divers desseins que la variété des sujets leur donne…Les choses qu'ils ont besoin de faire pour y arriver constituent ce nécessaire, qu'il faut préférer au vraisemblable ou, pour parler plus juste, qu'il faut ajouter au vraisemblable dans la liaison des actions, et leur dépendance l'une de l'autre' (LF, 118–19; GC, III, 170–1). Corneille's example here is Cinna, whose plot is 'necessary' to the subject of the play, but whose remorse and hesitations before Auguste's generosity are no more than 'vraisemblables' because he might not necessarily have reacted in that way – he might have been obdurate and hard-hearted. 'Le nécessaire' thus relates to credibility of behaviour in those aspects of the play which have to do with the poet's imitation of history itself. More interesting still are the passages in the second *Discours* where Corneille extends the concept of 'le nécessaire' to the broader issue of what the poet himself has to do in order to achieve a telling imitation of his subject. Once again the argument makes no reference at all to what Chapelain had called the poet's obligation to 'donner beaucoup à la morale'. Instead it turns on the central aesthetic issue of presenting a subject clearly and forcefully. The two most obvious 'nécessités' binding the poet in this respect are the unities of time and place – twin means to economy and force which override even previous necessities of verisimilitude of character or plot, should there be any conflict. For instance Corneille notes that, since his tragic subject-matter is so extensive, it is sometimes necessary discretely to compress events in order to present the action within the twenty-four-hours rule, 'et un auteur scrupuleux se priverait d'une belle occasion de gloire, et le public de beaucoup de satisfaction, s'il n'osait s'enhardir à les mettre sur le théâtre, de peur de se voir forcé à les faire aller plus vite que la vraisemblance ne le permet' (LF, 120; GC, III, 171). Once again the very Castelvetran ring of the passage tells us much of Corneille's view of the poet's powers, intent as he is on creating the most compelling and entertaining drama of which he is capable.

Elsewhere Corneille twice discusses these qualities of force and lucidity as necessary prerequisites to success, first on the matter of the clear exposition of his material and secondly on the importance of clarifying the lines of moral conflict which underpin the interest of his drama. Dealing with the problems and constraints of setting out his material in the second *Discours*, Corneille chooses *Horace* as an illustration of the unavoidable strains which may arise between the principle of verisimilitude and the poet's choice of the dramatic form of poetic imitation. In order to achieve a clear exposition in Act II of various individual reactions to Horace's nomination to fight for Rome, Corneille observes that it was necessary to introduce a series of entries, even if this risked offending verisimilitude, thus ensuring that the spectator could compare and evaluate each character's different reaction to events (LF, 110–11; GC, III, 164–5). The same concern to balance poetic necessity with verisimilitude is apparent when Corneille discusses the poet's need to realize a certain brilliance and force of imitation under the novel heading of 'les nécessités d'embellissement' – understood in Corneille's second sense of 'useful to the achievement of the poet's ends', even if not 'absolutely' necessary:

Le but du poëte est de plaire selon les règles de son art. Pour plaire, il a besoin quelque fois de rehausser l'éclat des belles actions et d'exténuer l'horreur des funestes. Ce sont des nécessités d'embellissement où il peut bien choquer la vraisemblance particulière [*probability judged in relation to known historical particulars*] par quelque altération de l'histoire, mais non pas se dispenser de la générale, que rarement, et pour des choses qui soient de la dernière beauté, et si brillantes, qu'elles éblouissent. Surtout il ne doit jamais les pousser au delà de la vraisemblance extraordinaire [*that credibility which derives from rare historical precedents*], parce que ces ornements ne sont pas d'une nécessité absolue [*here it would seem that they are 'utile à parvenir à quelque chose' by enhancing the delight and comprehension of the spectator*], et qu'il fait mieux de s'en passer tout à fait que d'en parer son poëme contre toute sorte de vraisemblance. (LF, 119; GC, III, 171)

This develops Corneille's earlier recognition that an audience experiences certain moral preferences in relation to the fortunes of the *dramatis personae* in the course of the play. But such alterations to history also clarify to advantage the major lines of dramatic conflict which link or prepare a series of brilliant and unforeseen dramatic effects. As was already to be inferred from the well-realized effect of 'la naïve peinture des vices et des vertus', this kind of clarification, once related to Corneille's discussion of 'les mœurs', will play an important role in the poet's creation of pleasurable and telling drama.

HEROIC CHARACTERIZATION AND 'LA NAÏVE PEINTURE'

Corneille's very personal understanding of characterization, and of what Aristotle had meant when he said that the tragic poet portrayed men as 'better', is much coloured by his conviction that the poet needs to ensure maximum clarity and breadth of moral significance in his imitation of an action. The first *Discours* rejects out of hand the doctrinaires' reading of the passage in the *Poetics*: 'Je ne puis comprendre comment on a voulu entendre par ce mot de bonnes, qu'il faut qu'elles [les mœurs] soient vertueuses'. Instead he ventures the more properly aesthetic reading that character imitation should possess a certain heightened nobility of presentation: 'Je crois que c'est le caractère brillant et élevé d'une habitude vertueuse ou criminelle, selon qu'elle est propre et convenable à la personne qu'on introduit' (LF, 54–5; GC, III, 129). For all that this is a strikingly independent position for the times, Corneille is certainly closer to the spirit of Aristotle than were his opponents. The *Poetics* had originally commended 'better' tragic characterization in a comparison of poetic imitation with individual portraiture: '"Comme les peintres font souvent des portraits flattés, qui sont plus beaux que l'original et conservent toutefois la ressemblance, ainsi les poëtes, représentant des hommes colères ou fainéants, doivent tirer une haute idée de ces qualités qu'ils leur attribuent, en sorte qu'il s'y trouve un bel exemplaire d'équité ou de dureté; et c'est ainsi qu'Homère a fait Achille bon."' This is Corneille's own version of the *Poetics* and it is clear that, despite the reference to the 'goodness' of Homer's Achilles, he does not intend to take 'qualités' in an exclusively laudatory sense. In fact he goes on to point out that Aristotle cannot have meant 'more virtuous', since Achilles is hardly a paragon of virtue in the *Iliad*: 'Ce dernier mot est à remarquer, pour faire voir qu'Homère a donné aux emportements de la colère d'Achille cette bonté nécessaire aux mœurs, que je fais consister en cette élévation de leur caractère' (LF, 55–6; GC, III, 130). Unenthusiastically he concedes that the vexed passage might mean that: [les mœurs] doivent être vertueuses tant qu'il peut, en sorte que nous n'exposions point de vicieux ou de criminels sur le théâtre, si le sujet n'en a besoin'. But he sets aside this reading, together with Castelvetro's proposal that attractive virtuousness be limited only to the 'premier personnage'. After a review of possible interpretations Corneille's position remains unaltered: the passage simply commends a kind of elevation which comes from force and lucidity of character portrayal, good or bad, so long as it is appropriate to the type of man or historical figure in question:

Le poëte doit considérer l'âge, la dignité, la naissance, l'emploi et le pays de ceux qu'il introduit: il faut qu'il sache ce qu'on doit à sa patrie, à ses parents, à ses amis, à son roi; quel est l'office d'un magistrat, ou d'un général d'armée, afin qu'il y puisse conformer ceux qu'il veut faire aimer aux spectateurs, et en éloigner ceux qu'il leur veut faire haïr; car c'est une maxime infaillible que, pour bien réussir, il faut intéresser l'auditoire pour les premiers acteurs. (LF, 58–9; GC, III, 131–2)

What is revealing here is the way Corneille has again preserved the option of improper behaviour as a means to estrange audience sympathies if it suits his poetic purpose. This makes it clear that the

principle of 'convenance' is not simply envisaged as one of the means
available to the poet to offer an 'improved' view of the world. Not
surprisingly Corneille has no interest in a line of argument which
quickly leads into binding prescriptions of 'bienséance'. Instead he
treats various kinds of moral characterization as the means whereby
spectator involvement may be enhanced through a sharpened
awareness of differing standards of behaviour. The poet is free to
illustrate proper or improper behaviour and thereby engage
audience sympathy or distaste before the spectacle of worthy or
unworthy conduct. The manoeuvre is typical of Corneille's constant
determination to escape the constrictions of a moralizing view of
imitation and at the same time enhance the profounder possibilities
of moral insight available to him in the drama.

Corneille's two remaining categories of characterization – 'semblables' and 'égales' – are straightforward and equally uncon-
strained by moralizing preoccupations. He relates similitude directly
to 'le vraisemblable particulier', in the sense that historical
knowledge must be respected in both good and evil characters. For
instance, Medea can only be shown as the cruel woman she was in
legend, and the poet has no obligation to trouble himself with
protecting the moral sensitivities of the spectator. As for 'l'égalité',
this simply obliges the poet 'à conserver jusqu'à la fin à nos
personnages les mœurs que nous leur avons données au commencement' (LF, 60; GC, III, 132). By this common-sense
recommendation even inconsistent characters should remain consistently inconsistent, as Aristotle had originally suggested.

A coherent poetics now begins to emerge, once these principles of
characterization are set against Corneille's view of the necessities
which govern his elaboration on historical fact. Its most salient
feature is a preoccupation with producing all the pleasures of an
urgent and vivid perception of conflicts of moral values in a poetic
universe which, even in the case of extraordinary and shocking
human behaviour, is both comprehensible and credible because it is
seen to be fundamentally coherent with the spectator's own
experience. In this lie the reasons why the second *Discours* suggests
that occasionally it may also be necessary to alter certain criminal
episodes in the historical material. These 'nécessités d'embellissement' certainly take something back from Corneille's original
combative use of Aristotle's commendation of certain histories of
domestic violence when he had argued that the best tragic subject-

matter exceeded the 'vraisemblable'. But he remains quite consistent
with the general tenor of his argument, if not with its detail, since he
directly links these alterations to the equally important factors of
credibility and moral clarity. A subject such as Orestes avenging his
father's death by the murder of his mother offers historical facts so
atrocious that they run the risk, despite all the dramatist's skills, of
alienating the spectator and so producing that worst of all practical
failures, 'une répugnance à les croire'. Furthermore such a sequence
of crime upon crime has the major disadvantage of blurring the
deeper moral significance of the play. The last thing Corneille wants
is to confuse the moral sympathies of the spectator by alienating him
from a 'premier acteur' around whom, in the interests of the larger
moral truth, the dramatist has sought to crystallize audience
goodwill: 'Je passe plus outre, et pour exténuer ou retrancher cette
horreur dangereuse d'une action historique, je voudrais la faire
arriver sans la participation du premier acteur, pour qui nous
devons toujours ménager la faveur de l'auditoire' (LF, 103; GC, III,
160). Such alterations relate less to a desire to edify the spectator –
or to pander to an actor's vanity – than to a search for that moral
comprehensibility which derives from consistency of characterization. Corneille is well aware that his own drama centres on
brilliant oppositions of moral values and that it would be
aesthetically disastrous if he permitted one figure in his play, who for
four acts had resolutely opposed certain values, suddenly to go back
on all his previous behaviour. So inexplicable a betrayal of principle
would forfeit all the sympathy earned by earlier conduct and reduce
the action to 'meaninglessness'. Given that Corneille aspires to
involve the spectator's interest through an enhanced appreciation of
the issues at stake in the dramatic conflict, it does indeed become
necessary to avoid inconsistencies of sentiment or conduct which
would so estrange or confuse the audience.

Corneille's position sharply reminds us that poetic drama is not
slavishly to be identified with the historical particulars from which
it starts, and that only through the poet's ability to shape and select
can he clarify the larger significance of these events. If certain of
Corneille's plays show the providential limits which govern human
action, this does not mean that he did, after all, intend his work to
serve as the moralizing vehicle for a preconceived message. It is
axiomatic to Corneille's view of his art, as also to the theory in which
it belongs, that poetic imitation makes evident a higher truth about

the order of things in ways quite specific to itself. Thus the manner in which a play imitates history may quite properly be seen to express certain convictions about the 'true' nature of human endeavour and its destinies. Were Corneille thinking of the drama in essentially propagandist terms like those with whom he disagreed, he would have raised the 'dénouement en leçon morale' to the dignity of prescriptive necessity and not left the poet free to choose his effect on his audience. It is not surprising then that, with regard to these 'necessary' alterations to history, he observes that the freedom 'd'embellir les actions historiques par des inventions vraisemblables n'emporte aucune défense de nous écarter du vraisemblable dans le besoin. C'est un privilège... et non pas une servitude' (LF, 105; GC, III, 161–2). The difference between a poet who holds that truth should be made apparent within the dramatic imitation of particulars and a doctrinaire who holds the poet obliged agreeably to convey directly conceived higher truths through chosen *exempla* may seem very fine. It might not even seem all that important were it not for the fact that it vitally affects our appreciation of the subtlety of the modes by which a greater truth may be made apparent. Because thought and action were presented in a particular way and within a particular moral climate and political context, Corneille believed that his plays might be left to speak for themselves through their 'naïve peinture des vices et des vertus'. The spectator, caught up in events, would be alert to the challenge which the stage spectacle offered him and, in the light of reason and experience, would draw his own conclusions on human strength and frailty. The moral element in such a 'naïveté' of effect is neither incidental nor moralizing but, as Corneille had said from the start of his *Discours*, consubstantial with a full and immediate enjoyment of the play's meaning.[22]

In Corneille's scheme of things, the forceful illustration of certain gifts of heroic personality is specific to the effect of tragedy, as the spectator recognizes and judges the true quality of the *dramatis personae*. For those of Corneille's seventeenth-century admirers who deplored the vogue for more 'soupirant' heroes in the latter part of the century, this 'naïveté' – once combined with a specifically tragic elevation of presentation – produced a sense of 'admiration' which should be understood as something closer to awed comprehension than simple moral approval or unreflective wonder.[23] What would appear to be involved in such an audience response is a double evaluation of heroic character in which the spectator appreciates both individual force of personality and also subjects the conduct displaying such heroic grandeur to a social and moral critique. This twin assessment – first of heroic personality and secondly of action within the social and political order – is that which Corneille himself urges upon us in his celebrated example of 'les mœurs bonnes' as 'élévation de caractère' in the first *Discours*. Here he invites us to consider the significance of what he calls 'le caractère brillant et élevé d'une habitude vertueuse ou criminelle':

Cléopâtre, dans *Rodogune*, est très méchante; il n'y a point de parricide qui lui fasse horreur, pourvu qu'il la puisse conserver sur un trône qu'elle préfère à toutes choses, tant son attachment à la domination est violent; mais tous ses crimes sont accompagnés d'une grandeur d'âme, qui a quelque chose de si haut, qu'en même temps qu'on déteste ses actions, on admire la source dont elles partent. (LF, 55; GC, III, 129)

The opposition of the two appreciations, one which condemns her in the light of the social repercussions of her behaviour, the other which commends her for the beauty, courage, and energy of her personality, carefully defines two simultaneous but different responses in the spectator, both of which are essential to his enjoyment of the larger meaning of the play.[24] Thus Corneille's second 'utilité' specific to the drama – the clear depiction of vice and virtue – exploits concepts of moral propriety only in so far as they underpin his calculations of the effect which the dramatic action will have on his spectator's judgement. The playwright is content to rely on the immediate impact on the spectator of 'la naïve peinture des vices et les vertus', as they may be seen to be conjoined in his hero's personality and in so far as that hero affects the world in which he moves. 'Naïveté' allied with 'élévation' in the drama provokes not only awed respect for the possessor of rare and formidable gifts but also judgement on the way those gifts are used within the community of men.[25] Within the confines of the 'beau sujet', Corneille's heroic characterizations have a claim to excellence not simply by virtue of their brilliance or power to astonish but because they immediately move the spectator to judgement in heightened understanding of the significance of good or evil conduct.[26]

Corneille's own views on this elevated contrast of forces and character in action are perhaps most clearly expressed in the 'Au Lecteur' and 'Examen' of *Nicomède*. Here Corneille sets out the consequences of a poetic founded on the assumption that every spectator shares in an instinctive and immediate perception of the good and the bad, the beautiful and the ugly. On this basis of a common participation in Right Reason Corneille claims to offer a tragic experience in which 'admiration' and its obverse 'indignation' supplant the effect of pity which Aristotle commended. After a description of the play's basic opposition of qualities of behaviour, Corneille describes his subject as an illustration of imperialist ambition and opportunism in conflict with a passionate commitment to legitimacy, freedom, and moral integrity: 'Mon principal but a été de peindre la politique des Romains au dehors, et comme ils agissaient impérieusement avec les rois leurs alliés, leurs maximes pour les empêcher de s'accroître, et les soins qu'ils prenaient de traverser leur grandeur.' To realize the imitation of this political subject he has drawn a brilliant comparison between the behaviour of a variety of *dramatis personae*, each showing the nature of the values they serve:

C'est le caractère que j'ai donné à leur république en la personne de son ambassadeur Flaminius, qui rencontre un prince intrépide, qui voit sa perte assurée sans s'ebranler, et brave l'orgueilleuse masse de leur puissance, lors même qu'il en est accablé. Ce héros de ma façon sort un peu des règles de la tragédie, en ce qu'il ne cherche point à faire pitié par l'excès de ses malheurs, mais le succès a montré que la fermeté des grands cœurs, qui n'excite que de l'admiration dans l'âme du spectateur est quelque fois aussi agréable, que la compassion que notre art nous commande de mendier pour leurs misères. ('Au Lecteur', GC, II, 639–41)

When Corneille returns to his play in the 'Examen' of 1660 he enlarges somewhat on this tragic effect grounded in awed recognition of the importance of the moral issues at stake. This time he considers his play in the broader context of his general practice and interestingly perceives its relevance to earlier work. Recognizing that it was something of an overstatement when earlier he had written that Nicomède inspired no feelings of compassion, he observes:

Il en fait naître toutefois quelqu'une, mais elle ne va pas jusques à tirer des larmes. Son effet se borne à mettre les auditeurs dans les intérêts de ce prince, et à leur faire former des souhaits pour ses prospérités.

Dans l'admiration qu'on a pour sa vertu, je trouve une manière de purger les passions, dont n'a point parlé Aristote, et qui est peut-être plus sûre que celle qu'il prescrit à la tragédie par le moyen de la pitié et de la crainte. L'amour qu'elle nous donne pour cette vertu que nous admirons, nous imprime de la haine pour le vice contraire. La grandeur de courage de Nicomède nous laisse une aversion de la pusillanimité, et la généreuse reconnaissance d'Héraclius, qui expose sa vie pour Martian, à qui il est redevable de la sienne, nous jette dans l'horreur de l'ingratitude. ('Examen', GC, II, 643)

The supreme importance which Corneille attributes to the immediate moral efficacy of his political drama supplants both Aristotle's original description of a tragic *catharsis* through pity and fear for a flawed hero and its doctrinaire development into a pseudo-Aristotelian cautionary effect through the due punishment of wrong behaviour.

The replacement of a theory of purgation through pity and fear by his own 'tragique d'admiration' explains the lack of conviction with which Corneille discusses *catharsis* as a fourth possible 'utilité du poëme dramatique'. It also partially explains his lack of interest in the Aristotelian theory of the tragic flaw illustrated by a hero of 'middling' virtue. For Corneille himself, as for every other commentator in seventeenth-century France, *catharsis* and *hamartia* had become almost impossible to disentangle from each other, such was the prestige of a cautionary reading of the *Poetics*' discussion of tragic effect. If Corneille downgraded both theories it was because the kind of poetic significance and audience reaction for which he aimed was of a much more intense and ambitious kind than a mere cautionary lesson. As the retrospective application to *Héraclius* indicates, what Corneille avers of *Nicomède* holds good for earlier practice and it is not hard to see that the same principles already apply even to the plays he had written before *Héraclius*. From *Médée* to *Rodogune*, all had provoked and exploited the spectator's sense of awe as they stimulated him to a passionate moral judgement on the dramatic spectacle of a momentous conflict of values.

THE SUBJECT OF TRAGEDY AND ITS MORAL STRUCTURE

Aristotle had placed the tragic hero, neither entirely good nor entirely bad, and the excessive punishment of some error or character flaw at the centre of the tragic subject. The political concerns of *Nicomède* and very different characterization and fortunes of its eponymous hero make it apparent that we need to look more closely at what Corneille himself believed to be the appropriate subject-matter of comedy and tragedy. From *Le Cid* to *La Mort de Pompée* Corneille's work had already shown a marked divergence from the Aristotelian description of the tragic hero. But only with the 'Epître' prefacing *La Suite du Menteur* (1645) does Corneille first tackle the problem of what was characteristic of tragic and comic subject-matter, although his immediate concern was a none too honest defence of the morality of *Le Menteur*. As ever, the best arms to use against his critics were their own. Observing that Aristotle 'préfère la fable aux mœurs, seulement pour ce qu'elle contient tout ce qu'il y a d'agréable dans le poème', Corneille adds: 'Cependant quand on y mêle quelque utilité, ce doit être principalement dans cette partie qui regarde les mœurs, et que ce grand homme [Aristote] ne tient pas du tout nécessaire, puisqu'il permet de la retrancher entièrement, et demeure d'accord qu'on peut faire une tragédie sans mœurs' (GC, II, 97). Sliding about on the ambiguities of 'la comédie' and 'les mœurs', Corneille deliberately failed to clarify what he really understood Aristotle to mean by 'une tragédie sans mœurs'. It was sufficient to throw dust in his critics' eyes by pious – but far from innocent – invocations of a revered authority. By 1660, however, the first *Discours* gives the lie to such ruses and it becomes clear that Corneille now takes 'les mœurs' to mean 'une disposition morale', for he admits that he is unable to make sense of Aristotle's reference to a 'tragédie sans mœurs', 'vu que... c'est par les mœurs qu'un homme est méchant ou homme de bien, spirituel ou stupide, timide ou hardi, constant ou irrésolu, bon ou mauvais politique, et qu'il est impossible qu'on mette aucun sur le théâtre qui ne soit bon ou méchant, et qui n'aye quelqu'une de ces autres qualités' (LF, 61; GC, III, 133). This firmly replaces discussion of character and dramatic effect at the level of audience perception and judgement of good and bad conduct. With only the scapegrace Dorante to defend, he had quoted an obscure passage in order to argue that plot alone was the soul of the play. Now that he is also concerned with a definition of tragedy he makes it clear that characterization is of considerable importance in so far as it has a major bearing on the moral significance of the drama:

Les mœurs ne sont pas seulement le principe des actions, mais aussi du raisonnement. Un homme de bien agit et raisonne en homme de bien, un méchant agit et raisonne en méchant, et l'un et l'autre étale de diverses maximes de morale suivant cette diverse habitude. C'est donc de ces maximes, que cette habitude produit, que la tragédie peut se passer, et non pas de l'habitude même, puisqu'elle est le principe des actions, et que les actions sont l'âme de la tragédie, où l'on ne doit parler qu'en agissant et pour agir. Ainsi pour expliquer ce passage d'Aristote... nous pouvons dire que quand il parle d'une tragédie sans mœurs, il entend une tragédie où les acteurs énoncent simplement leurs sentiments, ou ne les appuient que sur des raisonnements tirés du fait, comme Cléopâtre dans le second acte de *Rodogune*, et non pas sur des maximes de morale ou de politique, comme

Rodogune dans son premier acte. Car, je le répète encore, faire un poème de théâtre où aucun des acteurs ne soit bon ni méchant, prudent ni imprudent, cela est absolument impossible. (LF, 62; GC, III, 133–4)

Here, at least, Corneille makes an unambiguous and important distinction between, on the one hand, abstract statements of moral principle and, on the other, the tragic poet's capacity to realize telling contrasts of principled or unprincipled conduct. This attempted solution to a difficult passage has all the stamp of a poet more interested in the full and lucid presentation of the realities of political decision than in his opponents' pseudo-Aristotelian conviction that tragedy should offer 'un sermon délicieux en vers' built on 'des maximes de morale ou de politique'.

If we look beyond Corneille's obfuscations in defence of *Le Menteur* he seems to have believed that, as a comic entertainment, the central interest of his play lay in 'les grâces de l'intrigue' which illustrated Dorante's ingenuities. This foreshadows those passages in the first *Discours* where Corneille contrasts the subject-matter and preoccupations of comedy and tragedy. In the interim, however, he was to find further reason to reflect and refine, and in the dedication of *Don Sanche d'Aragon* (1650) he proposed a variant kind of comedy – 'la comédie héroique'. This he did because, despite the high rank of major roles in *Don Sanche*, the play illustrated nothing 'de pitoyable, ni de terrible, et par conséquent elle n'a rien de tragique ... Il [Don Sanche] a de grands déplaisirs... mais nous ne voyons autre chose dans les comédies, que des amants qui vont mourir, s'ils ne possèdent ce qu'ils aiment, et de semblables douleurs ne préparant aucun effect tragique, on ne peut dire qu'elles aillent au-dessus de la comédie' (GC, II, 552). By the time of the *Discours*, ten years later, these various considerations have been brought together in a clearer definition of what Corneille believes to be appropriate to the comic and tragic modes of imitation: 'La comédie diffère... en céla de la tragédie, que celle-ci veut pour son sujet une action illustre, extraordinaire, sérieuse: celle-là s'arrête à une action commune et enjouée; celle-ci demande de grands périls pour ses héros: celle-là se contente de l'inquiétude et des déplaisirs de ceux à qui elle donne le premier rang parmi ses acteurs' (LF, 48; GC, III, 125). The implication is that, in the case of comedy, the moral issue is not the 'subject' simply because it does not constitute the central point of interest. Applied to *Le Menteur*, this suggests that the problems and consequences posed by Dorante's conduct are of interest to the poet and spectator only in so far as they offer the opportunity for a series of misunderstandings and ingenuities of plot manipulation which show the limited and essentially harmless repercussions of one man's fabulations on the little group with which he is involved. Corneille seems to rely on Aristotle here rather more closely than did his contemporaries, ingeniously exploiting the *Poetics*' definition of the ridiculous as a species of the ugly or bad, 'a blunder of deformity not productive of pain or harm to others'.[27] If the comic action raises any moral disquiet, this recedes in importance before the fun to be derived from the witty inventiveness of Dorante and, behind him, of Corneille himself. So the comic poet pleases by his own ingenuity in complicating and unravelling a plot which never invites us to reflect with any great earnestness on the merits of the actions represented.[28]

Perhaps Corneille's 1660 definitions of the comic subject are less than completely satisfactory because they are too closely related to his later practice. However he offers a much more successful and comprehensive definition of tragic subject-matter in which the moral interest of the drama is no longer secondary to intricacies of plot. The central importance he gives to the moral issue, rather than mere observance of generic convention, accounts for the way the protagonists of Corneille's serious drama are so illustriously and closely linked to the fortunes of state and the larger community of man. Corneille himself makes this clear when he asserts that matters of rank alone are not sufficient to distinguish between comedy or tragedy. This was why it was necessary to re-define *Don Sanche* as a 'comédie héroique', and he makes the point again in the second *Discours*. In the dedication of *Don Sanche* Aristotle is held to justify, if only by default, this contention that royal status of itself is not a precondition of the tragic subject: 'Quand il [Aristotle] examine lui-même les qualités nécessaires au héros de la tragédie, il ne touche point du tout à sa naissance, et ne s'attache qu'aux incidents de sa vie et à ses mœurs.' After summarizing Aristotle's location of the tragic subject in the spectacle of the hero of middling virtue in conflict with those to whom he is closely related, Corneille also envisages the possibility of a tragic hero of undistinguished social status. He speculates that it can only be because history has not recorded the lives of such men that preference has gone to heroes of royal rank (GC, II, 550). He even finds an instance of a 'commoner' hero in Hardy's *Scédase*, where a peasant's hospitality is abused by two courtiers who profit from their host's absence from home in order to rape his daughters and murder them. The peasant Scédase gets no redress from his King, who sides with the courtiers when called to pronounce on the affair. It matters little to Corneille that this blameless peasant of Leuctra does not fit Aristotle's definitions of the tragic hero of middling virtue. What is of significance to him is that Scédase's misfortune and suicide perfectly exemplify the view that a traditional involvement of kings and princes in tragic subject-matter has less to do with their rank than with extraordinary circumstances which force them to decisions of major social and political importance. In the case of *Scédase*, the guests' betrayal of good faith to their host and the king's betrayal of his subjects' claim to justice offers a potentially tragic subject because the humble father's misfortune calls into question the very bases of social order.[29]

Don Sanche however, for all the elevated rank of its major roles, is denied tragic status in the first *Discours* because it turns on a simple question of identity and, extraordinary though the situation is, its interest is restricted to personal problems of sentiment:

Lorsqu'on met sur la scène un simple intrique d'amour entre des rois, et qu'ils ne courent aucun péril, ni de leur vie, ni de leur Etat, je ne crois pas que, bien que les personnes soient illustres, l'action le soit assez pour s'élever jusques à la tragédie. Sa dignité demande quelque grand intérêt d'Etat, ou quelque passion plus noble et plus mâle que l'amour, telles que sont l'ambition et la vengeance, et veut donner à craindre des malheurs plus grands que la perte d'une maîtresse. Il est à propos d'y mêler l'amour, parce qu'il a toujours beaucoup d'agrément, et peut servir de fondement à ces intérêts, et à ces autres passions dont je parle; mais il faut qu'il se contente du second rang dans le poëme, et leur laisse le premier. (LF, 46; GC, III, 124)

Corneille repeats the point in the second *Discours* in a discussion of the unity of time and the problems which it poses in relation to the scale of tragic and comic subject-matter: '[Les actions] de la comédie partent de personnes communes, et ne consistent qu'en intrigues d'amour et en fourberies... Mais dans la tragédie les affaires publiques sont mêlées d'ordinaire avec les intérêts particuliers des personnes qu'on y fait paraître; il y entre des batailles, des prises de villes, de grands périls, des révolutions d'Etats' (LF, 121; GC, III, 172). Corneille's concern here is with the poetics of comedy and tragedy, and both statements on tragedy reflect his practice of placing major political issues at the heart of the 'beau sujet'.[30] As ever, his principal concern is that the moral issues be brought to the fore and that their widest implications be laid bare. Whatever the lucidity and elevation which the poet himself brings to his imitation of men's actions, a tragedy of profound political significance is likely to be best realized in the most exalted and consequential of contexts in which man exercises his moral freedom, namely the world of high responsibility and decision. The splendours and servitudes of princes and generals are the ideal material, in dignity and breadth of application, from which Corneille may create a drama brilliantly illustrating the necessities of choice and the consequences of individual free will, to which all men are subject.[31]

Discussing his general practice in the second *Discours*, Corneille points out that his tragic kings and princes are not a race apart, acting in a universe divorced from the experience of everyman and remote from the sympathy or moral judgement of his audience. On the contrary, they offer a striking illustration of humanity in general and participate in the experience of everyman writ large: 'Ces rois sont hommes comme les auditeurs, et tombent dans ces malheurs par l'emportement des passions dont les auditeurs sont capables. Ils prêtent même un raisonnement aisé à faire du plus grand au moindre' (LF, 77–8; GC, iii, 143). As the tragic situation challenges the strengths and frailties of these illustrious protagonists, their success or failure places them in peril of death and shows how the fortunes of a whole anonymous community depend on their hesitations and momentous decisions. In this distinctively Cornelian view of the tragic subject, a precondition of its moral profundity is that his heroes be shown to be essentially free in choosing between a number of courses of action, and that the larger implications of their situation and decisions show how, whether they wish it or not, they cannot help but choose for everyone else in a tragic enlargement of the servitudes of every man's sense of moral responsibility. As Corneille's heroes move to action, by virtue of their social position they launch themselves on a course which affects many more than themselves, and so show both the difficulties of heroic decision and how the consequences of heroic action – as they exceed or belie the hero's hopes or intentions – decide the destiny of other men.[32]

Bénichou observes that the seventeenth-century spectators did not merely sympathize with the tragic hero in his moral predicaments and responsibilities. By extending their own experience of the social order into the socio-political order of the play they were also interested parties themselves and passed judgement on the hero's conduct: 'Ils composent l'auditoire indispensable à ces créatures

faites pour l'admiration, dont la vie n'aurait aucun sens si elle
n'affrontait victorieusement l'épreuve du jugement public. Finalement le public est juge de la valeur des héros parce qu'il est le
premier intéressé à ce que les grands soient dignes de leur rang.'[33]
This valuably emphasizes the degree in which Corneille's serious
drama, in appealing to the individual spectator's sympathy or sense
of moral outrage, consistently exploits and challenges the social and
political awareness of its audience. Through the intensifications of
their poetic recreation of history his tragedies lay bare the individual
and social experience of man by submitting their heroes' actions to
the collective judgement of an audience which he describes as
'composé ni de méchants, ni di saints, mais de gens d'une probité
commune, et qui ne sont pas si sévèrement retranchés dans l'exacte
vertu, qu'ils ne soient susceptibles des passions et capables des périls
où elles engagent ceux qui leur défèrent trop' (LF, 79; GC, III, 144).
The two worlds of play and audience interpenetrate at this level of
poetic significance, making the spectator a perceptive critic of the
play in so far as it involves him emotionally and morally in an action
which condenses and highlights the complex relationship between
individual aspiration and the collective moral structures which
comprise every man's experience of the community of men.

Saint-Evremond, who believed that 'ce n'est pas tant la nature
humaine qu'il faut expliquer, que la condition humaine qu'il faut
représenter sur le théâtre', faithfully defended Corneille's manner in
the second half of the century. Racine had eclipsed Corneille, and
Saint-Evremond clearly perceived that a fundamental change had
come about in the preoccupations of serious drama. Wistfully he
observed that 'il y a eu des temps où il fallait choisir de beaux sujets
et les bien traiter, il ne faut plus aujourd'hui que des caractères…Racine est préféré à Corneille et les caractères l'emportent sur
les sujets.'[34] The opposition is clear enough between, on the one
hand, Corneille's attribution of prime importance to action in a
'beau sujet' which explores the necessities of political decision in a
historical situation and, on the other hand, Racine's subordination
of plot and situation to the illustration of passion. The two
dramatists are very different in their subjects and exploit two very
different veins within the conventions of seventeenth-century French
tragedy.[35] If, in turning to Saint-Evremond, we briefly revive an
exercise in comparison which has often led to partial criticism of one
or other of the two playwrights, it is because the comparison has at

least the merit of pointing up differences and incompatibilities of attitude on the nature and effect of tragedy which need to be recognized if we are to respect Corneille's manner as a dramatist.[36]

More recent Racinian criticism has rewardingly explored the relation between the tragic hero and his world, but Racine's prefaces tend to confirm Saint-Evremond's observation that the younger dramatist was first interested in the characterization of his heroes – an interest which resulted in the most successful exploitation of Aristotle's essentially character-orientated theory of the hero of middling virtue, punished beyond his deserts as a result of some inner flaw. Alone amongst seventeenth-century French theorists and dramatists Racine seems to have grasped the possibilities of this tragic subject and understood what Aristotle meant by its cathartic effect. The sparer structure of his plots reflects his concentration on a subject in which tragic constraints manifest themselves principally through the inner necessities of individual character. Dramatic interest centres on a small number of roles in plays which are in large part tragedies of compulsion, recording the inevitable collapse of hope in a progress towards catastrophe which, from the outset, the audience knows to be unavoidable. Personality reveals itself primarily through the poetic expression of suffering caused by a tragic inability to reconcile mutually destructive personal necessities in a drama which is above all expressive of human solitude and inner incoherence. If the gods oppress the Racinian protagonist they do so mainly through the inheritance of an imprisoning past and through the inner necessities of passion and its frustration. Political intrigue and public disgrace are shown to be more the consequence of such inner compulsions than the result of a free but misguided choice of principle. Even in a play like *Bérénice*, responsibility to an external order of Roman Imperial values is set at a discount before the slow recognition of the impossibility of individual fulfilment as the protagonists face the incoherence of their own nature and context.

The possibilities of so powerful and distinctive an exploitation of Aristotle's connected theories of the inner flaw and purgation by pity and fear go virtually unexploited by Corneille, for all that he spends a fair amount of time examining what Aristotle might have meant by *catharsis*. It is possible partially to apply Aristotelian tragic criteria to a few of his greatest plays and critics have laboured hard to do so, notably in the case of *Horace*, when they were not belabouring Corneille for his supposed lack of tragic sense. Ironically Corneille was the first to bring this kind of reproach upon himself when he spent so much effort in defence of *Le Cid*, arguing unconvincingly that his play met Aristotle's requirements as they had been redefined by Robortello in his prescription of the 'perfect tragedy'. Not surprisingly this left too much unaccounted for and was to lay Corneille open to the charge of insensitivity to the *Poetics*, since it is on this matter of the subject of tragedy and its effect that he is most notoriously at odds with both Aristotle and seventeenth-century theorists.

Since the rediscovery of the *Poetics* in the early sixteenth century, the concept of the flawed hero provoking pity and fear – and hence the purgation of 'such-like' emotions – had repeatedly been enlisted as part of the argument for the moral efficacy of tragedy as prudential admonition. *Catharsis* was held to be especially central to this 'utilité' of poetic drama because it was understood to describe the spectator's chastened final response to the cautionary spectacle of a pitiful but culpable hero's punishment. It is ironic that, such was the prestige of this reading, even the most faithfully Aristotelian Racine sought, in the 'Préface' of *Phèdre*, to parry the charge of positively stimulating morally suspect emotions, when he alone got close to appreciating a passage which may have been first intended to answer Plato's charge that tragedy was socially dangerous because of the passions it provoked in its spectators.[37] The cautionary interpretation of the *Poetics* held such sway that even an original like Corneille followed his times when he too placed his discussion of *catharsis* amongst the 'utilités' treating it with little enthusiasm as a fourth possible source of the kind of 'utilité' specific to dramatic poetry. But Corneille was less characteristic of his times in the care with which, in the third *Discours*, he tried to explain what *catharsis* really meant in terms of practical effect. Having unavailingly shown willing and some erudition in turning for help to a list of notable commentators, he cut the knot and looked at the problem in the light of his experience of the effect of his own plays on their audiences (LF, 75–7; GC, III, 142–3).[38] Predictably enough, the distance between his practice and Aristotle's original statements is such that his conclusions on *catharsis* indicate little more than a sense of dutiful respect for authority. After an unconvincing, but ingenious, attempt to apply something of Aristotle's original argument to his own practice he is finally brave enough – or rash enough – to express open scepticism about the reality of the suggested purgative effect, suspecting that it is nothing more than 'une belle idée, qui n'ait jamais son effet dans la vérité' (LF, 82; GC, III, 146).

But the way in which Corneille has tried to make sense of the theory in relation to his own practice, debatable though it may be as an elucidation of the *Poetics*, does tell us much of his own preoccupations. Drawing perhaps on an interpretation originally proposed by Castelvetro, he argues that the theory of purgation might be seen to apply where pity and fear were not produced simultaneously by one character but instead were stimulated by various individuals in the interaction of a group, one figure provoking pity while another stimulated fear (LF, 84–5; GC, III, 147–8). Above all others this passage has provoked critical derision and is frequently quoted as indisputable evidence that Corneille understood little of Aristotle and less of Greek tragedy.[39] Even were that the case – and it is not – it offers no reason, except to the most pedantic of Aristotelian sensibilities, to conclude that Corneille was incapable of writing tragedy himself. In fact his suggestion shows clearly how he is less concerned with tragedy as an exploration of inner fatality of character than with the tragic possibilities latent in the interaction of various *dramatis personae* of roughly equal importance in a play first concerned with the depiction of man's social and political condition. Corneille's theoretical formulations constantly argue for a drama of the group in which the individual hero claims our interest not through a flawed personality but as one amongst a number of major roles whose varying convictions and fortunes are to be judged within a carefully defined social framework. In so political a drama Corneille can argue for the acceptability of a 'perfect' tragic hero in so far as he falls victim less to his inner frailties than to exterior constraints, these even being generated by the effect of his own conduct through the fatal logic of cause and effect peculiar to man's nature and social condition (LF, 87–9; GC, III, 149–51).

In consequence Corneille gives a very high value indeed to situation and its development, just as his protagonists show an intense awareness of their social and political context. It has been remarked that the Cornelian tragic hero has 'almost no private dimension; he lives, he exists, he is, only as he stands in some clearly defined relationship to others'.[40] Of course individual characterization as it is illustrated in action remains important, but it is not, in itself, Corneille's primary concern in the drama. As his discussion of 'les mœurs' showed, it serves to contrast individual motivations and value systems within an evolving political conflict. If Racine's characterization resides first in the poetic revelation of disintegrating hopes and personality, Corneille's protagonists possess an undoubted freedom in pursuit of self-realization as they respond to the constraints of their situation, a freedom which even enables them to redefine themselves from one act to another, reconstructing earlier reasons for action into new accounts of previous behaviour. But if Corneille's heroes can 'create' themselves as victors, they also have a part in their destiny as tragic victims, in so far as their chosen actions shape a constantly developing situation over which they may not end the masters and which may even overwhelm them. They are certainly free to define and reveal their nature through what they choose to do, as they shape their destiny in a heroic effort to inflect the situation within which they find themselves. Yet even in this they remain prisoners of circumstance, as they fall subject to the remorselessly changing pressure of events and the necessity for decision. Indeed, even by their obstinate refusal to act, heroes as various as Polyeucte, Nicomède or Suréna still 'become themselves' in the course of five acts, establishing their identity for better or worse through their freedom to resist the pressure of events and the solicitations of others about them. Thus, if Corneille first charac- terizes his heroes by the freedom with which they will a course of action and accept responsibility for the consequences of that choice, their social situation in turn acts as a potent tragic constraint. It may even threaten the hero's identity, as in the final act of *Horace* where other men's free judgements redefine the quality of the deeds by which the defender of Rome had sought to make his nature and capacity apparent. Within such an illustration of the condition of man, Corneille's proposal that pity and fear be derived from contrasted characters makes very good sense since, in his view, the interplay between the collectivity and the individual forms the essential dynamic of the action. This distinctive aspect of Corneille's drama has long been recognized, for all that its tragic potential has not often been appreciated. As long ago as 1852 Guizot saw that 'chez Corneille tout tend aux effets de situation – c'est la situation qu'il cherche constamment à préparer et à mettre en saillie'.[41] Of its very nature, this kind of drama can make little use of the theory of a 'flawed' hero and even less of the proposed effect of purgation by pity and fear. Instead, its tragic presentation of men in conflict must positively welcome the strongest combatants, and particularly those 'perfect' heroes whose constancy even in failure will most strikingly illustrate the ineluctable external pressures that bear upon human aspiration in the free exercise of the individual will.

It has been noted how Corneille, preoccupied as he is with the multiple possibilities inherent in the extended development of a complex situation, persists throughout his life in constructing plot patterns decidedly more elaborate than those of Racine's drama.[42] This complexity is the necessary consequence of his interest in the ramifications of a political situation in which individual action begets inescapable social consequences. The form of such a drama is well defined in Corneille's novel conception of a 'unité de péril' which the third *Discours* presents as a 'necessity' obliging the poet to condense and focus basic historical material into the limited time-scale of twenty-four hours, even if this results in an extreme situation straining to the very limit previous considerations of verisimilitude: 'Dans la tragédie les affaires publiques sont mêlées d'ordinaire avec les intérêts particuliers des personnes illustres qu'on y fait paraître; il y entre des batailles, des prises de villes, de grands périls, des révolutions d'Etats; et tout cela va malaisément avec la promptitude que la règle nous oblige de donner à ce qui se passe sur la scène' (LF, 121; GC, III, 172). The ambitious scale of such subject-matter calls for a special kind of unity not founded on principal character-roles, but which instead emphasizes the intensity of the pressures brought into play by a number of other *dramatis personae*, each essentially free in action and judgement. In the course of such a play, a number of subordinate plots converge with increasing urgency and suspense, only to collide and suddenly be resolved in the concluding stages of the action. The drama closes when all the explosive possibilities contained in the original exposition have been traced out through a series of intermediate and contributory crises, all of which are brought to their extreme point of pressure and sudden release in the play's brilliant conclusion. Corneille outlines this very personal variant of the unity of action at the start of the third *Discours* and shows its different application to both comedy and tragedy:

L'unité d'action consiste, dans la comédie, en l'unité d'intrigue, ou d'obstacle aux desseins des principaux acteurs, et en l'unité de péril dans la tragédie, soit que son héros y succombe soit qu'il en sorte. Ce n'est pas que je prétende qu'on ne puisse admettre plusieurs périls dans l'une, et plusieurs intrigues ou obstacles dans l'autre, pourvu que de l'un on tombe nécessairement dans l'autre; car alors la sortie du premier péril ne rend point l'action complète, puisqu'elle en attire un second; et l'éclaircissement d'un intrique ne met point les acteurs en repos, puisqu'il les embarasse dans un nouveau. (LF, 123–4; GC, III, 174)

In such a chain reaction of cause and effect the general unity of the extended dramatic situation is preserved in so far as it follows to the end the various uncertainties posed by separate elements established in the original exposition: 'Il ne doit y avoir qu'une action complète, qui laisse l'esprit de l'auditeur dans le calme; mais elle ne peut le devenir que par plusieurs autres imparfaites, qui lui servent d'acheminements, et tiennent cet auditeur dans une agréable suspension' (LF, 123–4; GC, III, 175). Thus, by virtue of this complex unity of peril, his tragedy traces out the relationships between various factors contributing to a political crisis and only comes to an end when all tensions implicit in the play's point of departure have culminated in a crisis and resolution which retrospectively establish the meaning of all that has gone before.

Corneille's drama repeatedly offers this progression from the threatening confusion and suspense of secondary plots to their unification and resolution in often surprising twists to what had earlier seemed an inextricably complex series of events. But, however anxious Corneille is to impress his audience by the ingenious manipulation of complexity and his ability to dazzle them with unforeseen dénouements, the profounder significance of such brilliant conclusions is guaranteed by the poet's insistence that every event should be properly, if unobtrusively, prepared. If the action lacked that essential coherence of cause and effect, the spectator would lose his cumulative sense of the pressure of events and, with this, his perception of the hidden necessities which govern the affairs of men. Corneille's *Discours* and *Examens* place considerable importance on the classically coherent interplay of cause and effect which prepares his wonderful conclusions, since any arbitrary twist to the action would destroy the compelling sense of necessity essential to an understanding of the tragic dimension of political initiative. Such incoherences, being neither the necessary or even probable consequences of previous action and circumstance, could not be attributed to the true nature of things and would instead be perceived as the whims or clumsinesses of a poet incapable of expressing a unified moral significance in the play's depiction of human conflict. When judged according to the audience's 'mœurs et croyances' the poetic truth of even the most unexpected ending must retrospectively be recognized as the logical conclusion towards which the *dramatis personae* had been moving. Otherwise the spectator's earlier sense of apprehension and final acceptance of the fundamental unity of an extended political crisis would not be transformed into a perception of the larger moral order governing the unfolding of events. This requirement holds true both for Corneille's final acts of 'judgement' and for those many unforeseen and brilliant *coups de théâtre* which suddenly order and unify the series of reversals and complications which had earlier generated such anguish in the protagonists and enjoyable suspense in the spectator. There is a very Castelvetran flavour about the way in which Corneille values the dramatist's virtuoso ability convincingly to produce his brilliant resolutions out of such ingeniously tangled complexity, as he leads his audience to final comprehension and acceptance of how the extraordinary historical subject-matter had come about. In Corneille's drama, however, this virtuosity offers much more than simple dazzlement because, both in his poetics and in his practice, his art was constantly exploited in such a way as to illuminate the conflicts of values and political necessities inherent in the social experience of man. In so far as they continue to do so, Corneille's tragedies, rooted though they are in the ideological conflicts of seventeenth-century France, can still bring modern audiences to the same awed perception of the insoluble difficulties of our political condition.

PART III

Corneille's plays written in the reign of Louis XIII

3

Clitandre *(1630–2)* and Médée *(1634–5)*

By comparison with Corneille's later work, the political interest of his first excursions beyond the urban world of his early comedies is relatively slight. And yet the 'Préface' of *Clitandre* contains a mysterious passage which is the only occasion in Corneille's work where he suggests a 'one-to-one' relationship between his drama and contemporary political events (GC, 1, 96). The dedication to the Duc de Longueville, Governor of Normandy, also suggests that this enemy of the Cardinal influenced the composition of the last three acts. These two passages have led a number of critics to argue that *Clitandre, ou l'Innocence délivrée* reflects specific events which followed Richelieu's triumph over his adversaries on the Day of Dupes (November 1630).[1] This interpretation of the play needs brief examination.

The Chancellor, Michel de Marillac, who had previously led the opposition to Richelieu's policies in the King's Council, was placed under house arrest and was to die in prison in Châteaudun in August 1632. His half-brother Louis, Maréchal de Marillac, was also arrested on what many considered to have been trumped up charges of embezzlement. The Cardinal considered that the latter's trial and condemnation was being pursued with insufficient vigour, and (March 1632) set up another tribunal at his country estate of Reuil. After a summary trial the Maréchal was sentenced to death (28 April) and executed (10 May). It has been suggested that he was the real-life Clitandre, since the composition of the play dates from when he was still awaiting trial and when the Parlement de Paris had refused to register a royal declaration condemning the brothers as criminal conspirators. The *privilège* of *Clitandre* is dated 8 March, a mere twelve days before the play was available to the public in what looks like a rushed publication intended to cash in on public concern for Marillac. Since the theme of innocence unjustly accused comes to the fore after the second act and closely reflects Marillac's position, it is suggested that the spectacle of Clitandre – profoundly faithful to the king yet unjustly imprisoned due to the machinations of an unscrupulous rival – was intended to please Marillac's sympathizers.

Perhaps no specific political references had been intended in Corneille's first drafts of his tragicomedy, but the suggestion is that Longueville – once he had seen the first two acts – recognized a subject which could be interpreted in a way which was favourable to his own convictions. Hence Corneille's reference to Longueville's interest in the completion of the play, and a shift of emphasis in the plot which might support the theory that – whether the dramatist liked it or not – the subject had been 'hijacked' by the play's patron. Of course Corneille himself might not have been averse to 'selling' the interest of his first venture into print by prefatory hints that there was some correlation between dramatic fiction and real events. In the same spirit, his publisher may well have published quickly in order to maximize sales of the work of an author who had barely made his mark. Certainly it would not have been hard for the play's first audiences to believe that it contained a thinly veiled plea for the deliverance of a man whom many saw to be an innocent victim of Richelieu's personal ambition. But there critical speculation must stop, since natural prudence dictated that Corneille should make quite sure that neither the Cardinal nor anyone else could prove that a coded reference to contemporary events was hidden within the plot.

Tragicomedy was particularly favoured by the great families of the period and, at the most conventional level of the providentialism which is the hallmark of the genre, it is not difficult to see how the moral and political implications of *Clitandre* might have pleased those who professed fidelity to the traditional values and procedures of the Crown. By generic definition the play dealt with more than lovers' tribulations, and did so with a providentialism which inevitably chimed with the arguments of those who wished to exploit general disquiet about the Cardinal's conduct of affairs. If the matter of a coded political message cannot be proved one way or the other, this very conventionality with which *Clitandre* illustrates the triumph of virtue and failure of unprincipled artifice is not without interest to the modern reader, since it offers a useful 'primer' in the commonplaces of moral and political theory against which Corneille calculated his effects in the 1630s.

Abraham Bosse's delightful plate illustrating *La Galerie du Palais* usefully reminds us that, despite official condemnation, Machiavelli's political theory was available to the reading public, even if the most forthright of his seventeenth-century disciples wrote for the limited world of scholars and 'esprits forts'. The works of Machiavelli are prominently advertised by Bosse's bookseller but, as is proper to the frontispiece of a comedy, one fashionable young man is more interested in buying Tristan's *La Mariane* and his friends are eyeing the ladies. And certainly popular acquaintance with Machiavelli's ideas came less from reading his works than through their unfavourable presentation in more popular discussions of political theory and civil morality addressed to the broad reading public.

Marillac's imprisonment was widely considered to be a shocking instance of an unprincipled 'coup d'état', and it fuelled an upsurge in a long-running debate over the true nature of political morality in which Machiavelli had become a constant point of reference. As early as 1625 the Cardinal had sought to meet a rising tide of criticism by employing pamphleteers to stress the practical necessity of a balance between political realism and Christian devotion. Neither Machiavelli nor his seventeenth-century admirers held that the Christian values were entirely to be abandoned, for all that those who opposed them would have their readers believe they did. But, in arguing that the Christian virtues in action could prove expedient, these political realists offended idealist convictions that society was instituted for the moral and spiritual betterment of the citizen. Appealing instead to the history of political success or failure, these adherents of 'la raison d'état' sharply distinguished between 'l'honnête' and 'l'utile' and defended the practice of the 'coup d'état' as a prudent sacrifice of strict moral probity to the broader interests of State. History after all, if not the Church, taught that the authority of the Prince was best served by strict internal order and military strength.[2]

The audiences of *Clitandre* may have read the Cardinal's pamphlets, but more commonly their knowledge of such secular political theory would have been gained through the distortions of those who rejected Machiavelli's ideas. For those who believed that human prudence alone was bound to fail within the providential order of history, Innocent Gentillet's widely-read *Anti-Machiavel* (1576) offered a convenient, if inaccurate, primer in the misguided and ungodly modern theory of politics.[3] By isolating and refuting at

length a series of scandalous propositions supposedly taken from
Machiavelli's works, Gentillet had created a scarecrow 'Machiavellianism' which profoundly influenced many popular seventeenth-
century works of political theory or civil morality, like Marnix's
Résolutions politiques or Bardin's *Le Lycée*, which repeated the myth of
the wicked Florentine.[4] Furthermore, seventeenth-century opponents of a secular 'statecraft' were no longer content simply to set St
Augustine and St Thomas at loggerheads with Machiavelli's
supposed principles. Instead they sought to occupy the realists' own
ground, covertly sniping at the Cardinal's 'statecraft' in safely
general formulations which aimed to discredit the claim that only a
secular pragmatism in political decision brought success by asserting
the superior political efficacy of Christian political conduct.
Certainly the larger public would have been more at home with
these popular works, since every confessor followed Aquinas'
insistence that each of us participated in Divine and Natural Law by
the light of conscience. Inclined to harmonious co-existence through
Right Reason and the charitable promptings of a Christian
conscience, each citizen was imbued with 'une secrète affection' for
his fellows: 'Nous ne pouvons nous regarder seuls ni faire un tout
d'un chacun de nous sans nous déshumaniser en quelque sort et sans
faire un divorce particulier de l'union commune que nous avons avec
tous les hommes...Notre tout n'est qu'une partie d'un autre tout,
qui est la nature universelle.'[5] Our natural destiny was thus to
participate in a community which had its origin in the Divine Will,
and true virtue lay in worthy accomplishment of the obligations laid
on us by God through his servant the King. Since 'Dieu est comme
le principe formel des Républiques qui en leur police portent les
traits de sa sagesse éternelle', each subject was enjoined to 'prendre
la forme de sa vertu et la mesure de sa dévotion sur les devoirs et sur
les obligations de son état'.[6] No valid distinction could be made
between public and private morality, for Natural and Divine Law
gave each his place in a social order which was as natural as that of
the family.[7]

Whether describing the obligations of citizen or hero, Christian
apologists repeatedly asserted that history showed that within the
'chaîne d'or de la Providence' there was nothing 'de casuel dans le
monde'.[8] Thus man's peculiar dignity resided in his capacity to
know and work with that providential order. Set above the beasts
and but a little below the angels, he was called to fulfil his civil

obligations within God's greater providential design, and natural affection and Right Reason ensured his recognition of duties concordant with the collectivity's participation in God's higher purposes. All causes linked up with the First, and within that greater order man was free only in so far as any defiance of God's purposes led to enslavement to the passions. Such unreason providentially called down ruin and humiliation upon itself, whilst true liberty and self-fulfilment lay in service of the Divine Intention which shaped the destinies of the world. Although gravely weakened by the Fall, every man still possessed the original grace of love for the Good and the Beautiful within God's ordered creation, and Christian apologists were especially careful to distinguish between the nobler promptings of conscience and the infirmity of purely human prudence. Indeed Bardin's *Le Lycée* (1632–4) insists almost to the point of heterodoxy on the *honnête homme*'s natural perception of 'la Justice Naturelle' as the supreme guide to social conduct.[9] This same belief in man's innate perception of the good and the true in accordance with Divine and Natural Law – as opposed to his fallen use of the tainted 'reasoning reason' of common human prudence – is fundamental to the political and juridical argument of Bodin's enormously influential *La République*. Within the larger context of God's providential purposes, the Christian Kings of France displayed the most excellent form of 'la Monarchie Royale', guaranteeing 'la liberté naturelle' of their subjects and ruling as fathers towards their children in accordance with a natural order of authority.[10] Collective harmony under their just rule was sure evidence of 'une puissance intellectuelle en souverain degré', since the social hierarchy reflected the Creator's purposes and accorded to every man his place and duties within the kingdom's participation in the providential unfolding of history.[11]

This received view of things structures the unfolding of events in *Clitandre*, where the King's orders risk gross injustice because of the tissue of lies woven by Pymante. Clitandre does not dream of disobeying the King and does not even blame him for his sufferings in prison. The Prince may consider keeping Clitandre with him until he knows more of the reasons for the King's summons, but Clitandre himself obeys without hesitation: 'C'est à moi d'obéir sans rien examiner' (II, iv, 596). In prison he affirms his unshakable faith that, despite unpromising appearances, the King's justice and the truth will ultimately prevail (IV, vi, 1441–2 and 1459–62). And of course Providence justifies his confidence: Pymante's treachery is discovered, and Alcandre finally distributes true justice in accordance with the sacred character of his rank. Given the interpretations which have been laid on the play, it is notable here that Clitandre's conduct in adversity offers very little indeed to flatter the ambitions of men like Longueville. Other tragicomedies of the period contain passages clearly intended to please the high nobility by marking out certain limits to the King's powers over his vassals.[12] There is nothing of the sort, however, in Corneille's play, where Alcandre's authority is opposed only by the blackest of villains who is justly punished as soon as the truth is discovered. Whatever lay behind the mysterious dedication, it is clear that, if the play could be construed to offer some support for the imprisoned Marillac, Corneille made sure that it neither criticized the King nor suggested any limitations on the Crown's authority. At most it might be argued that the apology for Marillac – if apology there is – takes the most generalized form of refusal of any kind of conduct involving treachery or deceit. When, at the close of the play, Clitandre refuses Alcandre's offers of reparation, it is clear that 'gloire' is only to be associated with faithful obedience and service of the King:

> L'honneur de vous servir m'apporte assez de gloire
> Et je perdrais le mien si quelqu'un pouvait croire
> Que mon devoir penchât au refroidissement
> Sans le flatteur espoir d'un agrandissement.
> (v, iv, 1729–32)

Like Rodrigue in *Le Cid*, Clitandre illustrates a Christian ideal of glory in conformity with Bodin's celebrated definition of a 'grand capitaine' fully reconciled with the justice and authority of the Crown.[13]

Where realist theory admitted no relationship between the principles of social order and the individual's spiritual destiny, Christian theorists held that, since all social and political life was inextricably involved in the extra-temporal perspectives of man's individual salvation, only within a Christian social order might he achieve the highest virtue and spiritual fulfilment. Since 'le spirituel et le temporel dépendent l'un de l'autre et doivent marcher ensemble', society alone offered the context within which man might live 'honnêtement, c'est à dire selon les préceptes de la vertu'.[14] Thus the King was particularly to be revered, for his just rule made the providential designs of God apparent in the social order, so offering his subjects the means to complete their own spiritual destiny through loyal service to the Crown.[15] Indeed the King's conduct offered the noblest illustration of the obligations of all, as he too laboured to perfect the social order:

C'est l'ouvrage de Dieu et la réflexion de sa lumière, comme le Roi est son image... Il faut donc croire que quand les hommes se sont attachés à leurs Princes par les liens du respect et de l'obéissance, ils ont été animés du désir de s'acquérir la perfection, en se soumettant à ceux que Dieu faisait régner sur eux, auxquels il communiquait les secrets conseils de sa divine Providence.[16]

Priézac's *Discours* show how traditional theory was later turned with especial emphasis to the glorification of the young Louis XIV, but this stress on the architectonic importance of the monarchy is characteristic of many earlier works. All insist on the identity of political and spiritual values, presenting the heroic virtue of service as most brilliantly embodied in the King's own exercise of monarchical authority. His successful rule is much more than the result of good fortune; it has the awesome quality of reflecting God's own glorious purposes on earth and shows that the King is possessed of a 'secrète et inconnnue puissance... soumise aux décrets de Dieu'.[17] In serving his King's devotion to the common weal, the hero also enjoyed something of that glory, for his actions in turn participated in his master's mystic sense of a providential vocation. The hero's soul was 'forte et généreuse' – and cherished no flattering illusions of self-sufficiency – because it was conscious of 'la divinité de son principe' and acted under the influence of 'le rayon immortel du premier soleil des esprits'.[18] Whether the hero was king or subject, his 'génie' resided in this grace of assuming the role which God had given him to further His purposes.

Within such a divinely instituted social order it was natural that God should prevail over the aberrant artifice of unprincipled men who defied Him and troubled social harmony. Such 'esprits pernicieux', 'se rebellent contre nature et semblent renoncer à leur condition en se détournant de la fin pour laquelle ils ont été engendrés... [Ils] ne sont hommes qu'en apparence.'[19] Their reliance on human prudence alone was bound to fail and cause suffering both for themselves and others. Life might often be confusing, but that was a natural consequence of man's freedom to reject or accept God's purposes in the world. Those who abused that freedom set in motion a series of causes and unexpected effects, the results of which provided sorry evidence of sinful man's capacity to obscure the Divine Intention. Since 'il est certain que les événements qu'on dit de fortune procèdent de Dieu', only wilful ignorance permitted men to term 'hasard' or 'fortune' what was in reality the 'effets occultes' of Providence.[20] All men should dispense with 'ce vain nom de fortune qui est un spectre plein d'inanité...qui n'a son existence qu'en la folle imagination de l'homme'.[21] With specious reasoning men tried to justify their carelessness of Natural and Divine Law, but all they succeeded in doing was to set the universe in travail before the truth would finally out and make God's purposes spectacularly apparent in the providential punishments which invariably ensued.[22] Judging the world like ignorant pagans, they termed 'blind fortune' or 'fate' those events which were in reality the providential consequences of their own perverse instigation of second causes within God's over-riding order.[23] Everything, no matter how mysterious, had its place within God's wisdom at work in the world, and we were no more the creatures of blind fortune than we were its slaves, impotent to affect the course of public events:

C'était l'erreur des païens estimant que le destin n'accablait pas moins les résolutions et les conseils des hommes, que la fange les cailloux d'une rivière: et une erreur de machiavélistes qui est facile à convaincre, car ce destin et fatalité ainsi entendus comme ils l'entendent ne dénotent rien d'autre qu'une pure nécessité, laquelle est diamétralement opposé au franc arbitre de l'homme.[24]

From parish pulpit to university chair Christian apologists were prepared only to valorize individual initiative within a world in which all was subject to the higher purposes of a merciful god: 'Nous voyons que Dieu ne se sert pas de l'homme comme d'un instrument inanimé, qui ne contribue rien de lui-même à l'action de l'ouvrier: il en use plutôt comme d'un instrument vivant et raisonnable, qui avec lui conduit l'ouvrage à sa dernière perfection.'[25]

Thus the conventional providentialism of *Clitandre*, in which Pymante is the chief proponent of the powers of wilful artifice, traces out the villain's course to unavoidable failure and the final salvation of a hero who trusts not in himself but in the justice of his King's sacred authority. Clitandre's disinterested glory in service is sharply contrasted with the ambitions of those who pursue a baleful kind of 'gloire' based on a single-minded and violent pursuit of criminal ends. Wrongly believing that Rosidor has betrayed her for Hippolyte, Caliste attributes to him 'une honteuse gloire' founded in pride and the *libido dominandi* (I, i, 24–8). Such conduct will have no place under Alcandre's just rule, and the plot shows how it will always be punished by a greater power. As Dorise observes, there is a dangerous necessity in misdeeds:

> Si tu veux empêcher ta perte inévitable
> Deviens plus criminelle, et parais moins coupable,
> Par une fausseté sache t'en dégager.
> Fausseté détestable, où me viens-tu réduire?
> Honteux déguisement, où me vas-tu conduire?
> (II, v, 617–22)

Pymante himself acknowledges this when finally he is brought to justice:

> Un crime attire l'autre, et de peur d'un supplice
> On tâche en étouffant ce qu'on en voit d'indice
> De paraître innocent à force de forfaits.
> (v, iv, 1769–71)

True to his kind, he first imagines his reverses to be no more than the mysterious caprice of blind destiny, but the dawning suspicion that he is struggling against Providence itself only prompts him to further defiance (II, i, 385–6 and 399–404). Dorise's appearance in the forest disguised as a peasant warns him again that he may be calling down upon himself an inevitable process of Divine retribution:

> Toutefois plus j'y songe, et plus je pense voir
> Par quelque grand effet de vengeance divine
> En ce foible témoin l'auteur de ma ruine.
> (II, vi, 712–14)

This depiction of aberrant conduct makes it very clear that Pymante has within him the seeds of salvation, when fleetingly he recognises the providential order to which he is opposed, yet lust and pride lead him into further defiance and final ruin.

This replacement of capricious destiny by the perception of an operative providential order structures the entire play and is a thoroughly conventional feature of the tragicomic climate of action. Equally conventional is the portrayal of Pymante as one of those damned souls whose pride contemporary moralists repeatedly presented as perverting the nobler possibilities of human reason: 'Ils n'appartient qu'à [Dieu] de ne dépendre que de soi, n'être obligé à suivre en ses divines opérations autres desseins que les siens. L'orgueilleux pour le contr'imiter à sa ruine ne voulant reconnaître aucun de qui il prenne loi, il fait à sa guise.'[26] Like Le Moyne's 'amoureux brutal', Pymante refuses to acknowledge the divine intimations of Justice which are his natural birthright. Prompted to action by the basest of passions, he destroys everything in his way and, when his artifices inevitably fail, he falls into hate and despair, soliciting nature and all the powers of 'le Ciel et l'Enfer, la Religion et l'Impiété, la Messe et le Sabat, dans un mesme cercle'.[27] If heroic virtue stems from Divine Illumination and can raise man to the level of 'demi-dieux', this opposite extreme of enslavement to the passions degrades Pymante to the level of brute animal.[28] Thus Caliste describes her vengeful intentions in the opening scenes:

> ... Déjà dépouillant tout naturel humain
> Je laisse à ses transports à gouverner ma main.
> (I, iv, 131–2)

The Prince speaks up for Dorise in similar terms as the play draws to its end:

> ... Un ver de jalousie
> Jette souvent notre âme en telle frénésie
> Que la raison tombée en un aveuglement
> Laisse notre conduite à son dérèglement.
> (v, iv, 1797–800)

This typology of criminal motivation is commonplace in contemporary tragicomedy, but one memorable episode in the fourth act of *Clitandre* lifts Pymante well beyond common stage convention. Spectacularly it illustrates the theme of brute perversity in a manner remarkably similar to the popular iconography which seventeenth-century *moralistes* used in their attacks on the 'athée' or 'machia-véliste' as a social outcast. Olivier's virulently misogynist *Alphabet* is characteristic, as it describes the evils of criminal vengeance: '[Il] arrive fort souvent que son coup ne porte pas, et que, pensant crever l'œil de ce qu'il n'aime, lui-même se blesse par malheur sans y penser; craignant la justice et le châtiment, il estime la campagne félicité, et la fuite le seul asile de sa vie et de sa meilleur fortune.'[29] Still trusting to his own resources, Pymante also takes flight into the forest where, disguised as a peasant, he finds refuge in a cave. Blinded in one eye by the girl he attacked in lust and vengeful anger,

Corneille's villain even openly invites the audience to 'read the moral' of his physical misfortune, standing centre-stage and pointing to his blindness as condign punishment for his lust and pursuit of vengeance through crime:

> Mon forfait évident se lit dans ma disgrâce.
>
> (IV, ii, 1201)

Pymante's appearance and fate spectacularly mark him out as one of those enemies of Providence whom Caussin attacked as men who 'remuent toutes sortes de machines pour combattre leur bonheur, et se crèvent les yeux pour ne pas voir ce grand Œil qui poursuit les impies jusques dans l'ombre de la mort'. Those who construct their own vengeance '[détruisent] le droit de nature, et [font] d'une vie civile une vie de cyclopes, qui n'aura point d'autre raison que la force, ni d'autres bornes que la pointe de l'épée'.[30] Dressed in rough peasant clothes and emerging half-blinded from a cave after trying to rape Dorise, Corneille's villain appeals to a long and – to the contemporary spectator – instantly recognizable emblematic interpretation of the secret moral significance of the race of Polyphemus. This 'reading' of the brutish figure of the Cyclops is well illustrated in Blaise de Vigenère's translation and annotation of Philostratus and in Natale Conti's *Mythologie ou explication des fables*. For Blaise de Vigenère the Cyclops represent pre-social barbarism and gluttonous sensuality; they were 'gens injurieux et violents ... insolents et outrageux ... [Ils] n'ont connaissance ni de marché, ni de palais ou de Cour, ni de maison particulière; ains font leur demeure dans les cavernes des montagnes'.[31] Conti expresses the same view, but is more concerned with Polyphemus – 'homme non seulement sauvage, et félon, mais aussi du tout brutal et inconsidéré ... luxurieux et lascif au possible', to be numbered 'entre les bêtes brutes plutôt qu'entre les hommes'. The image of Polyphemus portrays 'celui qui ne veut entendre raison, qui n'a cure aucune ni de Dieu ni des hommes, qui ne craint ni loi ni justice'. His major characteristics are ingratitude and arrogance and his blinding by Odysseus shows how 'cette importune outrecuidance a finalement senti la main et vengeance divine'. The Cyclopean race were 'gens impies profanes et méprisant la religion et le service des Dieux, et adonnés à toute espéce de cruauté et barbarie'. Polyphemus was 'contempteur de piété et de sainteté. Mais d'autant que Dieu venge sévèrement telle impiété et profanation de son service, il reçut pour tout le temps de sa vie telle punition que méritoit sa témérité et cruauté.'[32] Elsewhere, the image of the Cyclops is frequently exploited as an emblem of political rule which has thrown over reliance on reason and is governed solely by the baser passions.[33]

Critics have observed that, by 1632, the atrocity of Pymante's blinding was already decidedly unusual on stage.[34] If Corneille chose so to shock his audience, it can only have been because it offered a particularly arresting scenic illustration of a theme central to the moral argument of his play. Certainly what follows (IV, ii, iii and iv) spectacularly illustrates the anarchical and anti-social character of Pymante's impiety. The storm conventionally reflects the moral and social confusion he has caused, but Nature in turmoil still respects the sacred person of the Prince, even if a thunderbolt kills his horse as he arrives on stage (IV, iii, 1275–8) and the half-blinded Pymante turns on the heir to the throne who has run to Dorise's defence:

> Je ne connais ici ni qualités, ni sang,
> Quelque respect ailleurs que ton grade s'obtienne,
> Pour assurer ma vie il faut perdre la tienne.
> (iv, iv, 1316–18)

This cyclopean outlaw has indeed no respect for Court, palace or temple, 'alliance ni parenté…il ne distingue le sang d'avec le sang…les parricides ne sont pas plus noirs ni plus horribles à ses yeux que les meurtres innocents qu'ils font à la chasse. Il n'y a point de crime qui lui fasse peur pourvu qu'il le mène où sa passion l'appelle.'[35] Le Moyne's topic here is the nature of lust and, if Pymante is well beyond the desire for Dorise which had originally driven him to crime, this description of the brutish anarchy of passion is apt enough to his motives and conduct in the course of the play.

Survival and success are the only values in Pymante's cyclopean world. Obstinately refusing providential justice its full share in his failure, even if he admits to the bankruptcy of his conduct he persists to the end in calling 'le sort' the mysterious force which confounds him:

> Je ne suis criminel sinon manque d'effets,
> Et sans l'âpre rigueur du sort qui me tourmente
> Vous pleureriez le Prince, et souffririez Pymante.
> (v, iv, 1772–4)

His grandeur lies not so much in denying the existence of that contrary force as in the determination with which he pursues an impossible victory. Crude though his characterization may be, his revolt against Alcandre's fairytale court hidden deep in the Scottish forests offers Corneille's first illustration of the extent and limits of man's heroic claim to self-sufficiency and foreshadows his first tragedy, *Médée*.

Médée, first performed in the winter of 1634–5, was published in 1639. Even if Corneille had not been anxious to follow Rotrou's spectacular supernatural effects in *Hercule mourant* of the season before, the subject was a natural choice as a development on Pymante's emphasis on vengeance in love, the powers of artifice, and the darker side of individual self-assertion. Seneca's 'Medea ferox' already offered a terrible image of heroic criminality, and Corneille contrives to transform her into a still more formidable figure by further emphasizing her self-sufficiency and pride. Yet Corneille also borrows from Euripides, who had presented Medea as an object of pity crushed by callous injustice, and his heroine never totally forfeits our sympathy in so far as she is presented as an abandoned wife driven by the baseness of others to the appalling excess of killing her own children. The resultant combination of terror and pity, as Corneille himself remarks in the 'Examen' of 1660, offers a telling political lesson by contrasting the moral stature of his heroine and the treachery of those on whom she takes her vengeance (GC, 1, 540).

Créon, King of Corinth, is the first and perhaps most ignoble of a number of pusillanimous rulers in Cornelian tragedy, unjust and weak kings who betray the dignity of their rank through an inability to rise above personal concerns. Seneca's Creon was little more than brutally hard-hearted, but Corneille enhances the political interest of the role by emphasising the self-defeating character of Créon's policy of deceit. Like Corneille's heroine, Seneca's Medea had accused the King of bad faith but, in the face of his callousness, had also stooped to the hope that by admitting her guilt she will be able to beg more effectively for refuge with Jason in an obscure corner of Créon's lands. In contrast Corneille's impenitent Médée retains a much greater moral force in her searing criticism of Créon's politic betrayals (II, ii, 393–5 and 442–6). Even where the political realities and popular convictions of seventeenth-century France precluded inclusion of an original passage where Seneca's Medea had openly proclaimed her scorn for kings, Corneille preserves the political lesson by inserting six lines of his own in which Créon fatuously protests at Médée's exposure of his unworthiness to rule (II, ii, 503–8). By remarking on Médée's indomitable courage, the King diminishes his own stature and unwittingly reminds the spectator how badly he wears the dignity of the crown. Médée's unflinching assumption of responsibility shames her betrayers and brilliantly contrasts with Créon's evasions and hypocrisy.[36] The ironic effect of such rhetorical flourishes of orthodox political sentiment is unmistakeably Cornelian but, like so much in this uneven exercise in the grand style, its political interest derives principally from Corneille's unexpected adaptation of comic talents to the task of displaying the values of a corrupt court playing at 'les grands intérêts'. Similar effects are achieved by the figure of Ægée, Corneille's most questionable addition to the original plot. The role is barely justified by the need to indicate Médée's legendary refuge and there is little that elevated diction can do to disguise this old king's ancestry in the traditional comic type of 'le vieillard amoureux', for all that he gives valuable relief to Créon's political ineptitude and lack of principle. So again Créon's homespun Machiavellianism in telling his daughter how to break her word shows how uncertain Corneille still was in controlling a tone appropriate to tragedy (II, iii, 534–40).

In contrast, Médée steals the play with her unshakeable assertion of the untrammelled force of the will. Even in so extreme a characterization, Corneille's first tragedy contains the beginnings of a more searching political argument which reveals the force for anarchy latent in vengeance, as Médée repays betrayal with betrayal through unnatural crime. A supreme artist in wrong-doing, she cuts herself off from the city of man by transforming vengeance into a final onslaught on nature and the social order. In the sacrifice even of her children, she realizes her terrible identity to the full and liberates herself from all social and sentimental ties by surpassing that earlier criminal sacrifice to love when she and Jason had escaped their pursuers by throwing her younger brother piecemeal into the sea:

> Il faut faire un chef-d'œuvre, et qu'un dernier ouvrage
> Surpasse de bien loin ce foible apprentissage.
> (I, iv, 249–50)

In one respect alone does Corneille preserve his heroine's humanity. True to the central interest of the play as a tragedy of passion, she can neither deny the love she feels for Jason nor bind his faithless heart to her, despite all her superhuman powers:

> La flamme m'obéit, et je commande aux eaux,
> Et je ne puis chasser le feu qui me consomme,
> Ni toucher tant soit peu les volontés d'un homme!
> (III, iii, 920–2)

She will only find freedom from that humiliating limitation in a last sacrifice of love which tears from her heart the passion which has ruled her life. In all her sufferings and hesitations which prepare the final scenes of vengeance, Médée's main claim to nobility lies in her fidelity to a love which she cannot and will not deny. With Jason lost, Corneille's heroine sets herself beyond the community of men, even as she resolves the conflict between the will to triumphant self-assertion and the servitudes of the heart. Blasphemously she sacrifices her love for both children and father in the name of outraged marital fidelity and, like all blasphemies, the deed is done in reverence of that which it destroys.[37] Until that final choice of exile from the human community (III, iii, 793–6), every betrayal by others only serves to prepare the grandeur of a heroic 'arrachement' by which seventeenth-century moralists believed the will could break free of the common bonds of humanity.[38] In sombre anticipation of more glorious future metamorphoses of heroic self-mastery, Médée accomplishes her 'chef d'œuvre' by abandoning everything but an awesome assertion of her unbounded pride. Transcending at last the pathos of her frailty as a woman rejected but still in love, she ascends to the horror of a final crime which both destroys her past self and creates herself anew.

Corneille later asserted that Médée's infanticide was a 'justice' which she 'se fait elle-même de ceux qui l'oppriment', although he did not deny that this vengeance was a criminal act (First *Discours*, LF, 43; GC, III, 122). But in 1634, an awareness of the moral susceptibilities of his public inspired him to make a major alteration to Seneca's closing scenes where Jason had protested that the impotence of the Gods before Medea's crimes called their very existence into doubt. In keeping with the conventional moral lesson of *Clitandre*, Corneille replaces this by a less blasphemous speech in which Jason stresses the excess of Médée's vengeance. Recognizing that he is powerless against the supernatural resources of a wife who has after all spectacularly escaped in 'un char tiré par deux dragons', Jason renounces all thought of vengeance, decides on suicide, and piously leaves retribution to the Gods (v, vi, 1649–52 and 1655–8). In a tragedy which had turned principally on the extremity of passion but which relied on the discrepancy between power and justice to produce the required elements of pathos and terror, Corneille concludes with the scandal of unpunished crime only to assert in the last fifteen lines that justice will ultimately prevail.[39] This last-minute deference to the providential convictions of the day is so unexpected that it can only strike us as a lame and incoherent conclusion to a work which impresses above all by illustrating the ways in which justice is invoked, but in its violation rather than its observance.

Because Médée's final self-sufficiency is only possible through her exceptional arts, and because Corneille sets so much emphasis on the supernatural and on spectacular stage effects in order to illustrate her powers, it is inevitable that, apart from a few fine moments of 'forensic', confrontation, the play's political argument lacks vigour. As prison doors fly open and chains fall at the touch of her wand, Médée can never do more than illustrate a dream of heroic autonomy couched in spectacular fictions. Médée herself reveals the degree in which moral significance has been sacrificed to this pursuit of the awesome and marvellous:

> Emprunter le secours d'aucun pouvoir humain
> D'un reproche éternel diffamerait ma main.
> En est-il après tout aucun qui ne me cède?
> Qui force la nature a-t-il besoin qu'on l'aide?
> (IV, v, 1255–8)

Voltaire was surely right to point out that Médée's claim to self-sufficiency loses much of its splendour once we are so constantly reminded that her powers are not restricted to purely human resources.[40] Since her magic, quite as much as her crimes, sets her outside the city of man, the larger moral significance of Corneille's play is constantly falsified by an emphasis on supernatural atrocity and terror which, in the early 1630s, was still believed to be the essential ingredient of tragedy.

Both Pymante and Médée develop a heroic characterization which, in variously illustrating the darker resources of the individual will to self-assertion, already raises moral and political issues of importance to Corneille's later drama. As yet, however, those issues are but superficially explored or imperfectly integrated into the action. Furthermore, the idealist depiction of Alcandre and the undignified Machiavellianism of Créon do little more than illustrate the most conventional of political arguments. In the last analysis, like the one-act tragedy contained in *L'Illusion comique*, both *Clitandre* and *Médée* are essentially dramas of passion rather than political drama, and both are seriously flawed by their excessive reliance on generic or textual models. *Médée* in particular represents a type of spectacular 'tragédie d'arrachement' which others were practising with equal success. On occasions the language promises better things, and never more so than in the brilliant set pieces of Médée's confrontations with Créon over statecraft and good faith, but the political context of Corneille's first essays in serious drama is too nebulous a fiction to carry any true applicability to present experience. Neither Alcandre's romanesque forest kingdom nor the magical and legendary universe of *Médée* provides the appropriate context for a searching illustration of the relationship between power and justice. Even if Corneille had not been so concerned with illustrating the terrible force of passion in *Médée*, legendary Corinth could never have offered the clear sense of social order and historical continuity so vital to his later political tragedies. The insufficiencies and incoherences of the moral argument of *Médée* may be partially masked by a heavy emphasis on the awesome and spectacular, but Corneille's first tragedy does at least show that his interests were moving – if somewhat uncertainly – towards the graver expressive possibilities of the stage. Greater social precision and the historical setting of *Le Cid* will at last ensure a solidity of moral and political argument which exceeds the conventional limitations of tragi-comedy, and bring forcefully to life what was to become Corneille's enduring tragic preoccupation with the freedoms and necessities of man's social experience.

4

Le Cid *(1637)*

The political significance of *Le Cid* gives it an intermediate position between Corneille's earlier dramas of passion and his subsequent tragic development of the historical 'beau sujet'. Corneille underlined the play's affinity with his later work when, in 1660, he maintained that if love 'se contente du second rang dans le poëme' – and he was writing of tragedy here – this was true even of *Le Cid*, 'qui est sans contredit la pièce la plus amoureuse que j'aie faite' (LF, 47; GC, III, 124). In this first *Discours* Corneille was writing of a work so polished up that it has been argued that we should distinguish two plays, a tragicomedy of 1637 and a 'classicized' tragedy after 1660.[1] However the seeds of Corneille's future development were there from the play's beginnings, for the love theme itself carried within it a broader political significance, since Rodrigue and Chimène's sufferings exposed irreconcilable tensions between their individual aspirations and the collective necessities of a state which, like France, was at a turning-point in its institutional development. *Le Cid* is so often discussed in Corneille's later statements about his practice (and so many later modifications to the original text affirm and clarify elements which foreshadow his later political tragedies) that there can be little doubt that he quickly came to see that his later distinction as a writer of tragedy had its origins in this play which he first presented as a tragicomedy.

While we have to be careful not to project Corneille's later preoccupations back on to the 1637 text, the original play's political argument suggests that it is excessive to speak of a 'second' *Le Cid*. Later changes certainly reveal a desire for greater elegance of expression, but they do not alter the original sense. Indeed some of these modifications of style contribute to our understanding of the original since greater clarity gives better relief to substantive issues which had been present, but less cogently expressed, from the start.

For instance the simple alteration of 'Ce qui fut bon alors ne l'est plus aujourd'hui' (1637) to 'Ce qui fut juste alors ne l'est plus aujourd'hui' (1648), produces a more harmonious line and also refers us more directly to the central political issue – namely the nature of justice and its relationship to time and circumstance. Other more substantial alterations of 1660 may be thought less welcome, since they mute the vigour with which politically contentious views had first been expressed, but even then they never run counter to the essential argument of the first version. This is particularly true of the Count's robustly disobliging expression of his views on the character and function of kings in a speech which gave rise to the earliest alteration of all – the omission in the first printed edition of a passage which had been spoken at the first performances of the play. This exclusion is recorded by Fortin de La Hoguette:

On a supprimé du manuscrit avec beaucoup de sagesse ces vers:
    'Ces satisfactions n'apaisent point une âme
    'Qui les reçoit n'a rien, qui les fait se diffame,
    'Et de tous ces accords l'effet le plus commun
    'Est de perdre d'honneur deux hommes au lieu d'un.'
Ce poison était bien subtilement préparé pour ne pas s'insinuer dans l'esprit de la noblesse qui n'en est déjà que trop infecté.[2]

Later variants, trimmed to the taste and political climate of the closing years of Mazarin's ministry, neither change the substance of the Count's arguments nor obscure the implications of the position he adopts. Elsewhere more extensive re-workings show that, with experience, Corneille could see how to make yet more striking his illustration of the political issues first raised in the 1637 text. An alteration of this kind is the revised layout of the opening scenes of Act I, which valuably sharpens the contrast between public and private concerns that is a central feature of the play. Most importantly, Chimène's first direct appeal to the King is clarified in Act II, scene vii (this becomes II, viii in 1656), and Corneille reinforces the objections she makes in her last speech in response to Don Fernand's command that she marry Rodrigue. Both changes give greater weight to Chimène's protests: indeed they give such relief to an issue already posed in the original that they suggest that Corneille, far from misunderstanding his play's political significance, wished to make its expression yet more telling, even as he brought it into line with later critical taste.

Corneille's 1648 alteration of the play's description from tragi-

comedy to tragedy was more than a simple matter of changing
fashions in dramatic nomenclature. In all forms of the text, the play
lacks the essential characteristic of tragicomedy, 'un accord
providentiel ou merveilleux entre l'ordre établi et les intérêts de la
passion'.[3] The new subtitle recognizes the degree in which his
tragicomedy had exceeded the limits of its classification by the
prominence it gave to the political significance of the lovers'
entanglement in public affairs.[4] Later modifications to Chimène's
two speeches simply emphasize the insolubility of a conflict of values
in the action which was already apparent in the play's 1637 form.
On this issue it is unfortunate that in 1660 Corneille himself
contributed to critical confusion. He was then involved in polemics
on the morality of the stage and was so anxious to rebut the
Académie's dismissal of his historical subject as unsuitable for
imitation that, to carry particular points, he argued in two directions
at once over what kind of a future was implied for the lovers in the
play's conclusion. The first *Discours* argues for Chimène's tacit
acceptance of marriage (LF, 49–50; GC, III, 126), while the
contemporary 'Examen' suggests that Chimène concludes the play
still opposed to becoming Rodrigue's wife (GC, I, 701). In the
Discours Corneille was anxious to meet the criticism that *Le Cid* failed
to conclude properly according to his definition of a complete action,
while in the 'Examen' he was preoccupied with defending his
heroine against charges of a lack of 'bienséance'. In both cases the
need to deal with doctrinaire criteria which were basically
unsympathetic to his play leads Corneille to special pleading of
doubtful use in a discussion of the play's true concerns and effects.[5]
If it were really necessary to decide on 'events' which fall outside the
fiction of the dramatic action itself, we need surely simply observe
that history affirms that the lovers did marry and that is what all
forms of the text indicate. Corneille's suggestion in the 'Examen'
that, by remaining silent, Chimène implies an enduring refusal to
obey the King is simply not supported by the text, either in its 1637
or 1660 form. There is indeed precious little to confirm a later critic's
view that only the earlier version 'ne se prêtait pas à séparer
Rodrigue et Chimène'.[6] The sense of both is that she will obey the
King's command:

> Et vous êtes mon Roi: je vous dois obéir.
>   (v, vii, 1830: [1637], GC, I, 776)
> Et quand un Roi commande on lui doit obéir.
>   ([1660], GC, I, 1508)

In truth, the problem of what happens *after* the play can only be matter for speculation amongst those who fail to distinguish between 'character' as it emerges in the more fluid imaginative space of the novel and as it is apparent in a dramatic 'role' which only exists so long as the play holds the stage. In the last analysis it is dramatic effect which matters, and the modifications which Corneille brought to his original text suggest that he was at least certain that the action itself was concerned less with the marriage of the lovers than with the obstacles to their union.[7] Thus the major question at issue in the last act is whether Chimène is, or is not, fully satisfied with the Don Fernand's decision, and whether her expression of obedience completely sets aside any reservations which she – or the spectator – may have about the justice of his command that she marry Rodrigue. Both versions seem clear enough on this and suggest that she will obey, for all that she remains convinced that only partial justice has been done.

The transitional character of *Le Cid* is also apparent in its double illustration of the theme of inextinguishable love. Appropriate to the romanesque flavour of tragicomedy, the theme lies at the heart of the lovers' predicament and also has a variant illustration in the role of the Infante. The latter role concludes earlier explorations of the theme of a willed liberation from the power of love in *La Place Royale* and *Médée*. In keeping with the play's political preoccupations, the Infante's attempts to deny her feelings are inspired by motives of rank and her suffering results from obligations placed on her within the political order. However, as she openly admits to the futility of her efforts, the reasons she invokes are closer to resignation than heroic self-mastery (II, v, 525–6). In contrast, Rodrigue and Chimène will build their destinies on that same undeniable force of love, transforming the theme into an illustration of the endurance of heroic idealism which Corneille rightly insisted had greater importance than a matter of simple sentiment. Political and social pressures are so closely linked to the lovers' fortunes, and so strongly influence their feelings and behaviour, that it becomes impossible to consider the latter without regard to the evolution of their social context. This foreshadows Corneille's future development as a political tragedian, above all concerned with the relation between individual identity and social and political circumstance, and reveals for the first time the treacherous relationship between heroic aspiration and the shifting perspectives and pressures of the political context within which individual fulfilment is inextricably involved.

Significantly, Corneille's next play would be an historical tragedy which, instead of returning to the love theme of *Le Cid*, directly addresses the political difficulties posed by heroic initiative at a turning-point in the history of the State.

History enters the Cornelian hero's world with the processes of institutional change evoked by the Spain of *Le Cid*. Don Fernand is the first of his line to call himself King of Castile and needs to assert his primacy over erstwhile peers like the Count if he is successfully to govern his subjects and extend his authority over those parts of the peninsula which are still in Moorish hands. His domestic and military problems are to be compared to those of the French monarchy in the 1630s, as aristocratic pride, individual rights, and local traditions yielded before the King and Cardinal bent upon a 'politique de gloire'. The same counterpoint between dramatic fiction and seventeenth-century French context is also apparent in the roles of Don Diègue and the Count, both of which evoke the powerful nobility who served in the King's armies but whose jealousies and hasty recourse to violence constantly revealed the potential for anarchy implicit in their exclusive pride.

The King's choice between two great lords for a position of eminence at Court sparks off the whole dramatic conflict and at once reveals the essentials of the Count's self-esteem. As antagonistic pride spirals into violence, his sarcasms and exasperation brilliantly show how quickly such men become a force for disorder in the State. It is not immediately evident that Don Diègue's values are the same as those of the Count, but this will become apparent later in the play. In the meantime Rodrigue's father has been accorded a signal honour and, disinclined to question the King's decision, he simply preaches obedience to royal authority.[8] On the other hand, the disappointed Count has no doubts about the injustice of Don Fernand's choice and so attempts to discredit the royal Court, alluding to intrigue and corruption. He even declares – most forcefully in the 1637 edition – that the King is no better than his peers and commands no more respect than did his forebears. The King's ungrateful preference for Don Diègue as his son's tutor is very evidence that, whatever he may call himself, he has not shown the justice to be expected of his rank. The Count's indignation appeals to the common belief that great men may rightly aspire to positions of authority and eminence, and that a proper sense of worth is not to be condemned. As late as the second half of the century even

Daniel de Priézac, protégé of Richelieu and Séguier, wrote with approval of such 'generous' self-esteem: 'C'est le propre du magnanime d'entrer en un superbe sentiment de son mérite et de sa vertu…Celui qui ne s'estime digne que des choses médiocres, il est modeste, mais il n'est pas magnanime, puisque c'est le vrai caractère de la magnanimité de ne trouver rien qui soit au-dessus d'elle.'[9] However, if the Count appeals to the noble conviction that his certain superiority has been ignored, he quickly forfeits all sympathy as his pride leads him into a series of veiled threats which turn into outright disobedience.

Furthermore the Count's braggart humiliation of a man enfeebled by old age casts an unfavourable light on his belief that present prowess in battle assures his claim to a coveted position at Court. In the Count's view of things, the fact that strength is still undiminished by age is sufficient proof of his superiority over Don Diègue, and wisdom and devotion have little to do with his claim to preferment. That Don Diègue also accepts these grounds for self-esteem is apparent when, in the climate of anger and violence natural to both noblemen, he is so humiliated by the Count striking the sword from his shaking hand. His soliloquy – 'O rage, O désespoir! O vieillesse ennemie!' (I, v, 235–62) – is only fully comprehensible once we recognize how important to those of his kind is the power of the sword. And indeed, when Rodrigue draws his own sword on his father's behalf and looks to his youthful strength to level the score in the manner demanded by his caste, he too accepts the values of his forebears, but with tragic consequences. It seems strange, once we reflect on the way the elder generation is presented in *Le Cid*, that some have argued that Corneille celebrates the values of the feudal order. We are certainly not invited to sympathize with the Count, and the aged Don Diègue tries the patience even of Rodrigue. When the Count derides Don Diègue, he does so in the name of a cult, shared by both elder men, of physical strength in the field. Rodrigue's impatience, however, springs from a conflict of values of intense interest to the contemporary audience and which lies at the very heart of the play, namely a differing assessment of the importance of love to the 'homme d'honneur'.

The play's opening presentation to the climate of anger and force peculiar to this elder generation of grandees brings out all the violence latent in their cult of a glory founded on primacy through 'les faits d'armes'.[10] The structure of the first act, especially in its later form, spectacularly illustrates the socially disruptive nature of this older order of aristocratic pride, as the women's private hopes and fears yield abruptly to 'une place publique' in which a clash of arms calls both individual happiness and the King's authority into question. Subsequent events, however, quickly discredit the Count's sense of superiority, for his fortunes themselves reveal the insufficiency of the quality on which he most prides himself when, in his turn, he is overthrown by a yet younger and stronger man. In an interesting comment on what was an urgent problem in seventeenth-century France, life according to the Count's values is presented as ruthless, egocentric, precarious to the point of impracticality, and dangerous to the larger interests of the community. Because the Count's self-esteem is entirely self-referring, he can only belittle the King as sole fountainhead of honour in the larger context of the nation. Inevitably he comes into conflict with Don Fernand, as self-infatuation blinds him to that other kind of 'magnanimité' based on a just self-valuation in relation to established authority:

> LE COMTE: ... Pour conserver ma gloire et mon estime,
>   Désobéir un peu n'est pas un si grand crime.
>   (II, i, 367–8)

There can be no place in the well-ordered state for one who so presumes on his sense of quality, since there is only room for one at the top – whether 'the top' is the post of tutor or throne. Yet the Count will brook no superior, and the first two acts of the play perfectly 'paint' the necessities of his combination of arrogance and ambition, prompting the spectator to consider what does indeed found a proper sense of worth within the social order.

Ten years after the play's first performance, Cureau de la Chambre was still concerned with this problem of integrating 'les grands' during the early years of Mazarin's continuation of Richelieu's policies: 'Les arrogants et superbes ... pensent que toutes choses leur sont dues et ils veulent avoir la prééminence. Ils se vantent et parlent avantageusement d'eux-mêmes, d'autant que la chaleur de la passion allume le désir qu'ils ont pour la gloire'.[11] Such men are universally condemned, not for their passion for glory but for their refusal to integrate their ambitions into the perspectives of monarchical governance. As Saavedra Fajardo observed, their pride is bound to conflict with royal authority: 'Los ingenios grandes, si no son modestos y dóciles, son también peligrosos porque soberbios y pagados de sí; desprecian las órdenes y todo les parece que se debe gobernar según sus dictámenes. No menos embarazoso suele ser uno por sus excelentes partes que por no tenerlas, porque no hay lugar donde quepa quien presume mucho de sus méritos.'[12] Corneille's count offers a far from extreme illustration of the menace to public order constituted by the great nobility's exclusive sense of tradition in France during the first half of the seventeenth century. As Balzac wrote, they are 'brouillons' who make trouble for everyone: 'Ils veulent être arbitres de leur devoir et de leur obéissance... Ils veulent servir à leur mode... Ces gens-là... se cabrent aisément contre leur maître. Ils ne sont jamais rebelles de dessein formé et par inclination du mal, mais ils le peuvent être par dépit et par ressentiment. Voulant servir, ils veulent servir en souverains.'[13] Gormas' haughty service, in demanding to be trusted to the exclusion of all others, renders him quick to take offence – or even to revolt – once he has not been singled out for the greatest honours. He may submit his life to the King, but this is a formality accomplished in terms of menace and challenge to a ruler who dare not accept the offer (II, i, 363 and 380). As Don Fernand is quick to recognize, this arrogance constitutes an immediate challenge to his authority (II, vi, 565–6).

There can be no accommodation with such self-infatuated claims to pre-eminence, as the King makes clear to Don Sanche:

> Un Roi dont la prudence a de meilleurs objects
> Est meilleur ménager du sang de ses sujets.
> Je veille pour les miens, mes soucis les conservent,
> Comme le chef a soin des membres qui le servent.
> Ainsi votre raison n'est pas raison pour moi;
> Vous parlez en soldat, je dois agir en Roi,
> Et, quoi qu'il faille dire, et quoiqu'il veuille croire,
> Le Comte à m'obéir ne peut perdre sa gloire.
>
> (II, vi, 597–604)

This makes an important distinction between military glory and the glory of loyal service – the latter alone being compatible with the general good as envisaged by the Crown since the former refers only to a narrower self-exaltation. More important still, a distinction is drawn between justice as it may appear to the individual, and justice as it can only be perceived within a King's concern for the larger interests of the community he rules. As the lovers become entangled in a conflict of rights which was as much at issue in seventeenth-century France as within this historical fiction of eleventh-century Spain, Don Fernand's difficulties in handling the Count's unruliness will increasingly invite the spectator to reconsider the various kinds of justice evoked in the play.

We have begun with the Count's values and behaviour because, even as they raise a political problem involving the King's authority, they also define the world within which Rodrigue and Chimène live out their love. For the moment, however, we should pursue the issue of authority, and consider the working of the King's relationship to these potentially unruly great servants. Like Louis XIII, Don Fernand badly needs to harness the latter's energies to the task of defeating his enemies. The Count's behaviour may contain within it the seeds of anarchy, but he is a warrior on whose service the King relies. His present conduct makes it clear, however, that his services are not a question of free gift but form part of more politic calculations of service and reward.[14] In these calculations, Gormas is not alone, any more than he really was in the attitudes he struck at the time of the quarrel, even though on that occasion Don Diègue's new honour had ensured that he disagreed with his rival. As subsequent events show, the only reason for the quarrel between the two fathers was that they disagreed on who had the better claim to honour. In all other respects, caste ambition and pride will lead both men into the same presumptuous claims on the King's generosity in return for service.

Faced with the Count's defiance, the King had said that the only true honour lay in obedient service of himself, since genuine virtue and worth could not be at variance with the royal will, final guarantee of social order. But Gormas 'serves' as General of the King's armies not according to altruistic notions of *générosité* in obedience, but because this position gives him a lever to personal advantage and repute. High position confirms his own high self-esteem, increasing his glory by public displays of prowess and by such honours as success in battle brings. By reproaching the King for ingratitude he debases the traditional idea of 'le service du Roi' into more mercenary calculations of exchange, asserting that Don Fernand is in his debt and has denied him his just deserts. Despite his fine language, the Count's resentment reflects an essentially opportunistic assessment of the market-value of service in terms of honours and impunities:

> Monsieur, pour conserver ma gloire et mon estime,
> Désobéir un peu n'est pas un si grand crime.
> Et quelque grand qu'il fût, mes services présents
> Pour le faire abolir sont plus que suffisants.
>
> (II, i, 367–70)

Don Arias' warning to the Count goes straight to the point:

> Quoi qu'on fasse d'illustre et de considérable
> Jamais à son sujet un Roi n'est redevable…
> Qui sert bien son Roi ne fait que son devoir.
> Vous vous perdrez, Monsieur, sur cette confiance.
>
> (II, vi, 371–2 and 374–5)

This is the ideal thesis – but the Count remains convinced that political reality dictates that Don Fernand simply cannot afford to punish him. His services will protect him from the consequences of what privately he admits to have been an over-hasty action:

> LE COMTE: Il a trop d'intéret lui-mëme en ma personne,
>   Et ma tête en tombant ferait choir sa couronne.
> DON ARIAS: Souffrez que la raison remette vos esprits.
>
> (II, i, 383–5)

Don Arias may well be scandalized, but the Count's cynicism proves justified. For all his displeasure, the King is acutely aware of his servant's military importance: unable to ignore present political necessity, he hesitates to punish a subject so indispensable to the war against the Moors. In the event he is spared a final decision on the matter: the duel with Rodrigue ensues and Gormas dies by the code of his own caste, while the King remains a bystander. But this turn of events does not obscure the fact that events have shown how an uneasy and fragile accommodation may tacitly be established between 'grand seigneur,' and monarch, as political necessity, rather than a principled reverence for shared values, edges both parties towards a shared recognition of reciprocal advantages to be gained.

The outcome of the Count's duel with Rodrigue means that this conflict between the King and his overweening subject goes unresolved. Don Fernand may condemn his great servant, but that he is constrained to make the best of his subjects' opportunistic pursuit of glory is made quite clear by Don Diègue, whose later conduct strikingly confirms that he is of the same school as Gormas. This may not have been apparent in Act I but, by the end of Act II, he too is found weighing the advantages to be gained from services rendered. It is this which lies behind his plea on behalf of his son, when he assumes Rodrigue's guilt only to insist on his own past services in a process identical to Gormas' earlier claims on the King's gratitude. Still more telling is the way the same logic inspires Don Diègue to urge Rodrigue to make amends for killing 'du royaume le plus ferme appui' by saving the State in his turn. At first the father urges his despairing son to seek a heroic death in defence of the realm, but this is quickly replaced by more practical advice on how to exploit possible victory over the Moors. In terms singularly apt to the way in which Don Diègue's caste associates its rights with the power of the sword, he argues that, if Rodrigue returns victorious from the field, the King will have no choice but to pardon him:

> ...Reviens-en plutôt les palmes sur le front,
> Ne borne pas ta gloire à venger un affront,
> Pousse-la plus avant, force par ta vaillance
> La justice au pardon et Chimène au silence.
>
> (III, vi, 1101–4)

The last two lines clearly indicate the disruptive character of aristocratic pretensions within the King's new order. Their importance to the argument of the play is equally clear in the 1660 variant which preserves the original sense in a less abstract, and still more shocking, formulation: 'force...ce monarque au pardon et Chimène au silence'.

Despite all the fine theory that the King is under no obligation to his subjects in return for their services, Don Diègue's advice to Rodrigue proves remarkably successful – so successful indeed that it gives retrospective support to the Count's earlier cynicism. Whatever the nature of Rodrigue's own motives in defeating the Moors, the practical effect of his victory on the King is unmistakable. When it comes to a decision on Rodrigue's guilt and a choice – which the King had earlier been spared in the matter of the Count's disobedience – between punishing a factious subject or pardoning and preserving the victor over the enemies of Spain, Don Fernand does not hesitate:

> J'excuse ta chaleur à venger ton offense,
> Et l'Etat défendu me parle en ta défense.
>
> (IV, iii, 1263–4)

Rodrigue's total submission and a king's concern for the greater interest of his realm justify Don Fernand here, but only if we forget the personal predicament of the lovers. If we recall Chimène's passionate appeal in the second act: 'Sire, Sire, justice' (II, vii, 653), and if we also recall that the King had then considered her claim so serious as to deserve discussion 'en plein conseil', the peremptory nature of this pardon can only provoke admiration for Don Diègue's sagacity. Furthermore, so long as Chimène pursues her personal appeal for justice, the suddenness of the King's pardon must also arouse misgivings. For the moment, however, it is sufficient to note that Corneille's play, in addressing the problem of reconciling political realism with ideal conceptions of monarchical governance, has located a common ground of 'intérêt' upon which 'grand seigneur' and monarch can reach an uneasy coexistence. This revelation of the practical pressures of a realist political morality according to which both lord and king find it expedient to operate is essential to the pathos of the remainder of the action, and brings us close to problems best treated by direct discussion of Rodrigue's and Chimène's entanglement in a rapidly changing political situation.

Before we turn to the lovers, however, we still need to examine Rodrigue's own motives and behaviour in 'le service d'armes', for these are not to be identified with the calculations of his elders. His conduct alone realizes an exemplary reconciliation between individual aspiration to glory and the larger interests of the community under the benign rule of the absolute monarch. Rodrigue's situation is very similar to that of the Count, but, while his victory favourably influences the course of Don Fernand's justice, he himself never seeks to exploit that victory to his own advantage or to constrain the King's judgement. Instead he perfectly illustrates Bodin's description of the special relationship of the 'Grand Capitaine' to the Monarch, as he puts into practice the theory of glorious obedience which had left the Count so unimpressed. Not once does Rodrigue try to evade the King's judgement of his guilt or innocence in defending his family honour: instead in obedience, faith, and homage, he lays his victory at his liege-lord's and sovereign's feet (IV, iii, 1243–6). Where both the Count and Don Diègue are exclusively concerned with their personal sense of worth, all that Rodrigue has, even to his victory, is the King's. By equating his honour with the satisfaction of serving Don Fernand, he becomes the very embodiment of 'le sage capitaine [qui] pour triomphe au retour de sa victoire, baissant la tête devant son Prince, dit "Sire, votre Victoire est ma gloire"'.[15] By his victory over the Moors, Rodrigue is content to add 'l'éclat à la majesté de [son] Prince' and his greatest glory is to have become the King's sword-arm, 'son épée et son bouclier, l'appui du sceptre... l'honneur et le rempart de son Etat'.[16]

What had been mere surface show in the case of the Count becomes spectacular reality in the great narration scene of Act IV where the national hero stands purged of any taint of opportunism. Rodrigue may have been called 'Le Cid' by the Moors, but the King has no reason to mistrust such a title and will urge Rodrigue to yet greater conquests (v, vii, 1851-4). The king knows that if Rodrigue is a great and powerful lord who, in the words of a contemporary panegyrist, 'mérite et possède les hommages des peuples... adorateurs de sa vertu', he is still his loyal subject. Far from threatening the Crown, the hero's personal triumph enhances its authority, since his conquests of lands and hearts are only 'pour accroître les vassaux de son Prince. Notre Héros est quelque chose de notre Roi'.[17] Thus, for the public hero at Court, all is well. But the news that Chimène is on her way to call for justice produces a sudden drop from victorious exhilaration to the constraints of harsh reality, making it brilliantly and cruelly apparent that the King can only reward the saviour of the State by abolishing his original offence at the expense of the one other person whom Rodrigue, this time as lover, most seeks to serve.

Within this socio-political context, Rodrigue and Chimène illustrate for the first time what will become Corneille's characteristic preoccupation with the tragic theme of the hero constrained by factors beyond his control. Corneille later saw how *Le Cid* foreshadowed his mature work when he cited the play in the second *Discours* as the first illustration of the subject-matter of his tragedies, where

[Les personnages tragiques] font de leur côté tout ce qu'ils peuvent, et qu'ils sont empêchés d'en venir à l'effet par quelque puissance supérieure... L'action de Chimène n'est... pas défectueuse pour ne perdre pas Rodrigue après l'avoir entrepris, puisqu'elle y fait son possible, et que tout ce qu'elle peut obtenir de la justice de son roi, c'est un combat où la victoire de ce déplorable amant lui impose silence. (LF, 92-3; GC, III, 153)

As this implies, Rodrigue's and Chimène's fortunes show how the values to which they hold and by which they seek to live as lovers will only imperfectly be recognized or acknowledged, either within their fathers' code of values or within the practical necessities which govern Don Fernand's nascent state. That exchange of advantages which defined the common ground upon which the King achieved some degree of reconciliation with his jealous and powerful subjects becomes the reef upon which the lovers' ideals founder, leaving Rodrigue and Chimène unfulfilled and unreconciled within a community wedded to expediency and harnessed to the necessities of changing time and circumstance. The unique quality of *Le Cid* lies in the way in which, as a tragicomedy, it evokes intense sympathy for the young lovers yet, through that very sympathy, also evokes in the spectator a tragic perception of their vulnerability to the pressures of their social and political context. In the care with which Corneille's tragicomedy shows how those conflicting pressures each appeal to an order of values which contains within it some partial perception of justice, *Le Cid* not only invites us to suffer with the lovers but conveys through their misfortune a profoundly tragic insight into the treacherous relationship between heroic idealism and political necessity.

In order to see how this is achieved, we need first to look back to Rodrigue's and Chimène's conduct prior to the victory over the Moors. At this point a conflict of family honour unfolds without regard to the King's displeasure. Caught up in a rivalry which was none of their making, first Rodrigue and then Chimène are forced to choose between upholding or rejecting the paternal values which had caused their present misfortune. Since Corneille's choice of subject-matter is intent upon profounder truths than the illustration of irresistible love, both Rodrigue and Chimène acknowledge themselves to be inextricably part of the order from which they spring. Both recognize that their sense of personal worth can only be confirmed in action within the order which surrounds them and that their love must be expressed in fidelity to their participation in that order. But this recognition brings with it a bitter paradox, since they can only give practical expression of their feelings for each other through a code of honour which accords so little importance to love that it sets at risk any hope of union. Both are quick to see the peril of their situation, Rodrigue in his *stances*, and Chimène implicitly in her appeal for justice to the King and explicitly in her private confidences to Elvire. However, their meeting at dead of night (III, iv) establishes a new dimension to a conflict which, until then, had simply been a tale of love sacrificed on the altar of filial piety and family honour. Both come to see that by upholding the point of honour they do not destroy their love, but find the only way to sustain it at its most elevated level. Thus, while they remain faithful to the point of honour, their conduct invests it with a nobler significance than had previously been apparent in their fathers' behaviour. By following the course of honour they demonstrate

much more than fidelity to family pride: instead they find in
personal integrity the means to show the heroic quality of a love
which transcends the flawed morality of the vendetta.

Rodrigue is the first to set out the procedures of this 'amour
héroique', but he does so without fully expressing the higher morality
with which such honour in love may be invested.[18] Either from
despair or for reasons of sentimental blackmail he falls back upon the
harsh principles of traditional vengeance:

> Je t'ai fait une offense, et j'ai dû m'y porter,
> Pour effacer ma honte et pour te mériter.
> Mais, quitte envers l'honneur, et quitte envers mon père,
> C'est maintenant à toi que je viens satisfaire.
>
> (III, iv, 905-8)

Chimène follows suit, but only in so far as Rodrigue's conduct
challenges her to match him in courage:

> Tu n'as fais le devoir que d'un homme de bien;
> Mais aussi le faisant, tu m'as appris le mien...
> De quoi qu'en ta faveur notre amour m'entretienne
> Ma générosité doit répondre à la tienne:
> Tu t'es, en m'offensant, montré digne de moi,
> Je me dois par ta mort montrer digne de toi.
>
> (III, iv, 921-2 and 939-42)

At this point she raises their conflict to a higher level than that of a
heroic demonstration of love through the accomplishment of the
bloody code of the point of honour. Explicitly she refuses the
destructive hopelessness of that crude and imperfect kind of justice
which lies at the heart of vengeance, that talion law which repays
wrong with wrong and death with death. Instead she finds room for
hope by invoking a justice as constant and perfect as is her love for
Rodrigue. When Rodrigue killed her father he committed an
'offense' because, regardless of who first provoked the conflict, the
justice of that death was never more than partial. In recognition of
this, Rodrigue has now offered Chimène the chance to 'level the
score'. But Chimène sets this aside as a reciprocity of 'offenses', even
as she acknowledges that, in justice, Rodrigue must expiate the
wrong he has done her. Refusing the sword, that violent symbol of
feudal pride, she fuses the language of justice with that of love:

> Va, je suis ta partie et non pas ton bourreau.
>
> (III, iv, 950)

This offers a crushing moral judgement on the tainted quality of feudal vengeance and is not to be dismissed either as an evasion of Rodrigue's challenge or as the weak procrastination of a woman in love. Indeed, if we are to believe history and the period's many *galleries* of 'femmes fortes', there were many heroines who would not have hesitated to act as Rodrigue proposes. Chimène, however, makes it clear that love itself defines her future course of action, rather than the violent ethos of the point of honour. By setting aside the sword which Rodrigue presses upon her, she rejects the partiality of a code in which the avenger is plaintiff, judge and executioner. Listening to her love for Rodrigue, as well as to love of father and respect for family pride, Chimène initiates a call for a more inclusive justice which alone offers hope of a resolution to their conflict. As she explains to Rodrigue, in appealing to the Crown, she remains true to a love which is not to be associated with the brutal imperfections of the vendetta:

> Si tu m'offres ta tête, est-ce à moi de la prendre?
> Je la dois attaquer, mais tu dois la défendre,
> C'est d'un autre que toi qu'il me faut l'obtenir
> Et je dois te poursuivre et non pas te punir.
> (III, iv, 951–4)

Looking beyond private vengeance, she places all their hopes in the King, the one person in the State who claims to embody a higher and reconciling justice which can fully resolve this conflict rooted in the feudal order which his rule has superseded.

This transference of the seat of justice from the avenging hand of the offended party to the decisions of the Crown reflects a critical aspect of the institutional evolution of seventeenth-century France. Avoiding contemporary controversy over official condemnation of feudal 'satisfactions' by the sword, Chimène's appeal for justice in Act II had simply contrasted Don Diègue's values with her faith in the inclusive justice of the monarchy.[19] There the great lord's belief in his freedom to settle a vendetta was opposed to the King's obligation to defend the rights of his individual subjects:

> CHIMÈNE: Au sang de ses sujets un Roi doit la justice
> DON DIÈGUE: Une vengeance juste est sans peur du supplice.
> (II, vii, 659–60)

On her return from Court, hard pressed as she is by Rodrigue,

Chimène will not be seduced from her position by his abrupt recourse to pathos:

> Rigoureux point d'honneur! hélas! quoi que je fasse
> Ne pourrais-je à la fin obtenir cette grâce?
> Au nom d'un père mort, ou de notre amitié,
> Punis-moi par vengeance, ou du moins par pitié.
>
> (III, iv, 767–70)

That appeal to pity may lead her first to deny any such hate and later to admit that she still loves him, but vengeance has no place in her aspirations. The fine litotes of her reply movingly balances a confession of love with her desire for a higher equity:

> CHIMÈNE: Va, je ne te hais point.
> RODRIGUE: Tu le dois.
> CHIMÈNE: Je ne puis.
>
> (III, iv, 973)

She will not follow a bloody ethos which defies natural justice and dishonours her love by piling one 'offense' upon another. She will not act alone and from some narrowly personal view of her wrongs, taking in hate and anger yet another life she loves as payment for a life she loved.

By insisting that Rodrigue expiate his offence, Chimène upholds an ideal of justice which is of the same order as are her feelings for Rodrigue and which – if it does indeed inform the order of the society within which she lives – permits her without shame to express her love for him (III, iv, 980–2). Loving Rodrigue by this heroic pursuit of a more perfect and inclusive justice, she resolves to follow, but in her own way, the harsh path upon which their fathers have set them. There is indeed some justice in her father's cause and to that she must hold true, not least because adherence to that cause is itself proof of her love for Rodrigue – even though that proof carries with it the risk of death. At last a unity of purpose which will govern all their future conduct is established between the lovers, as argument gives way to a common understanding of their predicament:

> RODRIGUE: O miracle d'amour!
> CHIMÈNE: Mais comble de misères.
>
> (III, iv, 995)

Rodrigue may still exult in the sublimity of a love which points the only way towards hope, but Chimène knows that the future will bring further suffering. Harmony is only achieved in the perception that their love must be expressed in terms of a procedure of honourable conflict which is alien to love and from which the King alone can offer them hope of deliverance. From now until the end of the play Chimène cannot – and will not – abandon her appeal for that conciliating justice, both because she is truly her father's daughter and because she loves Rodrigue. Tragically, only Rodrigue – because he loves her as well as he is loved – appreciates the importance of her appeal to the King. Far from momentarily grasping the significance of Rodrigue's exposition of 'l'amour héroique', Chimène has not only understood it but, by appealing to the Crown, has invested it with a nobler significance than could ever be contained within the exclusive preoccupations of feudal pride. In no sense is her pursuit of Rodrigue a simple reaffirmation of feudal honour in the salving of her 'gloire'. It stems instead from a love for Rodrigue which is at one with what has been rightly called a 'terreur sacrée' rising from the very roots of her being in the urgent conviction of the operative reality of Divine and Natural Justice.[20] We will understand little of the deeper significance of her pursuit – and feel nothing of the pathos of the lovers' situation – if we do not recognize how complementary are the moral force of her love and her natural sense of outrage and rightness. Henceforth both will support her in repeated appeals for a dispensation of royal justice which alone can put an end to conflict.

If we look to Chimène's series of appeals to the King we are faced with a number of lines the later variants of which set out the issues more cogently than did the 1637 text and show how keen the later Corneille was to give relief to issues which had always been central to the deeper moral significance of his play. Chimène's first appeal is a case in point. In place of a confused exchange of half-lines between Chimène and Don Diègue, in which she first calls for justice, then calls for vengeance, and finally cries out that Rodrigue has killed her father (ii, vii, 653–8), the more cogent text of 1660 systematically lays down the three counts on which Rodrigue must be judged:

> D'un jeune audacieux punissez l'insolence.
> Il a de votre sceptre abattu le soutien,
> Il a tué mon père.
> (1660 edition: ii, viii, 650–2)

Moving as it does from public offence to private wrongs, the order of this series of accusations proves significant, since it is to the last charge alone that Chimène will adhere and on this charge alone she will not receive satisfaction.

At this point in Act II the King, anxious to avert the anarchy of two families at war with each other rather than confronting the greater threat of the Moors, is impressed by the arguments on both sides and recognizes an issue not lightly to be decided. He responds with courtesy and gravity and, as fountain-head of justice, makes a solemn promise:

> L'affaire est d'importance et, bien considérée,
> Mérite en plein conseil d'être délibérée...
> Je vous ferai justice.
> (II, vii, 743–4 and 747)

This undertaking acknowledges that Chimène has challenged him to uphold his claim, in the immediately preceding scene, that his just rule has superseded the order of feudal pride by virtue of a higher wisdom (II, vi, 599–604). But as we have seen, Rodrigue's victory over those invading Moors and his return to submission transforms the King's response to Chimène's appeal. For all that Rodrigue still acknowledges himself guilty of having wronged one who, as the King's ward, has as urgent a claim on Don Fernand's justice as any of his subjects, the King abolishes the 'offense' in the light of Rodrigue's signal service to the State. Forgetting his earlier conscientious gravity, the King perfunctorily decides the matter by brushing individual rights aside:

> Crois que dorénavant Chimène a beau parler,
> Je ne l'écoute plus que pour la consoler.
> (IV, iv, 1265–6)

At the news of Chimène's arrival, Don Fernand's embarrassment is as good as an admission that this is not to have fulfilled his subject's trust:

> DON ALONSE: Sire, Chimène vient vous demander Justice.
> LE ROI: La fâcheuse nouvelle, et l'importun devoir!
> (IV, iv, 1340–1)

The bitter irony of this turn of events is that Rodrigue, by virtue of his services to the King, has himself become the unwitting cause of Chimène's isolation. Yet Don Fernand's sudden pardon of Rodrigue has made much clearer that the 'reason' which perforce governs his justice is 'la raison d'état', in consideration of which he must set aside the individual rights of his subjects. Rodrigue's present obedience and victory over the Moors have certainly cleared him of Chimène's first two charges, but her third charge – that he must pay for the death of her father – still stands. It has become clear that, if Chimène had earlier gained the King's attention, this was as much because Rodrigue had flouted the royal will and endangered the State as because he had killed the Count. Now that Rodrigue has returned as saviour of the State and made full and proper protestations of submission, his misdeeds are set aside in recognition of the greater good. In this Don Fernand is perfectly consistent with his earlier claim to represent the larger interests of his Kingdom but, as his embarrassment makes clear and Chimène's protests at Rodrigue's present immunity show, it is equally apparent that he has sacrificed his subject's individual right to justice on the altar of political advantage.

It is not as if the spectator has not been well prepared for the King's decision to pardon Rodrigue and set the interests of State over Chimène's claim to justice. In Act II, scene vi, Don Fernand had invoked the traditional comparison of the human body and the body politic, explaining how the royal head acts upon a perception of Right which is denied to his subject members.[21] None in the seventeenth century would have disputed the natural good sense of this. Royal prudence was not only more comprehensive; its decisions were also held to express the principles of a Natural and Divine Justice which originally established and now maintained the order and hierarchies of society. After Rodrigue's exhilarating account of his victory, the King's grateful pardon immediately strikes the spectator as justified, and is likely to have had the same effect in 1637. But the sudden announcement of Chimène's arrival offers an early example of a characteristically Cornelian use of reversal which abruptly faces the spectator with the need to reconsider the deeper implications of what he has just witnessed. Chimène's return to Court at once raises the question of how far Don Fernand's abolition of Rodrigue's offence in killing the Count may be held entirely to satisfy those dictates of Divine Law and Natural Justice which guarantee his own position. It was no less than Natural Justice which Chimène came to claim of him, and now her protests raise grave uncertainties about the sufficiency of a decision which seems to owe too much to political expediency. In truth the King can only appear to be both just and unjust: by pardoning Rodrigue he has undoubtedly served the general interest, but he has also laid himself open to the reproach that his decision is tainted with an opportunism which makes short shrift of the individual rights which he has sworn to protect.

Presentation of such a conflict voices rather more than seventeenth-century doubts about the justice of 'lettres d'abolition' and special royal pardons.[22] Its ambiguities tellingly reflect contemporary uncertainty before institutional changes which had been precipitated by a national emergency and which increasingly revealed a divergence between, on the one hand, an essentially religious concept of monarchical governance and, on the other, more executive forms of governance in response to the demands of 'la nécessité évidente'. We have seen in the first part of this study how disquiet on the matter grew as Richelieu's ministry wore on, and how it had become a primary concern of those more courageous theorists who strove to reconcile ideal conceptions of public morality with the realities of effective political decision.[23] Five years before *Le Cid*, the Conseiller d'Etat Cardin Le Bret had argued in his *Traité de la souveraineté du Roi* that the subject had to recognize and obey the superior wisdom of royal commands. While acknowledging that obedience might be limited by individual conscience when the King's commands were unjust, he also held that exceptional cases of extreme necessity still obliged the subject to carry out orders which, if unjust, still served the public good.[24] This firm argument that 'necessitas...omnem legem frangit' did little to reassure other theorists who, neither diehard idealists nor harsh realists, remained uncomfortably aware of both sides of the argument and tried unavailingly to reconcile Christian morality with a pragmatic recognition of the necessity for invoking 'la raison d'état'.[25] Trying to find a proper place for prudent statecraft within their Christian convictions, they called it a supreme art of government given only to kings and held that such vice-regents of God on earth exercised a wisdom wider in its providential perspectives than that of the individual subject. But this was simply to re-invest that special royal prudence with all the aura of a Right Reason emphatically to be opposed to expedient decisions offensive to Christian morality. Priézac typifies such embarrassments as he tries to preserve some political realism within his Christian convictions. He introduces a category of positive royal prudence – 'une raison universelle' or 'raison dominante' – which, if ultimately sanctioned by Natural and

Divine Law, permits him to flirt with more pragmatic traditions of political theory. A king's prudent concern for public welfare is only subject 'par accident' to the Divine and Natural Laws which ultimately underpin the public good. The area in which this 'raison dominante' may function is strictly limited to necessary inflexions of 'les loix ordinaires', or man-made positive law.[26] But since Priézac recoils from entirely setting aside the dictates of Natural and Divine Law, all he has achieved by this is to give the Prince licence to claim higher inspiration in bending such man-made laws. Despite all his efforts, Priézac has still not succeeded in actually justifying such 'prudence'. Given his over-riding conviction that Providence is at work in the world, it would even seem to follow that any inflexion to positive law would be of little practical benefit, since, by setting positive law at odds with Divine and Natural Law, the King has disserved the long-term interests of the community.

Priézac's tortured reasoning illustrates the extreme difficulty encountered by Christian theorists who grasped the nettle of finding some place for political pragmatism within their larger providential vision of the nature and destiny of the State. Don Fernand's pardon of Rodrigue might seem to be just such an instance of 'la raison dominante' at work, as Rodrigue's 'offense' is set against his present importance to the nation. But Chimène's claim to justice is there constantly to remind us that, by discounting Rodrigue's killing of her father and by leaving him unpunished, the King has done much more than waive mere man-made law. He has set aside God's own commandment, 'Thou shalt not kill', and failed to mete out that sovereign justice which the sanctity of his rank was held to enshrine. Already in Act III, iv, where Rodrigue claimed he had done 'une bonne action' according to the feudal code of honour, he had also admitted that the same deed wronged Chimène as an individual and was one for which he should be punished (III, v, 911). As the action moves to a close, he alone recognizes the enduring validity of Chimène's third accusation (that he had killed her father), and does so because his love for her makes him the only one to share her conviction that the appeal for justice must be satisfied. By passing over this 'crime', the King has dashed the lovers' hopes in him as the inspired repository of a wisdom finally capable of fully reconciling public and private perceptions of what is just.

That Chimène is not simply locked in a demand for feudal vengeance is made clear once the King has told her that, after all,

Rodrigue had not died in battle. That revelation is met with bitter protestations against the tyranny of a governance which sets the interests of State above the satisfaction of individual rights. Chimène is reproved for her vehemence but, after the King's deceit over Rodrigue's supposed death, her misery and confusion forcefully remind the spectator that any royal decision, no matter how well meant, can only raise misgivings once it operates beyond the constraints of natural justice:

> Pour lui [Rodrigue] tout votre Empire est un lieu de franchise,
> Là, sous votre pouvoir, tout lui devient permis,
> Il triomphe de moi, comme des ennemis;
> Dans leur sang épandu la justice étouffée,
> Aux crimes du vainqueur sert d'un nouveau trophée,
> Nous en croissons la pompe et le mépris des lois
> Nous fait suivre son char au milieu de deux Rois.
>
> (iv, v, 1388–94)

The King quickly rejects this one-sided presentation of his treatment of Rodrigue, claiming that, by tempering the rigour of the law, it is he who has equity on his side:

> Ma fille ces transports ont trop de violence.
> Quand on rend la justice, on met tout en balance:
> On a tué ton père, il était l'agresseur,
> Et la même équité m'ordonne la douceur.
>
> (iv, v, 1395–8)

This appeal to the traditional royal virtue of 'douceur' is persuasive but exceptional in a play which, considering that it is set in the Christian society of medieval Spain, depicts a world strikingly short on the virtues of forgiveness and charity. However Don Fernand's argument proves insufficient not only to convince Chimène but even to confirm himself in the belief that Rodrigue has no case to answer. After further hesitation, he agrees to Don Diègue's proposal of a judicial duel in which God's authority alone will decide the matter, and further compounds the lovers' difficulties by the command that Chimène must marry the victor.[27]

By the end of Act iv the lovers' misfortune is complete and the tragic trap has been sprung. Through his victory Rodrigue has become 'Le Cid' and the indispensable guarantor of the King's authority. But that same victory and its consequences have made Rodrigue himself into the insuperable obstacle to his and Chimène's hopes of reconciliation, totally dependent as they are on the resolving equity of the King's decision. There is nothing left for Rodrigue to do but support Chimène's appeal and submit to a duel which is the consequence of the King's own inability to resolve their conflict. This is a cruel irony indeed, since Chimène finds herself once again subject to a decision by the sword when it had been she who first turned to the King in hopes that his wisdom could deliver them from such a process. Rodrigue can do no more than win the duel, thereby winning and losing Chimène yet again, and limit the bloody consequences of the combat by sparing Don Sanche's life. Thereafter he is a powerless bystander in a final act principally given over to Chimène's refusal to accept the sufficiency of the King's justice in commanding her to marry the victor of the combat.

As the initiative passes from Rodrigue to Chimène, a difficulty in performance of the play is the way in which the latter's repeated protests can seem unnecessarily to defer the final reconciliations which the spectator expects of tragicomedy. However, if we consider the last two acts of the play in the light of the political issues which have already been raised, Chimène's persistence foreshadows a dramatic process which Corneille will use to yet more disquieting effect in *Horace*. By pressing the moral issue to the extreme in the final act of *Le Cid*, Corneille leads events to a disconcerting conclusion which forces the spectator to reassess the quality of previous action and reveals the intractability of the moral and political problem inherent in the King's failure fully to resolve a conflict created by that feudal order which he seeks to supplant. With the opening of Act v, and Chimène's desperate appeal to Rodrigue to save her from an imposed marriage (v, i, 560–7), the lovers' claims on the spectator's sympathy are never stronger, since the painful paradoxes of their situation vividly illustrate the human price to be paid in this conflict between the individual's claim to justice and political expediency. Furthermore, in the anguish and confusion produced in Chimène by the prospect of this second duel and its outcome, we are never allowed to lose sight of the fact that the Count's death is not something which can conveniently be forgotten. To the end it remains both a heroic proof of Rodrigue's love and an 'offense' which, if not expiated, will separate him and Chimène for ever as unsatisfied litigants and lovers.

But before the result of the duel is known, the Infante's attempts to bridge the public and private worlds of the play establish that balance of argument which will become the hallmark of Corneille's political tragedy. Trying to bring Chimène to accept a 'reasonable' compromise after Rodrigue's victory over the Moors, she echoes her father's pragmatism by arguing that, since the public good is constantly to be redefined in relation to time and circumstance, so the character of what is just or unjust must change. Had Corneille permitted Chimène to accept this view that justice is subject to the needs of the moment, he would have betrayed her characterization and undone all of the profounder political argument of his play. It is no surprise that Chimène's fiercely idealistic identification of her love with unbending moral integrity leads her once again to protest:

L'INFANTE: Ce qui fut bon [juste: 1660 edition] alors ne l'est plus
               aujourd'hui.
               Rodrigue maintenant est notre unique appui...
               Tu poursuis en sa mort la ruine publique...
               C'est générosité quand, pour venger un père,
               Notre devoir attaque une tête si chère:
               Mais c'en est une encor d'un plus illustre rang,
               Quand on donne au public les intérêts du sang...
               Que le bien du pays t'impose cette loi;
               Aussi bien, que crois-tu que t'accorde le Roi?
CHIMÈNE: Il peut me refuser mais je ne me puis taire.
               (IV, ii, 1185–6, 1192, 1207–10, and 1213–14)

The Infante's own experience may discredit her advice that Chimène should simply stop loving Rodrigue, but her contention that the pursuit of private vendetta must yield to the greater 'générosité' of service to the country remains a powerful one, both in its dramatic context and in its application to France in the late 1630s. But the argument assumes that Chimène still persists in a position which she herself had long since rejected in Act III, iv, when, for love of Rodrigue, she had been the first to set aside the old order of feudal vendetta and put her trust instead in the King's wisdom. Because the King has still not satisfied Chimène's call for justice, love itself for Rodrigue must impel her to refuse this advice. Were she to accept it she would both dishonour the quality of her love and, in weary disillusionment, accept that the many affirmations of the sacred character of Kingship were nothing but empty words disguising the sorry truth that a perfect and inclusive justice can never inform the order of human affairs.

Subsequent news of Rodrigue's victory over Don Sanche should speedily have brought matters to a happier ending, but Chimène still pursues her lover in a manner which shows that, by the closing scenes of the play, the future author of *Horace* and *Cinna* has become less intent on bringing about a comfortable resolution to his tragicomedy than on pushing to the bitter end the tragic illustration of a moral impasse. After Chimène's tragicomic confusions over the identity of the victor in the second duel and Rodrigue's safe return from the field, the final scene seems at last to promise a long-awaited tragicomic reconciliation. Instead, with Rodrigue's explicit understanding and approval, Chimène persists in her challenge to the King that he has not done her justice. Since Corneille has now removed all other possible motives for resistance, this continued opposition to marriage shatters the conventional tragicomic pattern and emphasizes once again how the political argument has led to tragic impasse. Chimène has no reason to fear for her reputation since her conduct has provoked public sympathy and even admiration, and the King speaks for all his Court when he assures her that

> Ta gloire est dégagée et ton devoir est quitte.
>
> (v, vi, 1792)

Did Chimène simply fear public condemnation, she could now marry Rodrigue. Yet still she protests, and Rodrigue alone does not expect her to yield since only he – because he loves her – knows that her refusal stems from the desperation of love itself. Because he too shares in that love, he understands the supreme importance of her appeal and offers once again to expiate his offence:

> Je ne viens point ici demander ma conquête:
> Je viens tout de nouveau vous apporter ma tête.
>
> (v, vii, 1803–4)

No matter who was 'l'agresseur', Rodrigue knows that by avenging his honour through the death of Chimène's father he had performed both an act of love and an as yet unpunished wrong. Neither King nor Court appreciate the fierce idealism which inspires both lovers, fuelling their certainty that, if Rodrigue married her now, this would force her to betray her love for him in betraying her debt in honour to her father. Were Rodrigue so to claim her as his prize, he would be taking her by that same sword which, still stained with her father's blood, she had physically and morally refused to coun-

tenance in Act III, scene iv.[28] As her equal in love he will not be party
to her humiliation while he is strong in his good fortune at Court. He
alone recognizes that, if Chimène were to heed the King and accept
him without reservation, she would be accepting a man ready to
profit from her helplessness and marrying a lesser man than the one
he is and whom she cherishes.

It is not surprising then that, as the play completes its illustration
of an insoluble dilemma, Chimène once again refuses Don Fernand's
advice. In the strongest of terms, but still to no avail, she challenges
Don Fernand to dispense that royal justice which alone satisfies and
reconciles both private and public interests. It is not difficult to see
why the original 1637 text was suppressed, since its reference to time
and the marital bed too blatantly exposed the scandalous nature of
the King's command that they marry – so scandalous indeed that
both Scudéry and the Académie considered it sufficient to render the
subject unfit for imitation on the stage:

> Sire, quelle apparence a ce triste Hyménée,
> Qu'un même jour commence et finisse mon deuil,
> Mette en mon lit Rodrigue, et mon père au cercueil?
>   (v, vii, 1832–4: 1637 edition)

Corneille's second version, by a process of artful omission, avoids
drawing attention to this impropriety of the King commanding a
daughter to marry her father's killer only a few hours after the duel.
Instead, its more abstract language turns our attention to the
substantive issue of the injustice of that command:

> Rodrigue a des vertus que je ne puis haïr,
> Et quand un Roi commande, on lui doit obéir.
> Mais à quoi que déjà vous m'ayez condamnée,
> Pourrez-vous à vos yeux souffrir cet Hyménée?
> Et quand de mon devoir vous voulez cet effort,
> Toute votre justice en est-elle d'accord?
> Si Rodrigue à l'Etat devient si nécessaire,
> De ce qu'il fait pour vous dois-je être le salaire,
> Et me livrer moi-même au reproche éternel
> D'avoir trempé mes mains dans le sang paternel?
>   (v, vii; GC, I, 1508: 1660 edition)

No final plea could more sharply remind us that the King's
command has failed to reconcile public and private interests.
Chimène's appeal to the inviolability of the individual subject's
rights goes unanswered, but in its emphatic eloquence it cannot go

unheeded by the spectator. Don Fernand, necessarily preoccupied with the moment and the changing pressure of circumstance, evades the question and offers hope of solace in the obscuring powers of passing time and the infirmity of men, whose memories fade and judgements change:

> Le temps assez souvent a rendu légitime
> Ce qui semblait d'abord ne se pouvoir sans crime.
>
> (v, vii, 1839–40)

The King's advice is kindly but, like his final words to Rodrigue as he refers to a point of honour transcended long ago in Act III, scene iv, is not of a kind to match the idealism and constancy of the two young lovers. It is nonetheless a memorable line with which he concludes the tragicomedy as best he can:

> Pour vaincre un point d'honneur qui combat contre toi
> Laisse faire le temps, ta vaillance et ton Roi.
>
> (v, vii, 1865–6)

Chimène will obey the royal command and Rodrigue will go on to a triumphant future which will make his name a legend of heroic valour. But nothing can disguise the fact that the central moral and political issue remains unresolved in this drama of lovers uncompromisingly united in love and conflict – a drama which leaves its audience more profoundly aware of the difficulty of living, of the limitations set upon all men by the march of time and circumstance, and of the pity and waste of that which, but for human frailty, might have been achieved.[29]

As the text stands in both its original and its later forms, the final scene of the play remains profoundly disquieting, for all that it winds up the action at the level of tragicomedy. If *Le Cid* still continues to enlist our sympathies for the suffering of the lovers, this is because it shows that neither the feudal order nor the new order of Don Fernand's State can satisfy their pursuit of an unchanging justice capable of conciliating both private and public experience. By illustrating the obstacles which changing political circumstances place in the way of the lovers' fulfilment, *Le Cid* shows how heroic self-fulfilment can never be fully realized so long as those ideal values are neither apparent nor operative in the society of men. In this sense it already announces the future political tragedy of *Horace*, built on the same irreducible conflict between, on the one hand, the hero's striving for a completeness of self-definition in which he may gloriously transcend the shifting perspectives of a nation's history and, on the other, his inextricable entanglement in time and changing political circumstance.

The strength of *Le Cid* lies in the way in which our sympathy for the lovers' predicament leads us to reflect on the nature and exercise of justice and shows how universal is the human longing for its realization in the world. Some narrow sense of justice impelled Rodrigue to support and defend his own and his father's honour, and this groping apprehension of justice is freely shown to lie behind even the bloody ramifications of the 'point of honour'. So again, an honourable perception of justice lies behind the King's prudence with its well-intentioned – but equally insufficient – preoccupation with the general welfare of the State to the denial of his individual subjects' rights. Furthermore, as lovers, neither Chimène nor Rodrigue can claim to have perfect justice on their side but, privileged in the moral idealism with which their love inspires them, they alone know that this is so. Instead of claiming justice to be their own possession, they alone seek it beyond themselves in calling for a royal justice the inclusiveness of which will bear witness to the sanctity of the King's authority. Sainte Beuve thought that Don Fernand speaks too often 'en bailli',[30] but this is not simply because he lacks experience in kingship or that 'il n'était peut-être pas assez absolu sur les grands Seigneurs de son royaume', as Corneille suggested in the play's 'Examen' (GC, I, 702–3). It is because the play has shown that his governance lacks the supremely conciliating moral authority which marks the true divinity of kings.

Le Cid offers neither an unqualified apology for the pretensions of a centralizing monarchical order nor an exaltation of the values of those who opposed that process. Instead the political impasse which lies at the heart of the closing scenes of *Le Cid* movingly reflects the disquiet of many before the Cardinal-Minister's sharp inflexion of French institutions towards firmly centralized government by King and Council. Vividly it expresses opposition not to that process itself but to the inequities and suffering which, as we have seen in the first part of this study, were caused by an order of governance which, in the name of expediency, invoked 'la raison d'état' at the expense of more inclusive and traditional definitions of legitimacy. In this sense the play may well reflect a cultured Rouennais lawyer's recognition of the realities and pressures of political decision, even as it expresses his hesitations before the practical implications of contemporary policy. Both reverence for the sacred origins of royal justice and a courageous recognition of the lessons of present necessity inform *Le Cid*. In the broadest of terms, Corneille's first masterpiece offers a moving insight into a critical moment when France was hard pressed by her enemies and when Frenchmen had good reason to be aware of the need for some sacrifice of individual and traditional rights in the interests of firm government. Unequivocally, Corneille's play recognizes this need for men to rise above particularist and factious jealousies if common enemies are to be driven back. But equally clearly the lovers' predicament affirms the need for the supremely harmonizing values which were traditionally held to be enshrined in the sanctity of royal authority, and reflects the anxieties of those who saw that any appeal to political expediency set at risk traditional and individual rights long guaranteed by the monarchy.[31] By so constantly moving the spectator to sympathy for the lovers, *Le Cid* also brings its audience to a heightened awareness of the need for an order of governance which can ensure individual fulfilment within the larger context of the collectivity.

But such echoes of contemporary concerns, no matter how poignant, are insufficient to explain the play's lasting appeal. That may better be understood if we recall the Infante's question when she asked Chimène what she hoped to obtain from the King, and if we in turn ask ourselves what is the nature of that justice which she seeks and what the nature of the expiation which Rodrigue must make. Not the least of the beauties of Corneille's play lies in the way it shows that, of himself, no man can give an answer to that question – for all that by our very nature we would long to be able to do so. The enduring emotional force of *Le Cid* stems from the way it leads us into that longing, as its young lovers illustrate the universality of our aspiration to justice and the impossibility of its satisfaction within the flawed terms of the world that men have made for themselves. Seventeenth-century religious conviction held that man could only find fulfilment within the social order when both individual and public good were clearly seen to be complementary, for only then could he realize himself in love and service of a community ordered and informed by the eternal and unvarying dictates of God.[32] If men are to achieve such a political harmony, as Mugnier observed, heroes and kings need a wisdom given to few indeed:

une sagesse par laquelle l'homme se conduit sans faute et sans reproche non seulement dans la vie particulière mais encore... publique, exposé à la censure de tout le monde qui le regarde. La politique est une science qui enseigne comme il faut gouverner les peuples, comme l'on doit se comporter dans les hautes dignités et dans les grandes charges, et comme l'on peut se démêler des intrigues qui embarrassent les affaires publiques et en sortir à son honneur.[33]

The emotional force of *Le Cid* draws us far beyond conventional adherence to the idealist convictions which lie behind this heroic programme. It is to that more perfect order that Rodrigue and Chimène unavailingly aspire, and the thrust of the play's political argument still leads us to wish that the wider circle of 'le Bien Politique' could indeed be brought into harmony with 'le Bien Moral', even when we perceive how often it is not. The lovers' final impasse in *Le Cid* reflects the same idealism, but with a poignancy which foreshadows the way Corneille's future political tragedies were again to explore the significance of his times. As he began work on *Horace* in the midst of fierce debate over this play, Corneille could have been in no doubt that he had made a worthy beginning to what was to become a lifelong preoccupation with the tragic history of the triumphs and failures of idealism and ambition in the face of political necessity.

5

Horace *(1640–1)*

For seventeenth-century Frenchmen, the history of Rome embraced the most spectacular illustrations of heroic achievement and offered a supreme example of civic order. The Roman citizen was a very model of public service, combining the individual virtues of constancy and patriotic devotion with a military genius and political skill which might now ensure for France its own universally civilizing exercise of power. Balzac added to these qualities Rome's achievements in painting, sculpture, architecture, and political thought, and the ideal of Roman civism acquired a further gloss of French *honnêteté*, combining heroic *gravitas* with the urbanity of a seventeenth-century salon. This celebration of civic virtue, elegance, and eloquence was to inspire the ideals and taste of the age of Louis XIV, but its first major development occurred in the closing years of Richelieu's ministry.

A major initiative in this government-led attempt to redefine the nation's military and cultural perspectives was the Cardinal's foundation in 1635 of a literary Académie, to establish and propagate the manner which would be a noble successor to Roman eloquence.[1] A number of historical, and particularly Roman, plays appeared shortly after that date, presenting a renewed image of France through their evocation of Rome's earliest days and of its transformation from Republic into Empire. Thus *Horace* (first performed in the early months of 1640 and published in January 1641) was not the first tragedy to exploit Roman history in order to illuminate the moral and political significance of the country's widening military ambitions. But *Horace* is exceptional in this revival of historical tragedy for the moral inclusiveness and breadth of historical vision with which it illustrates Rome's ascent to power. In its more problematic treatment of the political significance of Rome's first steps to Empire, Corneille's first Roman tragedy rises far above his rivals' more narrowly programmatic re-interpretations of history and illustrates political issues which are much more broadly representative of the ideological debates of the day.[2]

After Mairet's *Sophonisbe* (1635) a number of dramatists had looked for the same successful mix of sentiment and high politics in the history of other *femmes fatales* of antiquity. Typical is Benserade's *Cléopâtre*, dedicated to Richelieu in 1636 and prefaced by a dedicatory sonnet in which the poet even raises Cleopatra from the dead so that she may march in Richelieu's triumph. Similarly Scudéry's *Didon* of 1637 presses the Carthaginian Queen into defence of Richelieu as the enlightened liberator of nations subject to the hegemony of the house of Austria. In the same season even Lucretia was twice revived, first in Chevreau's politically confused *La Lucresse romaine* and, more interestingly, in Du Ryer's fiercely anti-tyrannical *Lucrèce*, dedicated to the Duc de Vendôme who was involved in a series of conspiracies against Richelieu before his disgrace and exile in 1641.[3] In the case of those dramatists who sought to create a more austere political tragedy in service of Richelieu, the great heroes of Roman antiquity seemed ideally suited to a valorization of the Cardinal's political vision. Livy, Dionysius, and Plutarch were primary sources of their subject-matter and, in the context of Corneille's creation of *Horace*, the most interesting hero to be re-exploited was Coriolanus, a subject which twice appeared in 1638 in plays by Chapoton and Chevreau.

Instead of exploiting the rich ambiguities of right and wrong inherent in Plutarch's history of this Roman hero turned enemy of Rome, both playwrights present Coriolanus in a manner carefully tailored to suit the political education of their public. Chapoton's *Le Véritable Coriolan* (1638) was dedicated to the Cardinal himself and much praised by Richelieu's côterie of dramatists. Since the play is far from regular in form and shows an archaic predilection for high-flown rhetorical set pieces, this favourable prejudice in a quarter critical of the irregularities of *Le Cid* can only be explained by its political content. The play condenses the action to Coriolanus' banishment from Rome and his return as besieger, his rejection of the people's delegation, his final yielding to his mother's entreaties, and his murder by the Volscian chief Aufidius. Chapoton's principal intention seems to have been to flatter the Cardinal and woo the nobility by stressing the superior wisdom of a patrician senate which has no sympathy for the folly and ingratitude of 'ce monstre jaloux',

the common people. To the clear advantage of Richelieu beleaguered by popular discontent and the multiple conspiracies of the
disaffected great families of France, he presents Coriolanus' sense of
personal worth as a pride which no longer has its place in the new
order of the State. This angle suited Ministerial apologetics, but is not
easy to integrate into a coherent development of the action, and
Chapoton has some difficulty in keeping his audience's allegiances
clear. The closing scenes are obviously intended to warn rebel
noblemen of the risks and contradictions of disaffection, but
Coriolanus is also presented as a well-intentioned man whose pride
has led him into the destructive folly of treating with the enemies of
Rome, just as Gaston d'Orléans treated with Spain in the 1630s. As
Coriolan bitterly observes:

> Je me suis laissé choir au bas du précipice:
> Vos propres ennemis sont devenus les miens.
> J'ai perdu pour vous plaire, et l'honneur et les biens.
>
> (IV, vii)

Despite such occasionally striking lines, Chapoton's characterization
of Coriolan is too thin and inconsistent to support what might have
been an interesting mix of arrogance and frailty, as the audience
seems variously invited to pity and detest both the disdainful hero
and an ungrateful Roman people.

Equally disappointing is Chevreau's *Coriolan*, dedicated to the
diplomat Bautru, in 1638. This varies the theme of an attack on the
unruliness of the 'grands' by presenting Coriolan as an unnatural
war-machine consumed by selfish pride and a lust for vengeance. In
a remarkable exercise in hyperbole he longs to punish his
countrymen:

> Démolir leurs remparts, et briser leurs autels,
> Et faire enfin que l'air devienne si funeste
> Que même les corbeaux y meurent de la peste.
>
> (I, i)

Set on revenge, even if this be at the expense of Rome and his family,
Coriolan is driven by an insatiable 'faim de gloire' which expresses
itself most intensely in his fury at the people's ingratitude. Once
again, however, Richelieu's *protégé* fails to achieve affective and
intellectual coherence in his play. This monster abruptly mutates
into a figure of pathos: ruminating on the extremity of his situation,

he prepares for his edifying final redemption in *stances* reminiscent of
Le Cid:

> Maudite et coupable patrie
> Faut-il encor que je te prie
> De pardonner mes mouvements?
>   (III, iii)

Hereafter he is shown to be seduced into disloyalty by the Volscian
Aufidius and belatedly is given a noble line to describe the necessities
in which he has become entangled:

> Ayant mal commencé je dois finir de même.
>   (IV, vi)

With the close of the play Coriolan courageously faces death after
reconciliation with his mother and his country. The audience is now
invited to regret his assassination by perfidious Volscians when, to an
understandably angry Volscian senate, this 'reborn' servant of
Rome has made a clean breast of his patriotic and filial reasons for
deserting his new allies and defending again the interests of his native
city:

> Il est vrai que j'ai tort, et je dois l'avouer,
> Obligeant des ingrats on ne m'en peut louer.
> Ce peuple m'a banni, je soutiens sa querelle:
> Il fut impitoyable, et je lui suis fidèle.
>   (V, v)

All of this amounts to a considerable impoverishment of a powerful
and richly ambiguous subject, as the historical facts are used to put
the common people in their place and persuade the nobility, more
by rhetorical effects than by coherent dramatic argument, that love
of motherland and natural love of the family are entirely compatible
with aristocratic self-esteem. As treatments of the historical material,
both plays offer a poor contrast with the thought-provoking even-
handedness which was already a characteristic of Plutarch's *Life of
Coriolanus*.

We have to look to Corneille's *Horace* (1640, published 1641) if we
are to find any such moral comprehensiveness in another play of the
period concerned with Rome's earliest history and with a Roman
hero who became the enemy of the city. As the long-awaited
successor to *Le Cid*, *Horace* was almost certainly intended to show
Corneille's critics how a more independent-minded and more gifted
poet might treat the ambiguities of heroic pride and military
ambition caught in the complexities of political necessity. Thus the

play picks up a number of major themes voiced in the earlier
Coriolanus plays, notably that of the exceptional individual's
relation to a 'peuple stupide...qui voit tout seulement par l'écorce',
and of the difficult integration of individual heroic valour into the
collective interest. However, in exploring the theme of national glory
and the relation between violence and valour, Corneille distinctively
broadens the political argument by illustrating with unusual
emphasis the human cost of Rome's advance to universal empire.

In order to see how *Horace* reflects the way in which contemporary
perceptions of Roman achievement came to be modified in the harsh
light of the French experience during the closing years of Richelieu's
ministry, we must look elsewhere than to inferior historical tragedies
by Corneille's rivals. Of other roughly contemporary accounts of
Rome, the most favourable is Balzac's *Discours sur le romain*, composed
and circulated in the late 1630s and first published in 1644. This has
often been likened to *Horace* as a celebration of a heroic ideal of
devotion to the State, but it was conceived less as an exhortation to
patriotic loyalty than as a literary showpiece in which Balzac could
display both learning and eloquence to Madame de Rambouillet's
salon. Since publishing *Le Prince* (1631) Balzac no longer enjoyed the
Cardinal's goodwill, but in the late 1630s he still supported
Richelieu's foreign policy because he was convinced of the need to
overcome the external threat of Spain. Accordingly *Le Romain*
celebrates Rome as 'la boutique où les dons du Ciel étaient mis en
œuvre et où s'achevaient les biens naturels', and praises a civic
virtue in which self-discipline was 'le fondement de l'Empire et la
source des triomphes'. The Roman hero's supreme virtue was his
unswerving devotion to the interests of the city: 'Il estime plus un
jour employé à la vertu, qu'une longue vie délicieuse, un moment de
gloire qu'un siècle de volupté...Il ne connaît ni nature, ni alliance,
ni affection quand il y va de l'intérêt de la Patrie...il n'aime ni ne
hait que pour des considérations publiques.'[4]

This very literary exposition of an ideal virtue contrasts sharply
with Balzac's insistence elsewhere on the practical limits of human
capacity in the flawed world of political realities. Setting aside
Lipsius' providential vision of Roman glory, *Le Prince* had already
placed the history of Rome within a much less confident interpretation of the history of human endeavour and presented the
pursuit of empire in a more critical light, arguing that Rome's
dominance was built on a lust for power which respected neither

Divine nor Natural Law. More chasteningly he pointed to the moral
ambiguity of the heroic devotion upon which Rome's grandeur had
been built and unfavourably contrasted her military ambitions with
those of Louis XIII, whose only wish was to bring justice to the
oppressed: 'Les particuliers étaient vertueux, mais la République
était injuste. L'utilité qu'ils méprisaient au logis, était la fin de leurs
délibérations au Sénat: et quoiqu'ils donnassent de beaux noms à
leurs entreprises et les colorassent d'une générosité apparente, elles
étaient pourtant toutes remplies d'intérêt, et allaient ou tout droit,
ou par quelque route détournée, à l'accroissement de leur Empire.'[5]
By the very last years of Richelieu's ministry a completely
disenchanted Balzac sharply distinguished between the prosecution
of war for just ends and what he saw as the tyrannical and
vainglorious ambitions of the man he privately called a purple-robed
Tiberius. No longer convinced of the justice of a war which only
prolonged divisions between the Catholic brotherhood of Europe, he
shared in widespread hopes that Richelieu's death and Mazarin's
new ministry would bring a change of policy. In 1643 he wrote to the
Queen Regent, urging her to try diplomacy and persuasion: 'La
politique profane a beau déclamer sur le chapître de la réputation et
des avantages: elle a beau préférer un peu de bruit et un peu d'éclat
à la solidité du bien public...Ce ne peut point être votre dessein
d'acharner les fidèles contre les fidèles.'[6] The only way he could now
reconcile his desire for just government and peace with national pre-
eminence in Europe was by calling for a victory over brother
Catholics through the persuasiveness of moral superiority.

The author of *Horace* has often been presented as pre-eminently
the poet of Roman virtues in keeping with Balzac's more positive
view of Rome in *Le Romain*, but it has rightly been observed that
Corneille's idealism 'se révèle beaucoup moins simple, et simplifiant,
qu'on ne le croit trop volontiers'.[7] Certainly we miss the full breadth
of the political argument of Corneille's first Roman tragedy if we
only listen to the confident voices of Horace, his father, or Tulle, and
Balzac's changing perception of Roman civic virtue and imperial
ambition is as relevant to Corneille's *Horace* as it is to the later
depictions of Rome to be found in *Cinna*, *Polyeucte*, *La Mort de Pompée*
and *Nicomède*. This is less a question of debt or influence than a
matter of common experience and common ground, as both authors
responded to contemporary events in the light of a shared humanistic
culture. That culture also belonged to other writers of the 1630s and

1640s, who also expressed their admiration of Rome and their reservations about the morality of its Imperial conquests.

In the case of *Horace*, the most telling text is Du Bois Hus's *Le Prince illustre* (1645). Having in vain solicited the patronage of Richelieu, its author attached himself to the Condé family and, in this panegyric of the young Duc d'Enghien, holds that antiquity offers nothing to compare with his patron's heroism at Rocroi. Central to this argument is the belief that every past act of heroism was morally tainted. Thus Du Bois Hus calls on Rome to consider the evidence of her most venerated heroes:

> Recherche avecque soin tous leurs faits héroiques
> Tu les verras tâchés de marques tyranniques,
> D'un esprit qui ressent ton premier fondateur,
> On voit bien qu'ils ont eu des brigands pour leur pères,
>   Qu'un fratricide est leur auteur,
> Et qu'un rapt violent leur a donné des mères.
>
>   Le plus noble de leurs combats,
> Et le plus bel endroit de tes vieilles histoires,
> C'est ce coup où le Ciel te donnant trois victoires,
> Fit Albe ta sujette, et mit son trône à bas,
> Deux rivales cités au front de leurs armées,
> Albe et Rome en six corps, parurent enfermées,
> Jalouses d'emporter le droit du premier rang,
> Trois guerriers contre trois, ayant choisi leur homme,
>   Rachetèrent avec leur sang
> L'honneur de leur pays, et le sceptre de Rome.
>
>   On vit six escadrons vivants,
> Six parents divisés en deux partis contraires,
> Six soldats alliés, six amis adversaires,
> Six frères devenus leurs propres poursuivants;
> Un cruel généreux, le reste des Horaces,
> Porta son fer rougi du sang des Curiaces,
> Au sein de leur amante, et de sa propre sœur.
> La nature, et l'amour sortirent de son âme,
>   Et pour être ton défenseur
> Un mari fit mourir trois frères de sa femme.[8]

The last line shows that, if Du Bois Hus has chosen the history of the combat of the Curiatii and Horatii as his primary historical evidence, this is because he has recently seen or read *Horace*. By referring to a wife of Horatius who is sister to the Curiatii, the panegyric reflects its author's own response to Corneille's play, since this marriage is the dramatist's invention and Sabine, as Corneille's 'Examen' puts it, is 'un personnage assez heureusement inventé' (GC, I, 841).

In recounting the events of the combat and murder of Camille, Du Bois Hus comes so close to the language of Sabine and Curiace that he might well have had Corneille's text to hand:

> Que de crimes dans un bonheur,
> Où la loi d'amitié, du sang, de l'alliance,
> Du devoir, de l'amour, cède à la violence,
> Qu'exerce dans une âme un triste et fier honneur,
> Où même la valeur pour être sans égale
> A dû paraître enfin sacrilège, et brutale,
> Où l'on est plus prisé, plus on est inhumain;
> Pour être généreux, il faut être barbare,
>   Meurtrier pour être romain
> Et le moins de pitié rend la vertu plus rare.
>
>   Albe prise est un beau larcin.
> Horace est un vainqueur, quatre fois fratricide,
> Ce père qui le sauve après le parricide
> Tue encore sa fille en louant l'assassin:
> Rome n'est qu'une ingrate après cette conquête
> Ayant mis prisonnière une si noble tête,
> Et tenu le salut de son sauveur douteux,
> Et comme elle vient d'Albe, en domptant cette ville,
>   Son triomphe est toujours honteux,
> Où la mère paraît sous les pieds de sa fille.[9]

Proceeding to a discussion of Caesar's achievements, Du Bois Hus chooses Pompey's defeat and death after Pharsalus as his second major instance of the moral ambiguity of the great figures of Ancient Rome. The choice suggests that he had also seen Corneille's most recent Roman tragedy, *La Mort de Pompée*, in the season of 1643–4 (or had at least acquired the text when it came out in 1644) and put it to his own use in expanding on the heroism of the future Condé.[10] In fact, the text offers rather more than a contemporary view of the equivocal morality of Roman imperialism, giving us a rare indication of how *Horace* itself was understood by some of Corneille's contemporaries. We will recall Curiace's tirade, which concludes with the following lines:

> Je rends grâces aux Dieux de n'être pas Romain
> Pour conserver encor quelquechose d'humain.
>   (II, iii, 481–2)

At the original performance, Voltaire tells us, this speech 'fit un effet surprenant sur tout le public et les deux derniers vers sont devenus un proverbe, ou plutôt une maxime admirable'.[11] *Le Prince illustre* confirms that Voltaire was not projecting his own views back on to the seventeenth century in so warming to Curiace's opposition of humane values to the harshness of Roman virtue.

Equally interesting amongst contemporary judgements on Rome are Nicolas de Campion's *Entretiens*. These frequently refer to Rome in a debate which has the Cardinal's methods very much in its sights, and where both Richelieu and Rome earn a mixture of admiration and condemnation. In one of the discussions it is suggested that the prudent ruler should rely on force and fear if he is to govern with any efficacy – a principle 'dont on prétend que notre ministre se sert comme un parfait modèle de politique'. Discussion, however, is slow to start because none of the friends, not even the only *esprit fort* present, is willing to argue for such methods: 'Les sentiments se trouvaient pareillement tous si disposés à condamner le gouvernement présent que chacun garda le silence' (*Entretiens*, p. 351). One of the friends, however, finally agrees to defend the indefensible, since he has 'l'esprit tout rempli des maximes de quelques politiques de notre Cour' (p. 354). In support of his argument he cites Rome's foundation as proof that its grandeur was built upon a distinctive willingness to sacrifice natural ties of affection to the larger interests of State: 'La ville de Rome ne s'éleva si haut sur les dépouilles de ses ennemis, qu'après que les fondements en eurent été, s'il faut ainsi dire, cimentés avec le sang de celui qui avait voulu choquer l'autorité de son fondateur, quoiqu'il fût son frère' (p. 359). At once the objection is raised that, while Rome's greatness was indeed founded on Romulus' criminal disregard for natural law, this guilty past caused the city's final downfall. In terms carefully attuned to contemporary anxieties about Richelieu's foreign policy, it is explained that the seeds of later ruin were already present in the criminal violence with which Rome pursued imperial power: '[Elle] se fit payer à elle-même la peine d'avoir lâché la bride à son ambition, et changé le saint objet de défendre ses alliés et de protéger les plus faibles, à une profession presqu'ouverte de vouloir étendre les bornes de son empire' (p. 382). Another of the friends agrees and, like Du Bois Hus, observes that the greatest of deeds of Rome's greatest heroes were disfigured by criminal ruthlessness: '[Ils] ont donné sans doute des preuves de courage et de grandeur d'âme au

delà de toute croyance humaine; mais par combien de crimes n'ont-
ils point terni leur vie?...Ce mélange de mauvaises qualités et de
vertu ne défigure pas peu le beau génie de ces grands hommes'
(p. 388).

   Discussion of the Cardinal himself in the eleventh *Entretien*, 'De la
conduite du Ministre', enlarges on this moral ambiguity in heroic
achievement. Although Richelieu is condemned for the Machiavellian treachery of executing Chalais, the friends admit that he
possesses undeniable greatness. The key to Richelieu's contradictory
character and 'esprit de domination', as he enslaves even the Muses
with his new Academy (p. 453), is his 'soif insatiable de gloire' (p.
445). In this Richelieu is not as corrupt as some of his friends claim,
but neither is he beyond reproach. He is instead that rare
phenomenon of a man possessed by 'le propre génie'. Proposing the
same double evaluation of heroic personality, first in potential and
secondly in action, that Corneille was later to apply to Cléopâtre in
his first *Discours*, the speaker explains what he understands by this
term, offering a view of heroic ambiguity comparable with the
character of Horace, whose ambitions and conduct similarly provoke
both consternation and awe:

Il est certain que ceux qui s'y abandonnent [au propre génie] sont capables
de grands biens et de grands maux: tout le bien qu'ils font ne vient ni du
raisonnement ni de la réflexion sur les obligations auxquelles la vertu ou la
raison les engagent, mais du simple mouvement de je ne sais quel noble
instinct: tout le mal qu'ils causent ne procède ni d'une mauvaise inclination,
ni d'une malice affectée, mais d'une certaine impétuosité de nature qui veut
détruire tout ce qui s'oppose à eux. Et comme ils prétendent être envoyés
ici-bas pour conduire ou pour réformer le monde, sans se mettre en peine
des révolutions qu'ils y causent, ils élèvent ce qui leur plaît, ils rabaissent ce
qui leur fait ombrage, détruisent tout ce qui leur nuit; persuadés qu'ils ne
sont point obligés de rendre d'autre raison de leur conduite que leur mission
prétendue pour réduire les choses dans un meilleur état. (pp. 469–71)

   Despite this attempt at a balanced judgement, the general tenor of
the *Entretiens* is fiercely opposed to Richelieu, and we have not
quoted them as offering some kind of 'key' to the political
significance of *Horace*, for Corneille's position was very different from
that of active dissidents like the Campions. Nonetheless the *Entretiens*
again show how, in response to the times in which the play was
written, the glories of Roman history were also evoked as examples
of the darker side of military ambition and the politics of conquest.
This theme is so essential to *Horace* that the play cannot simply be

associated with the Cardinal's propaganda machine as a dramatic celebration of heroic devotion to a triumphant state. As we shall see, the play rises to tragic significance precisely because it also explores the moral ambiguity of the pursuit of empire, as its hero is called to triumph and to a final disaster which has its origins in the equivocal morality of the political order to which he has devoted his life.

The essential element in the argument of Corneille's later political tragedies – man's servitude to time and changing circumstance – came to the fore only in the last two acts of *Le Cid*, when Rodrigue's victory over the Moors insolubly complicated the lovers' fortunes. However the pathos of their final impasse was muted by the King's appeal to time as a friend, an evocation which provided the tragicomedy with its happy ending and looked forward to future contentment as bitter memories faded. The insult which caused the lovers' misfortunes may have represented a persistence of past values into the present political juncture, but *Le Cid* never invited the spectator to contemplate the future destinies of Spain – and with good reason, since the north of France had only recently been invaded by Spanish soldiery. Don Fernand was certainly concerned for the extension of his kingdom, but his decisions remained at the level of expedient response to the pressures of the moment. Only with the explicit comparison made in *Horace* between Rome and France do we encounter a temporal context which, by embracing past and future, permits the fullest development of Corneille's political argument. In evoking both Rome's origins and its destiny to be the mistress of the world, the play's presentation of history in direct comparison with the present French 'politique du gloire' represents a new departure which tragically generalizes the implications of Corneille's dramatization of the tensions between hero and state.

From the opening scenes of *Horace*, the theme of a transcendent order mysteriously at work behind the history of Roman achievement is strongly emphasized. Repeatedly both Romans and Albans reflect on past deeds in relation to the purposes of the gods and, in resolving to act in the present crisis, assume a role in a universe whose temporal perspectives stretch from the earliest days of the city to the divinely sanctioned glories of a universal *Imperium* and its final ruin. *Le Cid* began with premonitions of future unhappiness, but *Horace* powerfully develops the significance of this opening convention as Camille's dream is first misinterpreted, only to be finally understood as an inspired prefiguration of future events. Chimène

had only the uncomprehending, if well-intentioned, advice of Elvire
and the Infante; but from the start of *Horace* the women seek
illumination from the gods through augury and prayer and receive
reassurances which – like the dream – are misunderstood but prove
to be equally prophetic. This emphasis on the omnipresence of the
gods and on the inscrutability of their purposes is certainly important
to the tragic universe of the play and, by constantly recalling the
mystery of the providential perspectives within which present
tribulation has its place, it establishes the broadest of contexts
within which the spectator is invited to weigh the larger significance
of present events.[12]

In evoking, like Balzac, the obscurity of the providential forces
which shape the affairs of men, the play raises an issue of supreme
importance to the hero. If Horace is to realize himself to the full, he
must know his place within this larger purposive order. Seconded by
that ordering force he stands assured of success and public
recognition, just as – should evil fortune befall him – disgrace will be
providential punishment of a pride which has failed to recognize the
limits of human prudence unassisted by the gods.[13] Nowhere is this
mysterious dimension to individual initiative more apparent than
when the play evokes the theme of nascent empire. *Horace* never
permits us to forget the importance of the present conflict to the
accomplishment of Rome's future domination of the world. Destiny,
in Corneille's first truly historical tragedy, has become much more
than a conventional literary device. It is instead shown to be the
main cause of the rise and fall of states, constantly weighing upon
individual decision and influencing the course of the struggle
between Rome and Alba. This transforms the climate within which
Horace is called to act, since the gods themselves have prepared a
challenge which, if successfully met, will give him the historical
moment when individual greatness – until then no more than
aspiration and potentiality – may claim an enduring place in the
record of human achievement. For the first time in Corneille's
drama, destiny takes the form of opportunity and the promise
beckons of a full coherence between individual ambition and the
divinely sanctioned triumph of the city, as the hero fulfils himself in
action before a grateful and admiring people.

The vision of a state destined to rule the ancient world is stated
with emphasis from the outset of the play, forcefully echoing
seventeenth-century hopes that present hostilities heralded an era in

which Louis XIII's armies would establish his glory throughout the whole of Europe. In reply to Julie's confident assertion that

> Puisqu'elle [Rome] va combattre, elle va s'aggrandir.

Sabine agrees that the gods support Rome's ambitions:

> Je sais que ton Etat, encore en sa naissance,
> Ne saurait sans la guerre affirmir sa puissance...
> Que les Dieux t'ont promis l'Empire de la Terre,
> Et que tu n'en peux voir l'effet que par la guerre.
>
> (I, i, 22, 39–40 and 43–4)

The play's intended reference to contemporary French ambitions is at once made explicit in Sabine's discretely anachronistic allusion to present military campaigns against the Habsburg alliance:

> Bien loin de m'opposer à cette noble ardeur
> Qui suit l'Arrêt des Dieux et court à sa grandeur,
> Je voudrais déjà voir tes troupes couronnées
> D'un pas victorieux franchir les Pyrénées:
> Va jusqu'en l'Orient pousser tes bataillons,
> Va sur les bords du Rhin planter tes pavillons,
> Fais trembler sous tes pas les colonnes d'Hercule.
>
> (I, i, 47–51)

But Sabine does more than evoke future victory: her principal concern is the suffering caused by the prospect of this war against the city of her birth. By taking this first step on the long road to Imperial glory, Rome must disregard all claims of natural ties and humanity:

> Ingrate souviens-toi que du sang de ses Rois
> Tu tiens ton nom, tes murs, et tes premières lois.
> Albe est ton origine, arrête, et considère
> Que tu portes le fer dans le sein de ta mère.
>
> (I, i, 53–6)

This opening condemnation of a war tainted by unnatural crime reflects quite another aspect of the Cardinal's 'politique de gloire' and places the significance of all further development of the action within the general framework of both sides of the contemporary debate over the morality of France's involvement in the Thirty Years' War.[14] From the outset Sabine's protests give remarkable complexity to the play's illustration of military ambition, making it

clear that the spectator is not to expect a simple glorification of
Rome's early progress to universal dominion. Instead the ambiguous
morality of the values which inspire present hostilities will lie at the
heart of a tragic argument which recognizes the human cost of
conquest quite as much as its glory.

Corneille consistently elaborates on his historical sources in order
to stress the price in individual suffering exacted by Roman military
ambition. From the start, as Julie brushes aside Sabine's suffering as
so much weakness unworthy of a Roman (i, i, 20–4), he establishes
a contrast of characterization in which Roman patriots appear
ambitiously insensitive to the promptings of common humanity.
Julie's advice to Camille that she should regard her lover and
brother-in-law Curiace as no more than an enemy also shows how
small a place the bonds of love play in Rome's march to future glory
(i, ii, 147–50). In contrast with this patriotic insensitivity, the Albans
are shown to be incapable of setting aside the ties of love and nature.
Julie may set out the harsh ideology of Rome's conquering destinies,
but Sabine tellingly returns to the theme of a sister's suffering for her
Alban brothers and Camille, Roman though she is, will become yet
another enemy to be expunged from the city for having set her love
for Curiace before loyalty to the city.

Of all Corneille's modifications to history, the most important is
his invention of the role which sets the tone of the play in the opening
scenes.[15] In his 'Examen' Corneille considers Sabine to have been
'assez heureusement inventé' and compares her very favourably
with L'Infante. Whereas the latter contributed little to the action of
Le Cid, he ascribes the effectiveness of Sabine's paradoxically
ineffectual role to the fact that, as Horace's wife, she is intimately
involved in the course of events. It is certainly true that when Sabine
voices the pain of her situation and the human cost of Rome's
ambitions, her very inability to affect the course of the action makes
of her a striking image of humanity helplessly overtaken by events
and torn apart by war, just as her unique status as both Alban sister
and Roman wife gives her words a moral authority which cannot be
ignored in any assessment of the significance of subsequent events.
By so emphatically asserting that the present conflict offends all
natural claims of family love, she reminds the spectator that a
'matricidal' victory over Alba will not be Rome's first crime against
nature. The present war continues the sinister tradition of a city
whose very walls were built over the body of a victim of fratricidal

violence.[16] That original murder of Remus by Romulus heads a list of no less than eight unnatural crimes of central importance to the meaning of a play, the action of which contains six criminal and sacrificial deaths, all caused by Rome's unnatural onslaught on the mother-city whence Romulus and Remus came. Sabine's opening evocation of Rome's criminal origins returns again in the last act, once in Valère's speech (v, ii, 1532) and most importantly in Tulle's closing judgement:

> ... Que Rome dissimule
> Ce que dès sa naissance elle vit en Romule.
>   (v, iii, 1755–6)

Combining this allusion to the original fratricide with a closing variant on the complementary theme of a self-mutilating pursuit of military glory, the King turns a blind eye on Camille's death because the city has itself already countenanced so terrible a deed in its origins.

So disquieting a presentation of Rome's first steps to Empire must have seemed peculiarly apt to contemporary anxieties and debate over the rights and wrongs of Richelieu's belligerent foreign policy. Dionysius' history of Rome's origins offered Corneille some justification for this treatment of his subject, for the *Roman Antiquities* already distinguished between Alba's respect for a traditional order of legitimacy and the political efficacy of a belligerent Roman ethos which would ultimately lead Rome to triumph and universal dominion.[17] But Corneille also develops the contrast by ignoring or altering the play's sources. In discussing the origins of Rome's conflict with Alba, Livy apportions equal blame to both cities, while Dionysius recounts that the Alban Cluilius had begun hostilities by mischievously urging his compatriots to pillage Roman farms. In contrast, Corneille presents the Albans as the victims of Rome's determination to pursue its ambitions by force of arms. Again, Livy gives no details of the reactions of the Horatii or Curiatii on learning that they had been chosen to fight for their respective cities, and Dionysius relates that, since it was the Curiatii who first agreed to fight their Roman cousins, the Horatii followed suit.[18] Significantly Corneille reverses the roles, the better to maintain a contrast of morality essential to the larger significance of his tragedy. His Horace makes the initial break, as he describes the course of action which Curiace must follow:

HORACE: Avec une allégresse aussi pleine et sincère,
　　　　Que j'épousai la sœur, je combattrai le frère,
　　　　Et pour trancher enfin ces discours superflus,
　　　　Albe vous a nommé, je ne vous connais plus.
CURIACE: Je vous connais encore, et c'est ce qui me tue.

(II, iii, 499–503)

These changes, together with the introduction of Sabine, both clarify the broad lines of the play's political argument and so enrich the moral texture of the play that it becomes impossible to see in it an unequivocal call to self-sacrifice in the name of national glory. Following Dionysius' lead in contrasting the rival cities, Corneille grasps every opportunity to stress the inflexible harshness of Roman patriotism, whether it be in the confrontation of Curiace and Horace on hearing of the honour done them, or in Valère's account of Horace's victory in the field – a narration which is even more shocking than its model in Livy's vivid description of the savagery of the triple combat.[19]

But the most emphatic element of Corneille's depiction of the terrible cost of Rome's unflinching pursuit of empire is the way in which he presents the death of Camille.[20] In the teeth of semi-official opposition Corneille insisted that Horace deliberately kill his sister as an act of principle, almost before the eyes of the spectators who even hear Camille's dying 'Ah, traître!' off-stage (IV, v, 1321).[21] Nowhere else in the play is the balance of argument given more effective and morally disturbing scenic expression than here, as the triumphant Roman ethos embodied in an armed and exultant Horace is brutally contrasted with appalled humane values represented by the tearful and defiantly despairing figure of his sister. The dramatic effect of that murder is admirably calculated to express the splendour and misery of the kind of principled violence which has always been the accompaniment of war. But most important of all, this shocking turn of events casts its shadow over the remainder of the action and irreparably calls into question the hero's identification of himself with the values which guarantee Rome's future destiny as mistress of the world. This rift between the city and its 'criminal' saviour will lead to a tragic culmination which offers the spectator much more than an unequivocal endorsement of those great men whose unstinting service of the nation's interests (as some ministerial supporters argued in seventeenth-century France) set them above the laws which governed lesser mortals.

On learning of the identity of his adversaries in Act II, Horace had sensed that he was called to play his part in a greater order.[22] Knowledge that he will fight for Rome against his wife's three brothers brings with it the conviction that a force is at work which challenges him and Curiace to find the courage to grasp their chance of immortality:

> Le Sort qui de l'honneur nous ouvre la barrière
> Offre à notre constance une illustre matière...
> Et comme il voit en nous des âmes peu communes,
> Hors de l'ordre commun il nous fait des fortunes.
>   (ii, iii, 431–2 and 435–6)

This is to speak the same language as that of the devout moralists of seventeenth-century France, who affirmed that an active Providence gave to exceptional individuals the moment to play their part in furthering the Divine purpose. That moment has come, and it falls to Horace to welcome this necessity to fight his friend and brothers in law as a heaven-sent opportunity to show the qualities he knows himself to possess.[23] To fulfil himself he must act, and the more difficult the challenge to action the better the occasion to demonstrate his heroic capacities. From now on his over-riding concern will be to find the constancy to overcome all doubts or obstacles which might imperil the successful accomplishment of his role as a providential instrument in Rome's progress to domination of the world.

However the hero's ambition to realize his part in the larger purposes of the gods contains a tragic paradox. The seeds of final disgrace are already present in the fact that, by sanctioning Rome's triumph, the gods incomprehensibly also sanction deeds which – as the women never cease to point out – offend nature and the gods' own laws. Horace throws himself into unquestioning service of the city precisely because circumstance offers him the opportunity supremely to illustrate the heroic 'arrachement' of a Roman virtue which, from blood beginnings, has always disregarded the ties of natural affection. His determination on this self-mutilating sacrifice to the interests of the city is nothing if not logical, as he holds to what he will call 'des sentiments romains':

> Notre malheur est grand, il est au plus haut point,
> Je l'envisage entier, mais je n'en frémis point.

> Contre qui que ce soit que mon pays m'emploie,
> J'accepte aveuglément cette gloire avec joie,
> Celle de recevoir de tels commandements
> Doit étouffer en nous tous autres sentiments.
>
> (II, iii, 489–94)

He does not question the moral implications of such a sacrifice, for
the gods themselves have guaranteed Rome's conquering destiny. If
the role he has been called to fulfil entails yet another unnatural
severing of natural ties, so be it. Such a sacrifice both identifies him
totally with the governing values of the city and offers the extreme
challenge which will enable him to translate individual capacity into
the reality of an heroic action which will ensure immortal fame:

> Mourir pour le pays est un si digne sort
> Qu'on briguerait en foule une si belle mort.
> Mais vouloir au Public immoler ce qu'on aime,
> S'attacher au combat contre un autre soi-même...
> Une telle vertu n'appartenait qu'à nous.
>
> (II, iii, 441–4 and 449)

Curiace also accepts that circumstances offer them an opportunity
which they must grasp, but he does so with anguish:

> ...Votre fermeté tient un peu du barbare.
> Peu, même des grand cœurs, tireraient vanité
> D'aller par ce chemin à l'immortalité.
>
> (II, iii, 456–8)

In Horace's Roman perspective, to be a faithful servant of his city is
to be a faithful servant of the gods. Curiace may welcome the chance
to defend his mother city but, as an Alban, he cannot accept without
question that the heroic virtue needed to meet such a challenge is to be
defined by so 'Roman' a suppression of all natural ties of humanity.
Because fratricidal combat cannot be related to the humane values
of Alba, he cannot welcome the situation as an opportunity for
heroic self-realization. Instead he can only deplore 'Ce triste et fier
honneur' (II, iii, 478) as cruel necessity:

> Et si Rome demande une vertu plus haute,
> Je rends grâces aux Dieux de n'être pas Romain
> Pour conserver encor quelque chose d'humain.
>
> (II, iii, 480–2)

As potential heroes the two men agree: their difference resides in whether or not they believe that their ambition to distinguish themselves coincides with the morality of the role which fate has thrust upon them. In this Curiace's suffering reveals how – like all Corneille's heroes – the two men are free to choose but, because they are forced to choose, they have become tragic victims of circumstance.

That the two men's conflict of values has always seemed so telling is a measure of the force with which it confronts us with the central mystery of the play, namely the awesome incomprehensibility of the gods who confront men's ambitions with the challenge of events. For Horace there is no mystery, for the gods have promised the city universal dominion. But his certainty is contrasted both with Curiace's anguish and with the women's sharp awareness of the obscurity of the gods' intentions, as vainly they seek to comprehend this cruel turn which events have taken. The oracle had permitted Camille to see into the future only to misinterpret the truth, and both she and Sabine again offer prayers to Immortals who to the last remain incomprehensible and remote. The truce seems to answer Sabine's prayers that the battle between Alba and Rome be averted, but her hopes are dashed again as this apparent favour of the gods only results in a triple combat which completes her torment:

> Trop favorables Dieux, vous m'avez écoutée!
> Quels foudres lancez-vous quand vous vous irritez,
> Si même vos faveurs ont tant de cruautés?
> (III, i, 760–2)

Her unanswered questions challenge the scandal of the gods' cruelty and perfectly express the confusion into which she has been plunged. Constantly the presence of the gods is felt, but only through events which make a mockery of 'les vœux de l'innocence' and destroy the women's trust in the possibility of justice and happiness in this world of men at war.

A further delay, during which the gods pronounce through augury whether the triple combat should take place, is entirely an invention of Corneille's which further winds up suspense and again permits him to expand on the twin themes of heroic blindness and man's uncertainty before the gods' purposes (III, ii, 821–2). Sabine is sure that her prayers will be answered and that all will be well (III, ii, 828–30), but Camille offers sombre comment on the certainty of suffering and the obscurity of the gods. She does not believe that that popular outcry against an unnatural combat reflects the gods' providential intentions:

> ... La voix du Public n'est pas toujours leur voix.
> Ils descendent bien moins dans de si bas étages,
> Que dans l'âme des Rois, leurs vivantes images,
> De qui l'indépendante et sainte autorité
> Est un rayon secret de leur Divinité.
>
> (iii, iii, 842–6)

These lines prepare Le vieil Horace's later comparison between the folly of the people and the wisdom of the King and his great servants (v, iii, 1711–12 and 1717–18) in a speech which has been quoted as evidence of Corneille's support for his patron's policies. Here, however, Corneille's invention of a context in which Camille despairingly expresses the same sentiments has the contrary effect of making both gods and rulers seem yet more uncaring of individual suffering. That effect is at once confirmed by Camille's bitterly resigned dismissal of any attempt to fathom the higher purposes of the powers which dispose of events (iii, iii, 851–4). When Le vieil Horace announces that the gods have sanctioned the combat and that it is already taking place, Sabine's trust in Divine justice is destroyed:

> Je veux bien l'avouer, ces Nouvelles m'étonnent,
> Et je m'imaginais dans la Divinité
> Beaucoup moins d'injustice, et bien plus de bonté.
>
> (iii, v, 931–4)

By inventing this whole episode Corneille has produced yet another bitter reversal which forcefully illustrates the central mystery of the tragedy: the gods themselves approve a fratricidal conflict and, for reasons comprehensible to none but themselves, impose yet further suffering on those whose lives they govern.

Le vieil Horace does not try to understand this mystery. His prayers that the Albans would name alternative champions, thus preserving his sons from the pain of assuring Rome's triumph through the death of their brothers by marriage, had also gone unanswered. But he accepts the gods' incomprehensible 'prudence'[24] and, like his son, looks beyond present suffering to the comforting thought of a future world cowed by the might of Rome (iii, v, 797–80 and 987–91). For Horace, however, this wisdom of acceptance and hope is insufficient. A hero must act now – and has no choice but to act – if he is to take his place in the providential unfolding of Rome's glorious destiny.[25] This necessity brings with it a leap of faith into the certainty that he is right in his perception of the gods' purposes. This he had possessed ever since he had identified Roman conquest with Providence and accepted the call to fight for the city. It is in that sense that he sacrifices the last of the Curiatii to Rome:

> 'J'en viens d'immoler deux aux Mânes de mes frères,
> Rome aura le dernier de mes trois adversaires,
> C'est à ses intérêts que je vais l'immoler.'
> (IV, ii, 1131–3)

Here Corneille increases the horror of Livy's brutal account of the death of the last Curiatius by the still more disturbing, and poetically essential, image of human sacrifice to a city which has been raised to quasi-divine status. All the equivocal overtones carried by the theme of 'l'intérêt de l'Etat' in the context of contemporary ideological debate, not to speak of its presentation here as Horace's inspiration for human sacrifice, are heavy with consequence to the remainder of the action. The logic of that 'vertu digne de Rome' which Le vieil Horace so applauds in this culminating triumph (IV, ii, 1143) will be invoked later to justify the death of yet another enemy of Rome's future success when that son returns and kills his sacrilegious sister. But that same ruthlessness in virtue will also lead Tulle to praise and condemn a devotion criminal in its excess, and then pardon the disillusioned hero whom he calls once again to serve the city.

Camille's despair at the ruination of her hopes and her fury at the spectacle of Horace's bloody trophies culminate in two prophetic curses. The first – that Horace's glory will soon be tarnished – is accomplished within the tragic day. The second – that Rome's universal Empire will finally be over-run by barbarian hordes – again reminds the spectator of the relation of present events to the larger perspectives of Roman history. Horace responds to Camille's first onslaught by reasserting his faith in the rightness of his actions. He urges her to embrace a Roman virtue which sets the interests of state over any claim to individual happiness:

> HORACE: Aime, aime cette mort qui fait notre bonheur,
> Et préfère du moins au souvenir d'un homme
> Ce que doit ta naissance aux intérêts de Rome.
> (IV, v, 1298–1300)

But in response to Camille's subsequent evocation of Rome's future

destruction, the defender of the city finally sets aside a brother's
loving patience in favour of that same 'reason' of total sacrifice to
the interests of the Roman State. This is another crucial departure
from the historical sources and its only purpose is to make it quite
clear that, in killing his sister, Horace acted in principled fidelity to
Roman justice:

> HORACE,   *mettant la main à l'épée, et poursuivant sa sœur qui s'enfuit*:
> C'est trop, ma patience à la raison fait place.
> Va dedans les Enfers plaindre ton Curiace!
> CAMILLE,   *blessée, derrière le théâtre*:
> Ah, traître!
> HORACE,   *revenant sur le théâtre*:
>   Ainsi reçoive un châtiment soudain
> Quiconque ose pleurer un ennemi romain!
> PROCULE: Que venez-vous de faire?
> HORACE: Un acte de justice.
> Un semblable forfait veut un pareil supplice.
>   (IV, v and vi, 1319–24)

Dionysius, true to his theme of the ferocity of Roman 'virtue',
similarly presents Horatius as convinced that his killing of the
Curiatii was a principled act of civic duty. But, like Livy, Dionysius
interprets the actual murder of Camille as an action prompted by
uncontrolled hatred and anger.[26] Once again Corneille challengingly
modifies his sources in order to preserve the moral coherence of
Horace's devotion to the State and – in Horace's reply to Procule –
further develops Dionysius' lead on Horatius' Roman conduct as 'a
citizen who loves his country and punishes those who wish her ill,
whether they happen to be foreigners or his own people'.[27] Here
Horace himself asserts the 'rightness' of his action committed in
conscious sacrifice of self and family to the city's interests (IV, vi,
1328–34). Once right, always right, and in replying to the bitter
ironies of his wife – who wrongly believes that he could only have
acted in anger – Horace once again makes clear the Roman
principles which inspired him to kill his sister. In this, his
uncompromising certainty prefigures Polyeucte's exhortations to
Pauline, as he urges Sabine to embrace his devotion to the city:

> Embrasse ma vertu pour vaincre ta faiblesse,
> Participe à ma gloire au lieu de la souiller...
> Sois plus femme que sœur, et te réglant sur moi
> Fais-toi de mon exemple une immuable loi.
>   (IV, vii, 1356–7 and 1361–2)

But this personal ideal of right conduct according to an unchanging set of values is founded on Rome's 'intérêts' and, as the final act of the play will make tragically apparent, the latter are so closely wedded to time and changing circumstance that they can never be more than a treacherous and shifting basis for the hero's conviction that he acts in accordance with an absolute and unchanging moral law.

Corneille did scant justice to the haunting political argument of his tragedy when, in the 'Examen' of *Horace*, he condemned the last act for its lack of action and for the demands it made on the spectators' attention in weighing everything that has gone before:

Tout ce cinquième est encore une des causes de peu de satisfaction que laisse cette Tragédie: il est tout en plaidoyers, et ce n'est pas là la place des harangues, ni des longs discours... L'attention de l'Auditeur déjà lassée se rebute de ces conclusions qui traînent, et tirent la fin en longueur. (GC, 1, 843)

Corneille is right that the act is composed of a series of debates, but words on the seventeenth-century French stage are as decisive as actions and these impassioned exchanges force the spectator to judge between widely different evaluations of previous deeds. Horace's tragic destiny can only be accomplished once Tulle's final judgement completes the play's political argument. The opening scene of Act v offers the first of a series of judgements, as Le vieil Horace averts his eyes from the victim of yet another Roman fratricide and presents his son's fall from grace as a humiliation of pride and ambition (v, i, 1403–10). The father has no doubts that Horace has dishonoured himself by killing Camille, for all that he agrees with his son that she deserved to die. As a Roman *paterfamilias* he alone had the authority to ensure a death which in all other respects he approves (v, i, 1411 and 1415–18). Ever the rigorist in the exercise of Roman justice, Horace at once offers his life in submission to the paternal authority he had usurped in killing Camille. But his father, as Tulle will later do at the level of the State, flinches from the 'Roman' logic of his son's argument and cannot bring himself to kill him, preferring instead a shared guilt in 'dissimulation' of past criminal action. Infirmity and personal need are sufficient reasons for the old man staying his hand as, for the first time, he recoils from yet another sacrifice of natural bonds to the communal good. At the heart of this

touchingly private scene lies a terrible shared approval of Camille's
death – an approval which raises, at the level of the family, all the
moral issues which, in the context of the city, will be taken up again
by the King as he concludes the play's sombre exploration of the
relation between individual ambition and the collective interest.

Valère's speech against Horace repeats, in this broader political
context, the argument of familial authority according to which the
father had found his son guilty. He charges Horace with usurping
Tulle's sovereign prerogative by taking it on himself to kill a citizen
who had set herself apart from the city by the disloyalty of her
suffering. Through Camille's death, Horace threatens the whole
Roman body politic:

> Arrêtez sa fureur et sauvez de ses mains,
> Si vous voulez régner, le reste des Romains,
> Il y va de la perte, ou du salut du reste...
> Quel sang épargnera ce barbare vainqueur
> Qui ne pardonne pas à celui de sa sœur!...
> Faisant triompher Rome il se l'est asservie.
>   (v, ii, 1489–91, 1501–2 and 1507)

Balzac's ideal Roman hero has been placed in the real world of
political contingencies as Horace stands accused of a barbarism
incompatible with the survival of Rome itself. The enormity of
Camille's death offers yet another reminder of Romulus' original
crime and shows that, once natural ties are set aside in the interests
of state, such principles carry within them a terrible danger to those
they claim to serve (v, ii, 1531–4). By so arguing that action which
was good in the case of victory over Alba is unacceptable when
directed against the Romans themselves, Valère has exposed the
totalitarian character of the 'vertu digne de Rome' which Le vieil
Horace had so applauded when his son sacrificed the last of the
Curiatii to Roman 'intérêts'.[28]

Valère's eloquence contrasts sharply with the wearily reflective
tone of Horace as he disdains to counter these accusations.[29]
Submitting to the King's sovereign judgement, he requests that he
may take his own life in order not to fall further into ignominy (v,
ii, 1545–54). He has no need to defend an action which, by the
Roman logic of his 'triste et fier honneur', needs no defence. Instead,
as he stands accused and called to account for his deed, Horace
measures the extent of his failure to achieve his ambitions by this fall

from the splendour of general acclaim into present incomprehension and condemnation. At last Horace approaches the fulfilment of his personal tragedy, as he perceives how time and circumstance have worked to destroy his earlier hopes of heroic achievement. The heroic identity he had originally sought to realize in action has now been transformed and betrayed beyond redemption, and his references to time fall like hammer-blows as he reflects on the impossibility of sustaining his original glory:

> Sire, c'est rarement qu'il s'offre une matière
> A montrer d'un grand cœur la vertu tout entière;
> Suivant l'occasion elle agit plus, ou moins,
> Et paraît forte, ou foible aux yeux de ses témoins.
> Le Peuple qui voit tout seulement par l'écorce
> S'attache à son effet pour juger de sa force,
> Il veut que ses dehors gardent un même cours,
> Qu'ayant fait un miracle elle en fasse toujours.
> Après une action pleine, haute, éclatante,
> Tout ce qui brille moins remplit mal son attente:
> Il veut qu'on soit égal en tout temps, en tous lieux,
> Il n'examine point si lors on pouvait mieux,
> Ni que, s'il ne voit pas sans cesse une merveille,
> L'occasion est moindre, et la vertu pareille.
> Son injustice accable, et détruit les grands noms,
> L'honneur des premiers faits se perd par les seconds,
> Et quand la Renommée a passé l'ordinaire,
> Si l'on n'en veut déchoir, il faut ne plus rien faire.
>
> (v, ii, 1555-72)

'L'entier et pur honneur d'une bonne action' has been stripped from him as he stands accused of guilt in an action prompted by the same moral ideal which all had applauded in the triple combat. In bitter recognition of the fragility of glory, Horace perceives the chasm which has opened between his clear individual conscience and other men's judgement of his conduct. From no weakness in himself he has failed to conquer that heroic immortality which is founded in public recognition of the hero's noble motivation. Horace's perception of the necessity represented by the freedom of others to judge him offers a tragic insight into how much of personal identity is defined not by the inner certainty of what he knows himself to be, but by what other men – subject as they must also be to the vagaries of the moment and circumstance – 'make' him as they too pronounce on the quality of his actions.[30] Measuring the gulf between heroic intention and its

realization in action, Horace knows that he has lost that unquestionable glory which resides in the conquest of other men's
judgement by the successful projection of his inner truth into
action.[31] Reputation is as inseparable from action as the shadow is
from sunshine, yet the original virtues of an 'action pleine, haute,
éclatante' have fallen subject to the mysterious advance of time:

> Votre Majesté, Sire, a vu mes trois combats,
> Il est bien malaisé qu'un pareil les seconde,
> Qu'une autre occasion à celle-ci réponde,
> Et que tout mon courage, après de si grands coups,
> Parvienne à des succès qui n'aillent au-dessous;
> Si bien que pour laisser une illustre mémoire,
> La mort seule aujourd'hui peut conserver ma gloire:
> Encore la fallait-il sitôt que j'eus vaincu,
> Puisque pour mon honneur j'ai déjà trop vécu...
> Si ce que j'ai fait vaut quelque récompense,
> Permettez, ô grand Roi, que de ce bras vainqueur
> Je m'immole à ma gloire, et non pas à ma sœur.
>   (v, ii, 1574–82 and 1592–4)

Horace's present disgrace makes it clear that his instrumental role
ended with Rome's victory over the Albans. Having lost his role, he
can seek no other place in history than in the fragile permanence of
past memory. The glory which the gods gave they have now taken
away, and all of Horace's earlier dedication to a glorious future is
transformed into desire for a death which alone can enable him to
salvage something of heroic immortality from the destructive
servitudes of a hateful life, subject to the mutabilities of time and of
other men's judgements.[32] After that request to die, the man of
action stands silent and alone, while the beneficiaries of his devotion
argue about the nature of a guilt which he does not acknowledge.
Abandoned by the gods and accused of betraying the city to which
he has sacrificed everything, he has lost all but the inner certainty of
his personal integrity.

   As in *Le Cid*, the hero's only hope lies in the King's recognition of
the justice of his appeal. Corneille congratulates himself in the
'Examen' that, 'le Roi...est mieux dans sa dignité que dans *Le
Cid*...et...il ne laisse pas d'y agir comme Roi' (GC, 1, 842).
Certainly the benign gravity of Tulle's entry and assumption of the
duties of a King expresses all the prestige which seventeenth-century
France accorded to the dignity of his position:

> Je ferai justice.
> J'aime à la rendre à tous, en toute heure, en tout lieu,
> C'est par elle qu'un Roi se fait un demi-Dieu.
>   (v, ii, 1476–8)

Le vieil Horace further emphasizes the weight to be accorded to Tulle's final judgement when later he attempts to console Horace with the assurance that, while popular opinion is of no account, the King in his wisdom will recognize the nobility of his intentions in killing Camille (v, iii, 1711–12 and 1717–26). With greater dignity and firmness than Don Fernand, Tulle responds with a formidable lesson in the political skills of kingship. In a judgement which again preserves the hero in the interests of the state, but this time by an open sacrifice of the law, his speech puts an end to all uncertainty about Horace's 'péril'. For that reason above all it has been cited as evidence that the play expresses the political convictions of a dramatist profoundly committed to Richelieu's policies.[33] Certainly the realism of Tulle's concern for present advantage and political necessity invites comparison with that of the Cardinal's policies, but we can hardly ignore the fact that previous debate in the play had only moved the spectator in so far as it set out the full spread of moral responses to the events and actions presently under judgement. Any attempt to settle the significance of this most problematic of tragedies by an appeal to propagandist purpose is bound to fall far short of explaining the enduringly challenging effect of the play's cumulative exposition of values in conflict.[34] Few would disagree that *Horace* still means considerably more to its audiences than an authorial declaration of commitment to Richelieu's methods, and this is because, in disclosing the gulf between individual idealism and the realities of public necessity, Corneille's tragedy presents human and political issues no less important and disturbing today than they were at the time of its composition.

Direct identification of the dramatist's intentions with the single voice of Tulle can only diminish the more humane political truth contained in its larger illustration of conflicting principles. Before we accept that Tulle's intervention was indeed intended to be received as an unconditional endorsement of the politics of the Cardinal and sets aside any broader interpretation of the moral significance of previous action, we should recall that the accommodation which Tulle proposes is one which entirely disregards the convictions and aspirations of Horace himself. Where Horace had acted as a true

Roman in killing his sister, the King accepts Le vieil Horace's inexact contention that Camille was killed on impulse, but sees in this no excuse:

> Cette énorme action faite presque à nos yeux
> Outrage la nature, et blesse jusqu'aux Dieux.
> Un premier mouvement qui produit un tel crime
> Ne saurait lui servir d'excuse légitime,
> Les moins sévères lois en ce point sont d'accord,
> Et si nous les suivons, il est digne de mort.
>
> (v, iii, 1733–8)

Where Horace had trusted that the King in his wisdom would comprehend his conduct, Tulle refuses his plea that he be allowed to die and instead condemns and pardons him for a crime of which the hero knows himself to be innocent. In Tulle's view the Curiatii, for all that they were 'cousins' to Horace, were also the enemies of Rome whose death is to be applauded by the city. On the other hand, Camille's death offends because, as Valère has said, she was herself a member of the Roman body politic. And yet the terms in which he condemns Horace invoke the same Divine and Natural Laws which the Roman ethos had consistently set aside in pursuit of future power and glory. Faced with an extreme illustration of a 'vertu digne de Rome' which should have guaranteed the hero's immortality in memory, Tulle recoils before the truth of the motives which inspired this last of a series of 'Roman' sacrifices to the destiny of the city. Acknowledging the deed only on condition that it be forgotten, he evokes Rome's interests for the last time and, in the same breath, invokes those same gods who had approved a conflict which offended every dictate of Natural Law. But now that invocation is made in condemnation of the man who had earlier served the gods' own will and whose heroism the city had applauded when he set nature aside in service of future Roman glory. What has not ceased to be 'un acte de justice' in the eyes of Horace is now adjudged a crime by a State whose future success has only been assured by that same sacrificial violence. Concerned as he must be with the practical political problem of accommodating the hero within the general interests of the city, Tulle has no choice but to pass over Horace's true motivation, condemn his 'anger', and pardon this 'guerrier trop magnanime' so that he may serve Rome again, for all that he has lost all personal conviction in future service to the city.

As Tulle once more invokes these remote and mysterious gods, justice is again manipulated in recognition of the changing nature of political advantage.[35] Tulle's pardon of Horace, which to the latter is both irrelevant and unwanted, reflects a realist's acceptance of the shifting perspectives of political decision. Even as the pardon is justified by invoking the precedent of Rome's tainted establishment, it is clear that the hero's sacrificial devotion is above all necessary to the future ambitions of the city:

> Ce crime, quoique grand, énorme, inexcusable,
> Vient de la même épée, et part du même bras
> Qui me fait aujourd'hui maître de deux Etats.
> Deux sceptres en ma main, Albe à Rome asservie,
> Parlent bien hautement en faveur de sa vie...
> ... L'art et le pouvoir d'affermir des Couronnes
> Sont des dons que le ciel fait à peu de personnes,
> De pareils serviteurs sont les forces des Rois,
> Et de pareils aussi sont au-dessus des lois.
> Qu'elles se taisent donc, que Rome dissimule
> Ce que dès sa naissance elle vit en Romule;
> Elle peut bien souffrir en son libérateur
> Ce qu'elle a bien souffert en son premier auteur.
> Vis donc, Horace, vis, guerrier trop magnanime,
> Ta vertu met ta gloire au-dessus de ton crime,
> Sa chaleur généreuse a produit ton forfait,
> D'une cause si belle il faut souffrir l'effet.
> Vis pour servir l'Etat, vis, mais aime Valère.
>
> (v, iii, 1740–3 and 1751–63)

Horace's aspiration to a hero's glory through total adhesion to the values of Roman conquest stands revealed, once expressed in action, as a noble illusion for which he suffers the inevitable betrayals which future circumstance held in store for him. In assuming the criminal origins of the order which he sought to serve, the hero had aspired to an immortal *stasis* in unfading glory. Instead, and by his very mortality, Horace has fallen victim to the unending process of time which structures the history of the city.

The 'caractère quasi clandestin' of the King's final verdict has been noted even by critics who argue for the essential equity of Tulle's judgement.[36] In his reading of the play, equating Tulle's judgement with an apologetic for Richelieu's policies, Couton remarks that this 'mise en vacances de la légalité' would certainly have gratified the author of the *Testament politique*. But, by

countenancing an injustice done in the interests of State and setting
the nation's greatest servants above the law, Tulle's approval would
also have disturbed those many seventeenth-century spectators who
distinguished between the ministerial conduct of government and
the sacred character of the French monarchy. In such a perspective,
Tulle's decision does little to enhance the dignity of the Crown. But
for the modern spectator these seventeenth-century political differences recede in importance before the way Horace's final solitude
reminds us of how wide is the gulf between political realism and a
truly conciliating justice. This desolate end to the tragedy of Horace
is remote indeed from the triumphant final reconciliations which
Corneille will present in *Cinna*. In the meanwhile, the moral
ambiguity of Tulle's decision, grounded in present necessity and
criminal precedent, can only leave the spectator partially satisfied.
The King's last words may accommodate a recognition of human
strength and frailty with the necessities of the moment and so bring
the play's 'unité de péril' to a resting-point, but the weary figure of
Horace remains a potent presence on the stage and his heavy silence
reminds the spectator of the individual catastrophe represented by
that pardon and second call to arms. Horace's revulsion from life
remains too apparent in his brooding presence for us unreservedly to
endorse an unwanted pardon which condemns him to live on with
the consequences of his acts, a stranger to his wife and in service of
a city to which he has sacrificed everything but which itself shrinks
from the ruthless idealism to which it owes its triumph and
expectations of future glory.

By leaving substantially unresolved the moral and political
problem posed by the close relationship between violence and
Roman virtue, Tulle's judgement completes the hero's individual
misfortune and poses the supreme problem of whether Horace had
been wrong to identify service of Rome with service of the gods' will.
All that he had achieved was a moment of glory, before forfeiting the
immortality which every hero seeks in unclouded remembrance of
glorious achievement. At the level of individual ambition and its
realization in action *Horace* tragically illustrates the heights and
limits of human capacity, as the hero's desire for permanence stands
betrayed by the march of history and the mutabilities of political
circumstance. This it does not by condemning the will to transcend
the bounds of our condition but by prompting the spectator to
question whether, in the comfortless world of the Roman gods, it

were ever possible fully to penetrate that providential order in which the hero sought his place and which alone could have ensured him unfading glory. Only in the strong possession of such a truth could Horace have escaped the limits of his mortality, achieving that absoluteness which only the constant and immutable justice of God can give to the deeds of mortal men. Horace's tragedy lies less in his aspiration to be a hero than in his failure fully to achieve his ambitions for lack of participation in the Divine intentions which shape man's destinies and mysteriously summon the hero to action.[37] In himself Horace was capable of great deeds, but he was forever prevented from their fullest realization because the Roman virtue which prompted him to sacrifice his sister to the city left Rome itself appalled and was finally adjudged insufficient.

Even as it acknowledges the hero's courage, Tulle's verdict makes Horace the victim of prudent calculations of political opportunity and advantage. As such it also proposes a solution to the play which is essentially dramatic in so far as it looks forward to future perspectives of national glory.[38] However, at the level of the hero's aspiration to fulfilment within the city, the play closes with tragic finality on the eternal paradox implicit in a Christian perception of the strength of man's will and the frailty of his perception of the right. As Niebuhr observes:

Man is mortal. That is his fate. Man pretends not to be mortal. That is his sin. Man is a creature of time and place, whose perspectives and insights are invariably conditioned by his immediate circumstances...Human pride is greatest when it is based on solid achievements: but the achievements are never great enough to justify its pretensions. This pride is at least one aspect of what Christian orthodoxy means by 'original sin'. It is not so much an inherited corruption as an inevitable taint upon the spirituality of a finite creature, always enslaved to time and place, never completely enslaved and always under the illusion that the measure of his emancipation is greater than it really is.[39]

Horace powerfully reflects this tragic dichotomy, as the moral paradoxes posed by the gods undo the hero even as they create the moment for heroic achievement. That mystery calls into question the very possibility of Horace's realization of his ideals in action, betrayed as he is by the uncertain perspectives of a world which he seeks simultaneously to transform and transcend in glory. There were many like Priézac who asserted that, without heroic participation in a constant and enduring perception of the good,

ambition could only lead to terrible results.[40] Only in a full
conciliation of heroic strength with knowledge of a transcendent
order of justice could Horace be sure that the perilous leap from
intention into action would not bring with it an abuse of the very
qualities which made great achievement possible. But were such
heroic moralists merely dreaming when they affirmed that true
valour was invariably informed by a sense of right which the
Divinity alone assured? In the original text of the play, a final scene
had returned to this theme, as Julie was left to reflect on heaven's
purposes, seemingly forever hidden to our understanding:

> Mais toujours du secret il cache une partie
> Aux esprits le plus nets et les mieux éclairés...
> Sa voix n'est que trop vraie en trompant notre sens.
> (1641 edition: v, iv, 1785–6 and 1790; GC, i, 1573)

Horace's situation was such that he would have been no less wrong
– and would wholly have betrayed himself and his ambitions – had
he waited, ineffectual and passive, for that problematic truth to
make itself apparent. To the end of the play the purposes of the gods
remain a mystery to all but patriots who confidently enlist
Providence in service of national ambition. But any revelation of a
higher moral order in which justice and force stand reconciled
within an unchanging and ever-applicable code of values remains
stubbornly hidden, even in the judgement of the King himself.
Directly addressing the problem of integrating the hero into the
public order of the city, the early hopes and bitter ending of this first
of Corneille's historical tragedies richly develop the political
argument initiated in *Le Cid*. But not until *Cinna* will a conciliation
between individual and State be achieved: then only, in a
transformation of the hero himself and in an Augustan Rome which
is supremely the context of heroic action, will citizen and city be at
one.

If critical discussion of the political significance of *Horace* continues
with undiminished vigour, this is certain evidence of the even-
handedness with which Corneille's tragedy illustrates the quality
and the cost of the heroism and devotion on which Rome was built.
Painfully it shows how the pursuit of glory brings with it a terrible
threat to the humanity of which the body-politic is composed. The
theme had already lain unexploited in the subject of Coriolanus

when Chapoton and Chevreau had so botched the story of Rome's early beginnings in the interests of the Cardinal's propaganda. There a mother's pleas in favour of Rome had brought about her own son's death, but Corneille's *Horace* amplifies this theme of domestic violence fourfold as it shows the mother city defeated by her own progeny and measures the price of an ideal of civic devotion founded on man's destruction of his own humanity. In so inviting us to reflect on the tragic splendour of the Roman achievement, Corneille's *Horace* sets out with emphasis the exhilarating perspectives of future national grandeur. No less movingly, however, it also measures man's limits and weighs the cost of the Minister's 'politique de gloire' in which success could only be bought at the expense of justice and the brotherhood of man. The awesome themes of the violence inherent in valour and of the price of patriotic self-mutilation converge in this dramatization of the heroic devotion which opened the way to Rome's imperial destiny. By so illustrating how terrible was the courage necessary in sacrifice of self to the greater interests of the State, Corneille made a crushing riposte to his critics and rivals and showed that he alone possessed the capacity to express, through the history of Roman achievement, the complex moral issues of his times and the enduring truths of human capacity and human limitation. We are told that the seventeenth-century French audience looked to tragedy for the challenging pleasures of moral reflection, and never was there a play more apt to stimulate such agreeable meditation than *Horace*. As it concludes with the triumph of a political efficacy bought at the cost of heroic disillusion, the tragic force of *Horace* lies in the way Corneille eschews any imposed resolution of the tensions which his play discovers between its hero and his context. Instead he was content to move his audience to sombre reflection, triumphantly evoking Rome's advance from conquest to conquest at the same time as he illustrated the tainted character of any political order which sacrifices its own humanity to the pursuit of power.

In tragic illustration of the perils which the hero risks, once he moves from noble intentions to their manifestation in action, *Horace* turns upon the eternal problem of moral knowledge and moral responsibility. What values can we know to be eternally constant in the guidance of our lives, values upon which we may establish our identity and which will make us the masters of time and circumstance? Horace had the courage to commit himself con-

sistently to that which he believed himself to be and to what he
believed to be right. Refusing to entertain doubts about that
rightness in order to be able to act at all, the hero was proved wrong
and ended in solitude, subject to the incomprehension of the city in
service of which he had established his very sense of identity. In
courage and pride, man constantly renews his pursuit of permanence
in glory but, as Ophelia hauntingly reminds us in Act IV, scene v of
Hamlet, 'Lord, we know what we are, but know not what we may
be.' So also *Horace* confronts the spectator with a tragic perception
of the uncertainties and disenchantment unavoidably attendant on
man's entanglement in the ineluctable advance of time, as human
aspiration is constantly undermined and eroded by the processes of
that same history within which the walls of Rome were built and
would finally be laid waste. Corneille's 'guerrier trop magnanime'
commands our admiration even as we condemn and pity him for a
crime which was the inevitable consequence of his condition, as he
lost his way in the shifting perspectives of a world in which
mysterious gods constantly call men to choice and action. Repeatedly
those greater forces worked to the hero's exaltation and confusion in
a tragic celebration of courage, energy, and devotion which leads
remorselessly to the spectacle of individual hope in ruins. With the
close of *Horace* the ideal vision of man's individual fulfilment within
the necessities of his political context seems as remote as ever. This
greatest of all tragedies of heroic 'arrachement' shows how, in
Rome's comfortless world of violence and glory, individual devotion
could only end in greatness misdirected. As it leads us to deplore and
wonder at the consequences of conduct which could only have
stemmed from the noblest of personal qualities, Corneille's first
Roman tragedy never forces our judgement. Instead it powerfully
challenges us to draw our own conclusions on the dangerous
splendour of that will to distinction through honourable violence
which lies at the heart of man's pursuit of military glory.

6

Cinna *(1642–3)*

Between 1630 and 1660 many flattering comparisons were made between France's military and cultural achievements and Augustan Rome's ability to combine civilizing military conquest abroad with enlightened cultivation and generous patronage at home. This theme of literary patronage is extravagantly taken up in the dedication of *Cinna* to Montauron, which equates that parvenu's liberality with that of Augustus himself. The excess of the comparison earned Corneille even more mockery than good *louis d'or*, but his play won him the same compliment, made more acceptable by the wit with which it was expressed, when Balzac wrote (17 January 1643) to congratulate its author. It had been Augustus' boast that, if he found Rome built of brick, he would leave it clothed in marble: Balzac adapted the anecdote, praising Corneille as 'le réformateur du vieux temps, s'il a besoin d'embellissement, ou d'appui. Aux endroits où Rome est de brique, vous la rebâtissez de marbre: quand vous trouvez du vide vous le remplissez d'un chef-d'œuvre.'[1] Corneille was delighted rather than embarrassed by this extravagant compliment, and proudly inserted Balzac's letter before the text of his play in the editions of 1646 and 1656. Yet the comparison seems apt enough when we consider how his rival dramatists dealt with the crucial period when Roman Republicanism yielded to the Caesarian principate. As stage recreations of the conspiracies by which the defenders of the Republic tried to overthrow the personal rule of the Caesars, plays like Scudéry's *La Mort de César* (1636) and Guérin de Bouscal's *Suite de la mort de César, ou La Mort de Brute et de Porcie* (1637) provide a striking contrast with *Cinna*.

Both Scudéry and Guérin had dedicated their plays to Richelieu, prefacing them with declarations of devotion to the Minister which are barely less extravagant than Corneille's flattery of Montauron. The adoring Scudéry compares the Cardinal with Julius Caesar,

claiming the honour 'd'avoir pour maître un homme qui mériterait
de l'être de tout le monde'. In a comparison which will be the key
to the play's reinterpretation of its historical subject-matter,
Richelieu is portrayed as the protector of the people, whose conquest
of Alsace of 1635 is quite the match of Caesar's conquest of Gaul.
With a rare show of modesty Scudéry confesses that only Richelieu
– like Caesar before him – has literary skills adequate to describe his
personal perfections and military achievements. Nonetheless he
appends his own unworthy panegyric in praise of a writer and
patron of the muses, whose heroism outshines that of Caesar himself
and of whom Destiny herself has to admit,

> ....En voyant ce divin Cardinal,
>   Qu'il n'eut jamais d'égal,
> Parmi les grands Héros qu'on adorait à Rome.
>   (*La Mort de César*, 'Prologue')

In similar spirit, the play invites the spectator to favour Caesar on
the vexed matter of whether Brutus' Republic or Caesar's imperial
principate represented the 'true' Rome. Brutus, as a result, figures
less as the dignified Republican champion of ancient legitimacies
than as an outdated Stoic whose misplaced political nostalgia leads
him ungratefully to betray a good friend and benefactor. Obviously
Scudéry cannot totally disregard Plutarch, Livy, or Lucan – all of
whom had presented Brutus as the principled defender of the
Republic in opposition to Caesar's usurpation of power – and in the
play's opening deliberations Brutus makes a dignified exposition of
his political convictions. This also gives Scudéry the chance to
establish his own orthodoxy on regicide and tyrannicide. A clear
distinction is drawn between just rulers and tyrants: only the latter
may be killed, and in Brutus' view that category includes Julius
Caesar who has usurped the sovereignty of the Republic. But almost
at once the play moves away from the theme of Brutus' opposition
to illegitimate rule and stresses instead his personal ingratitude to
Caesar. We might recall, in comparison, how Shakespeare's *Julius
Caesar* also opens with the depiction of a noble Republican, only to
let the reality of Brutus' actions and their consequences degrade him
while Caesar gradually rises in stature as the play moves towards his
assassination and Antony's funerary oration. All such shaded effects
are absent from Scudéry's narrowly programmatic approach. Even
the complex figure of Antony is reduced to the exemplary role of a

sombre political realist advising mistrust and severity in repeated warnings about César's benevolence. Scudéry's Anthoine voices a theme particularly associated with the Cardinal's rule when he suggests that a prudent recourse to preventative 'justice' is necessary if the threat of César's death is to be avoided. Given our foreknowledge that César will trust Brutus despite these emphatic warnings, the effect is to make such advice look like the only true political wisdom – a lesson obviously intended for contemporary spectators who complained of Richelieu's severity. As for César himself, he is shown to prefer more gentle political skills:

> On doit tromper le peuple avec dextérité,
> Comme on ôte aux oiseaux la douce liberté.
>
> (III, i)

The coded message is clear: like César, Richelieu loves those he governs, but they are wayward children who would quickly transform liberty into disorder were they given more freedom. In an obvious contribution to contemporary debate over the Cardinal's rule, Scudéry's César is entirely devoted to the welfare of all the Romans. He wills the best but is fatally obstructed and betrayed by factious or misguided men bemused by an outdated political idealism. Misinterpreted by men envious of his power and who mislead a foolish common people, César's only mistake is to have refused to believe the worst of Brute. Scudéry's programmatic intentions are above all apparent in the way his play constantly identifies César with the fortunes of the State, just as Richelieu's apologists identified the Cardinal's will with that of the King – a flattering identification which appropriately culminates in the funerary oration of Act v, where César's death is ascribed to the treacherous ingratitude of the few.

Guérin de Bouscal's *Suite de la mort de César* again shows how propagandist intentions in the drama can impoverish the rich possibilities of Roman history. Here too a 'Prologue de la Renommée' praises Richelieu as literary patron, alluding to Caesar's death in a way which points accusingly at the conspiracies of those who would betray this hero devoted to the general weal. The battle of Philippi stands as a terrible warning to all 'ingrats' who plot against great men, and Brutus' suicide on the field is adjudged an exemplary punishment for perfidy. Like Scudéry's, Guérin's tragedy characterizes Brute as a Stoic whose old-fashioned idealism is out of touch with the times.[2] Brute's Stoic acceptance of misfortune again gives him a kind of nobility, but Guérin's play undercuts any posthumous admiration by showing how this champion of ancient Roman virtue is no less guilty of ambition than is César, and Brute's self-deceiving nostalgia is repeatedly contrasted with the new order's lucid recognition of the need for firm but benign monarchical rule. This political wisdom is principally expressed by Guérin's Anthoine, who is inspired less by high moral principle than hard-bitten political realism. But Guérin would also have us believe that the gods are on the side of this new order of political wisdom and that they sanction the *Imperium* of the future Augustus. In defeat, even Brute finally admits to the need to bend to changing times, conceding that the older political order is no longer applicable:

> Celui justement perd le titre de sage
> Qui veut choquer du temps l'infaillible passage.
>   (v, iv)

Guérin's desire to defend the new realism in political decision is constantly in evidence, as the coded lesson of his play sets the Cardinal's 'politique de raison' against those who cried scandal in the name of the traditional sanctities of the justice which St Louis had dispensed as he sat beneath his oak. Caesar was right to have replaced the traditional order and privileges of the Republic, for his 'coup d'état' inaugurated a new and glorious phase in Rome's destinies. Any appeal to ancient legitimacies has long since lost its usefulness: the only effective political order is the new dispensation in which one man's centralized rule can alone control factious elements and handle the problems of scale posed by a growing empire.[3] The argument (II, i) is made ostensibly in support of the monarchy but once again, in the characteristic strategy of ministerial propaganda at the time, the obvious beneficiary is the Cardinal who is identified with the Crown. Brute may have a certain *gravitas* in his fidelity to outdated principles, but Guérin never permits this to seem more than misguided nostalgia for times long gone, when perhaps it had been possible to respect Divine and Natural Justice in the conduct of great affairs.

Cinna draws all these themes together in its illustration of the moral and political significance of a turning-point in the history of Rome. Corneille himself suggested that the subject of his play was a crisis of political order when, in his first *Discours*, he carefully distinguished between the principal action and its contributory episodes:

Cinna conspire contre Auguste et rend compte de sa conspiration à Emilie, voilà le commencement; Maxime en fait avertir Auguste, voilà le milieu; Auguste lui pardonne, voilà la fin... La consultation d'Auguste au second de Cinna, les remords de cet ingrat, ce qu'il en découvre à Emilie, et l'effort que fait Maxime pour persuader à cet objet de son amour caché de s'enfuir avec lui, ne sont que des épisodes; mais l'avis que fait donner Maxime par Euphorbe à l'Empereur, les irrésolutions de ce prince, et les conseils de Livie, sont de l'action principale. (LF, 52–3 and 71; GC, III, 128 and 139)

This sets the threat to Auguste's life firmly at the centre of things and draws our attention to his evolution from tyrant to legitimate sovereign. All hinges on the way in which Auguste wields his authority, as the dramatic interest of the play shifts from Emilie and Cinna's conspiracy to the wider problem of Auguste's role in relation to Rome's past and future history. Thus the subject of an abortive plot to kill a tyrant-usurper who instead overcame that threat by establishing himself as 'Father of the Fatherland' brings together all the major themes – vengeance, the relation between violence and heroic ambition, the nature of monarchical governance and its powers of conciliation – which had been so important to Corneille's two preceding plays, concerned as they were with the place of individual heroism within an evolving social order. What is new, however, is the extraordinary richness and precision with which *Cinna* reflects contemporary political theory and debate.

In *Le Cid* and *Horace* the figure of the monarch served to conclude the action, rather than resolve the tensions between individual and State. But the episode of Roman history which established the legitimacy of Augustus' rule and finally put an end to the disorders of civil war offered Corneille a subject in which the figure of the monarch resolves a political crisis which he has himself precipitated by his own ambitions. As Auguste emerges from his past self as Octave, the final scene of *Cinna* fuses hero and monarch in an impressive celebration of the way in which royal authority can reconcile all interests and transcend partisan disunity within the community of men. By prefacing his play with Seneca's account of Augustus' pardon of Cinna (*De Clementia*, I, 9) Corneille was well aware that this situated his portrayal of Auguste within a tradition of political commentary for which Augustus had become a shining prefiguration of the efficacy of a Christian rule by 'douceur'. Seneca's text was a primary reference for those who condemned the sterility of personal vengeance and celebrated the conciliating political efficacy of the French monarchical tradition.[4] For these writers, the act of clemency with which Augustus put an end to Republican conspiracies showed how powerfully love bound together the society of man and supremely illustrated how the monarchy alone could establish and guarantee social harmony.

In Corneille's version of Seneca's celebrated account, Emilie is the only major role entirely of his own invention. It is characteristic of his practice that Emilie not only introduces the attractions of a love interest but also provides a telling contrast of values in the play's political argument. She opens with the great themes of personal vengeance and tyrannicide but concludes in wholehearted acceptance of her natural place within a renewed social order, breaking free of hatred in a personal endorsement of monarchical authority which completes the moral and political burden of the play. The 'impatients désirs d'une illustre vengeance' expressed in her opening monologue establish a *persona* which sets her amongst those black souls who are incapable of forgiveness.[5] Certainly she suffers in exposing Cinna to danger, and she is well aware of the price which she may have to pay for avenging her father's death, but the pathos of her position is counterbalanced by the ferocity of her hatred of an Emperor who has condemned her Republican father to death (i, i, 41–4). Her subsequent exchanges with Fulvie show how profitlessly destructive is her chosen course of action:

> Toute cette faveur ne me rend pas mon père.
> (i, ii, 69)

Leaving the spectator in no doubt about her determination, she puts a noble gloss on her vendetta by associating it with the more glorious motive of service to the general good.

> Joignons à la douceur de venger nos parents
> La gloire qu'on remporte à punir les Tyrans,
> Et faisons publier par toute l'Italie,
> 'La liberté de Rome est l'œuvre d'Emilie'.
> (i, ii, 107–10)

Nonetheless, from the start it has been made amply clear that her Republican zeal is little more than a front for private resentment.

The twentieth-century spectator is likely to have lost the sense of recognition experienced by Corneille's contemporaries before this confusion of private interest and public principle. They would have made an immediate comparison between Emilie and the aristocratic conspirators against Richelieu, whose defenders argued that it was no more than personal animosity which inspired these malcontents' high-minded appeals to tradition.[6] These contemporary overtones have been often noted, but they should not lead us to assume that, after all, Corneille's play is as partisan as those of Scudéry or Guérin. Emilie and Cinna's secret motivations are undoubtedly to be compared with those of contemporary plotters, but Corneille is equally careful to give their conspiracy some justification, presenting it as a consequence of the political disorder which Auguste brought upon Rome by usurping power and relying on repressive methods. This moral ambivalence is a major aspect of all the principal roles in the play which, after evoking some sympathy for the lovers, gradually shifts our allegiance to the role of Auguste. Even if Emilie plots what must have seemed a terrible crime to the seventeenth-century spectator, the opening scenes of the play also present her as a daughter wronged and appeal to our sympathies through the revelation of the personal cost she is prepared to pay to avenge her father in restoring the Republic. Similarly Cinna's long report of his speech to the conspirators, detailing the circumstances of the Emperor's usurpation, has the immediate effect of establishing a reasoned case for the Republican cause and emphasizes the worst traits to be found in historical accounts of the Emperor's character and rise to power. As soon as Auguste appears in Act II, however, we are confronted with a troubled but generous-hearted ruler who is clearly not the despot for whom we have been prepared. With this *coup de théâtre* of characterization, Corneille calls into question our expectations of the Emperor as tyrant and initiates a process of revaluation which will have its principal moral focus in Cinna's increasing hesitancy and misgivings about the rightness of the conspiracy.

The play's depiction of the self-serving motivations which inspire Emilie's and Cinna's Republicanism is greatly enhanced by the ambivalent effect in Act II of Auguste's own misery and disquiet. From his first appearance the Emperor appeals to our sympathies, but he also offers a fine illustration of the very fate which befalls the illegitimate ruler – a fate which many wished upon Richelieu for his abuse of the venerable traditions of governance in France. To see the

similarity between Auguste's 'déplaisirs et irrésolutions' and the
insecurities which many considered to be the natural consequence of
conduct tainted by 'l'esprit de domination' we may turn again to
the Campion brothers' verdict on Richelieu:

Comme le génie qui le conduit est le plus partagé et le plus indécis entre le
bien et le mal dont nous ayons peut-être eu connoissance, nous lui laissons
pour récompense du bien qu'il fait le pouvoir et l'autorité qu'il a d'en faire;
et lui ordonnons pour peine du mal qu'il cause, la continuation des
inquiétudes, des craintes, des chagrins et des remords qui tyrannisent
perpétuellement l'âme de ceux dont l'autorité n'est légitime, ni dans son
acquisition, ni dans son usage…Nous entendons que tous les gens de bien
en révérant les beaux talents dont Dieu a annobli de pareils génies,
détestent l'intention de ceux qui sans autre dessein que de laisser une belle
histoire à la posterité, font gémir leur siècle sous le poids de leur ambition.[7]

This condemnation of the Cardinal to the perils and uneasy
conscience attendant upon illegitimacy of rule dates from precisely
the same time as Corneille's depiction of Auguste, and is as relevant
to the political resonance of the play as are the similarities between
Emilie and the suspect motives of a factious seventeenth-century
nobility. In these two-sided echoes of contemporary debate over the
new order of France it is clear that its author aspires to something
more interesting than partisan apologetics and proposes a more
balanced reflection on the political issues of the day.

   Cinna is no more genuinely concerned for the true welfare of the
people than is Emilie, since he too is personally motivated by love for
a woman whose hand can only be won through the death of
Auguste. His dishonesty of purpose is tellingly illustrated when he
recounts to Emilie how he spoke to the conspirators, since the private
circumstances of this narration undercut the splendour of the public
parade of Republican principle. Cinna plots to please his lady, and
his motives are carefully contrasted with the more attractive
legitimist idealism of Maxime, who, at the start of the action, is the
only one unequivocally concerned to restore the Republic. Constantly Cinna speaks of heroic glory and as constantly he dissimulates
in its pursuit. If true heroism is to show publicly what one really is,
his exchanges with Maxime in the second act after the Council scene
leave us in little doubt that he is no hero:

MAXIME: Quel est votre dessein après ces beaux discours?
CINNA: Le même que j'avais, et que j'aurai toujours.
MAXIME: Un chef de conjurés flatte la tyrannie!
CINNA: Un chef de conjurés la veut voir impunie!

MAXIME: Je veux voir Rome libre.
CINNA: Et vous pouvez juger
          Que je veux l'affranchir ensemble et la venger.
                                              (II, ii, 647–52)

By this point in the action the audience knows that Cinna's love for
Emilie has led him to sacrifice the only true purpose of the
conspiracy – the liberty of Rome. Trying to disguise his true motives,
he claims to be the gods' chosen instrument in meting out justice,
even if Rome continues to suffer until he kills the tyrant:

          ...Le Ciel par nos mains à le punir s'apprête.
                                              (II, ii, 657)

Maxime's shock at Cinna's opposition to Auguste's proposed
abdication reveals an idealism and naiveté which leaves him baffled
by his friend's bluster. Later discovery of his friend's true motives will
destroy that innocence and provide his only excuse, when he too
betrays the Republic in the hope of winning Emilie for himself.

Long before that betrayal, however, the mutually destructive
nature of Emilie and Cinna's compact has exposed the inauthenticity
of their pretensions to heroism. Events inexorably reveal the gap
between Cinna's public claims to embody a principle of Divine
Justice and his personal reluctance to pursue a line of conduct which
draws him ever further into the secret shames of deceit and
ingratitude towards a ruler who does not act like a tyrant legitimately
to be overthrown. The confidences between the lovers show very
clearly how shakily their high principles correspond with their true
motives. By Act II, scene iv, Cinna can no longer ignore this
distinction between true and apparent 'générosité':

          Une âme généreuse et que la vertu guide
          Fuit la honte des noms d'ingrate, et de perfide.
                                              (III, iv, 969–70)

Emilie's reply to this traditional appeal to good faith strikingly
exposes the artificiality of her pose as liberator of Rome. In a series
of brilliant paradoxes she exalts an unnatural morality of fabricated
virtues which gives the lie to the authenticity of her heroism:

          Je fais gloire pour moi de cette ignominie,
          La perfidie est noble envers la Tyrannie,
          Et quand on rompt le cours d'un sort si malheureux,
          Les cœurs les plus ingrats sont les plus généreux.
                                              (III, iv, 974–6)

As Cinna observes, such self-created 'virtues' deny any rational perception of true justice:

CINNA: Vous vous faites des vertus au gré de votre haine.
EMILIE: Je me fais des vertus dignes d'une Romaine.
(III, iv, 974–6)

But Emilie holds Cinna to his word, forcing him into further paradoxes of honour in dishonour:

CINNA: Eh bien vous le voulez, il faut vous satisfaire.
Il faut affranchir Rome, il faut venger un père,
Il faut sur un Tyran porter de justes coups:
Mais apprenez qu'Auguste est moins Tyran que vous...
...L'empire inhumain qu'excercent vos beautés
Force jusqu'aux esprits, et jusqu'aux volontés.
Vous me faites priser ce qui me déshonore,
Vous me faites haïr ce que mon âme adore,
Vous me faites répandre un sang pour qui je dois
Exposer tout le mien, et mille, et mille fois.
(III, iv, 1049–52 and 1055–60)

This gallant language does nothing to disguise the fact that Cinna has offered a text-book definition of the true tyrant's violation of individual conscience, completing a very effective illustration of Emilie's profoundly unnatural inversion of values, both as a Roman citizen and as a woman in love.

The drama of Cinna and Emilie is that of self-deceit and heroic failure, in which honour becomes constraint and 'arrachement' in self-sacrifice can only show itself as inauthenticity. They both have the forced quality of those who 'se tuent pour aller plus loin que leur devoir en s'écartant de leur devoir... Il n'importe que leurs œuvres soient extraordinaires, qu'elles semblent avoir de l'éclat et de l'élévation: qu'elles demandent de la résolution et de la force... Il y a une résolution du désordre, il y a une force d'égarement'.[8] This element of strain is constantly suggested by the rhetorical stiffness of Emilie's language. Voltaire observed that 'Emilie ne touche point et elle inspire peu d'intérêt... Les sentiments d'un Brutus, d'un Cassius, conviennent peu à une fille.' Adjudging that Emilie's ingratitude towards Auguste severely limits 'la grandeur qu'elle affecte', Voltaire even suggested that the role raises doubts about Corneille's skills of characterization: 'N'est-ce point parce que ce rôle n'est pas tout à fait dans la nature? Cette fille que Balzac appelle "une adorable furie", est-elle si adorable?'[9] But Emilie's language may more justly be seen to be a subtle aspect of a portrayal of one who is indeed not 'dans la nature' and is capable only of striking heroic attitudes. Less sensitive to the play's larger political argument than to the conventional portrayal of female character, Voltaire has unwittingly isolated an important element in Corneille's depiction of a kind of heroism founded in artifice and obduracy of will rather than in the natural order of things.[10] For contemporary *moralistes*, such obduracy derived from a heroic self-deceit founded in 'la Hardiesse', source of great deeds but also of great wrongs.[11] Balzac may have been scarcely less enthusiastic about Corneille's heroine than his doctor friend who called her 'la belle, la sainte et l'adorable Furie' but, as the contrast between her strained ferocity and the Emperor's benignity becomes ever clearer, there can be little doubt that Emilie takes her place with Pymante, Médée, and Horace, amongst Corneille's striking illustrations of a heroism which has lost its way.

In the more abstract realm of political theory, French authorities were particularly uneasy about attempts on the life of the ruler, preferring to assert that unjust rule called God's wrath down upon itself. If men served as heaven's instrument in that punishment, Gentillet assures us, the initiative still remained with God since 'nulle chose violente ne peut être de durée. Tellement qu'il s'ensuit qu'un Etat fondé sur la cruauté ne peut longuement durer'.[12] But Aquinas *On Princely Government* and *On Natural Law*, like Bodin later in *La République*, had already examined the matter, and in seventeenth-century France they were the two most influential authorities on a difficult issue. Saint Thomas leaves the deposition of tyrants to God's initiative alone, considering the miseries of tyrannical rule to be a punishment for human sinfulness. However his *Commentary on Peter Lombard* does allow the oppressed subject the right to take back that which has been unjustly taken from him and affirms that there is no duty of obedience to a wicked ruler. St Thomas even goes so far as to state that 'it is permissible or even praiseworthy to kill' such a man, quoting Cicero's praise of the assassins of the usurping Julius Caesar. But in the case of a legitimate king who governs unjustly Aquinas is categorical: his subjects must suffer and obey him. Revolt is only permissible against those who have usurped power by violence, and even then God may legitimize their rule.[13] There is even less to justify Emilie's conspiracy in Bodin's *La République*, where we read that a legitimate king is plus sacré et plus inviolable que le père, étant ordonné et envoyé de Dieu...Jamais le sujet n'est recevable de rien attenter contre son Prince Souverain: pour méchant et cruel tyran qu'il soit: il est bien licite de ne lui obéir pas en chose qui soit contre la Loi de Dieu, ou de Nature, s'enfuir, se cacher, parer les coups, souffrir la mort, plutôt que d'attenter à sa vie, ni à son honneur.

Elsewhere in *La République*, however, Bodin offered some justification for Auguste's Republican enemies. As a 'politique' who had much in mind the ambitions of the house of Guise he asserted that those who would set aside a previous legitimate sovereignty should be put to death: 'Il n'appartient à homme vivant d'envahir la souveraineté, et de se faire maître de ses compagnons, quelque voile de justice et de vertu qu'on prétende: et qui plus est, en termes de droit celui est coupable de mort qui use des marques réservées à la souveraineté.' But even here Bodin observes that time may establish the legitimacy of a usurper, if only after at least a hundred years of uneasy rule during which the older claims of an original sovereignty are slowly forgotten.[14] It might be inferred from this that, since Auguste has not long seized sovereign power and rules by terror, Emilie's intention to restore the Republic justifies her conspiracy to avenge her father's death. But, as the action advances, her intended victim displays qualities of governance which set him increasingly apart from the usual illustrations of the tyrant and Emilie's claim that she has right on her side carries less and less conviction.

Conspiracies against the lives of the great may have had a privileged place in the political drama of the period, but public morality required that the dramatist made it crystal clear that the intended victim of conspiracy was indeed a tyrant, and so deserved his fate, and that a true king who escaped the knife of his enemies then dispensed due punishment. Cinna's harangue to the conspirators draws on the repertory of epithets which the seventeenth-century stage traditionally reserved for execration of the tyrant (I, iii, 167–68). If we are to believe him – and at this stage in the action we have no reason not to – Auguste has ruthlessly exploited civil discord in order to achieve his usurping ambitions (I, iii, 215–20). As in *Horace* the theme of human sacrifice to the pursuit of power is even evoked when Cinna (I, iii, 207–8) recalls Octave's sacrifice of his enemies on an altar raised to Julius Caesar. In similar manner contemporary descriptions of tyranny turn upon the ruler's respect or scorn for Divine and Natural law.[15] In this Bodin is characteristic, and his comparison of tyranny with 'la Monarchie Royale' served as an influential model for every dramatist in the period:

La monarchie tyrannique, est celle où le monarque foulant aux pieds les lois de nature, abuse de la liberté des francs sujets, comme de ses esclaves, et des biens d'autrui comme des siens...J'appelle bon et juste Roy qui met tous ses efforts d'être tels, et qui est prêt d'employer ses biens, son sang et sa vie pour son peuple. Or la plus noble différence du Roi et du Tyran est que le Roi se conforme aux lois de nature: et le Tyran les foule aux pieds: l'un entretient la piété, la justice et la foi: l'autre n'a ni Dieu, ni foi, ny loi: l'un fait tout ce qu'il pense servir au bien public et tuition des sujets: l'autre ne fait rien que pour son profit particulier, vengeance, ou plaisir: l'un s'efforce d'enrichir ses sujets...l'autre ne bâtit sa maison que de la ruine d'iceulx...l'un fait état de l'amour de son peuple: l'autre de la peur...l'un mesure ses mœurs et façons au pied des lois: l'autre fait servir les lois à ses mœurs: l'un est aimé et adoré de tous ses sujets: l'autre les hait tous et est haï de tous.[16]

This celebrated passage has much to tell us of the difference between what the Cinna of Act I wants his friends to believe of Auguste, and what the spectator himself begins to suspect once the Emperor appears on stage in the following act. Corneille's characterization of Auguste in Act II deliberately suspends the spectator's judgement between Bodin's two patterns of governance, the first exemplified by a tyrannical past and present reign of fear and the second by that nobler form of rule foreshadowed by Auguste's concern for Rome and his search for a way out of the morass into which the pursuit of power has plunged him.

The Council scene of Act II draws heavily on contemporary theory which repeatedly asserted that he who usurps power by violence provokes his own providential punishment. Accordingly Auguste offers a traditional, if touchingly eloquent, depiction of a tyrant's exercise of power:

> Dans sa possession, j'ai trouvé pour tous charmes
> D'effroyables soucis, d'éternelles alarmes,
> Mille ennemis secrets, la mort à tous propos,
> Point de plaisir sans trouble, et jamais de repos.
>
> (II, i, 373–6)

But the very pathos of this account hints that nobler ambitions lie behind Auguste's disenchantment. His rule is 'Odieuse aux Romains et pesante à moi-même' (II, i, 398), and, in confiding his awareness that he is reaping what he has sown, Auguste belies the conventional assertion that a tyrant's cruelty is matched only by his mistrust of others.[17] In the very first scenes of the play, Fulvie had also depicted Auguste's tyranny in a context which suggested a gentler side to the Emperor as Emilie's adoptive father, who has showered her with loving kindnesses (I, ii, 87–94). By the end of the Council scene, when Auguste responds to the advice of trusted advisers, this usurper's uncharacteristic capacity for love will be seen to reach beyond even personal ties and inspire his concern for the faceless multitude of those he governs – thus belying the stock contention that the tyrant knows nothing of love, either in his personal dealings or in his government.[18] However, because Maxime's and Cinna's advice to Auguste is immediately overtaken by discovery of their plot, the principal dramatic interest of Act II, scene i derives from the motives which inspire the conspirators, in a fine illustration of the skill with which Corneille could bring vividly to life the more theoretical implications of contemporary debate. Contrasting Cinna's treachery, Maxime's political naiveté, and Auguste's generosity and good faith, it dramatizes a conflict of political convictions which carries within it important distinctions between the insufficiencies of Auguste's present exercise of power – in the tradition of an unenlightened and pagan 'monarchie seigneuriale' – and the traditional sanctities of the 'Monarchie Royale' of the 'most Christian' Kings of France which will be exemplified in his final apotheosis.

Cinna's opening reply to Auguste has none of the theoretical solidity of his later interventions. Its hastily improvised arguments aptly suggest guilty relief and surprise at the unexpected nature of Auguste's concerns. In order to defend the Emperor's present position he first confuses the rights of legitimate foreign conquest with the wrongs of a civil usurpation of sovereignty:

> C'est sans attentat
> Que vous avez changé la forme de l'Etat.
> Rome est dessous vos lois par le droit de la guerre.
>
> (II, i, 419–21)

In terms of contemporary theory this was a quite unacceptable argument, for Bodin's authoritative discussion of the 'forme de l'Etat' had clearly set out the differences between tyranny, the 'Monarchie Seigneuriale' of pagan antiquity, and the 'Monarchie Royale' of Christian France:

La Monarchie Royale, ou légitime, est celle où les sujets obéissent aux lois du Monarque, et le Monarque aux lois de nature, demeurant la liberté naturelle et proprieté des biens aux sujets. La Monarchie Seigneuriale est celle où le Prince est fait Seigneur des biens et des personnes par le droit des armes, et de bonne guerre gouvernant ses sujets comme le père de famille ses esclaves. La Monarchie Tyrannique est où le Monarque méprisant les lois de nature, abuse des personnes libres comme d'esclaves et des biens des sujets comme des siens... Ne doit pas la Monarchie Seigneuriale être appelée tyrannie: car il n'est pas inconvénient qu'un Prince Souverain, ayant vaincu de bonne et juste guerre ses ennemis ne se fasse seigneur des biens et personnes par le droit de la guerre, gouvernant ses sujets comme esclaves, ainsi que le père de famille est seigneur de ses esclaves et de leurs biens, et en dispose à son plaisir par le droit des gens: Mais le Prince qui par guerre, ou par autres moyens injustes fait des hommes libres ses esclaves, et s'empare de leurs biens, n'est pas Monarque Seigneurial ains un vrai tyran.

This defines the tyrant in terms close to Cinna's earlier description of Auguste's rule, while Bodin's account of the pagan 'Monarchie Seigneuriale' clearly lies behind the specious argument that the Emperor has legitimately acquired power.[19] But it is also clear that Cinna's speech flies in the face of Bodin's definition of the French 'Monarchie Royale' and his more general strictures on the character of tyrannical usurpation. Bodin had traced a progress from the unenlightened first 'Monarchies Seigneuriales' to a nobler form of governance exemplified in the Christian monarchy of France:

Or les Princes et peuples adoucis peu à peu d'humanité et de bonnes lois n'ont rien retenu que l'ombre et l'image de la monarchie seigneuriale, telle qu'elle était anciennement en Perse... Le Monarque Royal est celui qui se rend aussi obéissant aux lois de nature comme il désire ses sujets être envers lui, laissant la liberté naturelle, et la propriété des biens à chacun... le Roi doit obéir aux lois de nature, c'est à dire gouverner ses sujets et guider ses actions par la justice naturelle qui se voit et fait connaître aussi claire et luisante que la splendeur du soleil.[20]

Once considered in the light of these definitions, Auguste's seizure of Republican sovereignty can no more be considered a just victory over another country than it may be argued that his present rule of fear legitimizes his usurpation of power. And yet this is what Cinna argues:

> Tous les conquérants,
> Pour être usurpateurs, ne sont pas des tyrans.
> Quand ils ont sous leurs lois asservi des Provinces,
> Gouvernant justement ils s'en font justes Princes.
>
> (II, i, 423–6)

If we discount Cinna's insincerity here, Auguste is at best an
unenlightened 'Monarque Seigneurial', but what we have earlier
been told about him better matches a tyrant's use of proscription and
terror after seizing power through civil war against his fellow
citizens. By confusing a civil war against the Republic with just
conquest of a foreign country, Cinna has come close to grounding the
Emperor's legitimacy on force alone. Since the spectator is well
aware that Cinna's desire to win Emilie is the real motive for
advancing so scandalous a point of view, the realism of his advice
seems particularly brutal and foreshadows Livie's later contention
that the acquisition of power is enough to justify whatever means are
used to achieve it:

> Tous ces crimes d'Etat qu'on fait pour la Couronne,
> Le Ciel nous en absout, alors qu'il nous la donne,
> Et dans le sacré rang où sa faveur l'a mis,
> Le passé devient juste, et l'avenir permis.
> Qui peut y parvenir ne peut être coupable,
> Quoi qu'il ait fait, ou fasse, il est inviolable.
>   (v, ii, 1609–14)

Neither of these overtly Machiavellian passages can be held to
represent the dramatist's own convictions. Cinna's speech is not
directly rebutted and is only implicitly discredited by its motivation,
but Maxime, given his circumstances, can hardly reply that
Auguste's own record gives the lie to Cinna's argument, although he
comes close to doing so later. Instead he passes over the vexed matter
of Republican or Imperial legitimacy by means of a formula which
still clearly expresses the illegitimacy of Auguste's exercise of power
through conquest. Echoing Bodin's description of the 'Monarchie
Seigneuriale' of pagan antiquity, 'entièrement seigneur des personnes et des biens', Maxime urges Auguste to take the nobler path of
renunciation:

> Rome est à vous, Seigneur, l'Empire est votre bien,
> Chacun en liberté peut disposer du sien...
> Votre gloire redouble à mépriser l'Empire,
> Et vous serez fameux chez la Postérité
> Moins pour l'avoir conquis que pour l'avoir quitté.
>   (ii, i, 451–2 and 474–6)[21]

Significantly this idealist argument is backed by an appeal to
practical experience: abdication would avert the risk of assassination
by subjects who secretly detest the monarchy and consider every

king a tyrant. His advice is of course rich with dramatic irony, as the spectator sees how trustingly Auguste listens to counsellors whose real motivations correspond to just such covert resentments.

Maxime's honest defence of Rome's Republican tradition prompts a reply from Cinna which falls back on the safest of all seventeenth-century political *dicta*. All parties, whatever their other differences, condemned 'l'Etat populaire' and agreed that only a monarchy was capable of imposing security and order and ensured a just attribution of responsibilities and honours.[22] Democracy invariably drifted into faction and civil confusion, and Cinna repeats the lesson:

> Mais quand le peuple est Maître, on n'agit qu'en tumulte,
> La voix de la raison jamais ne se consulte...
> Le pire des Etats c'est l'Etat populaire.
> (ii, i, 509–10 and 521)

This speech may be built on received seventeenth-century opinion, but its dramatic effect is again ambiguous when placed, as here, in the mouth of a hypocrite. Cinna's dishonesty so scandalizes Maxime that he launches into a refutation which appeals to geography as the determinant of every nation's political institutions:

> J'ose dire, Seigneur, que par tous les Climats
> Ne sont pas bien reçus toutes sortes d'Etats,
> Chaque Peuple a le sien conforme à sa nature,
> Qu'on ne saurait changer sans lui faire une injure:
> Telle est la loi du Ciel dont la sage équité
> Sème dans l'Univers cette diversité.
> (ii, i, 535–40)

It has been suggested that these lines foreshadow eighteenth-century developments of a theory of climate first enunciated by seventeenth-century Jesuits, but the context in which they appear renders them much more interesting for the way they echo contemporary debate over the 'alien' character of a ministerial government which ignored the characteristic virtues and institutions of the French monarchy.

The conviction with which Maxime champions the Republic's constitution as particular to Rome would certainly have struck a chord with traditionally-minded spectators in the seventeenth-century French audience, just as his defence of his countrymen's right to liberty must have delighted those who deplored the Cardinal's 'Machiavellian' encroachments on ancient freedoms enjoyed in France for more than 1200 years. It is not surprising then that the dramatic cut and thrust of the scene's political argument has so much in common with the exchanges in the Campion *Entretiens*. Hypocrite though Cinna is at this point in the action, his argument is at one with that of the political realist in the *Entretiens* who also argues from experience that Richelieu's authority alone can constrain 'une nation si folle à devenir sage' and curb the people's taste for unbridled liberty.[23] To a contemporary audience, Cinna's appeal to the recent evidence of the warring ambitions of the great patrician families would have had the same familiar ring:

> La liberté ne peut plus être utile
> Qu'à former les fureurs d'une guerre civile,
> Lorsque par un désordre à l'Univers fatal
> L'un ne veut point de maître, et l'autre point d'égal.
> Seigneur pour sauver Rome il faut qu'elle s'unisse
> En la main d'un bon Chef à qui tout obéisse.
>   (II, i, 585–90)

But those first spectators of *Cinna* are likely also to have known something of Bodin's celebrated eulogy of the distinctive sanctity of the French monarchy, of the inviolability of its 'Lois Fonda-mentales', and of the dignity of its Sovereign Courts. They would have relished Maxime's reminder of the suffering which a new and unfamiliar order of governance had brought with it, and noted how lame is Cinna's reply to a point equally tellingly made in the *Entretiens*:

> MAXIME: Les changements d'Etat que fait l'ordre céleste
>   Ne coûtent point de sang, n'ont rien qui soit funeste.
> CINNA: C'est un ordre des Dieux qui jamais ne se rompt,
>   De nous vendre un peu cher les grands biens qu'ils nous font.
>   (II, i, 557–60)

Furthermore Cinna's argument that 'cet ordre des Cieux / Change selon les temps comme selon les lieux' (II, i, 547–8), like his dismissal of the people's reverence for institutional tradition, were all recognizable arguments from those who valorized the superior political wisdom of the few and echoed the ministerial apologists' conviction that old-fashioned ideals must yield to the reality of changed times.

Seventeenth-century French monarchical convictions, together with the necessities of the plot, ensure that Maxime's Republicanism carries little weight. However, the dramatic context is such that Cinna's arguments prompt serious reservations – and not least because his last and most effective speech had opened with a betrayal of his Republican uncle, Pompey, which sharply reminded the spectator that not even Cinna believed in what he was saying (II, i, 563–70). It is also characteristic of Corneille's careful balancing of the argument that the scene closes with victory going to neither political thesis. Auguste cuts the debate short as he responds to Cinna's appeal that he take pity on the sufferings of his subjects:

> N'en délibérons plus, cette pitié l'emporte,
> Mon repos m'est bien cher, mais Rome est la plus forte,
> Et quelque grand malheur qui m'en puisse arriver,
> Je consens à me perdre afin de la sauver.
> (II, i, 621–4)

With this decision, prompted by 'l'amour du pays', Auguste already hints at qualities which will enable him to transcend Cinna's harsh vision of order by constraint and reveal an authority which will relegate present disagreement to nothing more than a memory of an unhappy past.

But Cinna himself will not forget that his appeal to Auguste's compassion brought the latter to follow a course in which personal interest was sacrificed to the public good. This altruism, followed by the trusting conferment of honours and the hand of Emilie, undermines Cinna's own belief in the justice of the Republican charge of tyranny. In the scene immediately following Auguste's departure Cinna may justify his behaviour to Maxime by a show of Republican fervour, but when he next returns to the matter of Auguste's rule he already makes a distinction between degrees of iniquity in tyranny. Reluctant to honour a promise which forces him to betray Auguste's trust and generosity, he bitterly protests that Emilie is the greater tyrant in insisting that he kill their benefactor (III, iv, 1052–3). It is significant that, by showing this effect of Auguste's 'douceur' on his betrayer, the play once again echoes the anti-Machiavellians' argument of political efficacy, when they contended that love and trust were more powerful principles of authority than the coercive exercise of force.

That this fundamentally Christian ideal of monarchical rule is indeed central to the play is also apparent in Corneille's evocation of the loneliness of the Emperor. Auguste's desire to escape his past provokes a sense of pity which ill accords with the horror normally associated with stage illustrations of the unjust ruler whose fear of retribution drives him from cruelty to cruelty.[24] Seneca's *De Clementia* had itself observed how this fatality of violence and cruelty resulted in as much misery for the ruler as for those he governed: 'Il faut maintenir les forfaits par nouvelles méchancetés: mais saurait-on trouver homme plus malheureux que celui à qui force est d'être méchant?'[25] It seems likely that Corneille, in gradually increasing our sympathy for Auguste, recalled these original reflections on the logic inherent in the criminal exercise of power. After the unexpected benignity of the Emperor's first appearance, this element of pathos becomes ever more important, reaching a high point in Auguste's desperate sense of isolation in Act IV, scene ii:

> Ciel, à qui voulez-vous désormais que je fie
> Les secrets de mon âme, et le soin de ma vie?
> Reprenez le pouvoir que vous m'avez commis
> Si donnant des Sujets, il ôte les amis.
>
> (IV, ii, 1121–4)

As constant threats to his authority force him into repression and cruelty, Auguste faces an unending struggle to eliminate his enemies:

> Mais quoi! toujours du sang, et toujours des supplices!
> Ma cruauté se lasse, et ne peut s'arrêter.
>
> (IV, ii, 1162–3)

His experience offers bitter confirmation that coercive methods only set the whole country into 'confusion et péril... car dès que la justice va mal, tout va mal, et quand elle va bien, tout va bien'.[26] But if the Emperor longs to give up his old ways, his problem is a double one. Not only does he need to discover the secret of just governance, he also needs to know how to make that justice evident in an action which breaks so completely with the past that the purity of his motives cannot be misinterpreted as yet another tyrannical ruse. In the meanwhile he must suffer all the consequences of his earlier assault on Republican legitimacy. The perspective is bleak, and small wonder that he contemplates abdication and suicide rather than await so remote an opportunity. Even in the final scenes of the play, when he has acknowledged that his own seizure of power makes him no better than those who conspire against him, the temptation to revert to tyranny is still there, as anger drives him yet again to threats of terrible reprisal.

Thus, from the Emperor's first appearance as a deeply troubled and indecisive figure, Corneille has developed a searching portrait of a 'tyran malgré lui' who, if only he could break free of the necessities of his past, gives repeated indications that he has the makings of all the qualities of the ideal monarch. But even as Auguste sacrifices his own hopes of personal peace to the contentments of his Roman subjects and takes his first step towards that nobler exercise of power, he has accepted the advice of his most deceitful counsellor. He has still to escape from the confusions fatally associated with illegitimacy of rule and, such are the consequences of his past, even his noblest instincts lead him closer to the assassin's knife. If we are to believe contemporary arguments in favour of a 'Politique chrétienne... enfermée dans le sein de la charité', this powerful dramatic irony is very evidence of the tyranny of a governance which relies only on the resources of the world: 'Commander, juger et faire du bien à autrui sont des actions vraiment royales et divines, qui toutefois sans la sagesse sont aveugles et produites à l'aventure: sans elle la puissance souveraine ne saurait agir, et sera comme un bras destitué de la conduite de l'œil.'[27] And yet this bitterly troubled and indecisive usurper has begun his search for the truth, even if constantly it eludes him. Auguste will soon discover the treachery hidden beneath the prudent advice of other men, but he will not cease to search for wisdom until the very last moments of the play. Only then will he come to deliverance in possession of a truth to be found neither in himself nor in the advice of others. Instead it will be made apparent in an exercise of clemency which, by transcending 'la gloire du temps sur la terre', at last permits him to enact his nobler qualities and enjoy 'la gloire de l'éternité... la vraie gloire qui se fait des vertus solides et utiles au public... qui fait les Augustes et les Tites, les héros de l'histoire, et les délices des peuples'.[28]

That act of clemency, as it was retold in the seventeenth century, was almost unanimously interpreted as a master-stroke of policy with which, once and for all, Auguste consolidated his position. With the sole exception of Corneille's *Cinna*, all accounts dating from the first half of the seventeenth century follow Seneca in relating how Augustus gratefully accepted Livia's advice that he pardon the plotters. This received interpretation of events, while it did not go so far as to propose a Machiavellian explanation of the Emperor's motives, at least suggested that Augustus' clemency was the considered enactment of a policy intended to serve him better than repression. Bodin is characteristic, noting the difficulty posed by factious nobles for whom civil discord is an opportunity to fish in

troubled waters. In considering what should best be done with such
rebels once they are called to account, he considers exile to be a
dangerous policy since that leaves them free to return at the head of
a foreign army. In Bodin's view, they should either be killed or made
good friends, and he cites Augustus' pardon of Cinna as a memorable
instance of the latter choice of policy, by which 'il voulut...essayer
si par douceur il pourrait gagner les cœurs des hommes: depuis il ne
trouva jamais personne qui osât rien attenter contre lui'.[29] This
interprets the pardon in the same spirit as Seneca's Livia proposed
it, as a manoeuvre to be used by a prudent king in the complex
strategy of asserting his royal authority. Rather closer to the date of
Cinna, the *Recueil Général du Bureau d'Adresse* also cites Augustus'
clemency in its discussion of the relative merits of retribution and
forgiveness. Majority opinion sides with punishment if it is a matter of
state security, but it is also observed that a king may take the nobler
and often more effective course of pardoning the offender.[30] Setting
the pardon somewhere between political calculation, heroic generosity, and noble statecraft, the *Recueil* is of much the same opinion as
Du Bosc, for whom the pardon is both evidence of Augustus'
generosity of heart and a master-stroke of political subtlety which
qualified Livia for a worthy place amongst his *Gallerie* of heroines.[31]

Twenty years later Georges de Scudéry took a different line and
placed the episode amongst his lists of royal acts of bravery. Despite
Livie's advice, he writes, Augustus pardoned Cinna as a personal test
of his own valour, deliberately choosing to prove his nerve by taking
an enormous risk.[32] But this characteristically idiosyncratic interpretation is likely to have derived from Scudéry's greater
familiarity with *Cinna* than with Roman history for, apart from
Corneille's version of events, his is the only other account in which
Augustus, against the historical record, rejects his wife's advice.
Where Seneca, in Goulart's translation, had recounted that the
Emperor, 'tout joyeux d'avoir rencontré un tel avocat, remercia sa
femme', Corneille's Auguste refuses Livie's advice as the fruit of
subtle but unheroic calculations inspired by weakness (IV, iii).[33] This
crucial alteration has not prevented a number of commentators from
interpreting the final pardon as a political stratagem, for all that it sets
aside all possibility of reading a taint of opportunist calculation into
the pardon and leaves open the possibility of a nobler motivation.

If we are fully to understand the final scene of the play, we need
to return to the Emperor's first appearance, where he longs to reject

his former self and break with the oppressive methods which events seem to force upon him. Between then and the clemency of the last act Auguste takes only two decisions, both of which indicate a refusal of that kind of statecraft which is based on an opportunist calculation of 'l'intérêt'. Pity for the people led him to a first decision valorizing altruism over self-interest when he decided not to abdicate but to sacrifice himself to the general good (II, i, 621–4). This prepared his second decision to reject his wife's advice as unworthily continuing the calculations of personal advantage which had carried him to his present possession of power (IV, iii, 1245–6). The anti-Machiavellian character of these two decisions had already been prepared at the start of the Council scene, when Auguste had explained that the lessons of history were too contradictory to offer him a key to wise political decision. The conflicting examples of Sylla and Caesar were of little use to him in deciding whether to abdicate or not:

> L'exemple souvent n'est qu'un miroir trompeur,
> Et l'ordre du Destin qui gêne nos pensées
> N'est pas toujours écrit dans les choses passées.
>
> (II, i, 388–90)

Such disenchantment with history as a useful, but insufficient, instrument of political decision strikes at the root of 'realist' political theory in which Machiavelli's commentary on Livy offered the most prestigious model of a pragmatic appeal to the historical record of success or failure.[34] Furthermore, the two occasions when Auguste seeks and receives advice also offer convincing evidence of the inadequacy of purely human prudence. The Council scene first showed this, since Auguste rejected the only honest advice offered him in that inconclusive debate and persisted in a governance detested both by himself and by his counsellors. The irony of this mistaken trust is clear from the privileged point of view of the spectator, but Auguste will come to realize how insufficient was that human counsel only when he learns of Cinna's treachery. Yet another indication of the anti-Machiavellian implications of the Council scene is apparent in Auguste's reference to 'l'ordre du Destin'. This supposes an active and purposive force working against the Emperor and suggests a context for political decision very different from that of Machiavelli's Prince, for whom destiny was no more than the blind chance against which he measured his 'virtu'. In fact Auguste's dissatisfaction with the politics of force and constraint by fear is rooted in this conviction that a higher power, whose purposes are hidden from him, actively opposes the achievement of his ends. As a ruler, he already senses that an understanding of that higher purpose would deliver him from a vicious circle of crises and repressive expediencies: as a man, he longs for that knowledge as the key to a personal peace and fulfilment which will surpass the hollow splendours of his present position (ii, i, 359–70).

To audiences familiar with contemporary Christian political theory, the reasons for Auguste's difficulties would not have been hard to see. Expanding on the theme that 'Le Prince Chrétien ne se peut arrêter à la politique humaine', Mugnier is amazed at the difficulty of decisions which, without God's help, are sure to confound the best of rulers:

Pour réussir dans le gouvernement des peuples et dans l'emploi des grandes affaires, il faut une sagesse qui soit au-dessus de l'esprit, et de la capacité d'un homme...Le Prince ne se peut arrêter à une politique qui soit purement naturelle et humaine...Sages du siècle, politiques mondains, entendez-vous ces paroles?...Que pensez-vous faire vivant détachés de la Sapience Eternelle? Vous ne pouvez non plus subsister avec toutes vos finesses et vos tromperies, que le rayon de lumière séparé du corps lumineux...Il est indubitable que la loi de Dieu étant la véritable sagesse, toute prudence qui ne coulera point de cette source se tarira, ou bien si elle a cours, elle infectera tous ceux qui en voudront user. Dieu est le maître du conseil et de la prudence.

Such are the uncertainties of government that the wise monarch can only turn away from reliance on human resources. He must 'appeler le Ciel au secours et prier quelque intelligence de lui donner les instructions nécessaires pour comprendre un secret qui surpassait la capacité d'un esprit humain'.[35] This wisdom, far superior to the frailties of human reason, is still closed to Auguste, and yet an entry to it seems essential if he is to find his legitimate place within the providential unfolding of history. Thus Auguste, betrayed by those he most loved, turns for the second time to the advice of others, only to be disappointed again by a wife whose prudent counsel he considers to be grounded in weakness and ambition (iv, iii, 1256). All that remains is for him to look to heaven in the hope of obtaining that wisdom which still eludes him:

> Le Ciel m'inspirera ce qu'ici je dois faire,
> Adieu, nous perdons temps.
> (iv, iii, 1258–9)

The significance of Auguste's rejection of the prudent calculations of men, like the importance of his appeal to heaven for the grace of a higher political wisdom, must have been obvious to those who so admired the play. Balzac's *Le Romain* had also celebrated another, heavenly authority, 'distincte et séparée de l'autre autorité qui naît du pouvoir... Ce caractère et cette lumière corrigent les défauts et imperfections de la nature... Ce caractère... est à cette personne une sauvegarde du Ciel contre les violences de la terre, la rend inviolable à des ennemis irrités... lie les mains des traîtres qui viennent à elle avec un mauvais dessein.' In a lengthy development on the theme of the hero's semi-divine power of command, Balzac's text invites constant comparison with Auguste's ascent to legitimacy in the course of the play:

La puissance est une chose lourde et matérielle qui traîne après soi un long équipage de moyens humains sans lesquels elle demeurerait immobile... Elle fait un effort pour faire un pas. L'autorité, au contraire, tient de la noblesse de son origine et de la vertu des choses divines, opère ses miracles en repos... est toute recueillie en la puissance qui l'exerce, sans chercher d'aide ni se servir de second: elle est forte toute nue et toute seule: elle combat étant désarmée.[36]

At almost the same time as *Cinna* was performed and published, the Campion *Entretiens* also addressed the theme. Unaware of Corneille's play, the defender of the Cardinal's politics of severity quotes the early rule of Augustus as proof that a ruthless elimination of all opponents remains the most effective guarantee of safety for most rulers.[37] Very few manage to combine severity with 'douceur', and in such cases,

la fortune a peut-être autant de part que la prudence et la volonté; ou pour parler plus chrétiennement... cette harmonie est l'effet d'une grâce que Dieu ne confère qu'à un petit nombre de ceux qu'il choisit pour présider aux états qu'il veut combler de ses bénédictions: on peut conclure que le Prince n'ayant en lui que le choix entre ces deux moyens de se faire obéir, il doit s'arrêter à celui que son industrie lui peut le plus sûrement acquérir... Le sage politique qui a pour objet le bien de l'Etat en général ne doit point s'émouvoir de la douleur particulière des membres qui le composent, quand il est expédient qu'ils souffrent pour le salut du corps entier.

Some support for this argument is found in the example of Julius Caesar: 'puisqu'il avait déjà renversé toutes les lois, et qu'il avait par ses premières démarches laissé lieu de croire qu'il ferait céder toute sorte de droit divin et humain au dessein d'établir sa domination;

il est permis d'attribuer au défaut de sa prudence tout ce qu'il a omis de faire pour s'y maintenir'.[38] Other speakers acknowledge the realism of this but still reject the principle of prudent rule by fear. Since 'chaque cruauté que le prince cruel exerce est une semence de ruine', they call instead for a return to the combination of 'douceur' and 'sévérité' traditionally characteristic of the Kings of France.[39]

Everything in Corneille's characterization of Auguste's descent from tyranny to imperial apotheosis leads to a clemency which offers just such an illustration of the traditional values of the French monarchy. Those values alone offer him the means to escape from the benighted confusions of secular ambition and the tainted calculations of human prudence. The contrast between *Cinna*'s conclusion with Auguste's triumph and the closing disillusionments of *Horace* could hardly be more complete. The 'crime' on which Tulle had sat in judgement was the terrible product of the hero's courageous choice to uphold the equivocal values of a city destined to world domination at the cost of its own humanity, just as Horace's pardon was justified by simultaneous recognition and 'dissimulation' of the past in the criminal precedents of Rome's dark origins. In contrast, the Emperor's redemptive wisdom begins in a dark night of the soul recounted in Act II and experienced in the monologue of Act IV, scene ii. From that bitter experience comes a true humility born of self-knowledge and revulsion from a criminal past in which domination was won by force. With Maxime's confession of treachery, Auguste loses not only his last friend but also the last shred of comforting self-esteem (v, iii, 1665). In anger and despair he begins the last stage of his accession to a Reason higher than that of the world of men and which, in its eternity, transcends both past and future.

Paradoxical though it may seem, Auguste's desperation does not deny the rationality of his final clemency. All depends on what we understand by the 'reason' which motivates him. There existed in seventeenth-century France a distinctive analysis of heroic motivation and action in which 'la raison', in the specific context of heroic prudence, stood much closer to inspired action than a twentieth-century reader might first suppose. A good instance of this is to be found in a contemporary description of Condé in action on the battlefield:

Aussitôt conçu, aussitôt exécuté; ce Prince ne met point de milieu entre le dire et le faire; ses actions ont la promptitude de ses pensées; ses exploits ont la même activité que ses desseins; la conception et la naissance de ses victoires se font dans un même temps; ses méditations sont aussitôt des effets que des conseils... Sa valeur va aussi vite que son esprit... Dans lui vaincre et vouloir vaincre paraît quasi le même.[40]

This is but one of many references in the period to a passionately impulsive reason which inspires heroic deeds so astonishing as to confound the calculations of mere human prudence. 'La prudence héroïque' offers evidence of the grace of a mysterious but infallible exterior force which impels exceptional souls to action and ultimate success. Du Bosc, citing Aristotle on the man of noble genius, explains:

Les vertus héroïques sont à moitié divines: nous l'apprendrons encore bien mieux de leur principe, qui sans doute est bien plus relevé et plus extraordinaire que le principe des vertus communes de la morale... Aristote avoue en paroles expresses que *le principe de la vertu héroïque n'est pas la seule raison mais quelque chose de meilleur et de plus fort*. Et si la pensée de ce philosophe nous semble obscure en cet endroit, Saint Thomas l'explique admirablement, et nous enseigne que par ce principe si relevé, Aristote entend un instinct, ou un mouvement divin qui est extérieur et qui vient du Ciel: et ce qui est admirable, c'est qu'il est meilleur et plus certain à l'homme de suivre le mouvement de l'instinct que le mouvement de la raison même... Ce que la philosophie appelle instinct ou mouvement extérieur, la théologie l'appelle plus nettement grâce, don ou secours céleste, sans lequel, à bien parler, il n'y a point de véritables vertus héroïques.[41]

So also, in the noblest context of the Monarch, Balzac's *Le Prince* exploits the Platonic theory of recognition in describing the heroic prudence of Louis XIII:

La plupart des grandes résolutions qu'il a prises lui ont été envoyées du Ciel. La plupart de ces conseils partent d'une prudence supérieure, et sont plutôt des inspirations venues immédiatement de Dieu que des propositions faites par des hommes. Il trouve la vérité sans prendre la peine de la chercher et le plus subit mouvement de sa pensée est d'ordinaire si raisonnable et si concluant, que le discours qui vient après ne fait qu'approuver ce premier acte, sans y rien ajouter de nouveau.[42]

Balzac's Louis is undoubtedly more fortunate than Auguste, but then he is both hero and unquestionable King by Divine Right, which – before the final scene – the Emperor is not. But both Balzac and Corneille draw on a mystical theory of heroism and kingship in which this higher and impulsive reason is believed so suddenly to illuminate individual action that it offers incontrovertible evidence of heroic rightness and, in the case of the ruler, of royal legitimacy. In pardoning Cinna, Auguste senses to the full this passionate spur to action and at last achieves a harmony with the highest kind of Reason in the grace of a full understanding of God's providential purposes in the world.

In 1646 Cotin dedicated *Théoclée* to Condé (then Duc d'Enghien). He recounts the heroic consequences of passions as intense as those of Auguste when, just before the moment of pardon, he is lost in a turmoil of anger and despair. For Cotin, as for Du Bois Hus, the young prince is one of 'ces hommes divins, qui ont su … connaître les grandes vérités et faire les grandes actions. Car … quoi qu'on ait voulu dire des vertus contemplatives et des vertus morales, elles sont trop bien unies pour les séparer jamais'. By snatching victory from the jaws of defeat at Fribourg, Enghien gave evidence of an 'incroyable valeur' which overcame 'la nature et le temps, et faisait elle-même sa destinée'. This dazzling success offered a heroic example of

ces illustres désespoirs qui n'abbattent pas le courage, mais qui l'élèvent et le transportent; qui ne troublent pas la raison, mais qui l'éclairent et la purifient; qui dans les grandes extrémités savent prendre les grands et les importants partis; qui sont pleins d'une fureur céleste et sacrée, et par leurs admirables succès surprennent les politiques médiocres, qui jugent trop humainement des choses divines … Leur invincible courage, libre de toutes les passions basses, épuré des lâches intérêts, témoin à soi-même de ce qu'il est digne et de quoi il est capable, égal à toute la grandeur du monde, et à toute l'étendue des siècles, connaît ce qu'il doit à sa réputation, à la gloire de sa patrie, à la divinité de son principe.[43]

Despite the windiness of this passage, Cotin's conclusion has an obvious affinity with Auguste's words as he rises above his own 'illustres désespoirs'. Setting aside conspiracy and betrayal, the Emperor outstrips the reasoning of ordinary mortals and fully realizes himself and the glory of his station in a clemency inspired by the serene truths of Eternity:

> En est-ce assez, ô Ciel, et le Sort pour me nuire
> A-t-il quelqu'un des miens qu'il veuille encor séduire?
> Qu'il joigne à ses efforts le secours des Enfers,
> Je suis maître de moi comme de l'Univers.
> Je le suis, je veut l'être. O Siècles, ô Mémoire,
> Conservez à jamais ma dernière victoire,
> Je triomphe aujourd'hui du plus juste courroux
> De qui le souvenir puisse aller jusqu'à vous.
> Soyons, amis, Cinna, c'est moi que t'en convie.
>
> (v, iii, 1693–701)

By this challenge to heaven and hell, Auguste heroically asserts his self-mastery in a supreme effort of the will – and with that the gods relent and a victorious knowledge of their higher truth bursts upon him.

Centrally significant to the political argument of the play is the way in which Auguste's first truly royal actions appeal to the unifying power of love over anger and violence. With his 'Soyons amis, Cinna', and his 'Aime Cinna, ma fille', he evokes the harmonizing powers of that *philia*, or mutual affection, which Aristotle had first discussed in Book VII of the *Ethics* and which devout political theory held, in its higher form of Christian charity, to be the essential unifying element in a just society ordered according to the will of God. The opening debate of the Campion *Entretiens* on 'le plus sûr appui de l'autorité souveraine' similarly expresses this belief in the fusion of sovereignty and spirituality, when one of the friends refutes the pragmatists' argument in favour of coercion by force and fear:

Chacun sait que l'amour est le principe de l'union de toutes choses... C'est lui qui les lie, les meut et les rejoint quand elles ont été divisées... [L'amour] meut le corps de l'Etat d'un mouvement libre et naturel... mais [la crainte] le traîne avec peine et avec violence. [L'amour] lui inspire un principe de vie qui lui fait exercer toutes ses fonctions avec facilité et même avec plaisir, et l'autre qui le trouve toujours répugnant, ne le remue pour ainsi dire que par ressort.[44]

Voltaire was badly mistaken to condemn Auguste's 'soyons amis' as inappropriate, for the reality is that Corneille has chosen a formulation central to the larger significance of his play and which marks the turning-point in the political drama when the binding power of love sets aside once and for all the coercive view of social order favoured by the worldly adepts of 'la raison d'état'.

But how could such a rule through love be reconciled with justice and prudence in the matter of conspiracy against the Crown? Bodin put the problem clearly when, on the one hand, he wrote that 'entre les grâces que le Prince peut donner il n'y en a point de plus belle que de l'injure faite à sa personne' but, on the other, had insisted that an attack on the Crown was unpardonable.[45] Following Christian teaching and traditional jurisconsults, Pierre de l'Hommeau concedes that 'c'est une marque de souveraineté que d'octroyer grâce et rémission', but he too makes the important reservation that the Prince should never pardon the crime of 'lèse-majesté divine et humaine'.[46] All seventeenth-century commentators, and the public stage in turn, repeatedly stressed the unforgivable character of the crime, as does Auguste when he reminds Livie of the Prince's obligation to punish such plotters:

> Tout son peuple est blessé par un tel attentat,
> Et la seule pensée est un crime d'Etat,
> Une offense qu'on fait à toute sa Province,
> Dont il faut qu'il la venge, ou cesse d'être Prince.
>
> (IV, iii, 1251–4)

Needless to say Richelieu himself had no doubts about the necessity to distinguish here between individual and public morality: 'Un chrétien ne saurait trop tôt oublier une injure et pardonner une offense, ni un roi, un gouverneur et un magistrat trop tôt les châtier, quand les fautes sont d'Etat.'[47] The implacable Cardinal-Minister who had been deaf to all appeals for the life of Montmorency reminds Louis XIII that, 'en matière de crime d'Etat, il faut fermer la porte à la pitié, et mépriser les plaintes des personnes intéressées, et les discours d'une populace ignorante, qui blâme quelquefois ce qui lui est plus utile et souvent tout à fait nécessaire'.[48] This hard-bitten realism needs to be contrasted with those traditional theorists whose idealist definitions of kingly rule made no distinction between private and public virtues and who praised the efficacy of reliance on the people's love, singling out clemency as the most sublimely effective of all the royal virtues.

While Seneca simply observed that clemency forged unbreakable bonds between ruler and subject, his seventeenth-century elaborators attributed to clemency the particularly royal quality of pure gift, devoid of any calculation of personal interest. Through this selfless creation of a new life for a subject who otherwise would have been dead, kings came closest to the creative powers of the Divinity who authorized and inspired their governance and whose power they represented on earth. That inveterate Aristotelian legalist Priézac considers the importance of *philia* and Christian charity to be so pre-eminent that they transcend even the law, should love and law conflict:

L'amitié [est] le nœud de la nature et l'âme de l'univers, la mère de la société, le rempart des cités et le génie des Etats... La loi même, quelque souveraine et impérieuse qu'elle soit, n'étend sa providence que sur les choses du dehors, et en cela elle demeure beaucoup au-dessous de l'amitié qui règle le cœur et la main, la langue et la volonté, et qui enfin n'est guère differente de l'union que sur toutes choses les politiques ont cherché dans la République.[49]

In no other royal act was the divinity of the Monarch more in evidence than in the exercise of clemency. Priézac may not have the eloquence of Portia in *The Merchant of Venice*, but he expresses the same convictions in opposing clemency to a reliance on fear and force:

A qui est plus nécessaire la clémence, qu'à celui qui n'a rien en sa fortune de meilleur que de vouloir, ni de plus grand que de pouvoir sauver les hommes et leur donner une nouvelle vie et un nouveau destin? C'est par la clémence que César et Auguste ont consacré leurs noms à l'immortalité, et que Rome s'est étonnée de ce que sous des princes si humains, elle avait pu regretter la perte de sa liberté. Si la clémence est à un Roi ce que l'humanité est au commun des hommes, il s'ensuit que la cruauté lui fait perdre non seulement la qualité de Roi, mais aussi celle d'homme. Si la clémence lui acquiert partout des amis et des sujets volontaires, la cruauté multiplie ses ennemis.[50]

With this ideal of royal governance Auguste's offer of friendship breaks away from his own guilty past and, in a new order of charity, rescues Cinna from treachery and confusion by giving him a new life:

> Soyons amis, Cinna, c'est moi qui t'en convie:
> Comme à mon ennemi je t'ai donné la vie,
> Et malgré la fureur de ton lâche destin,
> Je te la donne encor comme à mon assassin.
> (v, iii, 1701–4)

Auguste's appeal to love and his union of Emilie and Cinna in marriage are the public enactments of a conciliating power by which the sacred wisdom of a true Monarch leaves far behind it the vain differences and common calculations of lesser men.

Thus the *dénouement* of *Cinna* brings with it a long-awaited resolution to the conflicts of *Le Cid* and *Horace*. Individual heroic initiative is at last subsumed within a comprehensively just order of governance, as individual and public virtues coincide with the providential perspectives of a revolution authorized by the grace of God. Abolishing his bloody past of secular governance founded on wilful ambition and force, Auguste inaugurates a renewed monarchical order illuminated by a justice and love which have their origins in eternity. His discovery of the true nature of 'l'ordre du Destin' has

brought him consecration and legitimacy and his clemency bespeaks
an order of values within which his subjects unhesitatingly yield to
the indisputable evidence of his superiority. Emilie's hatred suddenly
dies, because the hero and Emperor

a fait connaître qu'il est animé d'une force plus divine qu'humaine. Une
vertu médiocre peut bien faire naître l'amour dans le cœur des sujets, mais
quand elle est extraordinaire et vraiment héroïque, c'est alors qu'elle
occupe l'entendement et qu'elle le remplit de la grandeur de son image. On
aime les égaux et les inférieurs, on respecte les grands, mais on décerne des
honneurs divins aux Héros qui ne sont nés que pour la gloire.[51]

It has been remarked elsewhere, but in terms which were not
accorded their full seventeenth-century resonance, that in *Cinna* we
witness 'le transfert de la puissance à l'être'.[52] Auguste's clemency
indeed bears witness to a royalty inspired by the spirit and not by the
principles of the world:

Son origine est plus haute, sa splendeur ne peut pas sortir des ténèbres de
la terre, et sa grandeur fait voir en telle trop de traits d'une main divine,
pour être mise au rang des inventions humaines... La source de la majesté
des Rois est si haute... et sa force si divine, qu'il ne faut pas trouver étrange
qu'à la façon des choses célestes elle se fasse révérer des hommes sans qu'il
leur soit permis de la connaître... Ne serait-elle point un rayon écoulé de
l'adorable majesté de Dieu, un rejaillissement de sa splendeur, et un éclat
de cette gloire qu'il fit autrefois luire sur la face du Prince des Hébreux?[53]

In this sense Livie's closing lines on the divinization of Auguste (v,
iii, 1765–74) look forward to what Priézac himself terms 'cet espèce
de culte civil' which is the adoration of the majesty and divinity of
an idealized Louis XIV.

Cinna culminates in a splendid act of homage to the sanctity of the
Kings of France as Auguste's clemency offers the supreme illustration
of sovereign independence from all solicitations but those of God.
Auguste had known only disenchantment before the revelation of a
truth which far outstrips men's tainted calculations of advantage,
and the preceding acts had shown how his present plenitude in the
achievement of true legitimacy began in the desolation with which
he had humbly recognized his personal lack of worth and finally
appealed to the heavens for help. Wrenching himself out of a morass
of rivalry, betrayal, and recrimination, he is motivated by nothing
other than the sudden revelation of what is eternally right, and acts
upon that perception with a freedom which alone gives his clemency
its true moral significance. With the last scene of the play the

monarch stands redeemed and ascends to the highest pinnacle of human achievement, confidently exposed to the judgement of the world and of future generations who will recognize and honour in him a hero divinely blessed as ruler of Imperial Rome. He has become one of those 'déités vivantes' of whom Colomby had written in his description of the establishment of the Capetian monarchy in France:

Il ne suffit pas que les Princes soient autorisés du Ciel, il faut que leurs sujets le croient afin qu'il les aiment et les révèrent comme si Dieu leur commandait en personne et n'était pas moins présent aux hommes qu'il l'est aux anges... La seule force peut fait craindre les Rois comme des lions, mais l'opinion qu'on a que leur puissance est légitime, les fait honorer comme des déités vivantes.[54]

Auguste has achieved no less than that sacred legitimacy to which Pépin le Bref referred when he became the first of the line of France's 'Rois très-chrétiens': 'Il faut être selon le cœur de Dieu... pour pouvoir s'affermir sur un nouveau trône... Il y a eu dans leur esprit plus d'inspiration que d'ambition: ils ont plutôt suivi les décrets éternels de Dieu, que leur vanité passagère et... ils se sont plutôt abandonnés à la providence, qu'à l'indiscret désir de régner.'[55] For all that he wears the Imperial purple, Corneille's Auguste stands before us at the end of *Cinna* a monarch by Divine Right and in the most hallowed tradition of the Kings of France.

7

Polyeucte *(1642–3) and* La Mort de Pompée *(1643–4)*

Criticism of *Polyeucte* has long affirmed the play's close relation to Corneille's preceding plays, but the Christian inspiration of its hero's characterization has been openly questioned ever since Nadal suggested that Polyeucte 'comme tout héros plus impatient d'être que de connaître...saisira Dieu par la violence'. Doubrovsky's indifference to the devotional element in *Polyeucte* forms part of his larger discussion of the heroic ethos, which argues that a Christian inspiration is quite foreign to Corneille's entire dramatic output. 'La "christianisation" de ses pièces constitue une totale erreur...De fait le projet héroïque est, par nature, *antichrétien*. Si donc *Polyeucte* est bien...en continuité avec le reste du théâtre de Corneille, ce n'est pas parce que ce théâtre serait chrétien, mais, au contraire, parce que *Polyeucte* n'est point, malgré les apparences, une pièce chrétienne'.[1] Prigent approaches Corneille's work through Pascal rather than Hegel, but comes to not dissimilar conclusions. His verdict on *Polyeucte* is that 'le héros principal est cornélien avant que d'être chrétien, il appartient à la même famille que Rodrigue, Horace et Auguste'. A 'Pascalian' unease before the ostentation and apparent lack of Christian humility in Polyeucte's resolve publicly to smash the idols leads Prigent to question conduct which seems to push individual self-assertion beyond the limits of Christian orthodoxy: 'le héros installe son fief au-delà de la nature. L'accès à cet héroïsme n'est pas un don du ciel.'[2] In both cases the critic's argument relates to a schema, whether it be that of a Hegelian master–slave dialectic or a Pascalian concept of orders, which is at some distance from more obvious and more natural referends in the moral theology of the period. As a result Corneille's first martyr-hero forces these critics into a drastic *prise de position*, since the play's perceived continuity with the nature of the values held to inspire its predecessors makes or breaks the validity of their earlier discussion of the hero in *Le Cid*, *Horace*, and *Cinna*.

No matter how seductive the arguments which deny the Christian inspiration of *Polyeucte*, they become impossible to follow once we perceive that play's obvious place within contemporary discussions of the theology of grace and of heroic virtue. Indeed we have seen that all of Corneille's plays written during Louis XIII's reign show the imprint of the Christian *moralistes* and political theorists of the period, if only in the degree in which their effects are calculated in relation to the expectations and understanding of the Catholic audiences for which they were written. This recognition of the ways in which the dramatist exploited a common ideological patrimony in calculating his drama's effect on the spectator in no way diminishes the distinctive and enduring interest of his plays, and one can only treat with some scepticism critical readings which either disregard that idealist tradition, or try to reduce it to so many 'sources' held somehow to confront or oppose his plays.[3] In both his secular dramas and his 'tragédies chrétiennes', there remains a clear continuity in their illustration of the hero, whether in the simple providentialism of *Clitandre*, the final moral impasse of *Le Cid*, the tragic disgrace and political 'recuperation' of Horace, the political 'grace' of Auguste's final clemency, or the overtly Christian grace which impels Polyeucte to martyrdom.

However, *Polyeucte* undoubtedly occupies a special place in Corneille's output in so far as it illustrates the exemplary journey of the hero's soul towards salvation and celebrates, as well as explores, the place of the Divine in the affairs of men.[4] In this celebratory aspect alone, Corneille's 'tragédie chrétienne' stands apart from the previous secular plays, although its effect is already foreshadowed in the closing scene of *Cinna*. Failure to recognize this distinctive characteristic seems to have been the main cause of critical confusion over the play's Christian inspiration and its relation to Corneille's previous work. And yet, as we have already seen in the second part of this study, Corneille makes it very clear in the 'Abrégé' prefacing *Polyeucte* that his play conforms entirely to a Counter-Reformation aesthetic. For once, he has put his art to the service of the prior truths of the Christian faith as they stand revealed in a martyr's life and death. In consequence his earlier more problematic presentation of political subject-matter – even that of *Cinna*, prior to Auguste's final apotheosis – takes second place to the necessity for exemplary clarity. This crucial change of poetics means that a critical reading of the play is itself forced to move from discussion to recognition of the clear devotional significance contained within the evolution and fortunes of a number of carefully contrasted roles. This does not mean that *Polyeucte* lacks interest as a political play: it records, after all, the establishment of a Christian order in Armenia. But that revolution is itself yet another unequivocal 'sign' of the play's higher purpose, and contributes to the play's illustration of the enduring and triumphant validity of a Christian life and death.

This celebratory note apparent in Auguste's final apotheosis and Polyeucte's martyrdom adapts to the stage a contemporary tradition which re-exploited ancient philosophy to the ends of Christian moral teaching, and did not hesitate to describe heroic virtue in overtly Christian terms of mystical inspiration. By adapting to the heroic *morale* a Platonic theory of the ecstatic recognition of Truth, these heroic moralists certainly come close to the limits of orthodoxy, both in their faith in the power of Right Reason and in their preoccupation with the theme of redemption at the expense of a corresponding recognition of the consequences of original sin.[5] In Corneille's case, however, it should be said that his depiction of the hero never strays beyond the bounds of Catholic orthodoxy.[6] *Cinna* already suggested that, of himself, Auguste could achieve no fulfilment and that his clemency was a special grace which, in legitimizing his rule, exceptionally crowned his natural participation in that Right Reason which was the common privilege of every man.[7] In conformity with those Christian *moralistes* who maintained that only such a 'transport héroïque' could permit the hero to outstrip the prudence of ordinary mortals, the play clearly showed that Auguste could only surpass himself once he had recognized the frailty of his own capacities and turned to heaven for help in rising above his own mortality. His sudden clemency illustrated that 'hardiesse louable' which Caussin believed to be unmistakable evidence of Grace at work in the individual soul: 'Tout habile homme, considérant ce qu'il est, ne peut être hardi de soi-même, à cause de l'incapacité et de la faiblesse de la nature humaine, et pour tant il faut avouer que s'il y a quelque hardiesse, elle lui vient nécessairement d'en haut.'[8] Such was our corruption that God alone inspired heroic daring which fell within the bounds of virtue. Without His aid no man, whatever his courage and determination, could achieve anything of lasting value.

Since the hand of God was at work in all such deeds of exceptional virtue, the difference between hero and saint becomes almost imperceptible in the works of many seventeenth-century *moralistes*. The twentieth-century reader may be disconcerted to find so many heroic 'galleries' fusing the moral philosophy of antiquity with Christian moral analysis and listing with equal enthusiasm pagan heroes and the saints and martyrs of the Church. For Du Bosc, however, the heroines of antiquity and those of the New Dispensation of Christ were all inspired by a 'mouvement extérieur [que] la Théologie appelle Grâce, Don ou Secours Céleste'.[9] Mugnier, for his part, invoked Plato and Aristotle to describe such heroic inspiration as 'une sagesse de l'esprit, qui donne la vie', transcending the insufficiencies of '[la] sagesse de la chair, qui enfante la mort':

Reconnaissons que la sagesse du monde n'est qu'une sagesse de terre, de boue, et de chair; qui la cherche est aveugle, qui la trouve est misérable, et qui la suit est perdu sans espérance de ressource ... Il est donc nécessaire que nous ayons recours à quelque sagesse supérieure à la nôtre, à quelque esprit divin qui nous éclaire et à quelque intelligence qui nous fortifie.[10]

The collapse of Horace's ambitions into benighted disillusionment and failure and Auguste's painful voyage towards self-knowledge had both suggested these limits to purely human initiative. Now *Polyeucte* takes its place in Corneille's dramatic 'gallerie' of heroic virtues but, as a natural successor to the final act of *Cinna*, does so in unambiguously Christian terms.[11]

Le Moyne's *Gallerie des femmes fortes* offers one of the fullest expositions of the grace which alone was believed to permit imperfect man the sublimities of heroic virtue. Describing the passionate reason which inspires both hero and saint, Le Moyne typically mingles Platonic terminology with a language more usually reserved for Christian accounts of the working of Grace:

Si le transport est de toute la personne, si la partie intellectuelle emporte l'appétitive, si l'âme enlève le corps: et que d'un commun effort elles aillent toutes, ou au bien divin et souverain, ou à cet honnête éminent qui est en cette vie le dernier terme de la vertu consommée: ce transport général qui est un transport d'action est l'enthousiasme qu'on attribue aux héros ... On ne fait point de doute que le transport soit nécessaire aux vertus héroïques.[12]

Elsewhere Le Moyne observes that the purest and greatest embodiment of such virtue was Christ himself upon the cross – 'le vrai trône de la vertu héroïque'.[13] But, according to its context and diverse action on the soul, heroic 'enthousiasme' could inspire many kinds of excellence in humbler mortals. It lay behind the philosopher's pursuit of the truth, or the eloquence of the orator or poet. In its most brilliant manifestation it was to be seen in 'un transport d'action', but even here the hero was never very far from

the contemplative virtues, since the spiritual values infused and
completed heroic action in the world: 'Quoi qu'on ait voulu dire des
vertus contemplatives et des vertus morales, elles sont trop bien unies
pour les séparer jamais: et quiconque n'excelle qu'aux unes ou aux
autres, n'est point une personne extraordinaire'.[14] Pierre Coton's
Sermons sur les principales et plus difficiles matières de la foi similarly exalt
the hero as inspired by an essentially mystical 'dépassement' of the
world:

L'homme spirituel encore qu'il parle, traite, et opère devant tout le monde,
il ne fiche pas ses yeux que sur le Roi du Ciel et de la Terre qui est là
présent, et en comparaison duquel tous les monarques et potentats de la
terre sont gens de basse étoffe… Et ce faisant, il acquiert une magnanimité
si héroïque qu'il foule aux pieds toutes les choses du monde.[15]

Coton is concerned here with the active virtues of the devout
Christian life and with the saintly 'unreason' which inspired a
number of Corneille's contemporaries to signal acts of devotion in
heroic self-sacrifice.[16] Similarly Balzac's reflections upon the lives of
the early saints and martyrs wonderfully express his awe before their
heroic devotion to God and scorn for the world:

Ces grandes âmes qui méprisaient la mort, comme si elles eussent eu des
corps de louage et une vie empruntée. O mon âme que d'honneur et de
gloire! O mon imagination que de délices et de douleurs, s'écriaient-ils au
milieu des flammes!… Ce n'était plus amour ni constance, c'était une
aliénation des sens… une sainte, une divine fureur.[17]

From such a sense of wonder it is but a short step to the exemplary
effect of *Polyeucte*, as the seventeenth-century audience witnessed the
public scandal of the Christian hero's iconoclasm, his private
sacrifice in abandoning his wife, and his joyful acceptance of
suffering and death.

But not all approved of such extreme behaviour, even at the time
of the play's composition. The lay *habitués* of the Hôtel de
Rambouillet thought it bad enough that Polyeucte attended a pagan
religious ceremony, but the saintly devotion which led him to treat
his wife with such a lack of gallantry made Sévère seem the only
possible hero of the play.[18] Communicating this unfavourable
verdict, Voiture rather quaintly let Corneille know that 'le
christianisme avait extrêmement déplu', while Godeau cited the
Christian Fathers' prohibition of revolutionary violence in condemning what was considered to be Polyeucte's unacceptably

fanatical behaviour. The public and political form taken by the play's illustration of saintly virtue has also disturbed more modern sensibilities, even if Claudel rather let his pen run away with him when he called the hero of the play a 'fiérabras grotesque qui affronte l'enfer avec des rodomontades'.[19] Thus Polyeucte's concern for his reputation and his seeming determination to conquer even heaven by abandoning the world for the glory of a martyr's crown led Nadal to question the spiritual effect of the play and has prompted Prigent to note a 'rhétorique de l'ostentation' which, in his view, has nothing to do with Christian humility.[20]

These twentieth-century reservations highlight the evolving nature of religious sensibility, but ignore the fact that many men of genuine devotion at the time considered a desire for glory and reputation to be an entirely legitimate spur to virtue. Many moral theologians believed that a hero's concern for glory in no way tainted his service of a higher good. Louis Richeôme is characteristic when he concludes his *Académie de l'honneur* with the resounding assertion that 'la gloire est bonne de soi et suit l'excellence de la personne comme la clarté la lumière: à la charge que l'homme la cherche en Dieu et pour Dieu, et pour quelque bonne fin'. This Jesuit also maintains that men have a legitimate claim on our gratitude and admiration when they respond to a desire for glory which later in the century will be condemned as vainglory born of 'amour propre':

On peut aimer, souhaiter et chercher la vraie gloire…L'instinct naturel, dont chacun est poussé à la gloire, nous acerte cette vérité, et Dieu a donné cet instinct à l'homme parce qu'il l'invite à la vertu et à son service par cette amorce…Si Dieu a créé les hommes à la gloire…et la nature raisonnable les y pousse, il est certain qu'on peut la désirer et chercher selon Dieu et selon raison.

The pursuit of virtuous glory, if it is for the honour of God and the public good, has the noble quality of service which sets an example for other men to admire and emulate: 'Il est selon Dieu de désirer, voire de procurer, que nos bonnes œuvres soient manifestées aux hommes, mais non pour notre gloire, ains pour celle de Dieu, et pour le bien du prochain.'[21] The *Recueil général*, in a discussion of why no man is content with his condition, similarly praises a desire for honour, but this time as evidence of man's healthy nostalgia for the perfections lost to him with the Fall.[22] Indeed, a desire for glory seemed so useful a stimulant to virtue that many laid considerable emphasis on the importance of the hero's admiring public, arguing

that public judgement served as a valuable stimulant and control on
an individual's pursuit of reputation.[23] Other moralists, of a more
Augustinian persuasion, left these apologists of glory in no doubt
that they were at some odds with the Church Fathers' reminders of
the sinfulness of the flesh and the beatitudes of private devotion.
Mugnier is well aware of this, but cites St Gregory of Nazianzus in
support of his conviction that 'le désir d'honneur est comme un petit
atome de la Divinité, qui se coule doucement dans les bons cœurs,
pour y jeter les semences de la vertu et de la félicité'.[24]

This matter of the legitimacy of a desire for glory, so long as it
flows from pursuit of the glory of God, underpins Corneille's
ingenious exploitation of dramatic suspense in structuring *Polyeucte*.
The second act includes an episode which has the effect of provoking
some uncertainty in the spectator about the motives which inspire
Polyeucte's intended iconoclasm. Upon the hero's return from
baptism, Néarque is shocked by his friend's conviction that he has
been called to smash the idols and expresses his reservations about so
sudden a resolve on death and glory:

> NÉARQUE: Ce zèle est trop ardent, souffrez qu'il se modère...
>   Ménagez votre vie, à Dieu même elle importe;
>   Vivez pour protéger les Chrétiens en ces lieux.
> POLYEUCTE: L'exemple de ma mort les fortifiera mieux.
>   (II, vi, 653 and 670–2)

At this point in the action the spectator is no more sure than is
Néarque whether Polyeucte is acting from vain-glory or upon the
genuine instances of 'une grâce particulière'. Polyeucte replies with
powerful counter-arguments, but beyond these assurances there is
nothing to allay the nagging suspicion that he has succumbed to the
last temptation of pride and is pursuing for himself the glories of
martyrdom. Not until the end of the play can the spectator, who has
been painfully aware of the sufferings Polyeucte causes Pauline, be
quite sure of the validity of the martyr's inspiration. By this early
exchange between Polyeucte and Néarque, Corneille deliberately
raises an issue which can only be settled by the efficacy of the
martyrdom itself – hence the canonically necessary twin miracles of
Félix's and Pauline's conversions which provide final proof that
Polyeucte was not, after all, prompted by 'temerarious zeal'.[25] The
traditional mechanics of suspense are already inherent in Corneille's
subject, since the audience is bound to fear that the martyr's moral

courage may weaken. But the dramatist has artfully prompted other, and more fundamental, doubts in the spectator, the better to prepare the confirmatory 'coups de théâtre' of the final miracles. This ingenious integration of hagiology and dramaturgy has the happy result of sustaining the audience's interest and profounder moral concern, in complete consistency with orthodox Christian teaching on the difference between a worldly passion for glory and the heroic ambitions of the saint. Godeau might have had his doubts, but Corneille could justly maintain that the conversion of Pauline and the miraculous illumination of Félix brought things to an exemplary close in a brilliantly satisfying fusion of the demands of theological orthodoxy, political significance, and dramaturgical skill, as the two conversions prove Polyeucte to have been inspired by God and not by pride. Through the efficacy of his death, the martyr finally conquers his audience as a true saint, whose death has brought about a Christian revolution in Armenia and earned him his place of honour in the providential history of the Church.

That political revolution in Armenia reminds us that the seventeenth-century religious revival and the vogue for 'la comédie sainte' in the 1630s and 1640s were not the only reasons why Corneille turned to the mystic zeal of this Christian saint.[26] His play's political argument is at one with its religious significance and, in exemplary illustration of the political efficacy of Christian values, crowns Corneille's earlier exploration of the relation between hero and State. The City of Man yields to the values of the City of God and, as in the three preceding plays, that argument is expressed through the dramatization of a crucial moment of political change. Set between the declining Roman empire and the diffusion of Christianity, *Polyeucte* ends with the first establishment of a Christian government in the providential history of mankind, repeating the revolution of the closing scenes of *Cinna*, but this time in an explicit affirmation of the earthly rule of Christ. If the play unfavourably contrasts Félix's unprincipled political prudence with Sévère's embodiment of the noble, but unredeemed, past virtues of a Brutus or a Manlius (v, iv, 1699–707), it also looks forward to the collapse of the benighted despotism of Décie (iv, ii, 1125–34) and the eclipse of the Roman *Imperium* by the Christian Empire of Byzantium. Thus Corneille's 'tragédie chrétienne' both refers us back to the two Roman plays which precede it and, in its evocation of the twilight period of a pagan empire ruled by a political order which has been

invaded by the bizarre cults of the Orient, introduces (IV, vi,
1419–34) the monstrous symbols of the moral confusion which will
haunt *La Mort de Pompée* and his later political drama.

Never were the moral bankruptcy and inner contradictions of
worldly politics more effectively illustrated than in the unregenerate
Machiavellianism of Félix, the subtleties of whose characterization
make an instructive contrast with Corneille's earlier depiction of
Créon in *Médée*. Behind this prudent representative of imperial
authority stands the despotic figure of Décie. If Félix protests his
loyalty to the Emperor even at the cost of his family, this is because
the pagan *Imperium* of a self-proclaimed god exercises a tyranny over
men's souls which constrains governor and subject alike to obedience
by terror (III, iii, 925–6). By smashing the idols in the name of the
supremacy of the one true God, Polyeucte strikes directly at a
Roman divinization of things mortal which can only regard the
Christians as criminal rebels against the city. When Félix bends the
law by sentencing Néarque to death while sparing his daughter's
husband in the hope that he will recant, the moral confusions of that
worldly order are evident to all. Should Sévère tell Décie of this
leniency, the Governor will stand accused of both injustice and
impiety in yielding to paternal love (III, iii, 987–900 and 932). Félix
may congratulate himself that his political skill in calculating
opportunities and advantages has brought him to his present
powerful position, but now he is impaled on the paradoxes of justice
and injustice inherent in Décie's pagan tyranny (III, v, 1016–18).
With his regrets at having so badly miscalculated the future power
of the politically insignificant soldier whom his daughter loved,
Félix's moral confusions are both domestic and public as he
reproaches Pauline for her obedience when he forced her to reject
Sévère:

> Ah, regret qui me tue,
> De n'avoir pas aimé la vertu toute nue!
> Ah, Pauline, en effet tu m'as trop obéi,
> Ton courage était bon, ton devoir l'a trahi,
> Que ta rebellion m'eût été favorable!
> Qu'elle m'eût garanti d'un état déplorable!
> (I, iv, 329–34)

Félix's undignified scramble for safety and his concern for worldly
position contrast sharply with the 'honnête' serenity of Sévère, the
selfless devotion of Pauline, and the heroic idealism of Polyeucte.
Yet, by marrying his daughter to a man of greater political

importance, he had simply obeyed the accepted rules of social advantage and ambition. Those same rules now force him to go back on his previous choice and cultivate this rejected suitor to his daughter who has become the Emperor's favourite. Polyeucte's crime now offers the shameful temptation of expediently invoking Décie's anti-Christian edicts in order to dispose of an inconvenient son-in-law and acquire a new and influential one in Sévère. The same calculations of political advantage which had earlier ensured general approval and respect now drive Félix towards action which can only meet with opprobrium, as the incoherences of his 'haute science' vividly display the insufficiency of conduct solely governed by considerations of worldly success and survival.

Félix's prudence impels him towards disaster rather than to safety, and the exchange between Félix and Albin at the start of Act V strongly emphasizes the self-defeating subtlety of the governor's Machiavellian reading of Sévère's true motives:

ALBIN: Dieux! que vous vous gênez par cette défiance!
FÉLIX: Pour subsister en Cour c'est la haute science.
      Quand un homme une fois a droit de nous haïr,
      Nous devons présumer qu'il cherche à nous trahir,
      Toute son amitié nous doit être suspecte...
ALBIN: Que tant de prévoyance est un étrange mal!
      Tout vous nuit, tout vous perd, tout vous fait de l'ombrage.
            (V, i, 1471–5 and 1502–3)

Félix's 'haute science' masquerades as wisdom, but stands revealed as that 'pusillanimité' enslaved to circumstance which idealist theory so firmly condemned as the primary source of weakness in the ruler.[27] Félix's conviction that men's motives are invariably self-serving precipitates the threat he most fears and, by the last scene of the play, Sévère has lost all patience (V, vi, 1747–50 and 1759–62). But, as Félix's subtle politics collapse in ruins, the miraculous power of God's Grace comes to his rescue and relegates to insignificance those worldly values which previously had been his only concern:

      Ne me reprochez plus que par mes cruautés
      Je tâche à conserver mes tristes Dignités,
      Je dépose à vos pieds l'éclat de leur faux lustre;
      Celle où j'ose aspirer est d'un rang plus illustre,
      Je m'y trouve forcé par un secret appas,
      Je cède à des transports que je ne connais pas.
            (V, vi, 1765–70)

Redeemed at last, Félix witnesses to the truth of the eponymous hero's vocation and to the absolute supremacy of none but God. Where the hidden logic behind Auguste's clemency had been carefully prepared, here the suddenness of Félix's conversion is a measure of the way in which normal Cornelian concepts of verisimilitude have been forced to yield before the need for an exemplary illustration of the miraculous power of Grace.

As for Sévère, his major role in the action is the sentimental one of 'honnête homme' and disappointed lover of Pauline. Primarily a secular 'galant' embellishment to the religious drama, Sévère's active interest in the political argument is limited to the degree in which Félix is intimidated by the Imperial favour he enjoys. His conduct, however, makes a telling contrast with the Roman Court's present decline into tyranny and with Polyeucte's illustration of a Christian heroic ideal. This soldier, saviour of the Roman armies and of the Emperor himself, has none of the ignoble traits of Décie's court and nothing in common with the expedient flexibility of the governor of Armenia. Risen from humble origins to distinction on the battlefield, Sévère illustrates all the noble but unenlightened integrity of earlier Roman virtue. Far more flatteringly presented than ever was Guérin's Brute, his qualities evoke an ancient Roman civism heavily overlaid with seventeenth-century 'honnêteté'. Sympathetic though his melancholy Stoicism is, Sévère's values prove totally ineffective in the play. The victim of 'la fortune et le sort', he remains a passive figure whose only remedy to personal disappointment lies in courageous acceptance and self-discipline. For all his qualities, his very reasonableness makes him incapable of comprehending the future significance of the Christians' exaltation and joyful acceptance of persecution. The most that this 'honnête païen' can appreciate, but without commitment, is the Christian community's fidelity to their god and courage in the face of death (v, vi, 1412–43).[28] Corneille's old teacher of rhetoric, the Jesuit father Claude Delidel, was later to explain the limitations of Sévère's philosophical reason and worldly graces when he opposed the 'mondanité' of 'les enfants du siècle' to the ways of Christ:

La seule raison et prudence humaine...quoiqu'elle ne combatte pas de front la Grâce, cependant indirectement est son ennemie, et pour le moins s'oppose à la perfection qu'elle inspire, et au mérite qui provient de sa conduite...En un mot, la nature est la grande ennemie de la Grâce, et quiconque se gouverne seulement selon qu'il est emporté de ses affections naturelles, quoique belles et généreuses, il bannit la Grâce de son cœur, et lui en empêche la conquête… C'est pour le plus, vivre en honnête paien, et rendre inutile la Croix de celui qui est descendu du Ciel non seulement pour corriger les défauts de cette nature corrompue, mais encore pour la sanctifier, et pour relever nos actions, qui n'ont autre principe qu'elle, par un principe incomparablement plus haut, qui est l'esprit de la Grâce.[29]

The very image of the fading qualities of a pagan world in decline, Sévère illustrates a 'reason' more concerned with the status quo and social harmony than with metaphysical certainties. His urbanity may set him apart from Décie's monstrous despotism, but it also leaves him blind to the future and unilluminated by the sacrificial devotion of the hero of the play.

In exemplary illustration of the Christian faith in action, Polyeucte alone fulfils the complete definition of the hero as he was celebrated by seventeenth-century Christian moralists. At least as gifted as Sévère, he possesses the essential further dimension of a mystical sense of purpose which leads him beyond mere worldly distinction to the martyr's crown. Like Sévère, he is himself a respected soldier 'dans la guerre éprouvé' (I, i, 3) and, as a prince of the family which once ruled Armenia, he also enjoys all the advantages of superior social status (II, i, 420). His qualities promise magnificent rewards in the world and yet he renounces them as 'des biens passagers' (v, iii, 1173–82 and 1185) to be set aside on the painful road which leads to eternal glory in service of God. Infused by the special Grace which calls him to attend the ceremony in the temple, this Christian hero's service of the purposes of God far transcends earthly ambition. Well aware of the price to be paid in fulfilling his heaven-sent role, the hero trusts in God alone to give him the courage he will need. Once he has discovered what he must do, the rest of the action will turn upon the constancy with which he repeatedly chooses to hold true to the promptings of Grace, as he wills himself to endure the consequences of an exemplary rejection of Décie's values. When Néarque first urged Polyeucte to baptism he had described the importance of sinful man's co-operation with Grace in terms which closely resemble Sabine's when she too had described the way the gods shape men's lives:

> Quand la faveur du Ciel ouvre à demi ses bras,
> Qui ne s'en promet rien ne la mérite pas,
> Il empêche souvent qu'elle ne se déploie,
> Et lorsqu'elle descend son refus la renvoie.
> (*Horace*, III, iii, 857–60)

But this time Néarque's language is better suited to context:

> Sa Grâce
> Ne descend pas toujours avec même efficace.
> Après certains moments que perdent nos longueurs
> Elle quitte ces traits qui pénètrent les cœurs,
> Le nôtre s'endurcit, la repousse, l'égare,
> Le bras qui la versait en devient plus avare,
> Et cette sainte ardeur qui doit porter au bien
> Tombe plus rarement, ou n'opère plus rien.
>
> (I, i, 29–37)

Corneille had good reason to be careful here, for the 'Querelle de la grâce' was beginning to become a matter of public interest and it is likely that he enjoyed expert advice on any allusion to so delicate a matter, since he maintained close relations with his old teachers at the Jesuit College in Rouen.[30] Polyeucte's attempts to stiffen Néarque's resolve to join him in smashing the idols make it clear that his decision is a free one, in which every effort of will will be necessary, both in choosing and in holding to the path of certain suffering. Without the faith which is God's gift through Grace he knows that he will not be able to hold true to his choice:

> J'attends tout de sa Grâce, et rien de ma foiblesse.
>
> (II, vi, 681)

Corneille's fidelity to his Jesuit teachers is apparent here, if we look to Delidel's equal emphasis on the theme that Grace alone completes the natural capacities of man: 'C'est une inspiration, une connaissance, une lumière surnaturelle que Dieu verse dans notre entendement... un attrait divin, un feu céleste qui se prend à notre cœur, et qui l'enflamme d'un saint désir d'exécuter fidèlement ce que Dieu demande de notre liberté'.[31] Like Polyeucte, who maintains that 'plus elle [l'action] est volontaire, et plus elle mérite' (II, vi, 658), Delidel also stresses the merit of a difficult course undertaken in knowledge that loyalty to God means a constantly willed resistance to earthly temptation. In his view, the miraculous effects of Grace strengthen that endeavour without ever calling into question man's essential freedom in service of Truth, as he wills the good in co-operation with God's prompting: 'Nous pouvons co-opérer à la grâce, ou la rejeter... parce que nous sommes libres... Il est en notre liberté d'obéir aux inspirations de Dieu ou de les rejeter.'[32] Polyeucte's 'stances' make the same point as he prepares to see Pauline:

Source délicieuse en misères féconde,
Que voulez-vous de moi, flatteuses voluptés?
Honteux attachements de la chair et du monde,
Que ne me quittez-vous quand je vous ai quittés?...
C'est vous, ô feu divin que rien ne peut éteindre,
Qui m'allez faire voir Pauline sans la craindre.

(IV, iii, 1105–8 and 1155–6)

All the exemplary effect and all the suspense of Corneille's play are built upon this repeated pattern of choice, as Polyeucte holds true to the call of God and steadfastly turns away from the attractions of the world.

Corneille's Christian hero embraces both life and death with triumphant optimism. Unlike Horace who, once he lost his way in the secular confusions of pagan Rome's ambitions, had turned to death in disillusionment and horror before the betrayals of future time, Polyeucte finds in God's strength the means to renounce the world and embrace eternity. In courageous ascension to a martyr's crown, he still loves the world – but through God, who is the source of life itself:

HORACE: D'autres aiment la vie, et je la dois haïr.
                    (*Horace*, v, ii, 1546)
POLYEUCTE: Je ne hais point la vie, et j'en aime l'usage,
                    Mais sans attachement qui sente l'esclavage,
                    Toujours pret à la rendre au Dieu dont je la tiens.
                    (*Polyeucte*, v, ii, 1515–17)

The perspective of immortality ensured by the martyr's death is undoubtedly far from the tragic finality of the closing scenes of *Horace*. Heaven sets Polyeucte free from every temporal constraint, as the heroic will, in co-operation with Grace, promises the splendid rewards of a self-fulfilment remote indeed from Horace's imprisonment within the necessities of mortal existence. The Roman hero's preoccupation with past glory and his indifference to all but his present loss of 'bonheur' had the tragic ring proper to the end of a noble illusion. In contrast, the hero of this 'tragédie chrétienne', strong in the receipt of Grace, marches confidently and without regret into eternity. All man's natural courage and generosity of heart are as nothing beside his possession of Grace, that 'don du Ciel, et non de la raison' (v, ii, 1554) which gives Polyeucte his certainty of purpose and alone authenticates the virtues he displays.

In so far as Polyeucte is infused with a truth which transcends the reason of common mortals, he offers an exemplary illustration of that heroic 'enthousiasme' which inspires the highest of individual achievements. But Corneille's play also has the larger purpose of showing how God is universally at work, and not least in the miraculous conversions of Félix and Pauline which conclude the drama. Félix, in doing no more than pretend to aspire to the knowledge of the Truth, had sufficiently opened his soul to the infinite charity of the one true God to be seized by the same irresistible conviction which brought Saul to his knees on the road to Damascus. Pauline's conversion at the moment of Polyeucte's death may not satisfy every last theological technicality on the conditions for baptism,[33] but her own *via dolorosa* to conversion offers an explicitly Christian illustration of the heroic ascent to a nobler order of existence and perfectly corresponds with contemporary descriptions of the way in which heroic illumination can lift us out of our despair in our own capacities. Vainly seeking the truth in her dreams, she increasingly dreads the future but is ever more certain of her love for a husband who seems set on rejecting her. By Act III, when she learns of Polyeucte's conversion and sacrilege in the temple, she resolves to plead with her husband and her father. Should those pleas fail – and indeed they will – Pauline steels herself in terms which, as yet unknowingly, indicate the way in which the Grace of understanding will come to her:

> Je ne prendrai conseil que de mon désespoir.
> (III, ii, 820)

This sentimental and marital drama crystallizes all that is at issue at the level of Christian doctrine in the play. Pauline's increasing desolation leads her to discover a strength of love for her husband which renders his rejections all the more painful for invoking a 'reason' which is as yet beyond her. Poignantly she expresses her love in the only language she knows, a language of the world which blindly foreshadows that of the higher devotion still hidden from her. While Polyeucte adopts the same intransigent language as Horace, her unillumined love drives her yet further into despair:

> PAULINE: Souffre que de toi-même elle [Pauline] obtienne la vie,
> Pour vivre sous tes lois à jamais asservie.
> Si tu peux rejeter de si justes désirs,
> Regarde au moins ses pleurs, écoute ses soupirs,

> Ne désespère pas une âme qui t'adore.
> POLYEUCTE: Je vous l'ai déjà dit, et vous le dis encore,
> Vivez avec Sévère, ou mourez avec moi,
> Je ne méprise point vos pleurs, ni votre foi,
> Mais de quoi que pour vous notre amour m'entretienne,
> Je ne vous connais plus, si vous n'êtes Chrétienne.
>
> (v, iii, 1603–14)

At the moment of Polyeucte's death Pauline plumbs the depth of humiliation and despair. But it is then that God rescues her *de profundis*, according her a Grace which at last makes everything clear, as a final extremity of despair brings her to the joys of Faith:

> Je vois, je sais, je crois, je suis désabusée,
> De ce bienheureux sang tu me vois baptisée.
> Je suis Chrétienne enfin, n'est-ce point assez dit?...
> Ce n'est point ma douleur que par là je fais voir,
> C'est la grâce qui parle, et non le désespoir.
> Le faut-il dire encor, Félix? je suis Chrétienne.
>
> (v, v, 1727–9 and 1741–3)

That 'enfin' not only tells us of Pauline's impatience before her father's incredulity: more poignantly it expresses the exemplary significance of her long journey from darkness, through despair, and into the light of a 'saint emportement' (*Polyeucte*, 'Examen', GC, i, 982).

The deed which caused a martyr's death, brought faith to Pauline and Félix, and thereby initiated Christian rule in Armenia, was a public declaration of the eternal supremacy of the Kingdom of Christ:

> Le Dieu de Polyeucte et celui de Néarque
> De la Terre et du Ciel est l'absolu Monarque,
> Seul être independant, seul maître du Destin,
> Seul principe éternel, et souveraine fin...
> C'est lui seul qui punit, lui seul qui récompense;
> Vous adorez en vain des Monstres impuissants.
>
> (iii, ii, 841–4 and 850–1)

By so witnessing to the power and Grace of the one true God, Polyeucte has begun a process of political reformation which will redeem even the tyranny of Rome. Christian definitions of heroic virtue combine with Christian teaching on grace in the final scenes, as the play spectacularly illustrates the bankruptcy of the values of this world and the triumph of that redemptive Grace by which man may devote himself to the establishment of the City of God on earth.

But that redemption will only be achieved at the cost of yet more suffering and the sacrifice of yet more lives upon the cross of Jesus. In its reminder of the price to be paid for man's inheritance of the sins of Adam, Corneille's 'tragédie chrétienne' offers a more sombre conclusion than that proposed by *Cinna*. Sévère may depart to plead the cause of the Christians, but the play does not disguise the enduring threat to happiness constituted by the pagan *Imperium* of Décie under the tutelage of its monstrous deities. Polyeucte's victory over man's benighted worship of things of clay and stone modelled in the image of his lusts and ambitions can be no more than an exemplary episode in the unending history of the tragic confusions of a fallen world. Even for twentieth-century audiences, less sensitive to the Christian exemplarity of the final triumphs of *Polyeucte*, Corneille's play still offers a humbling illustration of the suffering and death which originate in man's faith in the ways of the world and the frail resources of human prudence. For all that Armenia stands redeemed by the martyr's blood, the cost of that trans-formation and the fragility of that new order within a fallen world already announce the darkling horizons of *La Mort de Pompée*.

La Mort de Pompée was probably written in the very last months of Louis XIII's reign and first performed in late 1643.[34] While modern critical tradition has mainly considered this tragedy to be of secondary importance, Corneille's contemporaries ranked it amongst his greatest masterpieces, and this enthusiasm is easier to com-prehend once we recall the ideological tensions of the times in which it was written. In contrast with the final hopes of *Cinna* and the redemptive certainties of *Polyeucte*, the betrayal and death of Pompée, last champion of Republican Rome, plunge us back into the graceless confusions of man's own making and, for the first time in Corneille's work, the sufferings of the individual hero take second place to the illustration of high political argument within the broadest of historical perspectives.[35] As Corneille returns to the unregenerate bleakness of *Horace* in a play which ambitiously generalizes his reflection on the evolution of his times, the emphatic anti-Machiavellianism of this work dedicated to Mazarin was well attuned to contemporary hopes, after the death of Richelieu, for a return to a more traditional order of governance. Yet there is little to reassure the spectator in these tragic obsequies of traditional order abandoned and betrayed, where Pompée's ashes seem to be revered only as the symbol of a legitimacy embattled or even lost for ever. Alone amongst his contemporaries, Corneille had found in *Horace* and *Cinna* the means to express the darker significance of glory in pursuit of empire. Now, with *La Mort de Pompée*, he returns to the significance of Rome's historical destiny and, in a depiction of heroic virtue adrift in a graceless world, gives the most sombre illustration yet of a theme which was to play an increasingly important role in his later work.

Reverence in the first half of the century for the traditional legitimacies of French monarchical governance seems often to have gone hand in hand with admiration for Pompey and a preference for certain authors and historians with Republican sympathies.[36] Five years before *La Mort de Pompée*, however, another Norman dramatist had tried – somewhat perversely – to exploit Lucan's *Pharsalia* in a sense favourable to the Cardinal's policies. Entirely ignoring Lucan's Republican sympathies, Chaulmer's *La Mort de Pompée* (1638) follows Scudéry's and Guérin de Bouscal's depiction of Brutus, presenting Pompée as a 'galant' Stoic whose political idealism is out of touch with changing times when power needs to be consolidated in the hands of one man.[37] When Corneille, however, turned to the *Pharsalia* for its account of the events which followed Pompée's defeat, he alone would seem to have perceived the full tragic possibilities of the silver-age epic in further development of the anti-Machiavellian argument of his previous drama. Starting from Lucan's political sympathies and in tune with contemporary hopes for a return to more traditional forms of government after Richelieu's death, Corneille's *La Mort de Pompée* presents a view of Pompey's defence of Republican tradition in which even Ptolomée describes the defeated Pompée as 'ce déplorable Chef du parti le meilleur' (I, i, 15). As this wretched King of Egypt sets out the momentous context of the political drama to follow, the spectator is drawn into the disquieting perspectives of a world in which traditional orders of right and wrong yield to confusion, and where the only certainties of individual moral stature and of legitimacy of governance are expressed in terms of times past.

In contrast with Scudéry's flattering dramatization of Julius Caesar and his *Imperium*, Corneille builds his play around a much more complex and ambiguous portrait of the man whose future triumphs will be built on Ptolomée's treacherous assassination of Pompée. Corneille's César is close to the political opportunist depicted by Lucan and Plutarch, and it is notable how, in adapting

Lucan's account of Caesar's reaction at the crucial moment when he
was shown the murdered Pompey's severed head, Corneille offers a
highly disturbing account of opportunism masquerading as high
principle:

> César, à cet aspect, comme frappé de foudre,
> Et comme ne sachant que croire et résoudre,
> Immobile, et les yeux sur l'objet attachés,
> Nous tient assez longtemps ses sentiments cachés;
> Et je dirai, si j'ose en faire conjecture,
> Que par un mouvement commun à la Nature,
> Quelque maligne joie en son cœur s'élevait,
> Dont sa gloire indignée à peine le sauvait.
> L'aise de voir la Terre à son pouvoir soumise
> Chatouillait malgré lui son âme avec surprise,
> Et de cette douceur son esprit combattue
> Avec un peu d'effort rassurait sa vertu.
> S'il aime sa grandeur, il hait la perfidie;
> Il se juge en autrui, se tâte, s'étudie,
> Examine en secret sa joie et ses douleurs,
> Les balance, choisit, laisse couler des pleurs.
> Et forçant sa vertu d'être encor la maîtresse,
> Se montre généreux par un trait de foiblesse.
>
> (III, i, 769–86)

As César receives Pompée's widow with all the generous courtesies
due to a fellow-Roman, Cornélie's celebrated and richly ambiguous
praise again reminds how this hero is the fortunate recipient of the
fruits of Pompée's murder:

> O Ciel que de vertus vous me faites haïr!
>
> (III, iv, 1072)

Cornélie is the inheritor of a moral integrity which now can only
voice itself in protest or in warnings – even to her enemy – of the
treachery of others. With the corrosive dramatic irony which is so
characteristic of the play, César himself gratefully recognizes in her
conduct the true character of traditional values which his own
actions can never unambiguously embody:[38]

> O cœur vraiment Romain,
> Et digne du Héros qui vous donna la main!
>
> (IV, iv, 1363–4)

The spectator is made sharply aware that César is a beneficiary of
other men's crimes and generosities: he may be the perfect
'soupirant' as Cléopâtre's lover but, as Cornélie reminds us, as a

political figure he can all too easily afford the luxury of fine, but hollow, sentiments:

> O soupirs! O respect! Oh! qu'il est doux de plaindre
> Le sort d'un ennemi quand il n'est plus à craindre!
>   (v, i, 1537–8)

The moral ambiguities which so undermine the heroic stature of Pompée's opponents are the direct consequence of a battle which, leaving the Gods appalled and in disarray, has inaugurated a world in which justice is decided by force alone:

> Quand les Dieux étonnés semblaient se partager,
> Pharsale a décidé ce qu'ils n'osaient juger;
> Ses fleuves teints de sang et rendus plus rapides
> Par le débordement de tant de parricides,
> Cet horrible débris d'Aigles, d'armes, de chars,
> Sur ses champs empestés confusément épars,
> Ces montagnes de morts privés d'honneurs suprêmes,
> Que la Nature force à se venger eux-mêmes,
> Et dont les troncs pourris exhalent dans les Vents
> De quoi faire la guerre au reste des vivants,
> Sont les titres affreux dont le Droit de l'épée,
> Justifiant César a condamné Pompée.
>   (i, i, 3–14)

Eternally at war with itself, the post-Republican world of *La Mort de Pompée* is governed solely by ambition. In it César and Cléopâtre pursue their ambiguously ambitious love affair, competing under an appearance of honour with a foolish and dishonourable King of Egypt in a sorry scramble for power which spells the end of an older order of justice and heroic devotion. Pompée dies in vain for an ideal which was fatally betrayed once Caesar took his first steps to personal rule by crossing the Rubicon. That fatal act ushered in a world of ambition and violence in which the hero of Republican legitimacy can only find a posthumous place as the politics of force sweep aside traditional legality.

To illustrate the tragic finality of this eclipse of a nobler political order and the darkling beginnings of a sinister world of force and opportunism masquerading as heroic virtue and statesmanship, Corneille risks an extraordinary dramatic effect: the hero of his play never appears on stage. All we are permitted to witness are the sordid calculations of those who betray Pompée, and the equivocal reactions of others to his ignominious death. His physical absence and looming moral presence dominates the play's illustration of the irreparable consequences of Ptolomée's betrayal of the one man who embodied an indisputable moral integrity. Pompée's assassination occurs between the first and second acts, when this one undoubted hero is struck down by those who have gathered apparently to welcome him. His headless body is thrown into the sea which had carried him to Egypt:

> Pour comble à sa noire aventure,
> On donne à ce Héros la Mer pour sépulture,
> Et le tronc sous les flots roule dorénavant,
> Au gré de la Fortune, et de l'Onde et du Vent.
>   (ii, ii, 533–6)

As dishonourable men consign Pompée's body to the vagaries of unending and senseless flux, this terrible image of the disgrace of virtue spells the end of traditional stability and ancient order. More pious hands will later save the hero's remains for the proper honours of a funeral pyre, but when his widow carries his ashes on stage like the standard of a lost legitimacy the appalled spectator is well aware that her defiance will be in vain and that the Republic has been destroyed for ever. In apt comment on Corneille's previous tragedies and foreshadowing his future development of 'le beau sujet', Cléopâtre mourns the memory of the dead hero, splendidly inviting us to contemplate in Pompée's destiny the unending history of man's capacity both for the good and for the sordid betrayal of himself and others:

> Admirons cependant le destin des grands hommes,
> Plaignons-les, et par eux jugeons ce que nous sommes.
> Ce prince d'un sénat maître de l'univers...
> Les Monstres de l'Egypte ordonnent de sa vie...
> Ainsi finit Pompée, et peut-être qu'un jour
> César éprouvera même sort à son tour.
>   (ii, ii, 573–5, 582 and 587–8)

Pompée is truly the hero of time gone. The last champion of an integrity betrayed by the word of faithless allies and fallen victim to the opportunist ambition of lesser men, his ghost haunts the remainder of the tragedy, as its sumptuously rhetorical obsequies consign to memory a moral and political order to be revered even in its eclipse.

Permitting us no illusions about the recuperability of ancient virtues in modern times, the last of the plays which Corneille was to

write in the reign of Louis XIII rises to tragic effect because, like its
predecessors, it never betrays into 'lessons for the moment' the noble
and more philosophical human truths with which the history of
Rome challenged his times. Where Richelieu's dramatists had
sought with more servility to illustrate the interests of France, the
epic perspectives of *La Mort de Pompée* ensure a very different
judgement on present political uncertainties and repeatedly provoke
in the spectator that sense of awe and scandal which will become the
hallmark of Corneille's work to come. In a play in which images of
monstrosity and disorder form a constant *leitmotif*, 'les Monstres de
l'Egypte' decide the course of events and history seems to have lost
all sense of providential direction. But even as the penetrating
realism of the political *moraliste* recognizes that all hope of a return
to tradition has been overtaken by the pursuit of power and
advantage, Corneille's tragedy remains true to *Cinna* and *Polyeucte* in
presenting that past ideal of order as enduringly worthy of respect.
In its disquieting conclusion, so typical of Corneille's unflinching
political insight, the play announces a renewal of civil war from
which, as the spectator well knows, Rome will re-emerge transformed
into the formidable order of a glorious Empire. In this portrayal of
the greater meaning of Pompée's miserable betrayal and death on
the shores of Egypt, Corneille has singled out the decisive moment
when, on the ruins of an older legitimacy, Imperial Rome began her
ascent to world dominion. In a lesson of poignant relevance to the
evolution and ambitions of seventeenth-century France, the play
both celebrates the splendours of that ascent to power and shows the
price which must be paid for that future glory in betrayal of the past
and a descent into the moral ambiguities and covert violences of
political calculation and imperial intrigue.

La Mort de Pompée offers us what has rightly been called 'une longue
et fastueuse cérémonie funéraire'.[39] Its valedictory celebrations
mark the end of the serene vision of the City of Man which *Cinna* had
first celebrated in the triumph of moral values over force. With
Corneille's last tragedy written in the shadow of a great patron who
had irrevocably changed France's destinies, the redemptive ascent of
Corneille's drama is broken and the more chastening significance of
Polyeucte's triumphant death is brought to the fore, as the play
invites us to contemplate the future context of political ambition. As
Prigent observes, 'la raison d'Etat a envahi l'espace et le temps

cornéliens: il ne suffit plus d'être grand, il faut désormais être fort... C'est la grandeur qui condamne Pompée à mort'.[40] In the uncertainties of the next ten years under the Cardinal's successor, Corneille will offer a series of ideal resolutions to political conflict in increasingly desperate attempts, through the moral victories of his heroes over their opponents, to impose a providential interpretation on the events of history. With *Pertharite* in 1652, where virtuoso manipulations of dramatic effect have become Corneille's only means to imposing that political morality, the fragility of such an endeavour becomes unacceptably apparent. Eight years of silence and reassessment follow that failure, and Corneille will only return to the stage with a sobering series of tragedies of political intrigue, the effect of which is to transform a sense of awe into a sense of scandal before the tragic enormity of political corruption triumphant. The terrible sense of waste communicated by the desolate conclusion of *Sertorius* (1662) marks the beginnings of Corneille's last and impenitently idealist renewal of tragic creativity, as Pompée re-emerges degraded now into yet another opportunist survivor at the expense of Republican principle. That tragic renewal will in turn reach its conclusion in the elegiac despair of *Suréna* (1674) and the scandal of yet another ignominious assassination which shames the self-defeating politics of power. Despite the ideal apotheosis of Auguste as absolute monarch in *Cinna* and the hard-won triumph of the Christian God in *Polyeucte*, *La Mort de Pompée* illustrates a fatal turning-point in the history of human endeavour and tragically reflects the close of an era in France even as it signals the beginning of another in the poet's own development.[41] Henceforth, under a new King, Corneille will offer a long and valedictory celebration of political idealism in the face of the irresistible advance of that increasingly secular order of political theory and practice which, in the earliest days of his career, had been initiated by the greatest of his patrons.

Conclusion

In a profound sense, and one which does it no dishonour, all history is a fabrication: unavoidably it reflects the preoccupations of the age in which it is written. Particularly was this true of the historical drama of seventeenth-century France. If history is the imposition of form on things past – and to the Aristotelian habits of mind of the period it was only through form that truth could be made apparent – then the artifices of tragedy were especially apt to the expression of a transcendence more universally significant than the epiphenomena of which individual histories were made. Since history was also a part of rhetoric, its stage representation could become a particularly effective instrument by means of which the skilful dramatist might expound the past for the benefit of the present, as he captured his spectators' interest and directed their will. For both dramatist and audience, history was to be 'read' because it was a means to signify and persuade, and thence – in a century of *moralistes* – a means the better to know themselves and conduct their lives.

That is to describe historical drama at its highest level of significance, and it is hoped that this study of Corneille's plays has shown that it was not always the text with the most unambiguous meaning which exemplified the greatest literary achievement in the period. Those rival history-plays which Richelieu's protégés most applauded, because they seemed most successfully to marry the dramatist's art with a univocal political significance, now seem to us undeniably poorer than Corneille's more thoughtful, but problematic, recreations of history. In comparing Corneille's historical drama with that of his rivals, it has become apparent that the richest text will always be that which offers the greatest possibility of self-renewal, as it forces the spectator or reader to reflect upon the multiplicity of its complementary and contrasted meanings. Indeed the breadth and profundity of argument, so characteristic of

257

Corneille's manipulation of the raw material of history, remains the principal guarantor of the interest of his poetic transformation of recorded fact into a more enduringly telling exploration of man's social condition. As Gouhier has observed:

Si l'histoire inspire le poète, ce n'est pas pour le transformer en conteur d'histoires vraies, ce n'est pas pour l'inviter à mettre en scène ce qui a été réellement vécu, mais pour émouvoir le visionnaire et le prophète qui croit découvrir une histoire invisible dont l'histoire des historiens est l'apparence figurative. La transformation du fait en signe, telle est sans doute la métamorphose propre au théâtre dont l'action trouve ses personnages et ses situations fondamentales dans l'histoire, que la signification l'emporte sur le signe, qu'elle en arrive à créer d'autres signes pour se mieux manifester, c'est ce que montrent les plus grandes œuvres.[1]

The transformations and re-emergences of the great figures of Roman antiquity in the plays which Corneille wrote under Louis XIII offer an object-lesson in such an achievement. Constantly they refer their audiences to the enduring truth behind the history of human endeavour and aspire to a tragic view of human affairs in their refusal to exploit their sources for ephemeral answers in 'lessons of the moment'.

From the start, Corneille's serious drama repeatedly calls into question both the morality of individual action and the values which govern its social context. In this his plays certainly reflect the political climate of the first sixty years of the century, and it was perhaps inevitable that their morally challenging effect should have been less appreciated in the increasingly authoritarian social climate of the latter part of the century. Typically La Bruyère was ill at ease with the ideological focus of 'le beau sujet' when he compared Corneille's forcefulness with the less politically challenging plays of Racine.[2] The decline in Corneille's popularity in the latter years of the century has been attributed to a conflict between his manner and the triumph of a high classical taste which called for simplicity of plot and 'le pathétique des passions'.[3] There is considerable truth in this, but explanations which give primacy to manner over meaning are never wholly convincing. Corneille's poetics relate to plays which were written for audiences familiar with the ambitions and ideological tensions of the more 'open' political world of the ministries of Richelieu and Mazarin. The political preoccupations of Corneille's drama, no less than the distinctive modes through which they received their stage expression, were responsible for its gradual eclipse. We have seen how this Norman dramatist's personal position and *officier* culture gave him reason to dissociate his art from important tenets of a poetics too closely associated with an order of governance which indelibly marked both his province and his career as *officier*, and which was to triumph in the second half of the century. The challenging manner and effect of Corneille's dramatization of 'le beau sujet' were the natural expression of an independent and questioning spirit, pre-occupied with political issues ill-suited to the tastes of later audiences in a more sceptical and disillusioned age. Even in his last play, *Suréna*, where he seems most to trim his manner to a contemporary taste for elegiac simplicity, the action still communicates a sense of scandal before the spectacle of a 'généreux' destroyed by the sordid calculations of self-interest and 'la raison d'état'. Whatever concessions this last of Corneille's tragedies may have made to a rising taste for 'le sentiment', it still accorded a primary political significance to its fated lovers and was impenitently intended to quicken the spectator's awareness of his individual responsibility within the social and political context. For Corneille, the theatre was above all a means to stimulate his spectators to such political reflection, rather than lead them to acceptance of the way things were. If this is perhaps the secret of his enduring interest, it is also his most important difference from the major authors of the latter part of the century. The increasingly unfashionable complexity of his plays was the natural form of a drama which consciously reflected the ideological hesitations of an age of rapid institutional change and which sought to please in so far as it constantly provoked its audience to moral judgement.[4] Little wonder then that his work was later misinterpreted even by those who praised it, for it was of a kind which could only cause unease in a society governed by a monarchical bureaucracy unable to admit of criticism or reform.

We have seen how central to Corneille's treatment of the historical 'beau sujet' was his replacement of the 'Aristotelian' theory of the tragic flaw of a hero of middling virtue by the spectacle of the virtuous hero and his sufferings. That replacement removed the last alibi to the spectator's awareness of his political situation and responsibilities before a drama which invariably concentrates our attention on the ever-present tensions between individual aspiration and man's natural participation in the collectivity. So fundamental a difference between a later depiction of the fatalities of inner psychological frailty and Corneille's illustration of the social constraints which bind his heroes inevitably poses the question of how far he may be held to have expressed in his plays a tragic vision of man's condition. This tragic dimension is the quality most often denied to Corneille's work, even by many who admire it, and plays which are so concerned with man's social context are bound to run the risk of being referred to dramatic modes which, like comedy, are more obviously involved with the collectivity in exploiting the audience's moral response to the action. But Corneille himself had no doubts that, in his own distinctive way, he was heir to Æschylus, Sophocles, and Euripides. Indeed he spent a considerable amount of time in the second *Discours* confidently defining his own practice in relation to earlier theories and examples of tragedy.

While Aristotle was considered to be the supreme authority, both seventeenth-century theory and Corneille's practice are so often at variance with the *Poetics* that it is not surprising that his own theoretical reflections resulted in what he well knew to be an independent and original viewpoint. Part II of this study has shown how, unlike some who held that Aristotle had settled the matter once and for all, Corneille did not take so narrow a view of the nature of the tragic experience. In contrast with opponents who still claimed to follow revered authority even as they betrayed the spirit of the *Poetics*, he was both more loyal to inherited cultural tradition and more honest in admitting his differences. In the plays which Corneille wrote during the reign of Louis XIII we have seen how the dramatic action may be affected by other forces than one or a number of individual roles driven by some inner necessity or compulsion. Whether those other and external forces are evoked as the gods or destiny, they are repeatedly shown directly to constrain human aspiration and endeavour and manifest themselves above all in the social and political consequences of individual initiative. Furthermore, the effect of Corneille's dramatization of the momentous decisions of figures of high political responsibility is calculated in the conviction that the spectator also recognizes that those same consequences of choice and action subtend his own experience and understanding of beauty and ugliness in human conduct and of the servitudes and freedoms of his social and political experience. In such an exploration of our political condition we have seen how important time and circumstance are to the fortunes of Corneille's heroes. Inevitably those twin forces shape the destinies of men and illustrate constraints in the face of which individual constancy and courage may be of little avail.[5] The will of the Cornelian hero is never less than an essentially free cause and source

of action but, in pursuit of his chosen destiny, he can only act upon
the world in which he moves, and in this he falls subject to the
necessities inherent in a world of free men. Free in will, but fatally
enmeshed in the repercussions of the deeds whereby they seek to
realize their identity, Corneille's heroes offer a distinctively tragic
illustration of human strength and frailty. But the constraints which
bind them are never located within themselves. They lie outside
them, in their social and political condition, in the nature of the
world to which they are born, and in the ineluctably changing
historical situation within which they have to act. Constantly the
Cornelian hero's aspiration to realize himself in deeds falls subject to
the processes of that same history of human endeavour within which,
in defiance of time, men seek immortality in the judgement and
memories of their peers. In himself he is never less than free to
choose, yet he is subject to the tragic paradox that the march of
history forces him to choose.

In such a dramatic universe, heroic identity is so closely associated
with decision and action that the hero, while fully responsible for his
conduct, has little hope of controlling the consequences of his deeds
except in so far as he is both free and forced to define himself once
more in action. These paradoxes of freedom in Corneille's tragic
universe of moral responsibility have little place for psychological
necessity, or even for that spectacle of poetic justice offered by a
flawed hero punished beyond his deserts. Instead human capacity
and limitation become exhilaratingly and poignantly apparent in
the series of challenges which Corneille's dramatization of a political
crisis sets before the hero's ambition to fulfil himself in action. From
those trials he may emerge in triumph or in splendid failure, but he
is always a tragic figure in those plays where his fortunes exemplify
man's incapacity to escape the limitations to free self-realization
which are an essential part of his social condition. Certain of
Corneille's plays, like *Cinna*, *Polyeucte* and *Nicomède*, are undoubtedly
closer to heroic drama than tragedy in so far as they show how the
hero may finally transcend those limitations and transform the social
order in which he establishes his identity through a celebration of a
providential harmony between heroic initiative and the values
which govern its larger context. Other plays carry a more chastening
burden, and fail to reveal any such reconciliation. In these,
tragically, all hope of such a redemptive order is either abandoned
or destroyed. With these works in mind Corneille could later argue

convincingly for a tragic emotion grounded not in pity and fear but in 'admiration', that wonder and awe provoked by the dual spectacle of the indomitable courage of man's free spirit and of the fragility of his ambitions, once he aspires to assert himself in action and falls victim to the limits of endeavour which hedge us all.

In his second *Discours* Corneille proposed a formulation of political tragedy which is founded in just such a celebration of human liberty and the paradoxes of its triumphant failures. This very personal definition emerged as part of his condemnation of the kind of plot in which one protagonist seeks to destroy another but desists, 'par un simple changement de volonté', being neither constrained nor unable to carry out his original purpose:

J'ai déjà marqué cette sorte de dénouement pour vicieux; mais quand ils y font de leur côté tout ce qu'ils peuvent, et qu'ils sont empêchés d'en venir à l'effet par quelque puissance supérieure, ou par quelque changement de fortune qui les fait périr eux-memes, ou les réduit sous le pouvoir de ceux qu'ils voulaient perdre, il est hors de doute que cela fait une tragédie d'un genre plus sublime que les trois qu'Aristote avoue; et que s'il n'en a point parlé, c'est qu'il n'en voyait point d'exemples sur les théâtres de son temps, où ce n'était pas la mode de sauver les bons par la perte des méchants à moins que de les souiller eux-mêmes de quelque crime. (LF, 92; GC, 153)

This 'quatrième manière d'agir' is that which Corneille prefers, since he dares to suggest that it is 'plus belle que les trois qu'il [Aristote] recommande, et qu'il leur eût sans doute préférée, s'il l'eût connue'. Significantly the passage occurs in discussion of *Le Cid*, the play which had first set him on his distinctive road to fame as a master-tragedian. As further examples of this new kind of tragedy, Corneille refers us not only to Chimène, Cinna and Emilie, but also to *Rodogune* and *Héraclius*, and even – and less convincingly perhaps – to *Nicomède*. From this it is clear that he understood his personal definition of tragedy to be more generally applicable than might have seemed from his immediate reference to plays in which heroic criminality is brought to book. Certainly it is not hard to see that this notion of tragic constraint is centrally important to those of his plays which offer the paradoxical spectacle of human freedom and servitude, grandeur and frailty, energy and impotence.

Such a theory of heroic courage and tragic failure before the pressure of uncontrollable external forces explains why Corneille's poetics lay such emphasis on coherence of cause and effect within an extended political crisis, and firmly condemn all gratuitous events unmotivated by the original exposition's development. The seamless coherence with which Corneille disposes his material shows, through the action itself, how forces greater than the will and courage of his heroes are inherent in the nature of things and may confound their irrepressible pursuit of fulfilment and freedom. Only through our perception of how closely action relates to its consequences – whether the latter be apparent in the response of other free men to the hero's action, or in the working out of some greater necessity within the community – could Corneille's tragedies show how that external 'puissance supérieure' might manifest itself in the world of man and hedge the hero's freedom, as events force his decisions and necessarily follow from his deeds. Horace is genuinely free to choose as he thinks fit – but the choice itself, even as he welcomes its necessity, is unavoidable. And once he moves from the private world of ambition and intention into action upon the world about him, then the consequences of what may be termed his social fatality become tragically manifest. By acting in the world of men he perforce loses control of his deeds, as the tragedy traces out the social and political repercussions of his conduct. The very strengths of Horace reveal his frailties, for even as he seeks to rise above a series of exceptional challenges he is finally shown to be unable to escape the contingencies of his political context. Subject as he is to the free judgements of other men, his very realization of himself in action leaves him condemned and pardoned, a splendid but terrible victim of the ineluctable processes of time and changing circumstance which govern us all.

Corneille's careful definitions of the relationship between profit and delight, his insistence on the lucid and brilliant illustration of the specifically moral dimensions of his political subject-matter, and his confidence in the tragic effect of 'l'admiration', all have their natural place within this practice of a tragedy founded on a perception of the greatness and frailty of the hero as he measures himself against the challenge of his context. Just as Corneille's drama shows the limits and triumphs of man, so are its heroes defeated by, or in harmony with, forces which assume tragic significance only in so far as they mark out the boundaries of a constantly renewed progress to triumph or humiliation. In a brilliant spectacle of human aspiration and failure, Corneille's political tragedies provoke in the audience that sense of awe which flows from a heightened understanding of man's grandeur and frailty as he claims his place within the mysterious advance of history. Perhaps it was a basic sympathy with Æschylean tragedy which lay at the root of

Corneille's rejection of so much that was central to Aristotelian descriptions of the subject and effect of tragedy, for it is evident that the *Poetics* owe little to Æschylean tragic practice.[6] Indeed Corneille himself turned to the example of Æschylus when he wrote in defence of *Le Cid* – and this play, which so influenced the development of Corneille's reflections on his art, certainly has much in common, both in situation and preoccupation, with the *Oresteia*.[7] Corneille is perhaps no better than his contemporaries in the thinness of his references to Æschylus, but this appeal to the oldest of the Greek tragedians suggests a deeper affinity than was common in a century which more usually ignored Æschylus in favour of Sophocles and Euripides. One of the most sensitive of Corneille's critics was perhaps not too wide of the mark when he observed that Cornelian practice constantly tends to replace pity and fear by a kind of Æschylean awe proper to a deeply religious attitude to life founded in 'la croyance à la liberté humaine et à la justice divine'.[8] If we understand 'religious' in this broadest of senses then – for all that Corneille believed that he was offering an entirely new perception of tragedy – it might be said that his very originality in his own times belongs in the most venerable of tragic traditions, in so far as – like Æschylus before him – he was concerned less with the individual soul of man than with man's relation to the forces for order and disorder at work within the world about him.

Notes

INTRODUCTION

1 Georges Couton and André Stegmann have thrown considerable light
on the literary culture in Rouen, on Corneille's social standing and
financial circumstances, as well as on his contacts and links with the
world of patronage and letters in Paris: A. Stegmann, *L'Héroisme
cornélien: genèse et signification*; G. Couton, *Réalisme de Corneille: La Clef de
'Mélite': Réalités dans 'Le Cid'*; *Corneille et la Fronde*; *La Vieillesse de
Corneille*, pp. 3–29. For full details of these works and all others cited in
the notes, see Bibliography.
No less important to an understanding of Corneille as a political
dramatist is the work of historians who have studied the institutional
and ideological crisis which characterized the beginnings of early
modern Europe and, more locally, the popular disturbances and
institutional discontent which Corneille knew at first hand: R.
Mousnier, *La Vénalité des offices sous Henri IV et Louis XIII*; *Peasant
Uprisings in Seventeenth-Century France, Russia and China*; 'Recherches sur
les soulèvements populaires avant la Fronde', *Revue d'Histoire Moderne et
Contemporaine*; M. Foisil, *La Révolte des Nu-pieds et les révoltes normandes de
1639*; see also R. Mandrou, *La France aux XVIIe et XVIIIe siècles*.
Couton's edition of the complete works of Corneille has also assembled
a wealth of historical detail hitherto unknown or difficult to find:
P. Corneille, *Œuvres complètes*, edited by G. Couton. All quotations and
subsequent references will use this edition, henceforth referred to as GC.
The only exception will be reference to the *Discours*, where Forestier's
edition of the 1660 text seemed preferable: Pierre Corneille, *Trois
Discours sur le poème dramatique (Texte de 1660)*, edited by L. Forestier.
This edition is denoted as LF. For the convenience of the reader, I also
give page-references to the *Discours* in GC, the text of which derives
from the 1682 edition.
2 This neglect of Corneille's poetics continues in Poirier's remarkable
allegorical interpretation of the plays by direct recourse to Aristotle and
the Scholastics. Unconcerned by Corneille's extensive discussion of his
practice, the author asserts that the author remained mute and secretive
on the matter of his art: G. Poirier, *Corneille ou la vertu du prudence*,

pp. 173–4. However, both Marie-Odile Sweetser and Harry Barnwell are distinguished exceptions to the tradition, and both have shown how illuminating are so privileged a reader's comments on his own work and how useful Corneille's extensive theoretical statements can be in controlling the direction and methods adopted in studying his drama: see H. T. Barnwell's helpful, but incomplete, edition of Corneille's theoretical works, *Pierre Corneille: Writings on the Theatre*, his *The Tragic Drama of Corneille and Racine*, and M-O. Sweetser's examinations of Corneille's theory and dramaturgy, *Les Conceptions dramatiques de Corneille, d'après ses écrits théoriques* and *La Dramaturgie de Corneille*.

3 LF, 76; GC, III, 142. In addition to Stegmann's and Poirier's works, widely differing studies of Corneille published in the last forty years include: P. Bénichou, *Morales du grand siècle*; O. Nadal, *Le Sentiment de l'amour dans l'œuvre de Pierre Corneille*; S. Doubrovsky, *Corneille et la dialectique du héros*; J. Maurens, *La Tragédie sans tragique: le néo-stoicisme dans l'œuvre de Pierre Corneille*; M. Prigent, *Le Héros et l'Etat dans la tragédie de Pierre Corneille*.

4 A. Stegmann, *L'Héroisme*; M. Fumaroli, *L'Age de l'éloquence*; M. Fumaroli, 'Tragique païen et tragique chrétien dans *Rodogune*', *RSH*, 152 (1973), 599–631; M. Fumaroli, 'Rhétorique et dramaturgie: le statut du personnage dans la tragédie classique', *Revue d'Histoire du Théâtre*, 24 (1972), 223–50.

PART I 'UNE MUSE DE PROVINCE'

1 N. Vigneul Marville, *Mélanges d'histoire et de littérature*, I, 159–60. Fontenelle, 'Vie de Corneille', in *Œuvres*, III, 81–126.

2 J. Chapelain, *Lettres*, 1880–3, Letter CCCCLXXX (9 March 1640), I, 582–4 (p. 583) and Letter CCCCXXXIX (25 September 1640), I, 693–5 (p. 695).

3 *Horace*, 'Dédicace' (GC, I, 834).

4 According to D'Aubignac, Corneille only left Rouen 'pour faire des courses avantageuses dans le pays des histrions et des libraires', hawking his wares about for the highest profit and selling them three times over – once to the actors, once to the publisher, and once to the wealthy patron who would accept a dedication: F. H. d'Aubignac, 'Troisième Dissertation concernant le poème dramatique', in F. Granet, *Recueil de dissertations sur plusieurs tragédies de Corneille et de Racine*, II, 6–7. La Bruyère, in turn, lists Corneille among the human paradoxes to be seen at Court because of the disparity between his lack of personal distinction and the nobility of his plays: J. de La Bruyère, *Œuvres complètes*, 'Des Jugements', section 56, pp. 381–2. The charge of avarice is repeated in G. Tallemant des Réaux, *Historiettes*, II, 907.

5 J. Chapelain, *Opuscules critiques*, pp. 359–60.

6 Of many accounts of Chapelain's avarice, Tallemant's is particularly entertaining: *Historiettes*, I, 567.

7 See Corneille's own sonnet, probably of the mid-sixties, on the

confirmation of his nobility: GC, III, 559 and 1515–17. Perhaps the initiative for the ennoblement of Corneille's father came from the Queen, but Richelieu's niece, the Mme de Combalet to whom *Le Cid* was dedicated, has more recently been proposed as the lady responsible: A. Niderst, 'Corneille et Anne d'Autriche', in *Pierre Corneille* (Tercentenary Colloquium), pp. 189–96 (esp. pp. 189–90).

8 As Briggs observes, Richelieu's ministry, inaugurated by the 'Day of Dupes', was 'an unmistakable watershed in the evolution of the French state, heralding the great age of royal authoritarianism': R. Briggs, *Early Modern France: 1560–1715*, pp. 100–7 and 127–8. See also F. Dumont, 'French Kingship and Absolute Monarchy in the Seventeenth Century', in *Louis XIV and Absolutism*, pp. 55–84 (p. 67). For discussion of the reforms proposed by Marillac, see R. Bonney, *Political Change in France under Richelieu and Mazarin*, pp. 34–44. On the relation between internal unrest and taxation in the last ten years of Richelieu's ministry, see V. L. Tapié, *La France de Louis XIII et de Richelieu*, pp. 284–7 and 291.

9 Quoted by P. Gaxotte, *Histoire des français*, II, 77.

10 R. Mousnier, 'The Development of Monarchical Institutions', in *Louis XIV and Absolutism*, pp. 37–54. Mousnier defines as 'executive' an exercise of authority 'when public functions are entrusted by the holders of executive power to agents whose directives have coercive power and who are not subject to restrictions which a judge could impose on them' (p. 46). On the growth of bureaucratic autocracy, see also H. R. Trevor-Roper, 'The General Crisis of the Seventeenth Century', in *Crisis in Europe: 1560–1660*, pp. 59–96; G. Pagès, *The Thirty Years' War*, pp. 250–1.

11 J. Donne, 'An Anatomie of the World: The First Anniversary' (1611), in *Complete Poetry and Selected Prose* (p. 202).

12 Sir R. Fanshawe, 'An Ode, upon occasion of his Majesties Proclamation in the year 1630. Commanding the Gentry to Reside upon their Estates in the Country', in *The Metaphysical Poets*, pp. 168–72 (p. 168).

13 Fumaroli discusses the consequences to the institutions of France which flowed from Richelieu's indifference, in the name of 'la raison d'état', to moral and religious arguments against his conduct of government. Hence the discomfiture of the 'aristocratie de la robe': as Gallicans they were attracted by Richelieu's 'politique de gloire', but only at the expense of traditional philosophical and religious conviction: *L'Age de l'eloquence*, pp. 569–70.

14 *Lettre d'un gentilhomme français bon catholique à un sien confident touchant les affaires du temps et l'état de la France* (1632), p. 3. Quoted by W. Krauss, *Corneille als Politischer Dichter*, pp. 26–7. On this pamphlet, and on Mathieu de Morgues' strident criticisms of the Cardinal's ministry, see E. Thuau, *Raison d'Etat et pensée politique à l'époque de Richelieu*, pp. 120–9.

15 To Balzac, 10 May 1638: *Lettres*, CLXII, I, 233–6, esp. p. 235.

16 J-L. Guez de Balzac, *Œuvres*, I, 470–3. M. Fumaroli, 'Critique et

création littéraire: J-L. G. de Balzac et P. Corneille (1637–1645)', in *Mélanges Pintard*, pp. 73–89 (esp. 78–9).

17 *Relation à Ménandre*, in *Œuvres*, I, 546.

18 As Briggs observes, the end of the Frondes showed how the appeal to hierarchical principles and a divinely instituted social order had been overtaken by changed economic realities: *Early Modern France*, p. 193.

19 Church's general conclusion to his lucid exposition of the theoretical debate under Richelieu over the nature and role of 'la raison d'état' is that the Cardinal was convinced of the consonance of his use of discretionary power with higher purposes in accordance with Christian principles. However, in practising the politics of 'le coup d'état' and insisting that governments acted according to a morality which exempted them from ordinary canons of justice, he opened the way for a rationalization of political affairs increasingly divorced from moral and religious considerations. It was precisely this separation of moral orders for which Fénelon was to reproach Louis XIV in his celebrated letter to the King in the last years of the century: see W. F. Church, *Richelieu and Reason of State*.

20 O. A. Ranum, *Artisans of Glory*, pp. 159–64.

21 Corneille's connections with the provincial magistrature in Rouen extended more widely than might be suggested by his own line of direct paternal descent. An uncle had been *procureur* in the provincial Parlement and his mother, the daughter of another *procureur*, was related to the Le Pesant de Boisguilbert family. This numbered amongst its members magistrates whose attachment was to the important Cour des Comptes and one of them had held the considerable dignity of *lieutenant-général de police* in the *vicomté* of Rouen. *Officier* alliances continued into Corneille's own generation with the marriage of his two sisters, one to a *lieutenant* in the *prévôté* of Rouen and the other to a *procureur*.

22 His twenty years as a provincial *officier* at the Table de Marbre in Rouen remained a source of pride to him long after he had relinquished his *charges*. In 1661, famous poet and Academician though he was, Corneille still wrote after his name 'ci-devant avocat du Roi à la Table de Marbre', evidently considering this to be his major claim to social standing, when he signed the wedding contract of his daughter to the more distinguished family of Buat de Boislecomte.

23 The only known instance was an inherited interest in taxes farmed in Conches. This caused considerable litigation, which may explain why the family preferred to acquire neighbouring property to rent, or lent to others of their social standing against the solid security of further local property.

24 In *Le Cid* the term Corneille prefers is 'le pays', or 'l'Etat' in the case of the Crown, while in *Horace* 'la Patrie' is used for reasons of local colour entirely appropriate to the play's Roman context (*Horace*, II, iii, 447; II, vi, 644; III, ii, 784; III, v, 963).

25 On the limited scope of this sense of 'belonging' in the first half of the century, see J. H. Elliott, 'Revolution and Continuity in Early Modern Europe', in *The General Crisis of the Seventeenth Century*, pp. 110–33. See also Briggs, *Early Modern France*, p. 48; V-L. Tapié, 'Comment les français voyaient la patrie', and R. Mousnier, 'Conclusion', in *Comment les français voyaient la France au XVIIe siècle*, pp. 37–58 and 131–6. For an earlier and positive use of the term 'patriote' in connection with loyalty to the provincial *terroir*, see the Grenoblois in 1579–80 and the local community's desire to free itself of garrisons and fiscal inequities: E. Leroy Ladurie, *Carnival: A People's Uprising at Romans (1579–80)*, pp. 128–9.

26 Elliott, 'Revolution and Continuity', p. 123. Mandrou also points out that patriotism in the broader context of the realm 'resided upon royal authority and was inseparable from it': R. Mandrou, *Introduction to Modern France: 1500–1640*, p. 125. For a study of the way in which patriotism lost its 'monarchocentric' character in the closing years of the increasingly unpopular rule of Louis XIV, see W. F. Church's essay on France in *National Consciousness: History and Political Culture in Early Modern Europe*, pp. 43–65. See also Tapié, 'Comment les français voyaient la patrie', in *Comment les français*, pp. 43–6.

27 GC, I, 179. On the interpretation of this sonnet see my article: 'Pierre Corneille's Occasional and Circumstantial Writings relating to Cardinal Richelieu: 1631–1643', *FS*, 41, i (1987), 20–36.

28 G. de La Pinelière, *Hippolyte: tragédie*, 'Avis au Lecteur', and his *Le Parnasse, ou La Critique des poètes*, pp. 60–2.

29 On the Paris Parlement, see Coveney's 'Introduction', *France in Crisis*, pp. 32–7 and 41.

30 Normandy was not the only province to lay claim to such privileges. On the logic of absolutism as it manifested itself across seventeenth-century France by advancing the powers of the Crown at the expense of local privilege and customary law, see G. Durand, 'What is Absolutism?', in *Louis XIV and Absolutism*, pp. 18–36.

31 Mousnier has some eloquent pages on the Norman sense of *patria* and its role in the disturbances of 1639: *Peasant Uprisings*, pp. 107–10. As late as 1655, in the final year of their existence, the provincial Estates unsuccessfully invoked the Charter to support their claim to meet on a yearly basis: Bonney, *Political Change*, pp. 347–8. The popular prestige of the Charter is apparent well into the eighteenth century, when it still figures in a series of specific articles of exclusion in legal documents, the most familiar of which are publishers' *privilèges* which include the formula 'Car tel est notre plaisir; nonobstant Clameur de Haro et Chartre Normande, et lettres à ce contraires'.

32 Leroy Ladurie has documented the weather of the period in his *Histoire du climat depuis l'an mil*.

33 Outbreaks of plague in Rouen occurred in 1619–22, 1623, 1624, 1625, 1627, and 1637–9. The worst years were 1623, 1637, and 1639.

Recurring in 1647–9, it reached another high-point in 1650–1 and later returned in 1668–9: J-P. Bardet, *Rouen au XVIIe et XVIIIe siècles: les mutations d'un espace social*, I, 349.

34 The worst of these increased levies were the forced loan of 1637, the special levies of 1638–9 and the *taxe des aysés* of 1639.

35 On the profound consequences to political order and administration caused by Richelieu's fiscal increases and administrative measures, see Briggs' conclusions: *Early Modern France*, pp. 75–6. Coveney describes the Paris and provincial Parlements' role as one of constitutional remembrance and wishful thinking 'in the face of the ever-hardening outline of Richelieu's and Mazarin's sovereign monarchy': *France in Crisis*, pp. 35–7.

36 Fumaroli describes Bignon's convictions as follows: 'c'est le Parlement qui enracine l'Etat royal dans l'Etre, et qui fait de lui un corps mystique': *L'Age de l'éloquence*, p. 565.

37 See C. Loyseau, *Traité des seigneuries*, in *Œuvres*, 1656, II, sections 57–8 (p. 16). However the primary reference is J. Bodin, *La République*, pp. 270–97. Elsewhere Bodin stresses that the Monarch should give due heed to the counsel of his subjects (pp. 343 and 414–17). Book VI is of equal interest for the way in which it tempers, in the interests of 'la justice harmonique', Bodin's emphasis on monarchical absolutism. Dealing with the matter of taxation, he holds it necessary that the King have the good will of the Estates in any call upon their possessions. We shall have occasion to return to Bodin's distinction between the King's respect for Divine and Natural Law and the tyrant in the context of *Cinna*.

38 See A. Lemaire, *Les Lois Fondamentales de la monarchie française d'après les théoriciens de l'ancien régime*; also Dumont, 'French Kingship', in *Louis XIV and Absolutism*, pp. 55–7, and R. Mousnier, 'Comment les français voyaient la constitution', in *Comment les français*, pp. 9–36. In the earlier context of the Dauphinois magistrate Jean de Bourg's petition of 1576, Leroy Ladurie discerns the same relationship between humanist culture and popular protest in the name of traditional concepts of the judicial character of the monarchy: *Carnival*, p. 69.

39 Meuvret notes that the most violent outbreaks of popular protest related to indirect taxes, duties on the movement of goods and fiscal monopolies: J. Meuvret, 'Fiscalism and Public Opinion', in *Louis XIV and Absolutism*, pp. 199–225 (p. 203).

40 The most striking instance of these misfortunes is that of the Rouennais *officiers* concerned with the fiscal courts. These *élus* and *trésoriers* saw the payment of their salary delayed in 1636, cut in half in 1638 and then reduced by three-quarters in 1639. They also seem to have been most closely involved in a direct physical attack on a tax farmer in August 1639 and in the wrecking of the Office des Aides et Quatrième, which supervised the collection of indirect taxes on produce: Mousnier, *Peasant Uprisings*, pp. 91–3 and Foisil, *Révolte des Nu-Pieds*, pp. 229–67.

41 See G. MacGrath, 'Pierre Corneille avocat', in *Pierre Corneille* (Tercentenary Colloquium), pp. 171–8 (pp. 175–6).

42 V-L. Tapié notes later depredations by the Norman peasantry whom the local clergy had urged to recoup something of the taxes they paid to the King by taking what they might from the King's forests: 'Comment les français voyaient la patrie', in *Comment les français*, pp. 49–50. The precise facts of the matter in Normandy, however, have still to be established. Study of the much poorer Beauvaisis in the same period has shown how the starving peasantry was reduced to picking leaves, herbs, acorns and berries in contravention of forest owners' rights. Court records for the period show a considerable rise in offences against the forest laws, 'not to mention breaches of the laws relating to fishing and hunting': P. Goubert, 'The French Peasantry in the Seventeenth Century: a Regional Example', in *Crisis in Europe*, pp. 141–65 (pp. 157–8).

43 There is more than a hint of the miseries caused by the presence of such troops in Richelieu's observation that 'soldiers assembled disperse immediately if they are not paid'. See O. Ranum, *Richelieu and the Councillors of Louis XIII*, pp. 104–5 and 156.

44 Mousnier, *Peasant Uprisings*, p. 109. Since the *gabelle* involved the compulsory purchase of salt by all classes, the slogan was a particularly effective unifying call: J. Meuvret, 'Comment les français voyaient l'impôt', in *Comment les français*, pp. 59–82 (pp. 77–8).

45 Foisil has studied the government's reprisals after the Nu-Pieds disturbances in the third part of her *Révolte des Nu-Pieds*; see also Tapié, *La France de Louis XIII*, pp. 380–3.

46 Foisil, *Révolte des Nu-Pieds*, pp. 83–92. This instance makes it clear that the slow and costly advancement of France's military fortunes can hardly be attributed to some collective 'national effort': it was the achievement of the Cardinal's iron will, backed by the unquestioning loyalty and ingenuity of his 'creatures' on the King's Council: see Ranum, *Richelieu and the Councillors*, p. 158. As K. Hincker observes, 'L'ordre de Richelieu n'est point l'unité nationale, c'est l'autorité de l'Etat: la grandeur et l'expansion militaires ne sont point celles de la patrie, mais du prince': 'Le Temps de Corneille', *Europe*, 52 (1974), 15–25 (pp. 16–17). According to Couton, '*Le Cid*...est le cri de joie d'une nation qui s'est vue perdue et à qui sa victoire inespérée [à Corbie] donne toutes les confiances': GC, I, 147. This is to be contrasted with Mousnier's more realistic assessment of the peasantry's motives for rejoicing in Champagne after Fleurus and Steenkerque: 'Comment les français voyaient la France', in *Comment les français*, pp. 131–6 (pp. 134–5). On the unco-ordinated nature of popular rebellion in Normandy, see Foisil, *Révolte des Nu-Pieds*, p. 267.

47 For fuller discussion of these circumstantial pieces see my article: 'Pierre Corneille's Occasional and Circumstantial Writings', pp. 20–34.

48 C. Sarrau, Letter to Pierre Corneille, 12 December 1642: GC, I,

1054–55. Sarrau assures Corneille that, had Richelieu lived longer, 'volens, nolens' he would have crowned the poet with Apollo's circlet of laurel.

49 GC, I, 1061. Sentiments to be repeated in private with the celebrated quatrain's four lines of a 'silence' which speaks louder than words:

> 'Qu'on parle mal ou bien de fameux Cardinal,
> Ma prose ni mes vers n'en diront jamais rien:
> Il m'a fait trop de bien pour en dire du mal,
> Il m'a fait trop de mal pour en dire du bien.'
>
> (GC, I, 1062)

50 An opportunism apparent in his dedication of *La Galerie du Palais* in 1637 to Madame de Liancourt, who was compromised in the eyes of the Cardinal by her sympathies for Port Royal. But even if this dedication was 'un acte de courage, sinon de défi à l'égard de Richelieu', it offers no more evidence of the poet's political convictions than of his religious sympathies: see Stegmann, *L'Héroisme*, pp. 1, 42, 46–7 and 90–1. See also R. Pintard, 'Autour de *Cinna* et de *Polyeucte*: nouveaux problèmes de chronologie et de critique cornéliennes', *RHLF*, 64 (1964), 377–413.

51 Corneille could have had little regard for Charleville, the younger son of the Premier Président Faucon de Ris, who was a close friend of Sarasin, the first of Richelieu's protégés to attack *Le Cid*. For Charleville's possible contribution to the *Querelle* see A. Gasté, *La Querelle du 'Cid'*, pp. 203–25.

52 Probably composed in 1641, but unpublished until the eighteenth century: N. de Campion, *Entretiens sur divers sujets d'histoire, de politique et de morale*.

53 See my article: 'Echoes of a Provincial Discussion of the Morality of the Novel: Pierre Corneille's Sonnet and Nicholas de Campion's Preface to Alexandre de Campion's *Les Hommes illustres*', *MLR*, 84 (1989), 319–30.

54 Fumaroli, 'Critique et création littéraire', p. 80.

55 Discussing the problem of the obligations of seventeenth-century patronage, Ranum observes that 'in theory the writer felt more or less compelled to respect his patron's views. In practice this obligation was much less constraining than it might appear': *Artisans of Glory*, p. 150. See also W. D. Howarth's article, 'Mécénat et Raison d'Etat: Richelieu, Corneille et la tragédie politique', in *L'Age d'or du mécénat (1598–1661)*, 1985, pp. 59–68.

56 On the ill-timed appearance of *Cinna* in relation to the disgrace and pardon of Vendôme, and Corneille's evocation of contentious issues concerning the nature of grace at a time when the 'Querelle de la grâce' had come again to the fore in public awareness, see R. Pintard, 'Autour de *Cinna* et de *Polyeucte*', pp. 402–13.

57 Fumaroli's discussion of the emergence of a 'classical' French tradition of eloquence emphasizes Corneille's and Balzac's importance, during the final decade of Richelieu's ministry, as writers whose manner reconciled the contrasting traditions of 'la robe' and 'l'épée'. This fusion established a tradition distinct from the politically subservient

'magistère' of Richelieu's Académie: 'Il y a une part d'utopie généreuse chez Balzac comme chez Corneille qui les maintient en marge de la politique officielle, ou du moins en retraite. Chez eux pointe déjà le magistère moral de l'écrivain au sens moderne': *L'Age de l'éloquence*, p. 705. While I would not disagree with the final observation, it should be stressed – as Fumaroli does elsewhere – that the roots of that conception of the poet's moral authority lay in a humanistic erudition which set Corneille apart from the intellectual mediocrity of the majority of the Academicians of the 1630s: *ibid*, pp. 576 and 580-1. See also my article: 'Corneille's Differences with the Seventeenth-Century Doctrinaires over the Moral Authority of the Poet, *MLR*, 80 (1985), 550-62.

1 THEORETICAL CONTROVERSY: 1629-1643

1 J. Chapelain, 'Lettre sur le poème d'Adonis du chevalier Marino', and 'Lettre sur la régle des vingt-quatre heures', in *Opuscules*, pp. 71-111 and 113-26. See E. G. Kern, *The Influence of Heinsius and Vossius on French Dramatic Theory*, pp. 69-73.

2 GC, II, 625.

3 R. Tuve, *Elizabethan and Metaphysical Imagery*; J. E. Hagstrum, *The Sister Arts: The Tradition of Literary Pictorialism in English Poetry from Dryden to Gray*.

4 Quoted by R. Pintard, *Le Libertinage érudit dans la première moitié du XVIIe siècle*, p. 85.

5 F. R. Sutcliffe, *J-L. Guez de Balzac et son temps: littérature et politique*, p. 85; see also H. M. Davidson, *Audience, Words and Art: Studies in Seventeenth-Century French Rhetoric*, p. 3.

6 *Le Cid*, 'Avertissement' (1648-57), GC, I, 695.

7 As Jehasse observes of the 1630s and Balzac's fall from the Cardinal's favour: 'Les rapports des lettres et du pouvoir ont subi une transformation radicale. A la liberté des années vingt succède la discipline; à la fantaisie anarchique la convention; au particularisme un esprit centriste. L'ordre moral déjà régne. Un écrivain politique doit désormais prendre parti, choisir entre l'encens ou l'exil': J. Jehasse, *J-L. Guez de Balzac et le génie romain*, p. 244.

8 Balzac, 'Lettre à M. de Scudéry sur *Le Cid*' (first published together with Scudéry's reply and his letter to the Académie, Paris, 1638, pp. 13-14) in *Œuvres*, I, 453-57 (p. 457). Stegmann hypothesizes that *La Suivante* (published 9 September 1637) may have been dedicated in gratitude to Balzac: *L'Héroisme*, I, 105, n. 92. For Jehasse's conclusions on Balzac's critical independence, see *J-L. Guez de Balzac*, p. 487.

9 Chapelain, letters to Balzac of 13 June 1637, 22 August 1637, and 21 February 1638; to Boisrobert of 31 July 1637; to M. de Saint Chartres of 24 December 1637, in *Lettres*, I, 156-7, 159-60, 164-5, 185 and 203-4.

10 GC, I, 782.

11 Corneille to Boisrobert: 'Messieurs de l'Académie peuvent faire ce qu'il leur plaira; puisque vous m'écrivez que Monseigneur serait bien aise

d'en voir leur jugement, et que cela doit divertir Son Eminence, je n'ai rien à dire' (13 June 1637); 'Je me prépare à n'avoir rien à répondre à l'Académie que par des remerciments' (3 December 1637): GC, I, 803–8.

12 R. Bray, *La Formation de la doctrine classique en France*, p. 113; A. Adam, *Histoire de la littérature française du XVIIe siècle*, I, 516–17; M. FUMAROLI, 'La Querelle de la moralité du théâtre avant Nicole et Bossuet', *RHL*, 70 (1970), 1007–30.

13 Notably Fumaroli, 'Critique et création' , pp. 75–82.

14 See Fumaroli, *L'Age de l'éloquence*, pp. 576–81, 648–9, and 670–1. On the importance of Corneille's dissent in the development of a classical literary aesthetic and the traditional bases on which that 'magistère de l'écrivain' was grounded: *ibid*, pp. 693–5 and 705. A. Viala makes an interesting analysis of Corneille's 'alliance conflictuelle' with the literary institutions of the period (despite an underestimation of Corneille's debt to tradition and a tendency to anticipate later conceptions of the writer): 'Corneille et les institutions littéraires de son temps', in *Pierre Corneille* (Tercentenary Colloquium), pp. 197–204.

15 The dramaturgical evidence for this continuity between the two plays is presented in Sweetser, *Dramaturgie*, pp. 113–20.

16 Stegmann suggests that, during the period 1637–40, Corneille was at work on *Cinna* as well as *Horace* and conjectures that *La Mort de Pompée*, *Polyeucte* and even *Théodore* were already in the early stages of composition: *L'Héroisme*, I, 92–3 and II, 581.

17 *Lettres*, CIII, I, 147–8 (p. 148) and CIX, I, 154–7 (p. 156).

18 *Lettres*, CCL, I, 364–7 (p. 367).

19 Only Ogier had been as uncompromising, but that was in 1628 during the earliest days of the debate over regularity: 'Préface' to J. de Schelandre's *Tyr et Sidon*, p. 153. See H. C. Lancaster, *A History of French Dramatic Literature in the Seventeenth Century*, I, i, 314–19; also Bray, *Formation*, pp. 70–1, and Sweetser, *Conceptions*, p. 39.

20 'Lettre sur le poème d'Adonis', in *Opuscules*, pp. 85–7. Fumaroli notes the 'utilitarian' character of this Platonico–Augustinian tradition of eloquence deriving from *De Doctrina Christiana*; pertinently he observes that it carries within it 'la menace d'un asservissement au *docere* et d'une hegémonie intolérante du *rhetor ecclesiasticus*'. Elsewhere he shows how this neo-platonic current was allied in Roman eloquence to a certain monarchical tradition of Papal panegyric: *L'Age de l'éloquence*, p. 139 and pp. 206–7.

21 *Observations sur le 'Cid'*, in Corneille, *Œuvres complètes*, edited by C. Marty-Laveaux, XII, 441–61 (pp. 443 and 446).

22 *Les Sentiments de l'Académie sur 'Le Cid'* (first draft), in Chapelain, *Opuscules*, pp. 158–9.

23 Sutcliffe, *J-L. Guez de Balzac*, p. 244.

24 *Les Sentiments de l'Académie sur 'Le Cid'* (final version), in Corneille, *Œuvres complètes*, edited by C. Marty-Laveaux, XII, 465–6.

25 *Sentiments*, XII, pp. 468–9 and 472.

26 J. de la Mesnardière, *La Poétique*.

27 Scudéry, *Observations*, pp. 446–7.

28 Balzac, 'Lettre à M. de Scudéry sur *Le Cid*' (pp. 13–14 of the original 1638 publication), in *Œuvres*, I, 457. In 1639 Scudéry later made what he could of Balzac's letter, referring to Plato's *Republic* as a work which banished poets, 's'ils n'avaient point de meilleur emploi que celui de faire rire'. He seems also to have been impressed by Corneille's 'Epître' prefacing *Médée*, which must have appeared before he went to print. Referring his reader to Plutarch's 'traité de la Lecture des Poètes', he attempts a weak riposte to Corneille's confidence in his audiences' natural discernment of the good and the bad: *Apologie du théâtre*, 'Préface' (unpaginated) and pp. 13–16.

29 L. Cellot, *Panegyrici Flexiensis Ludovico XIII*. Quoted by Fumaroli, whose translation I use: 'Querelle de la moralité', pp. 120–1.

30 Bray, *Formation*, p. 81.

31 Predictably, Scudéry takes the same line in 1639: *Apologie*, pp. 13–14.

32 *Première Dissertation sur le poème dramatique*, in Granet, *Recueil*, I, 147.

33 F. H. d'Aubignac, *La Pratique du théâtre*, p. 73.

34 See also *Poétique*, pp. 120 and 325.

35 Sir Philip Sidney, *A Defense of Poesy*, p. 16. Compare La Mesnardière: 'Le Poète doit prendre garde à figurer ses héros les meilleurs qu'il sera possible, à l'exemple des grands peintres qui flattent toujours leurs portraits, et leur donnent des agréments que les naturels n'ont pas': *Poétique*, p. 46.

36 N. Boileau, 'L'Art poétique', Chant III, in *Œuvres complètes*, 167.

37 *Pratique*, pp. 37–9. Bray's equation of D'Aubignac's position with that of Corneille misleadingly ignores the continuity of D'Aubignac's utilitarian conception of poetry: *Formation*, p. 72.

38 *Troisième Dissertation*, in Granet, *Recueil*, II, 33. See Sweetser, *Les Conceptions*, p. 100–1.

39 'How a Young Man should study Poetry', in Plutarch, *Moralia*, I, 71–197.

40 Tuve and Hagstrum extensively discuss the history of this use of vivid concretion. See also B. Hathaway, *The Age of Criticism: The Late Renaissance in Italy*, pp. 11–12.

41 O. Nadal, 'L'Exercice du crime chez Corneille', *Mercure de France*, January 1950, 27–37.

42 See my article, 'Corneille's Differences', pp. 550–2.

43 P. Du Moulin, *La Philosophie mise en français*, Book III, 'Ethique', chapter 6, p. 303; see also R. de Ceriziers, *Le Philosophe français*, Book III, 'La Morale', pp. 95–7.

44 G. Forestier has persuasively argued that it was D'Aubignac who most tended to confuse stage representation with the illusion of 'real life': 'Illusion comique et illusion mimétique', *Papers on French Seventeenth-Century Literature*, 11 (1984), 377–91 (pp. 382–6).

45 In the analogous area of the Counter-Reformation painters' exploitation of the still life and emblematics, Martin usefully reminds us that 'the naturalism of seventeenth-century art is inextricably bound up with a metaphysical view of the world ... There is as great a gap between Velazquez and Manet as there is between Descartes and Darwin': J. R. Martin, *Baroque*, p. 119.

46 Tuve, *Elizabethan and Metaphysical Imagery*, p. 383.

47 As Tuve concludes, the poet's traditional aim pleasurably to communicate a truth simply did not make of a poem 'a decorated sermon, or an informative exposition trimmed with metaphors, or a set of precepts with examples to match. Least of all does such an aim ask poets to state, and make palatable, orthodox moral codes ... (As always a few persons, not usually poets or critics either, would like to have had it mean this) ... Poetry is concerned with truth, as carefully and sensitively seen as may be, and not with the Favourite Truths of the age. It may not be perfunctory and it may not be stupidly good': *Elizabethan and Metaphysical Imagery*, p. 409.

48 Adam, *Histoire*, II, 373–4.

49 See Chapelain to Balzac (18 November 1640): *Lettres*, I, pp. 721–2.

50 *Lettres*, I, pp. 573–6 (pp. 575–6).

51 Quoted by Stegmann: *L'Héroisme*, II, 80–1. P. du Ryer, *Saul: tragédie*, 'Préface'.

52 Gillet de La Tessonerie, *L'Art de régner, ou le Sage Gouverneur: tragicomédie*, 'Epître'.

53 Maurens, *La Tragédie sans tragique*, pp. 243–69. Pintard follows this view, describing Corneille as the panegyrist of Richelieu, despite a concluding discussion of Corneille's Rouennais acquaintances, which clearly reveals the ambiguities of Corneille's relations with his patron: 'Autour de *Cinna*', pp. 377–413. More recently the view that the Corneille of *Horace* and *Cinna* is 'le fidèle interprète des volontés et de la politique du cardinal' has been endorsed by A. Niderst in his 'Corneille et Anne d'Autriche', p. 191, and in his 'Tragédie et conflits sociaux au XVIIe siècle: Corneille et la sédition des Nus-pieds', in *Mélanges Couton*, pp. 289–97 (pp. 294–5). Couton also concludes that Corneille was 'profondément engagé dans la politique de Richelieu', and that his play celebrates 'la rigoureuse et exigeante morale de salut public que le temps, selon Corneille, demandaient': GC, I, 1548.

54 F. le M. de Boisrobert, 'Epître à Monseigneur le Cardinal: de l'ingratitude des gens de province', in *Les Satires françaises du XVIIe siècle*, II, 57–60. Boisrobert, in a reference which may recall the 1639 reading of *Horace*, is recorded as saying that, despite Corneille's clumsy reading of his work, he found his verse admirable: *Ménagiana*, I, 312.

55 La Mesnardière in his *Poétique*, Scudéry in his *Apologie du théâtre* (both of 1639) and J-F. Sarasin in his *Discours de la tragédie, ou remarques sur 'L'Amour tyrannique' de M. de Scudéry*, published after Sarasin's death in *Œuvres de Monsieur Sarasin*, pp. 301–44.

56 *Entretiens*, p. 443.
57 A line of argument which Molière adopts, and with equal wit, in his dedication of *Les Fâcheux* to Louis XIV in 1661: Molière, *Œuvres complètes*, I, 481–2.
58   Qu'on parle mal ou bien du fameux Cardinal,
        Ma prose ni mes vers n'en diront jamais rien:
        Il m'a fait trop de bien pour en dire du mal,
        Il m'a fait trop de mal pour en dire du bien.
                            (GC, I, 1062)
59 Gombauld even got away with 'Ce n'est pas ma faute', in reply to Richelieu's complaint that he could not understand Gombauld's work: *Ménagiana*, I, 372–3. Retz accords the Cardinal a lively sense of humour, but at the expense of others: P. de Gondi, Cardinal de Retz, *Mémoires*, p. 16.
60 For a Jesuit's fervent expression of such an aesthetic in service of religious values, see Pierre Le Moyne, *Hymnes de la sagesse divine et de l'amour divin, avec un Discours de la poésie*, pp. 3–41.
61 GC, II, 625 and GC, II, 549–53.
62 GC, II, 95–8, 195–8 and 354–8. These pieces will be considered in the following chapter.

2   TRADITION AND ORIGINALITY

1 'Lettre sur la règle des vingt-quatre heures' (29 November 1630), in *Opuscules*, pp. 113–126 (p. 115).
2 That Corneille's audiences were familiar with the use of such skills is apparent in Valère's allusion to the powers of *evidentia*, even as he refuses such artifices in presenting the murdered Camille to his hearers: *Horace*, v, ii, 1513–19; see Poirier, *Corneille*, pp. 176–77.
3 Barnwell, *The Tragic Drama*, p. 223.
4 See Tuve: 'It is no wonder that poetry as contemplation can come so close to poetry as urging well-doing, against this background…When the contemplation of universals in truly judged relation to particular events urges a reader to a particular course of action, the poet finds himself as a propagandist. Poetry moves to true knowing, and if knowing moved to the "ordinary forms of action", the Renaissance poet would not see that that put his poem into some meaner category. The theory erects bars against shoddy moralizing, wilful deceit, and the cheap short cuts of tricky appeals through the affections. Against other dangers – man's capacity for error and his insufficiently disciplined faculties – it simply takes its chances.' (*Elizabethan and Metaphysical Imagery*, pp. 402–3.)
5 *Ibid.*, p. 183. As Tuve observes: 'Right Reason, that sixteenth-century desideratum, does not involve the supplanting of the affections by intellectual activity, rather the rectifying of them…The Renaissance poet willed to move his reader's will' (pp. 399 and 402). Honoré d'Urfé

echoed a fundamental moral conviction of his age when he began as follows the 'Histoire de Célion and Bélinde' in the first part of *L'Astrée*: 'Il est tout certain...que la vertu dépouillée de tout autre agencement, ne laisse pas d'être d'elle-même agréable, ayant des aimants tant attirants, qu'aussitôt qu'une âme en est touchée, il faut qu'elle l'aime et la suive' (*L'Astrée*, I, 390.)

6 As Martin observes in his discussion of the allegorical character of much Counter-Reformation art, the Baroque artist's purpose was 'to give new force and meaning to received truths by transplanting them from the realm of the general and abstract into that of immediate, sensuous and concrete experience' (*Baroque*, p. 132).

7 R. Weinberg, 'Castelvetro's Theory of Poetics', in *Critics and Criticism*, pp. 349–71 (p. 351).

8 For a balanced and comprehensive review of Castelvetro's poetics, H. B. Charlton's *Castelvetro's Theory of Poetry* remains authoritative.

9 That difference was one of manner as well as content. As Bray observes, the doctrinaires' moralistic concern constantly tempts them into allegory, a process which Balzac explicitly rejects in the context of the drama: *Formation*, pp. 82–4; see also my 'Corneille's Differences', p. 561.

10 Martin, *Baroque*, p. 121. On the period's allegorical turn of mind, see G. Couton, 'Réapprendre à lire: deux des langages de l'allégorie au 17ème siècle', *Cahiers de l'Association Internationale des Etudes Françaises*, 28 (1976), 81–101.

11 Only in the specific case of the 'Préface' to *Clitandre* (GC, I, 96) does Corneille possibly invite an allegorical interpretation of his work as a direct reflection of seventeenth-century historical particulars (see Part III). See also, from a socio-critical perspective, K. Gronau's reservations about the propriety of applying allegorical methods to the elucidation of Corneille's plays: 'Matériau et fonctions sociales de la tragédie', *Papers on French Seventeenth-Century Literature*, 11 (1984), 447–73 (pp. 463–4).

12 'How a Young Man should study Poetry', *Moralia*, I, 101.

13 Otherwise Corneille gets tucked up with some unlikely bedfellows. Concluding a discussion of Galuzzi and Donati on the historical subject with the observation that their position is 'exactement la position de Corneille, et de ses contemporains, auteurs de tragédies historiques, Mairet, Du Ryer, Scudéry, La Mesnardière', F. de Daimville unacceptably confuses very distinct views of the function of the public drama: 'Allégorie et actualité sur les tréteaux des jésuites', in *Dramaturgie et société*, II, 433–43. Rossi's emphatic political utilitarianism, Del Rio's dated allegorizing and his proselytizing spirit, or Giasone de Nores' insistence on the cautionary function of the hero of mediocre virtue and his explanation of *katharsis* (which is surely the coarsest explanation of all in a period of crudely utilitarian excess), sit very oddly indeed with the spirit of Corneille's principles and practice, even if they concur with Corneille on points of detail.

14 L. E. Roux, 'Cent ans d'expérience théâtrale dans les collèges de la
Compagnie de Jésus en Espagne', in *Dramaturgie et société*, II, 479–523
(p. 522). As M. Gravier observes: 'Ce théâtre est un théâtre d'enseigne-
ment…La pièce jésuite est un sermon qu'illustre une action dramatique': 'Le Théâtre des jésuites et la tragédie du salut et de la
conversion', in *Le Théâtre tragique*, pp. 119–29 (p. 119 and 120).

15 The kinship between a Tridentine emphasis on edification and its
literary extension into the field of political education in France under
Richelieu has been noted by Fumaroli: *L'Age de l'éloquence*, pp. 141–2.

16 Caussin, *La Cour sainte* (collective edition of 1664); Stegmann,
L'Héroisme, II, 111.

17 Castelvetro, *Poetica d'Aristotele vulgarizzata e sposta*, p. 140: select
translation in A. H. Gilbert, *Literary Criticism: Plato to Dryden*, p. 317.
Such an over-enthusiastic identification mars Fumaroli's otherwise
informative article, 'Rhétorique et dramaturgie', pp. 223–50.

18 The continuity of Corneille's thought since the Querelle du *Cid* is
apparent in the way in which he describes the *Discours* in a letter (25
August 1660) to the Abbé de Pure: 'J'y ai fait quelques explications
nouvelles d'Aristote, et avancé quelques propositions et quelques
maximes inconnues à nos Anciens. J'y réfute celles sur lesquelles
l'Académie a fondé la condamnation du *Cid*' (GC, III, 6–7). After an
outline of the plan of the *Discours* he adds, 'après cela il n'y a plus guère
de question d'importance à remuer'. Clearly he intends once and for all
to settle matters which had been at issue for nearly twenty-five years.

19 *Sentiments* (final version), XII, 468.

20 Compare Balzac's robust conviction that, when he witnessed a tragedy,
he judged what he saw, rather than what he was expected to 'read into'
the action: 6th 'Discours', in *Œuvres*, I, 294–309 (pp. 300–8). See Bray,
Formation, p. 83.

21 After the early 'Epître' prefacing *Médée* and well before the publication
of the *Discours*, Corneille had returned to the kinds of 'utilité' proper to
drama in the 'Epître' prefacing *La Suite du Menteur* (1645):

> J'en trouve deux à mon sens, l'une empruntée de la morale, l'autre qui lui est
> particulière. Celle-là se rencontre aux sentences et réflexions que l'on peut
> adroitement semer presque partout; celle-ci en la naïve peinture des vices et des
> vertus. Pourvu qu'on les sache mettre en leur jour, et les faire connaître par leurs
> véritables caractères, celles-ci se feront aimer, quoique malheureuses, et ceux-là
> se feront détester, quoique triomphants. Et comme le portrait d'une laide
> femme ne laisse pas d'être beau, et qu'il n'est pas besoin d'avertir que l'original
> n'en est pas aimable, pour empêcher qu'on l'aime, il en est de même dans notre
> peinture parlante: quand le crime est bien peint de ses couleurs, quand les
> imperfections sont bien figurées, il n'est point besoin d'en faire voir un mauvais
> succès à la fin pour avertir qu'il ne les faut pas imiter. (GC, II, 98)

22 As Saint-Evremond observed, this 'naïvete' defined the special pleasure
of Cornelian drama: 'Chez Corneille la grandeur se connaît par elle-
même…Il lui suffit de bien entrer dans les choses, et la pleine image

qu'il en donne fait la véritable impression qu'aiment à recevoir les personnes de bon sens': C. de M. de Saint-Evremond, 'Sur les tragédies' (1669–70), in *Œuvres en prose*, III, 24–31 (pp. 25–6).

23 See, for instance, P. de Villiers, 'Entretien sur les tragédies de ce temps', in Granet, *Recueil*, I, 22–4, which is to be compared with Saint-Evremond's similar regrets about the success in the 1670s of gratuitous displays of disordered passion and the waning popularity of Corneille's depictions of 'la condition de l'homme': 'Défense de quelques pièces de M. Corneille', in Saint-Evremond, *Œuvres en prose*, IV, 429.

24 The moral psychology which lies behind this assessment of Cléopâtre's dramatic effect is by no means peculiar to Corneille: indeed it seems to have been something of a seventeenth-century moral commonplace. The preface to Books VII and VIII of Brébeuf's translation of Lucan's *Pharsalia* offers an important example of this. Far from original in both admiring and condemning Caesar, Brébeuf uses much the same categories as those which Corneille applies to Cléopâtre's effect on the spectator: Lucain, *La Pharsale*, Books VII–VIII, 'Avertissement'.

25 Plutarch, once more, may be a source for this analysis of the effect of heroic characterization. He had long ago described the combination of enhanced moral awareness and immediate affective response which was available to the spectator or reader from good poetic imitation. In a state of wonderment before the poet's invention, the reader (or spectator) feels 'elation and a sympathetic enthusiasm over noble deeds and an aversion and repugnance for the mean'. Plutarch's less happy commendation that the young man should cultivate the habit of exclaiming 'Wrong!' or 'Improper!' quite as loudly and frequently as 'Right!' or 'Proper!' obviously relates to the privacy of the study, but the principle itself foreshadowed the kind of enjoyment through alert moral involvement which Corneille particularly seeks to produce in the theatre. But then it was also Plutarch's comparisons of great men which demonstrated the value of an imitation of the character and lives of 'men who are not perfect or spotless', bringing out 'along with the actions, indications of both vice and virtue commingled': *Moralia*, I, 133–7.

26 That this response to Corneille's drama was experienced by the poet's contemporaries is shown by Scarron, who singles out the same telling contrast of characters in action as peculiarly characteristic of the pleasure he had derived from a performance of *Nicomède*: P. Scarron, *Le Roman comique*, in *Les Romanciers du XVIIe siècle*, p. 771. The effectiveness of such a brilliant and telling comparison of strengths and values was more recently described by C. Péguy as 'le perpétuel affrontement, la comparaison constante, la constante confrontation des êtres et des vies, des personnages et des thèses': *Note conjointe sur M. Descartes et la philosophie cartésienne*, in *Œuvres complètes de Charles Péguy, 1873–1914*, IX, 177.

27 Aristotle, *The Art of Poetry*, p. 13, n. 1.

28 G. J. Mallinson has examined the exceptional skill with which Corneille manipulates and exploits his spectator's awareness of an available repertory of registers, types and situations: see *The Comedies of Corneille: Experiments in the Comic.*

29 See also the second *Discours*: '[Les infortunes] des autres hommes [que les rois] y trouveraient place, s'il leur en arrivait d'assez illustres, et d'assez extraordinaires pour la mériter, et que l'histoire prît assez de soin d'eux pour nous les apprendre. Scédase n'était qu'un paisan de Leuctres: et je ne tiendrais pas la sienne indigne d'y paraître, si la pureté de notre scène pouvait souffrir qu'on y parlât du violement effectif de ses deux filles (LF, 78; GC, III, 144).

30 There may also be a trace of Castelvetro here, for the Italian had suggested that tragedy was particularly concerned with rights and wrongs as they may be called into question by the socially disruptive behaviour of great men. He had also said that a historical basis in the chronicles of kings and princes was necessary, if such a subject was to be credible: *Poetica*, pp. 188 and 221–2. See also Gilbert, *Literary Criticism: Plato to Dryden*, pp. 319 and 329.

31 H. T. Barnwell, *Les Idées morales et critiques de Saint-Evremond*, p. 161.

32 D. Sellstrom, 'The Structure of Corneille's Masterpieces', *RR*, 49 (1958), 269–77. See also J-P. Sartre, 'Forgers of Myths', *Theatre Arts*, 30 (1946), pp. 324–335.

33 *Morales du grand siècle*, pp. 21–2.

34 'Défense de quelques pièces de théâtre de M. Corneille', in *Œuvres en prose*, IV, 423–31 (p. 429).

35 For a carefully balanced discussion of Saint-Evremond's literary criticism see Barnwell, *Idées morales*, pp. 139 and 159–78. See also Bray, *Formation*, p. 314, and Sweetser, *Conceptions*, pp. 166–9.

36 My concern here is with the specific issue of the dramatists' chosen areas of tragic focus. This is not to discount, in the more general context of their craftsmanship and its relation to contemporary dramaturgy, the invaluable lesson of H. Barnwell's more recent extended study in comparison, which has shown the pitfalls of too easy an opposition. Pertinently he reminds us how much the two dramatists have in common within the seventeenth-century French dramatic tradition: *The Tragic Drama*, pp. 95–7.

37 J. Racine, *Œuvres complètes*, I, 745–7.

38 Corneille's list of commentators here looks rather more impressive than perhaps it really is, since he had used Beni, who had already done most of the work in reviewing the sixteenth-century theorists for various possible interpretations.

39 Compare Racine's more perceptive reading of the passage: 'La tragédie...ne se fait point par récit, mais par une représentation vive, qui, excitant la pitié et la terreur, purge (et tempère) ces sortes de passions. (C'est à dire qu'en émouvant ces passions, elle leur ôte ce qu'elles ont d'excessif et de vicieux, et les ramène à un état modéré et

conforme à la raison)' ('Fragment du premier livre de la poétique d'Aristote', in *Œuvres complètes*, II, 923).

40 D. Sellstrom, 'The Structure of Corneille's Masterpieces', p. 275.

41 M. F. Guizot, *Corneille et son temps*, p. 243.

42 See in particular Barnwell, *The Tragic Drama*, chapters 5 and 6, and G. May's less carefully shaded comparative study of structure: *Tragédie cornélienne: tragédie racinienne*.

3 *CLITANDRE* (1630–2) AND *MEDEE* (1634–5)

1 G. Charlier, *La Clef de 'Clitandre'*; L. Rivaille, *Les Débuts de Corneille*, pp. 76–81; see also GC, I, 1198–9.

2 For a defence of the distinction between private and political morality, see P. Charron, *De la sagesse*, Book 2, chapter 2; G. Naudé, *Considérations politiques sur les coups d'état*; L. Machon, *Apologie pour Machiavel*. For discussion of an extensive debate, see N. O. Keohane, *Philosophy and the State in France: The Renaissance to the Enlightenment*, pp. 151–82; E. Thuau, *Raison d'Etat et pensée politique à l'époque de Richelieu*; W. F. Church, *Richelieu and Reason of State*; P. Wyndham Lewis, *The Lion and the Fox*.

3 I. Gentillet, *Discours sur les moyens de bien gouverner et maintenir en paix un royaume ou autre principauté, contre Nicolas Machiavel, florentin*.

4 J. de Marnix, *Les Résolutions politiques ou Maximes d'Etat*; P. Bardin, *Le Lycée du sieur Bardin, où en plusieurs promenades il est traité des connaissances, des actions, et des plaisirs d'un honnête homme*. Noting Corneille's simplification of Machiavellianism into a politics founded on self-interest, Stegmann observes: 'Corneille ne semble connaître, comme la plupart de ses contemporains, que les ouvrages des moralistes qui attaquent Machiavel sur les principes isolés abusivement par Gentillet' (*L'Héroisme*, II, 346 and 369).

5 Fortin de la Hoguette, *Testament ou Conseils fidèles d'un bon père à ses enfants, où sont contenus plusieurs raisonnements chrétiens, moraux et politiques*, pp. 11–12 and 13; see also G. du Vair, 'Exhortation à la Vie Civile' in *La Philosophie morale des stoïques*, in *Œuvres politiques, morales, et mêlées*, p. 896; Marnix, *Résolutions*, pp. 367–70; Bardin, *Lycée*, II, 12, 776–7 and 881–2; Caussin, *Cour sainte* (collective edition of 1664), II, 76–8; P. Cureau de la Chambre, *De l'Art de connaître les hommes*, pp. 258–9.

6 Priézac, *Discours politiques*, p. 29; P. Le Moyne, *La Dévotion aisée*, pp. 28–9; see also Marnix, *Résolutions*, p. 37; P. Fortin de la Hoguette, *Testament*, p. 241; R. Bary, *La Morale*, p. 86–7.

7 B. Gracián, *El Oráculo Manual y Arte de Prudencia*, pp. 68–9 and Campion, *Entretiens*, p. 376.

8 Fortin de la Hoguette, *Testament*, pp. 360–1; see also Bardin, *Lycée*, I, 70. For an extended development on the Divine Harmony manifest in the world and an attack on the *esprits forts* who follow Lucretius, see J. de Silhon, *Les Deux Vérités*, and H. Mugnier, *La Véritable Politique du Prince Chrétien, à la confusion des sages du monde, et pour la*

condamnation des politiques du siècle, pp. 10–11. For presentation to a salon public of the same theme, see C. Cotin, *Théoclée, ou La Vraie Philosophie des principes du monde*. In the context of political and juridical theory, see the 'Préface' of C. Loyseau, *Traité des ordres et simples dignités*, in *Œuvres*; also F. de Colomby, *Discours de l'autorité des Rois*, p. 4. For its treatment in a moral work and a work of popularized philosophy, see F. N. Coeffeteau, *Tableau des passions humaines*, p. 416, and Du Moulin, *Philosophie*, Book II, 'La Physique', pp. 2–9.

9 Bardin, *Lycée*, II, 638–9, 657, and 766–7. Other widely read works which similarly emphasize the promptings of Right Reason are A. de Guevara, *Les Epîtres dorées*, p. 10; Caussin, *Cour sainte*, V (1645), pp. 510–11; P. Cureau de la Chambre, *De l'Art de connaître les hommes*, p. 258.

10 Bodin, *République*, pp. 11 and 16; P. Fortin de la Hoguette, *Les Eléments de la politique selon les principes de la nature*, p. 31. On the monarch's particular obligation to Natural Reason and Natural Justice, see Bodin, *République*, p. 156.

11 Caussin, *Cour sainte* (collective edition of 1664), II, 374; see also Colomby, *Discours*, pp. 4–6 and 35–6; Fortin de la Hoguette, *Testament*, pp. 360–1; Du Moulin, *Philosophie*, Book III, 'La Morale', pp. 172–80.

12 An instance is that of Scudéry himself, before he began to court the Cardinal's favour in 1636. Certain passages of *Le Trompeur puni* (1633), conventional though they are, sound out of context like cautions to the Prince in the exercise of his royal authority and even propose a discreet apology for duelling, asserting that individual honour is beyond the jurisdiction of kings (Act IV, i and iv). Even *Le Vassal généreux* (1636) explores the limits of a subject's obedience to his King and flatters the nobility's pretensions to political importance by presenting the King's authority as largely dependent on their support (Act V). For discussion of tragicomedy's contribution to this apology for 'feudal' attitudes see P. Butler, *Classicisme et baroque dans l'œuvre de Racine*, pp. 164–5.

13 Bodin, *République*, pp. 731–2; on 'le magnanime', see also Priézac, *Discours*, pp. 456–7.

14 Aquinas, *Selected Political Writings*, p. 75; Marnix, *Résolutions*, p. 52; Priézac, *Discours*, pp. 29–30.

15 'Si la justice est la fin de la loi, la loi œuvre du Prince, le Prince est image de Dieu, il faut par même suite de raison que la loi du Prince soit faite modèle de la loi de Dieu' (Bodin, *République*, p. 161).

16 Priézac, *Discours*, p. 96. See R. Mousnier, 'Comment les français voyaient la constitution', in *Comment les français*, pp. 18–20.

17 Priézac, *Discours*, pp. 147–8.

18 Cotin, *Théoclée*, 'Dédicace'.

19 Bardin, *Lycée*, II, 767.

20 A. Ammirato, *Discours politiques de Tacite*, pp. 130–1; Bardin, *Lycée*, I, 427; Caussin, *Cour sainte* (collective edition of 1664), I, 35–41; Marnix, *Résolutions*, pp. 23–6; F. Guicciardini, *Maximes populaires*, Part II, Maxim LXVI; Priézac, *Discours*, pp. 248–9.

21 Fortin de la Hoguette, *Testament*, p. 363. Du Bois Hus offers an excellent

example of the polemic urgency with which an increasingly 'libertin' secularity of thought was attacked:

L'Œil éternel n'agit point aveuglément et sans considération. Nous ne devons pas le premier instant de nos vies au caprice de la fortune mais aux arrêts du Ciel: nous ne sommes pas des assemblages animés de ces atomes fortuitement rencontrés que la philosophie libertine nous a donnés pour pères. Le hasard n'est point le dispensateur de nos années, ni le créateur des hommes: c'est la Providence seule qui manie tous les ressorts de l'horloge des temps et sonne quand il luy plaît l'heure de nos nativités. (G. Du Bois Hus, *Le Prince illustre*, p. 107)

22 Silhon, *Deux Vérités*, pp. 248–9; J. de la Noue, *Discours politiques*, p. 556.
23 'La fortune n'est autre chose que l'homme même lorsque sans y penser il se fait la cause accidentelle d'un effet non prétendu': Caussin, *Cour sainte* (collective edition of 1664), I, 36. See also Du Moulin, *Philosophie*, Book II, 'La Physique', p. 12.
24 Marnix, *Résolutions*, p. 23.
25 Priézac, *Discours*, p. 153; see also Bodin, *République*, pp. 19–20; Ceriziers, *Philosophe français*, Book III, 'La Morale', pp. 143–53. See C. Dejob, *De l'Influence du Concile de Trente sur la littérature*, pp. 88 and 150; H. Bremond, *Histoire littéraire du sentiment religieux en France depuis la fin des Guerres de Religion jusqu'à nos jours*, I, 10; also Mousnier, 'Comment les français voyaient la constitution', in *Comment les français*, p. 13.
26 E. Bauny, *Somme des péchés qui se commettent en tous états*, p. 759.
27 P. Le Moyne, *Les Peintures morales*, II, Book III, pp. 304–5 and 309.
28 Aquinas, *Selected Political Writings*, p. 19; C. du Bosc, *La Femme héroïque ou Les Héroïnes comparées avec les héros en toute sorte de vertus*, I, 13–14.
29 J. Olivier (A. Trousset), *Alphabet de l'imperfection et malice des femmes*, pp. 178–9.
30 Caussin, *Cour sainte* (collective edition of 1664), I, 103.
31 B. de Vigenère, *Les Images et tableaux de plate peinture de Philostrate*, II, 436–44 (p. 436).
32 N. Conti, *Mythologie ou Explication des fables*, pp. 809–11 and 886.
33 Among others: F. Schoonhoven, *Emblemata Florenti Schoonovii Goudani partim Moralia partim etiam Civilia*, no. 71, 'Pestis regni Rex, sine Prudentia', pp. 211–12. A century later Vico recapitulates on the Cyclopean symbolism of unbridled bestial freedom: G. Vico, *The New Science*, paragraphs 191, 338, 516, 644, 1012–13, and 1098.
34 C. Federici, *Réalisme et dramaturgie*, pp. 232–6.
35 Le Moyne, *Peintures morales*, II, Book III, p. 306.
36 An eighteenth-century critic was particularly shocked by Corneille's rendering of Seneca. In his view it was 'peu digne de la majesté royale': Le père Brumoy, *Le Théâtre des grecs*, II, 490.
37 On Corneille's early treatment of the paradoxes of love and love of self, see M. Margitiç, 'Mythologie personnelle chez le premier Corneille: le jeu de l'amour et de l'amour-propre de *Mélite* au *Cid*', in *Pierre Corneille*

(*Tercentenary Colloquium*), pp. 547–67. See also W. O. Goode, 'Médée and Jason: Hero and Non-hero in Corneille's *Médée*', *French Review*, 51 (1978), 804–15.

38 P. Le Moyne, *La Gallerie des femmes fortes*, Part II, p. 169.

39 Much later, Corneille was to show similar difficulty in adapting antique myth to the providential convictions of his seventeenth-century audience. *Œdipe* concludes with a moving narration of the King blasphemously accusing the gods of injustice, but the drama cannot end before 'rectifying' this with an anticlimactic final assertion of their providential purposes: *Œdipe*, v, ix; GC, III, 91–3.

40 Voltaire, *Commentaires sur Corneille*, in *The Complete Works of Voltaire*, LIV, 24.

4 LE CID (1637)

1 M. R. Margitiç, 'Les Deux *Cid*: de la tragi-comédie à la pseudo-tragédie classique', *Papers on French Seventeenth-Century Literature*, II (1984), 409–25 (p. 420). See also on the *dénouement*, R. Pintard, 'De la Tragicomédie à la tragédie: l'exemple du *Cid*', in *Mélanges Vier*, pp. 455–66.

2 Letter to Jacques Dupuy (12 May 1637), in R. Pintard, 'Un Témoignage sur *Le Cid* en 1637', in *Mélanges Chamard*, pp. 293–301 (p. 298). Excision of the Count's scornful reference to suppression of the duel in favour of royal arbitration on a point of honour has been held to indicate that 'le propos de Corneille [est] bien de servir ... la politique du Cardinal' (GC, I, 1475). Rather more obviously it would seem to indicate Corneille's political innocence when first he completed his play. Later removal of the lines shows no more than prudence once he had realized that, if the Count's sentiments were dramatically apt, they would also offend a patron whose policy favoured royal arbitration in matters of honour and who had recently issued an interdict on duelling.

3 '*Le Cid*', à la différence de tant d'autres tragi-comédies ... échappe à l'attraction du mensonge romanesque pour devenir le drame du choix et de la conscience': Maurens, *Tragédie sans tragique*, pp. 230–1.

4 A view confirmed from a socio-critical point of view by P. Burger, '*Le Cid* de Corneille et le matériau de la tragicomédie', *Papers on French Seventeenth-Century Literature*, 11 (1984), 427–45 (p. 434).

5 This is not the only occasion on which a preoccupation with the criticisms of his 'grammarian' opponents led Corneille into inconsistency and even inexactitude on *Le Cid*. The same thing happens in the second *Discours*, where, trying to apply a cautionary theory of purgation to *Le Cid*, he sets the lovers' sense of duty in opposition to their love for each other. 'Ils tombent dans infélicité par cette faiblesse humaine dont nous sommes capables comme eux', with the supposed effect of purging the spectator of 'ce trop d'amour qui cause leur infortune' (LF, 82; GC, III, 146). The 'Examen', however, does not present their love as a weakness and asserts, with greater fidelity to the play, that Rodrigue

'suit…son devoir sans rien relâcher de sa passion: Chimène fait la même chose à son tour' (GC, I, 700).

6 GC, I, 1469.

7 First *Discours*: LF, 49–50; GC, III, 126–7. *Le Cid*, 'Examen': GC, I, 701–2.

8 In the 1637 text, Don Diègue does express some sympathy with the Count's bitter conviction that kings are fallible and, in a formal gesture of modesty, concedes that the King might possibly have chosen better (I, iv, 155–8).

9 Priézac, *Discours*, pp 457–8. For discussion of this 'religion de l'orgueil' see Maurens, *Tragédie sans tragique*, p. 207, and Bénichou, *Morales*, pp. 16–24.

10 Couton, *Réalisme*, pp. 68–9 and C. Péguy, *Victor Marie, comte Hugo*, p. 158. It seems unnecessary to follow Couton's speculations here on a supposedly 'Hobbesian' pessimism about man as a social animal, or indeed to confuse Corneille's supposed personal beliefs with the dramatic illustration of but one value system and mode of behaviour which is contrasted with others within the play. Otherwise we obscure the carefully delimited problems the play poses on the integration of an individual sense of worth within the State. If *Le Cid* shows the fathers behaving in one way, Rodrigue and Don Fernand are also there to show that other men may act very differently.

11 Cureau de la Chambre, *Les Caractères des Passions*, II, 134.

12 D. de Saavedra Fajardo, *Idea de un Príncipe Cristiano*, Emblem 51, II, 10. Originally published in Madrid in 1595, the work appeared in a number of seventeenth-century French editions.

13 'Aristippe' (first published in 1642), in *Œuvres*, II, 229 and 230–31.

14 Marnix discusses this uneasy relationship between monarch and powerful subject, once 'le service d'armes' becomes degraded into a pursuit of rewards and immunities: *Résolutions*, p. 133.

15 Bodin, *République*, pp. 731–2 (p. 731).

16 Priézac, *Discours*, p. 64.

17 R. de Ceriziers, *Le Héros français, ou L'Idée du grand capitaine*, p. 19 (misprinted as p. 61).

18 See Nadal, *Sentiment*, pp. 168–74.

19 Couton, *Réalisme*, pp. 86–8.

20 Nadal, *Sentiment*, p. 178.

21 For a characteristic development on the subject, see Fortin de la Hoguette, *Eléments*, pp. 351–2.

22 Couton, *Réalisme*, pp. 70–1.

23 Even the subtle and experienced Montaigne had been unable to resolve this conflict between 'l'honnête' and 'l'utile', for all that he would not accept a radical distinction between public and private morality: 'De l'Utile et de l'honnête', in *Essais*, III, i, pp. 788–803.

24 Cardin Le Bret, *Traité de la souveraineté du Roi*, pp. 188–201 (notably pp. 193–5).

25 See Stegmann, *L'Héroisme*, II, 161–80.

26 'Elle [la raison dominante] appartient à la prudence politique et ne se
    rapporte à la vertu morale que par accident, c'est à dire en tant que le
    prudent gouverneur a besoin des vertus pour faire de bons citoyens et
    rendre les cités heureuses...[Elle] fait seulement que [les actions] qui
    par les loix ordinaires ne sont pas permises le soient par un principe plus
    haut, d'où dépend la conservation et félicité des Républiques' (Priézac,
    Discours, pp. 208 and 211).
27 Couton discusses the technical status of the already archaic concept of
    the judicial duel as a final appeal to God's judgement: *Réalisme*, p. 84,
    and GC, I, 1505, note 3 to p. 762. While seventeenth-century stage
    convention had it that no direct reference to God might be made,
    Chimène does once voice an unavailing prayer (v, iv, 1675–7) that this
    judicial duel between Rodrigue and Don Sanche prove inconclusive.
28 See Nadal, *Sentiment*, p. 169. Couton's notice to the play in his edition
    pertinently reminds us of the dramatically spectacular and symbolic
    function of the sword in *Le Cid*. 'L'épée est presque un personnage de
    la pièce, et non un accessoire. Elle est symbole' (GC, I, 1453; see also
    GC, I, 1501, note to p. 744).
29 Couton is of the view that 'ce dénouement amer, de nature à satisfaire
    les scrupules moralisants, a beau être inscrit dans le texte comme une
    virtualité, il reste néanmoins inaperçu de spectateur; comme du lecteur
    s'il ne scrute par les texte avec minutie' (GC, I, 1470). This
    underestimates the effectiveness of Corneille's exploitation of the
    audience's rational and emotional perceptiveness. Couton himself
    warns us elsewhere against just such an underestimation of the
    seventeenth-century audience's capacity to read the larger significance
    of the dramatic poem: GC, I, 1505. Corneille says no less than the truth
    in the second *Discours* when he points out that 'tout ce qu'elle
    [Chimène] peut obtenir de la justice de son roi, c'est un combat où la
    victoire de ce déplorable amant lui impose silence' (LF, 92–3; GC, III,
    153).
30 Sainte Beuve, *Les Nouveaux Lundis*, VII, 291.
31 Strictly speaking, since the King ruled 'by the grace of God' alone, the
    French concept of kingship was absolutist from its remotest origins. The
    matter at issue in the seventeenth-century development of absolutism
    was that the theory and practice of absolute rule tended to emancipate
    itself from the restraints of conscience which traditionally it was held to
    acknowledge. The most striking illustration of this is Louis XIV's
    legitimization of the royal bastards: see F. Dumont, 'French Kingship
    and Absolute Monarchy', pp. 56–7. While we would broadly agree
    with Couton's conclusions on the political relevance of *Le Cid* to times
    of military emergency, the political significance of the play is not to be
    limited to a supposed call for national unity addressed to those noble
    families which had felt the effect of the Cardinal's 'justice': '*Le Cid*
    sonne comme un appel à l'union sacrée adressé aux grandes familles ou
    à leurs éventuels imitateurs' (GC, I, 1476). The play's emotional impact
    goes considerably beyond that of a dramatic pamphlet intended to

support the Cardinal's designs and appealing to a select audience of costive aristocrats – and the poetic truth it expresses derives from a more even-handed (if ambivalent) response to the significance of contemporary events.

32 Aquinas, *On Princely Government*, chapter 14, in *Selected Political Writings*, p. 75. See also Aristotle, *The Politics*: 'The state is intended to enable all, in their households and in their kinships, to live well, meaning by that a full and satisfying life' (p. 120).

33 Mugnier, *Véritable politique*, p. 73.

5   *HORACE* (1640–1)

1 See J. Jehasse, 'Guez de Balzac et Corneille face au mythe romain', in *Pierre Corneille* (Tercentenary Colloquium), pp. 247–63.

2 For discussion of the place of Rome in that debate, see Jehasse, *J-L. Guez de Balzac*, pp. 289 and 405–6.

3 More commonly, those who opposed the Cardinal favoured tragi-comedies in which a variety of romanesque, rather than Roman, subjects could be exploited in allusion to the miseries resulting from Richelieu's belligerent foreign policy. Typical is Du Ryer's tragicomedy *Cléomédon* (1636), which derived its plot from *L'Astrée* and (III, v) portrays the King's anguish at the misery of his subjects and the harsh consequences of a 'politique de gloire'. Du Ryer's romanesque tragedy *Alcionée* (1637) more ambiguously attempts to elicit audience sympathy for a rebellious subject and still court the Cardinal's favour by supporting the over-riding claims of 'le bien de l'Etat', presenting morally suspect but necessary political decisions as the will of heaven (III, v).

4 'Discours sur le romain', in *Œuvres*, I, 212 and 214.

5 'Le Prince' (1631), in *Œuvres*, I, 104; see Jehasse, 'Guez de Balzac et Corneille', p. 248.

6 'Discours à la Reine Régente' (1643), in *Œuvres*, I, 361–85 (p. 377).

7 R. Jasinski, 'Sur *Cinna*', *Europe*, 52 (1974), 114–30 (p. 125).

8 *Prince illustre*, p. 14.

9 *Ibid.*, pp. 15–16. Compare *Horace*, I, i, lines 53–6; II, iii, line 456; II, iii, line 478; II, iii, lines 481–2.

10 *Prince illustre*, p. 18.

11 Commentaires, in *Complete Works*, LIV, 258.

12 G. Michaud, 'Structure et signification d'*Horace*', in *Annales Universitatis Saraiavensis (Philosophie, Lettres)*, *Mélanges Dimoff*, 1–2 (1954), 95–100 (p. 95).

13 For an important discussion of this aspect of the seventeenth-century heroic *morale*, see J-E. Fidao-Justiniani, 'Discours sur la raison classique', *Revue des Cours et des Conférences*, 38 (1937), 81–669 (p. 373).

14 Other historical parallels have been proposed, Couton even interpreting Tulle's pardon of Horace as evidence of Corneille's full adhesion to 'le style même de la politique de Richelieu' (GC, I, 1548). But the play's

more ambitious level of political significance renders otiose such attempts to reduce it to a coded recreation of specific historical referends or partisan political argument.

15 *Horace*, 'Examen': GC, I, 841. In the 1648–57 editions of *Horace*, Corneille includes Livy's account of events in his *History of Rome*, Book I, chapters 23–7. This establishes no blood relationship between the protagonists, but notes the Romans' and Albans' common origin in Troy: see Tite-Live, *Les Décades*, I, 19–23 (p. 19). Dionysius is the more important source here, although he differs from Corneille in describing the blood relationship between the Horatii and Curiatii as stemming from a common Alban grandfather Sicinius, whose twin daughters married into the Horatii and Curiatii families: Dionysius of Halicarnassus, *The Roman Antiquities*, II, 57.

16 Corneille follows Livy rather than Dionysius in preferring the popular belief that Romulus himself – rather than his supporters – killed Remus. In the interests of cogency he also presents victory over Alba as Rome's first step to universal empire, when his sources tell us that it was but one of a number of Roman conquests of neighbouring tribes.

17 According to Dionysius' Alban leader, 'The city of Alba has so far made no alteration in any part of its constitution, though it is already the eighteenth generation that it is being inhabited, but continues to observe in due form all its customs and traditions'; in contrast Tullus claims pre-eminence for Rome in 'strength in war and prudence in council' (*Antiquities*, II, 43 and 49).

18 In this account, the first of the Horatii addresses in the following terms his father, whose decision it is whether his sons should fight their cousins or not: 'As for the bond of kinship with our cousins, we shall not be the first to break it, but since it has already been broken by fate, we shall acquiesce therein. For if the Curiatii esteem kinship less than honour, the Horatii also will not value the ties of blood more highly than valour' (*Antiquities*, II, 69). See also H. Peyrtraud, 'A propos des Horaces et des Curiaces', *Revue Universitaire*, 48 (1939), 32–5.

19 *Décades*, I, pp. 21–2. Corneille follows Livy's account in leaving three Curiatii against the lone Horatius.

20 See Dionysius' commentary on the elder Horace's response to this enormity:

> But so averse to baseness and so stern were the manners and thoughts of the Romans of that day and, to compare them with the actions and lives of those of our age, so cruel and harsh and so little removed from the savagery of wild beasts, that the father, upon being informed of this terrible calamity, far from resenting it, looked upon it as a glorious and becoming action. (*Antiquities*, II, 85)

21 It would seem that Camille's murder had originally been performed on stage. Corneille's stage directions in the text thus made sure that this scandal did not occur in future performances; it was important not only that Horace's sword should not be drawn on stage, but that Camille's

body did not encumber the next two scenes. In 1660, in the 'Examen' of *Horace*, Corneille tries to exculpate his hero as less guilty than Medea and regrettably betrays his own text by describing the murder of Camille as 'l'emportement d'un homme passionné pour sa Patrie' (GC, I, 839).

22 J. Morel, 'A Propos du plaidoyer d'Horace: reflexions sur le sens de la vocation historique dans le théâtre de Corneille', *RR*, 51 (1960), 27–32.

23 'Dieu [fait] naître les occasions et [donne] les moyens pour exciter leur force, ou pour exciter le courage des gens de bien, confirmer leur espérance, exercer leur générosité et couronner leur constance' (Mugnier, *Véritable politique*, pp. 80–1). Gracián observes that the hero must 'conocer su estrella': *Oráculo Manual*, p. 135. See Michaud, 'Structure et signification d'*Horace*', pp. 95–6.

24 Among the host of seventeenth-century moralists who urge upon their readers the necessity to accept suffering and adore the mysteries of Divine Providence, see Mugnier, *Véritable politique*, p. 82.

25 'La vertu...n'est que pour l'action et le mérite...[Elle] ne peut se faire estimer que si elle ne se montre, et elle ne se peut montrer qu'en faisant des actions nobles et illustres...la vertu est une qualité agissante (Mugnier, *Véritable politique*, pp. 293–5). P. Le Moyne further observes that 'La vertu n'est pas une idée de la République de Platon: elle consiste moins en la spéculation qu'en la pratique (*Peintures morales*, I, Book V, p. 353).

26 'Since, therefore, you mourn, not for your brothers, but for your cousins, and since, though your body is with the living, your soul is with him who is dead, go to him on whom you call and cease to dishonour either your father or your brothers.' After these words, being unable in his hatred of baseness to observe moderation, but yielding to the anger which swayed him, he ran his sword through her side; and having slain his sister, he went to his father. (*Antiquities*, II, 83–5)

27 *Ibid.*, II, 83.

28 A powerful critique of such ruthlessness in patriotism had already been made early in the seventeenth century by Du Vair, who established the true character of patriotism in the twin sentiments of love and Christian charity. Love of country is not to be equated with service of an ideal which stifles the natural ties of affection; instead it reconciles human and divine values in service of those other fellow-selves who constitute the body politic: G. du Vair, 'Exhortation à la Vie Civile', in *La Philosophie morale des stoïques*, in *Les Œuvres*, p. 896. The preliminaries and repercussions of the Second World War prompted a number of modern critics to observe that *Horace* offers a judgement on patriotism once it degenerates into chauvinism: 'Il n'y a pas d'héroisme patriotique sans terrorisme chauvin': V. Vedel, *Deux Classiques français vus par un critique étranger: Corneille et son temps: Molière*, p. 96. See also W. H. Barber, 'Patriotism and Gloire in Corneille's *Horace*', *MLR*, 46 (1951), 368–78, and D. Trafton's assessment, marked by the moral uncertainties

of yet more recent conflicts: 'Horace turns to the extreme case in order to define the limits and essence of patriotism... To understand patriotism we must strip away its blandly pious garb of every day: we must lay bare the terrible paradox, the impious piety hidden in its heart': 'On Corneille's Horace', Interpretation, 2–3 (1972), 183–93 (pp. 192–3).

29 It is left to his father to match Valère with a display of forensic skill which, alone of the 'plaidoyers' of this last act, justifies Corneille's strictures in his 'Examen', since it adds little of substance to the debate. While Le vieil Horace's speech eloquently sets out the city's debt to his son, it is also less than honest in its assertions of Horace's innocence (v, iii, 1648). Both father and son know the speciousness of the argument that Horace acted on impulse in killing Camille: 'Un premier mouvement ne fut jamais un crime.' The second, and truer, claim that Horace acted as a Roman patriot is also developed (v, iii, 1655–62) in terms which contradict that earlier private exchange when the father had recoiled from the punishment his son pressed upon him. Le vieil Horace now makes a great show of his 'Roman' principles as paterfamilias, principles which earlier he had failed to sustain.

30 Approaching the play from a very different angle, Doubrovsky concludes in the same sense on the personal tragedy of Horace: Corneille, pp. 175–9.

31 Compare Gracián, Oráculo Manual, Maxim 130, pp. 90–1: 'Hacer, y hacer parecer. Las cosas no pasan por lo que son, sino por lo que parecen. Valer y saberlo mostrar, es saber dos veces: lo que no se ve es como si no fuese... La buena exterioridad es la mejor recomendación de la perfección interior.'

32 Scudéry was sufficiently impressed by Horace's disillusionment to re-exploit it in the Emperor Charles V's discourse of abdication: G. de Scudéry, Discours politiques des Rois, pp. 23–4.

33 Setting aside Corneille's equally eloquent presentation of a broad spectrum of arguments reflecting the many sides of contemporary political debate, Couton extrapolates from the speeches of Le vieil Horace and Tulle an interpretation of the whole play as an act of political adhesion by Corneille to his Cardinal's policies: GC, I, 1542–8. Both Doubrovsky and Prigent seem closer to the sense of the tragedy in stressing the personal catastrophe implicit in Tulle's recuperation of the hero in the interests of Rome: Doubrovsky, Corneille, p. 182; Prigent, Le Héros et l'Etat, pp. 137–8.

34 'The playwright is less concerned with drawing a specific moral than with giving us a deeper insight into an aspect of human life... Corneille has taken a situation familiar to his contemporaries and portrayed it as a whole, complete with the conflicts and contradictions inherent in it': E. Forsyth, 'The Tragic Dilemma in Horace', Australian Journal of French Studies, 4 (1967), 162–76 (p. 176).

35 As Prigent observes: 'Le silence des lois a légitimé le crime contre la nature: le héros ne sera pas une victime d'Etat mais un esclave d'Etat.

La liberté qu'Horace avait conquise se trouve aliénée à Rome: le libérateur de Rome est maintenant l'esclave de Rome' (*Le Héros de l'Etat*, p. 137).

36 Poirier's equation of Tulle's judgement with the Divinity of his rank fails to convince in the context of seventeenth-century idealist theory and is only possible by direct and selective recourse to the *Nichomachaean Ethics* and to Aquinas. His earlier examination of Corneille's illustration of the problem of the reconciliation of force and justice is remarkably interesting, if we accept the abstract terms with which he has chosen to approach the drama. But the grave disadvantage of his extra-temporal 'symbolic' method of interpretation is that it obscures the degree in which the play relates to contemporary French experience, whatever was originally written in the *Nichomachaean Ethics* or done in antiquity. For instance: 'Dans l'esprit d'un contemporain de Richelieu, la crise [d'un conflit entre la force et la justice] avait depuis longtemps pris fin: elle avait été miraculeusement dénouée par Auguste, modèle paien des rois très-chrétiens' (p. 162). The historical and textual evidence is there – in the experience and writings of Balzac, Mathieu de Morgues, or the Campion brothers – to prove the statement wrong: *Corneille*, pp. 158–69.

37 'Tout le problème pour le héros authentique est de savoir lire dans les desseins cachés de cette Providence... Le meurtre de Camille... pose le problème dans toute sa force. Y-a-t'il, oui ou non, une "justice"?... La Gloire est-elle un vain mot?': Michaud, 'Structure et signification d'*Horace*', pp. 96 and 99.

38 L. Goldmann, *Le Dieu caché*, pp. 357–63.

39 R. Niebuhr, *Beyond Tragedy*, pp. 28 and 29–30.

40 'La vaillance ne se trouve qu'aux seuls vertueux: elle veut être toujours conjointe et unie avec la justice, et quand elle s'en sépare ce n'est plus une source de biens, mais de crimes' (*Discours*, p. 454).

6 *CINNA* (1642–3)

1 Balzac, *Œuvres*, I, 471–2.

2 So unfavourable a presentation of Stoic integrity by two of the Cardinal's dramatic apologists must raise some doubts about the identification which has been proposed between neo-Stoic moral and political philosophy and those 'grandes idées' of the Cardinal to which Corneille holds himself indebted in the dedication of *Horace*: Maurens, *Tragédie sans tragique*, pp. 253–5.

3 An argument in favour of monarchy already rehearsed by Maecenas in Dio's account of his debate with Agrippa over whether Augustus should abdicate or not. This debate was the model for the Council Scene of *Cinna*, as Corneille indicates (II, i, 394): Cassius Dio, *The Roman History: The Reign of Augustus*, Book 52, chapters 1–41, pp. 88–124 (p. 100).

4 Caussin particularly commends the author of 'les divins livres de la Clémence', praising Augustus' solicitude towards his people and the creative and conciliating power of his clemency, and calling him 'le plus

sage des empereurs romains': Caussin, *Cour sainte*, v, pp. 803–4. Compare also the dedicatory 'Epître au comte de Harcourt' in N. Faret's *Des Vertus necessaires à un prince pour bien gouverner ses sujets*. For a later evocation of Augustus as the supreme example of the monarchy's capacity to unite different forces into harmony and concord, see Priézac, *Discours*, p. 412. Dio's account of Livia's advice to Augustus in favour of clemency is the other major Classical source here: *Roman History*, Book 55, chapters 14–22 (pp. 204–12).

5 Compare Caussin's description of such creatures 'qui exercent les haines, partie secrètes, partie publiques, et font gloire d'éterniser leur vengeance jusque dans l'éternité de leurs supplices' (*Cour sainte* (collective edition of 1664), I, 106).

6 'Quant au bien public c'est un masque si vieil et si usé c'est merveille que l'on s'en puisse encore aujourd'hui servir. Il n'y eut jamais brouillon factieux ny séditieux qui n'ait commencé par là. Un homme qui veut remuer, qui veut entreprendre, ne parle jamais de ses intérêts, il ne parle que du public': J. Sirmond, *Avis du français fidèle aux malcontents nouvellement retirés de la cour* (no place or date of publication), p. 3.

7 *Entretiens*, pp. 474–6.

8 Le Moyne, *La Dévotion aisée*, pp. 42–4.

9 *Commentaires*, in *Complete Works*, LIV, 147.

10 Du Bosc makes the same distinction between the heroism of Tanaquil – 'magnanime, aspirant aux grands honneurs dont elle était capable, et où elle ne voulait arriver que par des moyens honnêtes' – and Tullia's wilful heroics – 'orgueilleuse et insupportable, entreprenant des choses qui étaient au-dessus de son esprit, et par des moyens injustes... Aussi la fausse magnanimité... infecte tout ce qu'elle emploie et tout ce qui dépend de son empire porte les marques de sa tyrannie': *Femme héroïque*, II, 562–3 (see also pp. 607–8).

11 See Cureau de la Chambre: 'C'est une chose étrange, et qui ne se trouve guère dans les autres passions, que les plus mauvaises actions qu'elle [la hardiesse] produit lui paraissent glorieuses et dignes de louange'. To be driven by 'la hardiesse' is to become deaf to the solicitations of Right Reason: 'ne s'arrêtant plus à ce qui est honnête et n'ayant point d'autre guide que cet instinct qu'elle a pour la gloire, elle s'imagine qu'elle le doit rencontrer partout, et que c'est un prix qui est dû à toutes ses actions quelques mauvaises qu'elles soient' (*Caractères des passions*, II, 129 and 132).

12 Gentillet, *Discours*, pp. 348 and 349.

13 'Whoever possesses himself of power by violence does not truly become lord or master. Therefore it is permissible when occasion offers, for a person to reject such authority: unless in the case that it subsequently become legitimate, either through public consent or the intervention of a higher authority': *Commentary on the Sentences of Peter Lombard*, Book II, dist. 44, art. 2, qu. 2, in Aquinas, *Selected Political Writings*, pp. 181–3; see also *On Princely Government*, chapter 14, and *On Natural Law*, art. 9, qu. 104, in *Selected Political Wirings*, pp. 31–5 and 179. In the sixteenth

and seventeenth centuries only the Jesuit Juan de Mariana firmly endorsed the right to kill a tyrant and, notoriously, extended his argument to include justifiable regicide. All others agreed with St Thomas that none was justified in rising against a divinely sanctioned monarch, no matter how badly he ruled, but Mariana found sufficient grounds for the destruction of both tyrants and unjust kings in the contractual theory that sovereignty is first given by God to the people and thence delegated to the ruler. Thus the people has a right to reclaim by violence a sovereignty usurped or abused: J. de Mariana, *Del Rey y de la Institución Real*, in *Obras*, II, 482. These extreme views brought the Company political disgrace and enduring mistrust after the assassination of Henri IV.

14 Bodin, *République*, pp. 307 and 297–9. Compare, nearly a century later, Fortin de la Hoguette: 'Si quelqu'un vient à la Couronne comme un usurpateur, il est certain que les troubles qu'il aura causés en faisant ce changement ne s'appaiseront jamais jusques à ce qu'une longue suite de générations et d'années y ait apporté le calme' (*Eléments*, pp. 310–11).

15 Apart from Bodin, among a host of others see Saavedra Fajardo, *Idea de un Príncipe Cristiano*, Emblem 21, I, 191; R. Bellarmin, *Le Monarque parfait*, p. 91; Priézac, *Discours*, p. 431.

16 Bodin, *République*, pp. 287 and 289–90.

17 Marnix particularly praises the noble virtue of trust in other men as essential to a distinction between true kings and tyrants. He too cites Seneca's account of the pardon of Cinna as an example of the royal qualities which brought peace and were to earn Augustus his title of 'Father of the Fatherland: *Résolutions*, p. 226.

18 E. de la Boétie, *De la Servitude volontaire*, p. 98; Priézac, *Discours*, pp. 33–4.

19 Bodin, *République*, pp. 273–4. Couton correctly compares line 421 with this passage on just conquest. Unfortunately he betrays the political significance of the scene by truncating the quotation and failing to indicate that Bodin refers not to 'la monarchie royale' of France but to the unenlightened exercise of 'la monarchie seigneuriale' in pagan antiquity: GC, II, 1606–7, n. 3. On the importance of the distinction see Loyseau, *Des Seigneuries*, pp. 11–28; see also Mousnier, 'Comment les français voyaient la constitution', in *Comment les français*, p. 15.

20 Bodin, *République*, pp. 274–5 and 279–80.

21 Twenty years later Georges de Scudéry expropriated Maxime's argument here, as he had those of Horace, for his account of Charles the Fifth's abdication: 'Tout l'Univers doutera lequel me sera le plus glorieux, ou d'avoir si souverainement régné ou d'avoir cessé volontairement de régner' (*Discours politiques*, pp. 35–6).

22 Bodin condemned democracy as 'déborde en toute licence'. While he recognized that the ideal of total equality was a noble one, 'il n'y eut jamais de République [populaire] où cette égalité de biens et d'honneurs fût gardée... Comment pourrait un peuple, c'est à dire une bête à

plusieurs têtes sans jugement et sans raison, rien conseiller de bien?'
(*République*, pp. 945, 939 and 940); see also Ammirato, *Discours politiques*,
p. 139; Guicciardini, *Maximes populaires*, Maxim v, p. 18; Colomby,
Discours de l'autorité, p. 16; Saavedra Fajardo, *Idea de un Príncipe Cristiano*,
Emblem 46, 1, 424; J. F. Sénault, *Le Monarque ou Les Devoirs du Souverain*,
pp. 6–7.

23 *Entretiens*, p. 347.

24 'Le Tyran a cela de juste qu'il se punit soi-même, et il n'y a point de
loi naturelle plus équitable que celle qui ordonne que celui qui ravit à
tous la liberté et le repos, s'ôte à lui-même la confiance et la sûreté. Il
mesure sa peur par sa puissance, et appréhende d'autant plus qu'il est
élevé à une plus grande fortune.' He lives 'dans une affreuse solitude
d'où il ne sort jamais que pour en faire un autre par le bannissement,
et par le massacre des hommes': Priézac, *Discours*, pp. 177–8.

25 'De la Clémence', in *Les Œuvres morales et mêlées de Sénèque*, 1, 189^v and
193^r.

26 Gentillet, *Discours*, p. 396. Lines 1164–8 from the great soliloquy of Act
IV recall Guicciardini's popular work of political maxims which also
follows Seneca in asserting the futility of repression and sees in
Augustus' pardon of Cinna proof of the political efficacy of a royal
'douceur'. Compare Maxims IX and X: 'Encore que vous ôtiez la tête
à un ennemi, vous n'en éteignez pourtant pas la semence... Pour un il
en revient sept, ainsi qu'on dit de l'Hydre... Les troubles des Etats ne
s'appaisent pas à couper des têtes: parce que cela engendre plutôt une
plus grande quantité d'ennemis' (*Maximes*, p. 22).

27 Mugnier, *Véritable politique*, p. 395.

28 P. Le Moyne, *De l'Art de régner*, pp. 34 and 37.

29 Bodin, *République*, pp. 534–6.

30 *Recueil général des questions traitées ès conférences du Bureau d'Adresse, sur toutes
sortes de matières, par les plus beaux esprits de ce temps*, II, 144. This discussion
first appeared in the 1638 collection of the *Recueil général*.

31 Du Bosc, *Femme héroïque*, II, 477–8. Only in the second half of the century
does the cynical reading of self-serving political strategy come to the
fore. Jacques Esprit is characteristic, anxious as he is to show that all
human endeavour is tainted by concupiscence, when he ascribes
Augustus' clemency to 'la lassitude de la cruauté' and ranks it as little
more than a variation on his previous murders and proscriptions:
J. Esprit, *De la Fausseté des vertus humaines*, 1, 252–9.

32 Scudéry, *Discours politiques*, pp. 635–6 (p. 636).

33 Seneca, 'De la Clémence', 1, 191. Voltaire pointed out the discrepancy,
but without appreciating its significance: 'Corneille devait d'autant
moins mettre un reproche si injuste et avilissant dans la bouche
d'Auguste, que cette grossièreté est manifestement contraire à l'histoire.
Uxori gratias egit, dit Sénèque le Philosophe, dont le sujet de *Cinna* est
tiré': *Commentaires*, in *Complete Works*, LIV, 156.

34 The *Discorsi* themselves had argued that experience might justify the

kind of calculated pardon which Livie offers and Auguste later rejects: *Discours sur Tite Live*, III, xx, in N. Machiavel, *Œuvres complètes*, pp. 664–5.

35 Mugnier, *Véritable politique*, pp. 90 and 93 (see also pp. 91–2, 106–7 and 118–19).

36 'Discours sur le romain', in *Œuvres*, I, 220 and 221–2.

37 *Entretiens*, pp. 362–3. This speaker claims to be familiar with arguments favoured by the Cardinal's apologists, and his condemnation of misguided trust and benevolence tallies closely with sentiments expressed by Anthoine and Lépide in Scudéry's *La Mort de César* (II, i and III, i), a play whose very subject justified the reproach that Caesar's government 'pèche en douceur'.

38 *Entretiens*, pp. 355–7 and 362–3.

39 *Ibid.*, pp. 377 and 403–4.

40 Du Bois Hus, *Prince illustre*, pp. 323–4.

41 *Femme héroïque*, p. 6 (Du Bosc's emphases). The reference Du Bosc gives is Aristotle: *Morale*. 'A Eudemius', VII, 4: this presumably refers us to the *Nichomachaean Ethics*, x, 9: Aristotle, *Nichomachaean Ethics*, p. 310. Fortin de la Hoguette's *Testament* expresses much the same idea in the author's advice to his sons. Whenever they are torn between conflicting advice and hesitate on what course to take, they should act on first impulse, even when this seems unreasonable. Condé on the battlefield is again the model for this: his 'obéissance aveugle à l'impulsion de son génie' resulted in 'une audace divinement inspirée': *Testament*, pp. 264 and 266–7.

42 *Le Prince*, in *Œuvres*, I, 132.

43 *Théoclée*, 'Dedicace' (not paginated).

44 *Entretiens*, p. 376.

45 *République*, p. 241.

46 P. de l Hommeau, *Les Maximes générales du droit français*, p. 41.

47 Letter dated 13 January 1629: Richelieu, *Œuvres*, p. 152.

48 *Testament politique*, in *Œuvres*, pp. 66–72.

49 *Discours*, pp. 32 and 34.

50 *Discours*, pp. 436 and 442–3.

51 Priézac, *Discours*, p. 134.

52 Nadal, *Sentiment*, p. 199.

53 Priézac, *Discours*, pp. 96 and 111–12.

54 Colomby, *Discours de l'autorité*, 'Préface'.

55 Scudéry, *Discours politiques*, pp. 557 and 559. This last section expands on my article: 'Heroic Prudence and Reason in the Seventeenth Century: Auguste's Pardon of Cinna', in *FMLS*, (1965), pp. 328–38.

7   POLYEUCTE (1642–3) and *LA MORT DE POMPEE* (1643–4)

1 Nadal, *Sentiment*, p. 208; Doubrovsky, *Corneille*, p. 225.

2 Prigent, *Le Héros et l'Etat*, p. 77.

3 For such an argument, see Prigent, *Le Héros et l'Etat*, pp. 77–8.

4 As J-C. Joye observes, '*Polyeucte*...serait incompréhensible à qui n'entrerait pas dans la "théomachie" qui l'innerve et lui confère sa cohérence et son intelligibilité': *Amour, pouvoir et transcendance chez Pierre Corneille*, p. 187.

5 Bremond, *Histoire littéraire*, I, 37 and 358–77. A fine instance of such an emphasis is bound to be found in Bardin, *Lycée*, I, 10–19.

6 In his translation of the *Imitation of Jesus Christ*, Corneille emphasizes man's corruption, accentuating the pessimism of the original text by extending to reason a weakness which St Thomas à Kempis principally attributed to the will. Only the saving gift of Grace can raise us above our present imperfections: 'De la Corruption de la Nature et de l'Efficace de la Grâce', *L'Imitation de Jésus-Christ*, III, 55 (GC, II, 1099–1103). When Corneille re-used the poem in his *Instructions chrétiennes* of 1670, he marked this change by altering the title to 'De la Corruption de la Nature, et de l'Impuissance de la Raison': P. Corneille, *Œuvres*, edited by C. Marty Laveaux, IX, pp. 393–5; see H. Busson, *La Pensée religieuse française de Charron à Pascal*, p. 246.

7 Ceriziers, *Héros français*, pp. 103–4.

8 *Cour sainte* (collective edition of 1664), I, 131.

9 *Femme héroique*, pp. 4 and 7–8.

10 *Véritable politique*, pp. 120 and 123.

11 For a discussion of the rise in the first forty years of the century of this 'forme d'augustinisme, radicalement opposée au futur jansénisme', see Stegmann, *L'Héroisme*, II, chapter 4: 'La Philosophie morale', pp. 203–75 (p. 274).

12 *Gallerie des femmes fortes*, Part II, pp. 169–70 (see also pp. 132–4).

13 *Ibid.*, Part II, p. 142.

14 Cotin, *Théoclée*, 'Dédicace'.

15 P. Coton, *Sermons sur les principales et plus difficiles matières de la foi*, p. 447.

16 Bremond, *Histoire littéraire*, VI, 51. Calvet cites the contemporary instance of a son's comment on his mother who had abandoned him in order to spread Christ's message to heathen Canada: 'Les lumières surnaturelles quand elles éclairent les saints, qui n'agissent que par les mouvements de la grâce, font voir les choses d'une toute autre manière que ne font celles de la seule raison': J. Calvet, '*Polyeucte*', p. 99.

17 'Socrate Chrétien', in *Œuvres*, II, 29–30.

18 M. Magendie, *La Politesse mondaine et les théories de l'honnêteté en France au XVIIe siècle*, p. 401.

19 R. Brasillach, *Notre Avant-guerre*, pp. 315–17.

20 'Le machineries du christianisme...restent trop théâtrales pour nous convaincre de leur efficacité': Nadal, *Sentiment*, pp. 192–3 (p. 193). 'Le Dieu de Polyeucte répond trop exactement aux expériences métaphysiques de l'héroisme pour n'être pas soupçonné d'anthropomorphisme. Le créateur ressemble plus à la créature que la créature n'est l'image du créateur. Le tragique de Polyeucte est celui de l'adéquation du héros à Dieu': Prigent, *Le Héros et l'Etat*, p. 74.

21 L. Richeôme, *L'Académie d'honneur*, pp. 614, 320–5 and 327; see also Bardin, *Lycée*, II, 437–8.

22 *Recueil général*, I, 347–8.

23 Caussin, *Cour sainte* (collective edition of 1664), I, 9.

24 *Véritable politique*, p. 278. The results of this extrovert theology of honour can be disconcerting to the twentieth-century reader, but never more so than in the works of the Franciscan Guevara, where Christ's agony on the cross is interpreted more in terms of shame at the public opprobrium of His treatment as a felon than in terms of the spiritual desolation of the Son of Man: Guevara, *Epîtres dorées*, II, 146.

25 For discussion of the hagiological background to Corneille's play see Couton's 'Notice' to *Polyeucte*: GC, I, 1634–57.

26 Stegmann, *L'Héroïsme*, II, 81–92.

27 'Cette grande défiance est une croix à un Prince, encore plus à ceux qui ont affaire avec lui...La défiance procède de pusillanimité, car qui se défie des autres se défie volontiers de soi-même' (Marnix, *Résolutions*, p. 224).

28 Later editions omit this passage, since such 'reasonable' open-mindedness presented too complaisant a picture of pagan disbelief to be publicly acceptable on the seventeenth-century stage.

29 C. Delidel, *La Théologie des saints*, pp. 358–9.

30 In his *Ode au révérend P. Delidel*, a liminary poem dedicated to Delidel's *Théologie des saints* in 1668, Corneille acknowledges his debt to his master's teaching on Grace: GC, III, 721–2, lines 41–4. This was over twenty-five years after *Polyeucte*, and it is curious to note that it corrects a possibly contentious element in Néarque's speech where the latter refers to the diminishing generosity of God. For the rest Corneille emphasizes again the decisive importance of the will in relation to the efficacy of grace – and with reason, for he had built his play on the drama of that repeated choice. On Corneille's relations with the Jesuits and with Delidel, see Couton, *La Vieillesse*, pp. 302–4; M. Fumaroli, 'Rhétorique, dramaturgie et spiritualité: Pierre Corneille et Claude Delidel. S.J.', in *Mélanges Couton*, pp. 271–87.

31 *Théologie*, p. 23.

32 *Ibid.*, pp. 338 and 339.

33 See Couton's 'Notice' to *Polyeucte*: GC, I, 1648–50.

34 Richelieu died in the last days of 1642 and Louis XIII in May 1643. The first public performance of *Polyeucte* dates from early in 1643, and the first printed edition appeared 20 October 1643, a month or two before the first performance of *La Mort de Pompée* (November/December 1643).In the course of the summer following Louis XIII's death (14 May 1643), Corneille unsuccessfully tried to restrict to the Marais the performing rights of *Cinna*, *Polyeucte*, and *La Mort de Pompée*: GC, I, 1684–5. This would suggest that the latter play's composition was already well advanced in the spring of 1643.

35 Stegmann, *L'Héroïsme*, II, 591.

36 On the reality of Corneille's debt to Lucan in *La Mort de Pompée*, I follow
   Brébeuf's judgement in the 'Avertissement' to Books VII and VIII of his
   translation of Lucan's *Pharsalia* (1655). Stegmann's formulations here,
   for once, seem less than perceptive: 'Après Tite-Live et Sénèque,
   Lucain... Simple façade. Lucain n'a fourni que quatre-vingts vers et le
   républicanisme du poète roman ne passe en rien dans la pièce moderne'
   (*L'Héroisme*, p. 591). Earlier discussion of *Cinna* has already shown how
   the Republican theme had its own significance within the seventeenth-
   century Frenchman's loyal adhesion to the monarchy and contemporary debate over the nature of political legitimacy and the significance
   of a rapid extension of royal power. It is not by a simple line-count that
   Corneille's debt to Lucan can be so summarily dismissed. Couton, for
   his part, confirms the major importance of Lucan to the play and
   pertinently reminds the reader of Plutarch's account of the life of
   Pompey as an accessory source: GC, I, 1713–18.

37 C. Chaulmer, *La Mort de Pompée: tragédie*. Poor though it is, this play
   may have offered a model for Corneille's opening deliberation in which
   Ptolomée resolves on the 'illustre crime' which will put the fleeing
   Pompée to death; but Chaulmer's text has nothing of the epic
   perspectives which Corneille establishes as a framework to the rest of the
   action.

38 For a thoughtful discussion of this disparity between nobility of tragic
   utterance and the reality of action and situation, see Appendix C in
   Barnwell's edition of *La Mort de Pompée*, pp. 200–5. Joye also offers an
   acute analysis of the ambiguity of Corneille's characterization of César:
   Amour, pouvoir et transcendance, pp. 154–60.

39 GC, I, 1728.

40 Prigent, *Le Héros et l'Etat*, p. 180.

41 'A partir de cette pièce charnière qu'est *La Mort de Pompée*, il est
   manifeste que le mythe romain s'évide de l'intérieur': Jehasse, 'Guez de
   Balzac et Corneille', p. 262. See also: M. Prigent, 'L'Exercice du
   pouvoir dans les tragédies de Corneille', in *Pierre Corneille (Tercentenary
   Colloquium)*, pp. 593–604. In this context, Livie's commentary on
   Auguste's apotheosis: 'Vous avez trouvé l'art d'être maître des
   cœurs. / Rome avec une joie, et sensible et profonde, / Se démet en vos
   mains de l'Empire du Monde' (*Cinna*, V, iii, 1764–6) makes an
   instructive contrast with Suréna's protestations before the tyranny of
   Orode and Pacorus: 'Sans faire un nouveau crime oserai-je vous
   dire / Que l'empire des cœurs n'est pas de votre empire' (*Suréna*, IV, iv,
   1309–10).

CONCLUSION

1 H. Gouhier, 'Remarques sur le "théâtre historique"', *Revue d'Esthétique*,
   13 (1960), 16–24 (pp. 22–3).

2 'Corneille nous assujettit à ses caractères et à ses idées, Racine se
   conforme aux nôtres': 'Des Ouvrages de l'esprit': 54, in *Œuvres*, p. 104.

3 See R. Bray, *La Tragédie cornélienne devant la critique classique*.

4 As the faithfully admiring Saint-Evremond put it in his *Réponse à Corneille*, 'Il n'y a que vous qui sache penser': *Œuvres en prose*, III, 43; see also Barnwell, *Les Idées morales*, p. 173.

5 Barnwell, *The Tragic Drama*, pp. 229–30.

6 H. D. F. Kitto, *Form and Meaning in Drama*, pp. 231–5 and 258.

7 LF, 90; AS. 833.

8 L. Herland, 'La Notion du tragique chez Corneille', *Mélanges de la Société Toulousaine d'Etudes Classiques*, I (1946), 265–84.

Bibliography

EDITIONS

Corneille, P., *Œuvres complètes*, ed. G. Couton, 3 vols. Bibliothèque de la Pléiade. Paris, 1980–7

Corneille, P., *Œuvres complètes*, ed. C. Marty-Laveaux. 12 vols. and album. Editions des Grands Ecrivains de la France. Paris, 1862–8

Corneille, P., *Pompée (La Mort de Pompée)*, ed. H. Barnwell. Oxford, 1971

Corneille, P., *Trois Discours sur le poème dramatique (Texte de 1660)*, ed. L. Forestier. Paris, 1963

BIBLIOGRAPHICAL WORKS

Couton, G., 'Etat présent des études cornéliennes'. *L'Information Littéraire*, 8 (1956), 43–8

Jourda, P., 'La Bibliothèque d'un juge à Narbonne au 17e siècle', *Humanisme et Renaissance*, 3 (1936), 420–8

La Mothe le Vayer, F. de, *Du Moyen de dresser une bibliothèque d'une centaine de livres seulement*, in *Œuvres*. Paris, 1662

Leverdier, P., and Pelay, E., *Additions à la bibliographie cornélienne*. Paris, 1908

Margitiç, M., 'Corneille Comique: A Bibliographical Guide (1633–1980)', in *Corneille comique*, ed. M. Margitiç. Paris/Seattle/Tübingen, 1982, pp. 185–213

May, G., 'Sept Années d'études cornéliennes', *RR*, 43 (1952), 282–92

Mongrédien, G., *Recueil des textes et des documents du XVIIe siècle relatifs à Corneille*. CNRS, Paris, 1972

Naudé, G., *Avis pour dresser une bibliothèque*. Paris, 1627

Naudé, G., *Bibliographia Politica*. Venetiis, apud F. Baba, 1663

Picot, A., *Bibliographie cornélienne*. Paris, 1876

Ritter, A., *Bibliographie zu Pierre Corneille von 1958 bis 1983*. Erfstadt, 1983

Schérer, J., 'Activités cornéliennes', *Revue d'Histoire du Théâtre*, 1 (1950), 59–70

Sorel, C., *De la Connaissance des bons livres*. Paris, 1671

Sorel, C., *La Bibliothèque française, ou Le Choix et l'examen des livres français qui traitent de l'éloquence, de la philosophie, de la dévotion et de la conduite des mœurs*. Paris, 1664

Tancock, L. W., 'Work on Corneille since 1945', *Modern Languages* (Journal of the Modern Languages Association), 40 (1958), 109–14

Toinet, R., 'Les Écrivains moralistes au XVIIe siècle. Essai d'une table alphabétique des ouvrages publiés pendant le siècle de Louis XIV (1638–1715), qui traitent de la morale', *RHLF*, 23 (1916), 570–610; 24 (1917), 296–306 and 656–75; 25 (1918), 310–20 and 655–71; 33 (1926), 395–407

PRIMARY WORKS

POETIC THEORY AND LITERARY CRITICISM

[Chapelain, J.], *Les Sentiments de L'Académie sur 'Le Cid'* (final published version), in Corneille, *Œuvres complètes*, ed. C. Marty-Laveaux, XII, 463–501

Aristotle, *The Art of Poetry*, translated by I. Bywater. Oxford, 1940

Aubignac, F. H. d', *La Pratique du théâtre*, ed. P. Martino. Alger/Paris, 1927
'Trois Dissertations concernant le poème dramatique'. In F. Granet, *Recueil de dissertations sur plusieurs tragédies de Corneille et de Racine*, 2 vols. Paris, 1740

Balzac, J-L. G. de, *Lettre à M. de Scudéry sur 'Le Cid'*. Paris, 1638

Boileau, N., *Œuvres complètes*, ed. F. Escal. Bibliothèque de la Pléiade. Paris/Bruges, 1966

Brumoy, Le Père, *Le Théâtre des grecs*, 3 vols. Paris, 1730

Castelvetro, *Poetica d'Aristotele vulgarizzata e sposta*. Basle, 1576

Chapelain, J., *Opuscules critiques*, ed. A. C. Hunter. Paris, 1936

Dorsch, T. S. (ed.), *Classical Literary Criticism: Aristotle, Horace and Longinus*. London, 1965

Gilbert, A. H. (ed.), *Literary Criticism: Plato to Dryden*. New York, 1940

Granet, F., *Recueil de dissertations sur plusieurs tragédies de Corneille et de Racine*, 2 vols. Paris, 1740

Horace, *The Art of Poetry*, in Dorsch (ed.), *Classical Literary Criticism*, pp. 79–95.

La Mesnardière, J. de, *La Poétique*. Paris, 1639

La Pinelière, G. de, *Le Parnasse ou La Critique des poètes*. Paris, 1635

Le Moyne, P., *Hymnes de la sagesse divine et de l'amour divin, avec un Discours de la poésie*. Paris, 1641

Plutarch, *Moralia*, ed. E. Capps et al., translated by F. C. Babbitt et al., 15 vols. Loeb Classical Library, London/New York, 1927–69. ('How a Young Man should study Poetry', I, 71–197)

Saint-Evremond, C. de Marquetel de, *Œuvres en prose*, ed. R. Ternois, 4 vols. Paris, 1962–9

Sarasin, J-F., *Œuvres de Monsieur Sarasin*. Paris, 1694

Scudéry, G. de, *Apologie du théâtre*. Paris, 1639
Observations sur 'Le Cid', in P. Corneille, *Œuvres complètes*, ed. C. Marty-Laveaux, XII, 441–61

Sidney, Sir Philip, *A Defense of Poesy*, ed. A. Feuillerat. Cambridge, 1923

Villiers, P. de, 'Entretiens sur les tragédies de ce temps' (1675), in F. Granet, *Recueil de dissertations sur plusieurs tragédies de Corneille et de Racine*, 2 vols. Paris, 1740
Voltaire, *The Complete Works of Voltaire* (LIII–LV). 'Commentaires sur Corneille', ed. D. Williams, 3 vols. Banbury, 1974–5

DRAMA AND ASSOCIATED TEXTS

Benserade, I. de, *Cléopâtre: tragédie*. Paris, 1636
Chapoton, *Le Véritable Coriolan: tragédie*. Paris, 1638
Chaulmer, C., *La Mort de Pompée: tragédie*. Paris, 1638
Chevreau, U., *Coriolan: tragédie*. Paris, 1638
  La Lucresse romaine: tragédie. Paris, 1638
Du Ryer, P., *Alcionée: tragédie*. Paris, 1637
  Cléomedon: tragicomédie. Paris, 1636
  Lucrèce: tragédie. Paris, 1638
  Saul: tragédie. Paris, 1642
Guérin de Bouscal, G., *Suite de La Mort de César, ou La Mort de Brute et de Porcie: tragédie*. Paris, 1637
La Pinelière, G. de, *Hippolyte: tragédie*. Paris, 1635
La Tessonerie, G. de, *L'Art de régner, ou Le Sage Gouverneur: tragicomédie*. Paris, 1645
Molière, J-B. P., *Œuvres complètes*, ed. G. Couton, 2 vols. Bibliothèque de la Pléiade, Paris, 1971
Racine, J., *Œuvres complètes*, ed. R. Picard, 2 vols. Bibliothèque de la Pléiade, Paris, 1950–66
Rotrou, J., *Hercule mourant: tragédie*. Paris, 1636
Schelandre, J. de, *Tyr et Sidon*, ed. J. N. Barker. Paris, 1974
Scudéry, G. de, *Didon: tragédie*. Paris, 1637
  La Mort de César: tragédie. Paris, 1636
  Le Trompeur puni: tragicomédie. Paris, 1633
  Le Vassal généreux: tragicomédie. Paris, 1636

MORAL PHILOSOPHY, 'MORALISTES', AND THE HERO

Aristotle, *The Nicomachœan Ethics*, translated by J. A. K. Thomson. London/Tonbridge, 1953
Balzac, J-L. G. de, *Œuvres*, ed. L. Moreau, 2 vols. Paris, 1854
Bardin, P., *Le Lycée du sieur Bardin où en plusieurs promenades il est traité des connaissances, des actions et des plaisirs d'un honnête homme*, 2 vols. Paris, 1632–4
Bary, R., *La Morale*. Paris, 1672
Bauny, E., *Somme des péchés qui se commettent en tous états*. Paris, 1635
Caussin, N., *La Cour sainte*, Vol. v. Paris, 1645
  La Cour sainte. Collective edition, Paris, 1664
Ceriziers, R. de, *Le Héros français, ou L'Idée du grand capitaine*. Paris, 1645
  Le Philosophe français. Rouen, 1651–2

Charron, P., *De la Sagesse*. Bordeaux, 1601

Coeffeteau, N., *Tableau des passions humaines, de leurs causes et de leurs effets*. Paris, 1620

Cotin, C., *Théoclée, ou La Vraie Philosophie des principes du monde*. Paris, 1646

Coton, P., *Sermons sur les principales et plus difficiles matières de la foi*. Paris, 1617

Cureau de la Chambre, P., *De l'Art de connaître les hommes*. Paris, 1659
  Les Caractères des passions, 5 vols. Paris, 1648–62

Delidel, C., *La Théologie des saints*. Paris, 1668

Du Bois Hus, G., *Le Prince illustre*. Paris, 1645

Du Bosc, J., *La Femme héroique, ou les héroines comparées avec les héros en toute sorte de vertus*. (Two volumes bound as one volume, each paginated separately.) Paris, 1645

Du Moulin, P., *La Philosophie mise en français*. (Three parts bound as one volume, each paginated separately.) Paris, 1644

Du Vair, G., *Les Œuvres politiques, morales et mêlées*. Geneva, 1621

Esprit, J., *De la Fausseté des vertus humaines*, 2 vols. Paris, 1678

Fortin de la Hoguette, P., *Testament ou Conseils fidèles d'un bon père à ses enfants, où sont contenus plusieurs raisonnements chrétiens, moraux et politiques*. Paris, 1648

Gracián, B., *El Oráculo Manual y Arte de Prudencia*. Amsterdam, 1659

Guevara, A. de, *Les Epîtres dorées*, translated by Guterry. Paris, 1577

La Bruyère, J. de, *Œuvres complètes*, ed. J. L. Benda. Bibliothèque de la Pléiade, Argenteuil, 1934

Le Moyne, P., *La Dévotion aisée*. Paris, 1652
  La Gallerie des femmes fortes. Paris, 1663
  Les Peintures morales, 2 vols. Paris, 1643–5

Montaigne, M. de, *Essais*, ed. P. Villey. Paris, 1965

Olivier, J. (Trousset, A.), *Alphabet de l'imperfection et malice des femmes*. Rouen, 1630

Richeôme, L., *L'Academie d'honneur*. Lyon, 1614

Seneca, 'De la Clémence', in *Les Œuvres morales et mêlées de Sénèque*, translated by S. Goulart. Paris, 1595

Silhon, J. de, *Les Deux Vérités*. Paris, 1626

POLITICAL THOUGHT

Ammirato, S., *Discours politiques de Tacite*, translated by J. Baudoin. Paris, 1618

Aquinas, St Thomas, *Selected Political Writings*, ed. A. Passerin d'Entrèves. Oxford, 1948

Aristotle, *The Politics*, translated by J. A. Sinclair. Penguin Classics, Bungay, 1962

Bellarmin, R. Cardinal, *Le Monarque parfait*, translated by J. de Lannel. Paris, 1625

Bodin, J., *La République*. (1st edition in 8°.) Lyon, 1593

Campion, N. de, *Entretiens sur divers sujets d'histoire, de politique, et de morale*, ed. Abbé de Garambourg. Paris, 1704

Colomby, F. de, *Discours de l'autorité des Rois*. Paris, 1620

Faret, N., *Des Vertus nécessaires à un prince pour bien gouverner ses sujets*. Paris, 1623

Fortin de la Hoguette, P., *Les Eléments de la politique selon les principes de la nature*. Paris, 1663

Gentillet, I., *Discours sur les moyens de bien gouverner et maintenir en bonne paix un royaume ou autre principauté, contre Nicolas Machiavel, florentin*. Geneva, 1576

Guiccardini, F., *Maximes populaires*, translated by le Chevalier de l'Escale. Paris, 1634

L'Hommeau, P. de, *Les Maximes génerales du droit français*. Rouen, 1614

La Boétie, E. de, *De la Servitude volontaire*, ed. R. Bonnefon. Paris, 1922

La Noue, J. de, *Discours politiques*. Basle, 1587

Le Bret, C., *Traité de la souveraineté du Roi*. Paris, 1632

Le Moyne, P., *De l'Art de régner*. Paris, 1665

Loyseau, C., *Œuvres*. 2 vols. Paris, 1656. (Including *Traité des ordres et simples dignités*, Paris, 1655, and *Traité des seigneuries*, Paris, 1656)

Machiavel, N., *Œuvres complètes*, ed. E. Barincou. Bibliothèque de la Pléiade, Paris/Angers, 1958

Machon, L., *Apologie pour Machiavel*. Paris, 1643. (Published anonymously)

Mariana, J. de, *Obras*, 2 vols. Biblioteca de Autores Españoles, vols. xxx–xxxi. Madrid, 1854

Marnix, J. de, *Résolutions politiques ou Maximes d'Etat*. Bruxelles, 1632

Mugnier, H., *La Véritable Politique du Prince Chrétien, à la confusion des sages du monde, et pour la condamnation des politiques du siècle*. Paris, 1647

Naudé, G., *Considérations politiques sur les coups d'état*. s.l. 1752. (First published Rome, 1638)

Priézac, D. de, *Discours politiques*. Paris, 1666

Richelieu, A. du Plessis, Cardinal de, *Testament politique*, in *Œuvres*, ed. R. Gaucheron. Paris, 1929

Saavedra Fajardo, D. de, *Idea de un Príncipe Cristiano*, 2 vols. Valencia, 1786

Scudéry, G. de, *Discours politiques des Rois*. Chez Jacques le Gras. Paris, 1663

Sénault, J. F., *Le Monarque ou Les Devoirs du Souverain*. Paris, 1661

Sirmond, J., *Avis du français fidèle aux malcontents nouvellement retirés de la cour*. s.l. s.d.

MISCELLANEOUS

F. Fleuret and L. Perceau (eds.), *Les Satires françaises du XVIIe siècle*, 2 vols. Paris, 1923

H. Gardner, (ed.), *The Metaphysical Poets*. Harmondsworth, 1957

[Ménage, G.], *Ménagiana*, 2 vols. Paris, 1694

[Renaudot, T.], *Recueil général des questions traitées ès conférences du Bureau d'Adresse, sur toutes sortes de matières, par les plus beaux esprits de ce temps, 6 vols*. Lyon, *1656*

Cassius Dio, *The Roman History: The Reign of Augustus*, translated by I. Scott-Kilvert. Harmondsworth, 1987

Chapelain, J., *Lettres*, ed. P. Tamizey Larroque, 2 vols. Paris, 1880–3

Conti, N., *Mythologie ou explication des fables*, translated by J. de Montlyart. Rouen, 1611

Dionysius of Halicarnassus, *The Roman Antiquities*, translated by E. Cary, 7 vols. Loeb Classical Library, London/Cambridge (Mass), 1937–63

Donne, J., *Complete Poetry and Selected Prose*, ed. J. Hayward. London, 1962

Fontenelle, B. le Bouvier de, *Œuvres*. Paris, 1742. 'Vie de Corneille', vol. III, 81–126

Lucain, *La Pharsale*, translated by G. de Brébeuf. Paris, 1655

Retz, P. de Gondi, Cardinal de, *Mémoires*, ed. M. Allem. Bibliothèque de la Pléiade, Monaco, 1956

Scarron, P., *Le Roman comique*, in *Les Romanciers du XVIIe siècle*, ed. A. Adam. Bibliothèque de la Pléiade, Paris, 1958

Schoonhoven, F., *Emblemata Florentii Schoonhovii Goudani Partim Moralia Partim Etiam Civilia*. Goudae, 1618

Tallemant des Réaux, G., *Historiettes*, ed. A. Adam, 2 vols. Bibliothèque de la Pléiade, Paris, 1960–2

Tite-Live, *Les Décades*, translated by Blaise de Vigenère, 2 vols. Paris, 1606

Urfé, H. d', *L'Astrée*, ed. H. Vaganay, 5 vols. Lyon, 1925–8

Vico, G., *The New Science*, translated by T. G. Bergin and M. H. Fisch, 2 vols. Ithaca, 1948

Vigenère, B. de, *Les Images et tableaux de plate peinture de Philostrate*, 2 vols. Paris, 1578

Vigneul-Marville, N. (Bonaventure d'Argonne), *Mélanges d'histoire et le littérature*. Rouen, 1699

SECONDARY WORKS

HISTORICAL STUDIES

T. Aston (ed.), *Crisis in Europe: 1560–1660*. London, 1965

P. J. Coveney (ed.), *France in Crisis*. London, 1977

R. Hatton, (ed.), *Louis XIV and Absolutism*. London, 1976

R. Mousnier (ed.), *Comment les français voyaient la France au XVIIe siècle*. Paris, 1955. (Originally published in *17 ème Siècle*, 25–6 (1955))

G. Parker and L. M. Smith (eds.), *The General Crisis of the Seventeenth Century*. London, 1978

O. A. Ranum (ed.), *National Consciousness: History and Political Culture in Early Modern Europe*. Baltimore, 1975

Bardet, J. P. *Rouen au XVIIe et XVIIIe siècles: les mutations d'un espace social*, 2 vols. Paris, 1983

Bonney, R., *Political Change in France under Richelieu and Mazarin*. Oxford, 1978

Briggs, R., *Early Modern France: 1560–1715*. Oxford, 1977

Church, W. F., *Richelieu and Reason of State*. Princeton, 1972

Dumont, F., 'French Kingship and Absolute Monarchy in the Seventeenth Century', in Hatton (ed.), *Louis XIV and Absolutism*, pp. 55–84. (Originally published as 'Royauté francaise et monarchie absolue au 17ème siècle', *17ème Siècle*, 58–9 (1963))

Durand, G., 'What is Absolutism?', in Hatton (ed.), *Louis XIV and Absolutism*, pp. 18–36

Elliott, J. H., 'Revolution and Continuity in Early Modern Europe', in Ranum (ed.), *The General Crisis*, pp. 110–33

Foisil, M., *La Révolte des Nu-pieds et les révoltes normandes de 1639*. Paris, 1970

Gaxotte, P., *Histoire des français*, 2 vols. Paris, 1951

Goubert, P., 'The French Peasantry in the Seventeenth Century: a Regional Example', in Coveney (ed.), *Crisis in Europe*, pp. 141–65. (Originally published in *Past and Present*, 10 (1956))

Lemaire, A., *Les Lois fondamentales de la monarchie française d'après les théoriciens de l'ancien régime*. Paris, 1907

Leroy Ladurie, E., *Carnival: A People's Uprising at Romans (1579–1580)*, translated by M. Feeney. London, 1980
Histoire du climat depuis l'an mil. Paris, 1967

Mandrou, R., *Introduction to Modern France; 1500–1640*, translated by R. E. Hallmark. London, 1975
La France aux XVIIe et XVIIIe siècles. Paris, 1967

Mousnier, R., *Peasant Uprisings in Seventeenth-Century France, Russia and China*, translated by B. Pearce. London, 1971
'Recherches sur les soulèvements populaires avant la Fronde'. *Revue d'Histoire Moderne et Contemporaine*, 5 (1958), 81–113
La Vénalité des offices sous Henri IV et Louis XIII. Rouen, 1946

Pagès, G., *The Thirty Years' War*, translated by D. Maland and J. Hooper. London, 1962

Ranum, O. A., *Richelieu and the Councillors of Louis XIII*. Oxford, 1963

Tapié, V-L., *La France de Louis XII et de Richelieu*. Poitiers, 1952

Thuau, E., *Raison d'Etat et pensée politique à l'époque de Richelieu*. Athens, 1966

Trevor-Roper, H., 'The General Crisis of the Seventeenth Century', in Coveney (ed.), *Crisis in Europe*, pp. 59–96

CORNEILLE STUDIES

Barber, W. H., 'Patriotism and Gloire in Corneille's Horace', *MLR*, 46 (1951), 368–78

Barnwell, H. T., *Pierre Corneille: Writings on the Theatre*. Oxford, 1965
The Tragic Drama of Corneille and Racine: An Old Parallel Revisited. Oxford, 1982

Bray, R., *La Tragédie cornélienne devant la critique classique*. Paris, 1927

Burger, P., '*Le Cid* et le matériau de la tragicomédie'. *Papers on French Seventeenth-Century Literature*, 11 (1984), 427–45

Calvet, J., '*Polyeucte*', Paris, 1944

Charlier, G., *La Clef de 'Clitandre'*. Bruxelles, 1924

Clarke, D. R., 'Corneille's Differences with the Seventeenth-century Doctrinaires over the Moral Authority of the Poet'. *MLR*, 80 (1985), 550–62

'Echoes of a Provincial Discussion of the Morality of the Novel: Pierre Corneille's Sonnet and Nicolas de Campion's Preface to Alexandre de Campion's *Les Hommes Illustres*'. *MLR*, 84 (1989), 319–30

'Heroic Prudence and Reason in the Seventeenth Century: Auguste's Pardon of Cinna'. *FMLS*, 1 (1965), 328–38

'Pierre Corneille's Occasional and Circumstantial Writings relating to Cardinal Richelieu, 1631–1643'. *FS*, 41 (1987), 20–36

Couton, G., *Corneille et la Fronde*. Clermont-Ferrand, 1951

La Vieillesse de Corneille. Paris, 1949

Réalisme de Corneille: La Clef de 'Mélite': Réalités dans 'Le Cid'. Paris, 1953

Doubrovsky, S., *Corneille et la dialectique du héros*. Paris, 1963

Forsyth, E., 'The Tragic Dilemma in Horace'. *Australian Journal of French Studies*, 4 (1967), 162–76

Fumaroli, M., 'Critique et création littéraire: J-L. G. de Balzac et P. Corneille. (1637–1645)', in *Mélanges de Littérature Française Offerts à René Pintard*. Strasbourg, 1975, pp. 73–89

'La Querelle de la moralité du théâtre avant Nicole et Bossuet'. *RHLF*, 70 (1970), 1007–30

'Rhétorique et dramaturgie: le statut du personnage dans la tragédie classique'. *Revue d'Histoire du Théâtre*, 24 (1972), 223–50

'Rhétorique, dramaturgie et spiritualité: Pierre Corneille et Claude Delidel. S. J.', in *Mélanges Offerts à Georges Couton*. Lyon, 1979, pp. 271–87

'Tragique paien et tragique chrétien dans *Rodogune*'. *RSH*, 152 (1973), 599–631

Gasté, A., *La Querelle du 'Cid'*. Paris, 1898

Goode, W. O., 'Médée and Jason: Hero and Non-hero in Corneille's *Médée*'. *French Review*, 51 (1978), 804–15

Guizot, M. F., *Corneille et son temps*. Paris, 1852

Herland, L., 'La Notion du tragique chez Corneille'. *Mélanges de la Sociéte Toulousaine d'Etudes Classiques*, 1 (1946), 265–84

Hincker, K., 'Le Temps de Corneille'. *Europe*, 52 (1974), 15–25

Howarth, W. D., 'Mécénat et Raison d'Etat: Richelieu, Corneille et la tragédie politique', in *L'Age d'or du mécénat (1598–1661)*. Colloque international CNRS (Mars 1983), Paris, 1985, pp. 59–68.

Jasinski, R., 'Sur Cinna'. *Europe*, 52 (1974), 114–30

Jehasse, J., 'Guez de Balzac et Corneille face au mythe romain', in *Pierre Corneille (Tercentenary Colloquium)*, pp. 247–63

Joye, J-C., *Amour, pouvoir et transcendance chez Pierre Corneille*. Berne/Francfort-s. Main/New York, 1986

Krauss, W., *Corneille als Politischer Dichter*. Marbourg, 1936

MacGrath, G., 'Pierre Corneille avocat', in *Pierre Corneille (Tercentenary Colloquium)*, pp. 171–8

Mallinson, G., *The Comedies of Corneille: Experiments in the Comic*. Manchester, 1984

Margitiç, M. R., 'Les Deux *Cid*: de la tragi-comédie à la pseudo-tragédie classique'. *Papers on French Seventeenth-Century Literature*, 11 (1984), pp. 409–25

'Mythologie personnelle chez le premier Corneille: le jeu de l'amour et de l'amour-propre de *Mélite* au *Cid*', in *Pierre Corneille (Tercentenary Colloquium)*, pp. 547–67

Maurens J., *La Tragédie sans tragique: le néo-stoïcisme dans l'œuvre de Pierre Corneille*. Paris, 1966

May, G., *Tragédie cornélienne: tragédie racinienne*. Urbana, 1948

Michaud, G., 'Structure et signification d'*Horace*'. *Annales Universitatis Saravaiensis. (Philosophie, Lettres)*: *Mélanges Dimoff*, 1–2 (1954), 95–100

Morel, J., 'A Propos de plaidoyer d'Horace: reflexions sur le sens de la vocation historique dans le théâtre de Corneille'. *RR*, 51 (1960), 27–32

Nadal, O., 'L'Exercice du crime chez Corneille'. *Mercure de France*, 308 (1950), 22–34

Le Sentiment de l'amour dans l'œuvre de Pierre Corneille. Paris, 1948

Niderst, A., 'Corneille et Anne d'Autriche', in *Pierre Corneille (Tercentenary Colloquium)*, pp. 189–96

'Tragédie et conflits sociaux au XVIIe siècle: Corneille et la sédition des Nus-pieds (1639)', in *Mélanges Offerts à Georges Couton*. Lyon, 1981, pp. 289–97

(ed.), *Pierre Corneille (Tercentenary Colloquium, 2–6 October 1984)*. PUF, Paris, 1985

Péguy, C., *Œuvres complètes de Charles Péguy, 1873–1914*, 15 vols. Paris, 1917–24

Victor Marie, comte Hugo. Paris, 1934

Peyrtraud, H., 'A Propos des Horaces et des Curiaces'. *La Revue Universitaire*, 48 (1939), 32–5

Pintard, R., 'Autour de *Cinna* et de *Polyeucte*: nouveaux problèmes de chronologie et de critique cornéliennes'. *RHLF*, 64 (1964), 377–413

'De la Tragicomédie à la tragédie: l'exemple du *Cid*', in *Mélanges Offerts à J. A. Vier*. Paris, 1973, pp. 455–66

'Un Témoignage sur *Le Cid* en 1637', in *Mélanges Offerts à H. Chamard*. Paris 1951, pp. 297–301

Poirier, G., *Corneille ou la vertu de prudence*. Geneva/Paris, 1984

Prigent, M., 'L'Exercice de pouvoir dans les tragédies de Corneille', in *Pierre Corneille (Tercentenary Colloquium)*, pp. 593–604

Le Héros et l'Etat dans la tragédie de Pierre Corneille. Paris, 1986

Rivaille, L., *Les Débuts de Corneille*. Paris, 1936

Sainte Beuve, C. A. de, *Les Nouveaux Lundis*, 13 vols. Paris, 1864

Sartre, J-P. 'Forgers of Myths'. *Theatre Arts*, 30 (1946), 324–35

Sellstrom, D., 'The Structure of Corneille's Masterpieces'. *RR*, 49 (1958), 269–77

Stegmann, A., *L'Héroisme cornélien: genèse et signification*, 2 vols. Paris, 1968

Sweetser, M-O., *La Dramaturgie de Corneille*. Geneva/Paris, 1977
  Les Conceptions dramatiques de Corneille, d'après ses écrits théoriques. Geneva/
  Paris, 1962
Trafton, D. A., 'On Corneille's *Horace*'. *Interpretation*, 2–3 (1972), 183–93
Vedel, V., *Deux Classiques français vus par un critique étranger: Corneille et son
  temps: Molière*, translated by E. Cornet, Paris, 1935
Viala, A., 'Corneille et les institutions littéraires de son temps', in *Pierre
  Corneille (Tercentenary Colloquium)*, pp. 197–204

GENERAL STUDIES OF LITERATURE AND THE HISTORY OF IDEAS

Adam, A., *Histoire de la littérature française du XVIIe siècle*, 5 vols. Paris,
  1949–56
Barnwell, H. T., *Les Idées morales et critiques de Saint-Evremond*. Paris, 1957
Bénichou, P., *Morales du grand siècle*. Paris, 1948
Brasillach, R., *Notre Avant-guerre*. Paris, 1941
Bray, R., *La Formation de la doctrine classique en France*. Paris, 1951
Bremond, H., *Histoire littéraire du sentiment religieux en France depuis la fin des
  Guerres de Religion jusqu'à nos jours*, 12 vols. Paris, 1916–36
Busson, H., *La Pensée religieuse française de Charron à Pascal*. Paris, 1933
Butler, P., *Classicisme et baroque dans l'œuvre de Racine*. Paris, 1959
Charlton, H. B., *Castelvetro's Theory of Poetry*. Manchester, 1913
Couton, G., 'Réapprendre à lire: deux des langages de l'allégorie au 17ème
  siècle'. *Cahiers de l'Association Internationale des Etudes Françaises*, 28
  (1976), 81–101
Crane, R. (ed.), *Critics and Criticism*. Chicago, 1962
Daimville, F. de, 'Allégorie et actualité sur les tréteaux des jésuites', in
  Jacquot (ed.), *Dramaturgie et Société*, pp. 433–43
Davidson, H. M., *Audience, Words and Art: Studies in Seventeenth-Century French
  Rhetoric*. Ohio, 1965
Dejob, C., *De l'Influence du Concile de Trente sur la littérature*. Paris, 1884
Federici, C., *Réalisme et dramaturgie*. Paris, 1974
Fidao-Justiniani, J-E., 'Discours sur la raison classique'. *Revue des Cours et
  des Conférences*, 38 (1937), 81–93, 177–89, 277–87, 372–84, 561–76,
  659–69
Forestier, G., 'Illusion comique et illusion mimétique', *Papers on French
  Seventeenth-Century Literature*, 11 (1984), 377–91
Fumaroli, M., *L'Age de l'éloquence*. Geneva, 1980
Gilbert, A. H., *Literary Criticism: Plato to Dryden*. New York, 1940
Goldmann, L., *Le Dieu caché*. Paris, 1959
Gouhier, H., 'Remarques sur le "théâtre historique"', *Revue d'Esthétique*, 13
  (1960), 16–24
Gravier, M., 'Le Théâtre des jésuites et la tragédie du salut et de la
  conversion', in Jacquot (ed.), *Le Théâtre tragique*, pp. 19–62.
Gronau, K., 'Matériau et fonctions sociales de la tragédie', *Papers on French
  Seventeenth-Century Literature*, 11 (1984), 447–73

Hagstrum, J. E., *The Sister Arts: The Tradition of Literary Pictorialism in English Poetry from Dryden to Gray*. Chicago, 1958

Hathaway, B., *The Age of Criticism: The Late Renaissance in Italy*. New York, 1962

Jacquot, J. (ed.), *Le Théâtre tragique*. Paris, 1962
(ed.), *Dramaturgie et société*, 2 vols. Paris, 1968

Keohane, N. O., *Philosophy and the State in France: The Renaissance to the Enlightenment*. Princeton, 1980

Kern, E. G., *The Influence of Heinsius and Vossius on French Dramatic Theory*. Baltimore, 1949

Kitto, H. D. F., *Form and Meaning in Drama*. London, 1959

Lancaster, H. C., *A History of French Dramatic Literature in the Seventeenth Century*, 6 vols. New York, 1966

Magendie, M., *La Politesse mondaine et les théories de l'honnêteté en France au XVIIe siècle*. Paris, 1925

Martin, J. R., *Baroque*. London, 1977

Niebuhr, R., *Beyond Tragedy*. London, 1938

Pintard, R., *Le Libertinage érudit dans la première moitié du XVIIe siècle*. Paris, 1943

Ranum, O. A., *Artisans of Glory*. Chapel Hill, 1980

Roux, L. E., 'Cent Ans d'expérience théâtrale dans les collèges de la Compagnie de Jésus en Espagne', in Jacquot (ed.), *Dramaturgie et Société*, pp. 479–523

Sutcliffe, F. R., *J-L. Guez de Balzac et son temps: littérature et politique*. Paris, 1959

Tuve, R., *Elizabethan and Metaphysical Imagery*. Chicago, 1947

Weinberg, B., 'Castelvetro's Theory of Poetics', in Crane (ed.), *Critics and Criticism*, pp. 349–71

Wyndham Lewis, P., *The Lion and the Fox*. London, 1955

Index